£35.00 o

657.3 REI

Moreton Morrell Site

The meaning of company accounts

The meaning of company accounts

Eighth Edition

Walter Reid and D R Myddelton

GOWER

First published 1971
Second edition 1974
Third edition 1982
Fourth edition 1988
Fifth edition 1992
Sixth edition 1996
Seventh edition 2000
Eighth edition published by Gower Publishing Limited,
Gower House, Croft Road, Aldershot, Hants GU11 3HR, England

Gower Publishing Company, Suite 420, 101 Cherry Street, Burlington,
VT 05401-4405, USA

British Library Cataloguing in Publication Data
Reid, Walter
      The meaning of company accounts. –8th ed.
      1. Corporations – Accounting 2. Financial, statements
      I. Title II. Myddelton, David Roderic
      657.9'5

ISBN 0 566 08660 3

Library of Congress Cataloging-in-Publication Data
Reid, Walter.
      The meaning of company accounts / by Walter Reid and D. R. Myddelton. -- Ed. 8.
          p. cm.
      Includes bibliographical references and index.
      ISBN 0-566-08660-3
      1. Financial statements.   2. Corporations--Accounting. I. Myddelton, David Roderic.
II. Title.
HF5681.B2R37 2005
657'.3--dc20
                                                                    2004023638

Typeset in 10pt Times by Bournemouth Colour Press, Poole, Dorset and printed in Great Britain by TJ International, Padstow.

Contents

Preface

OBJECTIVES

This book aims to help people using company accounts to gain a firm grasp of what they mean and how they relate to business events and transactions. Managers without accounting or financial training should find the book useful. It will also provide a basic introduction to company accounts for those taking formal accounting or business studies courses.

We have taken care to make the book as brief as possible, but a superficial approach might lead to faulty conclusions about company accounts. And it would frustrate readers to discover in business practical aspects of which they had not been aware. The book thus needs to be thorough as well as concise.

WORKBOOK DESIGN

The Meaning of Company Accounts brings together both basic and detailed material within a 'workbook' framework. This comes somewhere between a normal textbook and a programmed text. It is structured and allows a high degree of reader involvement. At the same time, it is very flexible.

We have tried throughout to develop ideas in a logical sequence. In presenting them we also aim to make a strong visual impact. In this respect the side-by-side page layout is a great help and is still an almost unique feature of the book.

To aid learning further, the text of most sections includes detailed examples which we invite readers to work through. We expect that many who use the book may find at least some of the topics difficult. The opportunity to tackle examples at such points should help readers to achieve a suitable level of understanding.

Not everyone will have trouble with the same points, so we have divided each section of the book into two parts. The text provides a basic study of the whole subject, but moves quickly from topic to topic. In addition, there are plenty of exercises and problems (mostly with solutions), which readers are free to use as they think best.

SEQUENCE OF SECTIONS

Broadly the book consists of two parts. Sections 1, 2 and 3 cover general accounting issues, the structure of company accounts and some approaches to formal financial analysis. They illustrate the total package in published company accounts before we look at the supporting detail. Section 4 then deals (briefly) with recording business transactions.

Sections 5 to 13 go into more depth on theoretical and practical problems; they cover measuring income and expense, assets and liabilities, and presenting the profit and loss account, balance sheet and cash flow statement. This material forms the basis for understanding the meaning of company accounts. Section 14 then provides a review of how to analyse and interpret accounts, with a detailed worked example in the text.

HOW TO USE THE BOOK

In some sense no part of this book stands alone – the fourteen sections form an integral structure. For this reason, readers who are not taking part in a formal programme may prefer to read quickly at first to gain an overview before tackling topics in detail. Two complete readings may be more rewarding than a single in-depth study. Ideas which seem difficult to begin with may often become clearer after covering other parts of the book.

The same approach may be useful even within sections. A quick look through the text (or at the summary) will give a good idea of the areas covered in each section. This may well make it easier to understand the relevance and context of the detailed topics on a more careful reading.

Readers with little previous knowledge of accounting may wish to follow their study of the text of each section by extensive use of the various exercises and problems. This will help them acquire a substantial level of competence. For those who already know something of accounting, not all the exercises may be useful. The intention is that readers should be able to move at their own pace throughout; this will enable them to build up strength where weaknesses exist and move more quickly where they do not require further detailed work.

PROBLEMS AND SOLUTIONS

The additional material at the end of each section, after the text, consists of about a dozen exercises and problems. The first exercise in all sections contains ten definitions, for which we ask readers to *write down* answers in the space provided. (Or use a separate sheet of paper, if you prefer.) For most people this will be far more rewarding – though harder work – than merely 'thinking' your own answer. Suggested definitions, often with extra comments, then appear on the following page. We repeat: you will learn far more from attempting your own answers than limiting your effort to casual criticism of our versions!

We have treated the remaining exercises and problems in three ways. First in each section come some fairly basic problems on matters covered in the text. We have left space in the book for readers to use for their answers. Once again we strongly recommend taking the trouble to *write down* your attempted answers to problems. The suggested solution appears in detail on the following page, together with comments. In effect we are almost having a 'conversation' with each reader; and our notes to the solutions sometimes make extra points which do not occur in the text.

Then follow several rather more difficult problems, solutions to which appear at the end of the book. Here (for space reasons) we ask readers to use their own paper. These more difficult problems are in effect self-tests for readers on how well they have understood the material in the text. We show solutions at the back of the book, rather than straight after each problem. This is to minimize the temptation to look at the solutions too soon! Again you will usually gain more personal benefit from a serious attempt to work through each problem completely *before* looking at our solution.

Finally in most sections, we include two or three problems for which we do not publish solutions. These may serve as assignments on formal programmes in companies or business schools, or readers may care to attempt them for personal satisfaction. A few of these problems are 'essay type' questions for which there is no single 'correct' answer.

In total the problems and exercises (including the examples to work within the text part of sections) constitute about half the book. The workbook design clearly places more demands on the reader than a normal textbook. But the extra effort required to select and tackle the specific material which satisfies each reader's own needs should lead to the rapid development of a real competence to interpret accounting statements.

APPENDICES

Terminology can be a problem, especially for readers whose first language is not English. Appendix 1 lists synonyms (some of American origin) and Appendix 2 lists common acronyms. Appendix 3 lists current accounting standards, both UK and International. Appendix 4 gives details of the UK Retail Prices Index, a measure of inflation, since 1960.

Appendix 5 contains full details of the permitted formats for balance sheets and profit and loss accounts. The bibliography in Appendix 6 will help those who wish to extend their studies of related and more advanced aspects of accounting theory and practice. Finally we include, in Appendix 7 (pages 283 to 290) some skeleton forms covering an overview, financial ratios, segment analysis and cash flow statements. We would encourage readers to photocopy the forms in Appendix 7 for their own use.

Walter Reid and D.R. Myddelton

EIGHTH EDITION

The main (relatively minor) changes in this eighth edition are shown below:

- Sections 8 to 11 are as follows in this edition (compared with the 7th edition):
    - 8 Capital structure (9)
    - 9 Group accounts (11)
    - 10 Company taxation (8)
    - 11 Cash flow statements (10).
- 'Definitions' problems have been added for Section 10 Company taxation and Section 11 Cash flow statements.

- As always we have carefully reconsidered every page of text; we have changed the order of some pages and dropped some material. We have also added material where it seemed desirable.
- The treatment of dividends has been changed. Instead of deducting dividends paid *and proposed* from profit after tax, to leave 'retained profit for the year', we now show 'profit after tax' as literally the 'bottom line' in the profit and loss account. That amount is added to cumulative retained profits in the first instance, and any dividends paid are deducted as and when actually paid.

We have also, of course, updated the 'real' company accounts used, as well as the material in the Appendices, where necessary. In this edition we no longer provide a 'real' set of company accounts to analyse as a 'problem' at the end of Section 14 (though we do provide a detailed analysis of Tesco plc's accounts in the text). Company accounts, unfortunately, have become too voluminous to treat in this way.

For the eighth edition there is again an Instructor's Guide containing suggested solutions to all the problems for which no solution is published in this book. This is available free of charge to any teacher of accounting working in a recognized institution. Please write for a copy to:

Professor D.R. Myddelton
Cranfield School of Management,
Cranfield,
Bedford,
MK43 0AL.

In the five years since the seventh edition was published, four new Financial Reporting Standards have been issued, superseding three of the former Statements of Standard Accounting Practice. As a result, at 31 March 2004 there are 35 UK accounting standards in force [8 SSAPs and 21 FRSs, listed in Appendix 3 on page 275]. In view of the proliferation of accounting standards in the past 35 years we are rather proud of having fewer pages in the eighth edition in 2005 than in the second edition in 1974. We have deliberately continued to avoid excessive detail, especially on disclosure.

Walter Reid has been reducing his commitments for health reasons, so again I alone have been responsible for the changes in this latest edition.

D.R. Myddelton

The Authors

Walter Reid was Professor of Accounting and Financial Control at the London Business School from 1973 to 1988. He was for many years Chairman of Management Development Associates Limited (MDA), a management training consultancy with a primary focus on financial management.

D.R. Myddelton has been Professor of Finance and Accounting at the Cranfield School of Management since 1972. He has written books on tax reform, inflation accounting and accounting standards, and textbooks on accounting, economics and financial management. He is Chairman of The Institute of Economic Affairs.

Acknowledgements

We are grateful to all the companies from whose accounts we have reproduced extracts. Thanks too to the anonymous companies whose figures we use in Problem 2.5: The Secret Seven. We should stress that we remain entirely responsible for any simplifications and for the analysis and comments thereon.

BOC Group plc
British American Tobacco plc
Diageo plc
GlaxoWellcome plc
H. J. Heinz Company
Henkel
Rio Tinto plc
Royal Dutch Shell Group
Tesco plc
Unilever Group

We should like to thank the many students at the London Business School and the Cranfield School of Management who over the years have commented on the text and problems of various editions.

Section 1
Background and structure

DEVELOPMENT OF ACCOUNTING

At its simplest, business accounting recorded cash receipts and payments for a specific venture, such as a voyage overseas. Various shareholders contributed capital funds to get it started; and when the enterprise was over, any remaining assets were sold and the owners shared pro rata in the net proceeds. Some businesses, however, were more permanent 'going concerns' intended to last for many years. They needed 'interim accounts' to measure profits out of which to pay regular dividends and give shareholders a cash return on their investment.

As some businesses grew larger and more complex, so did the number and range of their transactions, and they began to need more elaborate records. In order to record revenues and expenses, assets and liabilities, 'double-entry' bookkeeping evolved some 500 years ago. This system was not only able to classify transactions but was also self-checking. Goethe called it 'the finest invention of the human mind', and it remains the foundation of modern accounting.

The Industrial Revolution brought the next major step in accounting. Most commerce had involved either sole traders or several partners, who bore the risks of the business up to the limit of their personal wealth. But by the mid-nineteenth century, larger concerns needed more capital resources than all but a few individuals or families could muster. This led to the increasing use of 'limited liability' companies, whose shares could be freely bought and sold. Their emergence divorced a firm's ownership from its day-to-day management, and led to regular stewardship reports from the managers to the dispersed owners.

At first it was feared that managers and part-owners enjoying the protection of limited liability might act with less prudence than wholly-liable sole traders and partners. As a result, company directors were conservative in what they let accounts reveal and balance sheets (which might be 'audited') emphasized financial soundness while often concealing secret reserves. These reserves were available to smooth out profits from year to year, which might mislead shareholders as to the true riskiness of the business.

In the twentieth century, public trading on stock exchanges of shares in companies greatly increased, especially in the UK and the US. At the same time, pension funds, insurance companies, mutual funds and other financial institutions largely supplanted individuals as shareholders in listed companies. Pressure from capital markets led to ever more extensive formal accounting rules ('standards') to help investors and others understand company accounts.

Finally, in the past 50 years many large 'multinational' companies have emerged, with operations and shareholders spread around the world. Combined with high rates of inflation, this has also led to complex problems of translating foreign currencies. Currently attempts are being made to harmonize different national accounting practices by means of International Accounting Standards.

'A TRUE AND FAIR VIEW'

Since 1948 the UK Companies Acts have required accounts to give 'a true and fair view' of a company's profit or loss for the year and of its state of affairs at the end of the year. This requirement now applies to all member-states of the European Union.

In accounting, 'a true and fair view' is a technical phrase. Its meaning can be expressed in three similar, but not identical, ways:

- appropriate measurement, classification and disclosure of items;
- consistent application of generally accepted accounting principles;
- compliance with official accounting standards.

A company's directors are legally responsible for ensuring that the company's accounts give 'a true and fair view' and comply with the Companies Act 1985. The company's auditors (see p. 9) then report whether or not, in their opinion, the accounts do so.

Financial results for a single year are often less useful as a guide to a company's performance than accounts for several years. Hence most large companies now publish five- or ten-year summaries of the main items in their accounts.

Between 1970 and 1984 UK inflation averaged nearly 12 per cent a year – a peacetime rate unprecedented in sterling's thousand-year history. In fifteen years the pound lost 80 per cent of its purchasing power. Such conditions distort historical money cost accounts, which as a result give a misleading view of companies' real assets and real profits. Interest in 'inflation accounting' (which Section 13 discusses in detail) has declined recently, due to the fall in the rate of inflation.

Under the going concern concept, current assets appear at cost (unless net realizable value is lower), while accounts normally show tangible fixed assets at original cost less depreciation (see Section 7), which may well be below current market value. So the phrase 'a true and fair view' should not tempt users of accounts to believe that a company's balance sheet discloses its real 'value'. It does no such thing, nor does it try to. Hence the American phrase 'net worth', used in balance sheets to refer to shareholders' interests, is highly misleading.

A balance sheet is merely a statement of those business assets and liabilities which the accounting rules recognize. It excludes many important items, for example such intangible assets as business 'know-how' and the value of its people. Thus the market value of a company's equity may often be very different from the 'book value' of its shareholders' funds in the balance sheet.

FUNDAMENTAL ACCOUNTING CONCEPTS

Over time, accountants have developed four generally accepted fundamental accounting concepts: going concern, accruals, consistency and prudence. Understanding them is essential to grasp the meaning of company accounts.

(a) The going concern concept

The going concern concept assumes that an enterprise will continue for the foreseeable future, and that there is no need or intention to close down the business. Thus accounts value work-in-progress at cost rather than at the (often lower) amount which a forced sale would yield. Companies use the 'liquidation' approach only when they are about to cease trading, or if there is serious doubt about the going concern assumption.

(b) The accruals concept

The accruals concept recognizes revenues and costs as a business earns or incurs them, not as it receives or pays money. Accounts include revenues and costs in the relevant period's profit and loss account, as far as possible 'matching' expenses against revenues. A different method would be cash accounting, which historically preceded the accruals concept (and which the British government has only recently abandoned).

(c) The consistency concept

Accounting requires each company to adopt consistent treatment for similar items within each accounting period and from one period to the next. Otherwise trying to compare an enterprise's accounts over time would be pointless. Companies must disclose fully any change in accounting treatment – and its effect – and, where suitable, restate prior years' figures on the new basis.

(d) The prudence concept

We have already seen that accounting tends to be conservative. This results from practical wisdom based on many years of commercial experience. Under the prudence concept accounts do not anticipate revenues and profits, instead the profit and loss account includes revenues (and hence profits) only when they are 'realized'. This may be either in cash, or else in the form of other assets whose ultimate cash proceeds are fairly certain. In contrast, accounts make full provision for all known expenses and losses, even where they are less certain and their amount has to be estimated.

Accounting policies

Accounting policies are the specific methods (based on the fundamental concepts) which an enterprise chooses as best able to present its financial results fairly. Businesses have become so complex and diverse as to rule out complete uniformity between them; but where more than one accounting method is possible, it can make a big difference which policy is chosen. A company must therefore state what its policies are [IAS1/FRS18] and stick to them, so that readers can understand its accounts.

THE ACCOUNTING TASK

At its simplest, accounting deals with receipts and payments of cash. If all transactions are complete at the accounting date, it is easy to summarize receipts and payments and calculate the closing cash balance. But problems begin to emerge when an ongoing business needs 'interim' accounts. For now some transactions will be incomplete.

At least once a year companies must publish three main accounting statements: a profit and loss account [income statement], a balance sheet [statement of financial position], and a cash flow statement. To prepare these statements, accountants must analyse the continuous stream of transactions at regular intervals in order to identify and measure the relevant sales revenues and expenses in a period, and the company's assets and their means of finance.

The results can only be approximate. Some items of revenue and expense may be easy to assign to accounting periods, but incomplete transactions raise problems. For example, those preparing accounts need to decide in which period to charge costs intended to benefit future periods. It is not enough to identify assets and liabilities at the balance sheet date: accountants must also attach a definite value to the various assets. This may involve partly completed stocks, partly worn-out equipment or unexpired intangible assets.

Problems of this kind do not yield uniquely 'correct' solutions. They depend partly on uncertain future events, so measurement is often a matter of judgement. Accounting is an art not a science.

Recording transactions: cash and credit

A retail shop normally buys goods on credit but sells for cash. Many companies, however, enter into only a few cash transactions. They buy and sell most goods and services on credit. To the extent that cash has not yet been received from a credit sale, the year-end balance sheet shows a debtor [account receivable]. Similarly, if a company owes money for goods or services bought on credit, this will show in the balance sheet as a creditor [account payable]. Any differences between credit transactions and related cash flows in a period will lead to changes in outstanding debtors and creditors.

A major function of the profit and loss account for a period is to show the operating profit or loss. It does this, to a large extent, by 'matching' against the revenues earned in a period the expenses incurred to generate them.

Some transactions may not relate entirely to the current period. For example, rent paid in advance will appear as a current asset ['prepayment'] in the closing balance sheet. Non-trading transactions, such as borrowing money or making a long-term investment, will cause changes to the balance sheet amounts for loans and fixed assets.

The diagram on the right shows the general structure of the three main accounting statements. Please study it carefully. We shall now consider each of these statements in more detail.

THE MAIN ACCOUNTING STATEMENTS

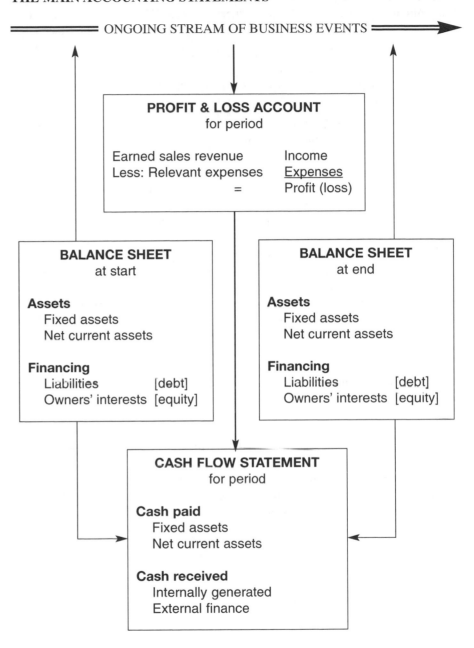

PROFIT AND LOSS ACCOUNT AND BALANCE SHEET

The profit and loss account and balance sheet of General Trading Limited are set out on the right. In looking at these statements, consider the following questions:

1 (a) Briefly what is the purpose of each financial statement?
  (b) What is the link between them?
2 How does the profit and loss account classify items?
3 How does the balance sheet classify items?

Please study the financial statements of General Trading Limited and formulate your answers to the above questions *before* reading on.

1 (a) Briefly what is the purpose of each financial statement?

The profit and loss account summarizes the turnover (sales revenue) and operating expenses of the business for the financial year, to reveal the 'operating profit'. It then deducts interest expense and tax and shows the resulting 'profit after tax' for the period.

The balance sheet is a classified summary at the end of the financial year showing how much the business has invested in fixed assets and in working capital, and how these amounts (= total assets less current liabilities) have been financed by long-term borrowing ('debt') and by shareholders' funds ('equity'). In total, uses of funds must always equal uses of funds, so 'net assets' must always equal 'capital employed'. That is why the balance sheet always balances.

1 (b) What is the link between them?

The profit after tax for the year (£110 000) increases 'capital and reserves'. In a sense this amount 'belongs' to the company's shareholders. It represents one of the company's sources of funds during the year. *This is the link between the profit and loss account and the balance sheet.*

Any dividends paid to shareholders during the year reduce the balance on the 'profit and loss account' under 'capital and reserves'. General Trading Limited paid dividends of £60 000 to shareholders during the year, so the net increase in the (cumulative) profit and loss account balance was £50 000 (that is, £110 000 profit after tax less £60 000 dividends paid).

GENERAL TRADING LIMITED

Profit and loss account for the year ended 31 March 2005

	£'000
Turnover	**2 400**
Cost of sales	1 500
Gross profit	900
Selling and administrative expenses	720
Operating profit	**180**
Interest expense	20
Profit before tax	160
Tax on profit	50
Profit after tax	**110**

Balance sheet at 31 March 2005

Tangible fixed assets		
Land and buildings		300
Plant and machinery		500
		800
Current assets		
Stocks	400	
Debtors	350	
Cash	150	
	900	
Less: **Current liabilities** (creditors due within one year)		
Trade creditors	270	
Tax	30	
	300	
Net current assets (working capital)		600
Total assets less current liabilities		**1 400**
Less: **Creditors due after one year**		180
Capital and reserves		
Called up share capital	1 000	
Profit and loss account (170 $^{b}/_{f}$ + 50)	220	
		1 220

PROFIT AND LOSS ACCOUNT CLASSIFICATION

2. How does the profit and loss account classify items?

Profit may be defined as turnover (sales revenue) less total expenses. (If expenses exceed turnover in a period, there is a loss.) The published profit and loss account splits total expenses between a number of headings:

● cost of sales
● selling and administrative expenses
● interest expense
● tax on profits.

The 'bottom line' is then profit after tax.

Thus the profit and loss account starts with turnover (sales revenue) for the period. It then deducts the 'cost of sales', which represents all the costs needed to bring the goods into a saleable condition. Turnover less cost of sales equals 'gross profit'. Selling and administrative expenses are the costs incurred by the business in selling the goods and running the business. Gross profit less selling and administrative expenses equals 'operating profit'.

Operating profit is sometimes referred to as 'Profit Before Interest and Tax' [PBIT], or as Earnings Before Interest and Tax [EBIT]. This is a key figure in analysing performance, representing as it does the (before tax) return earned on the assets employed in a business. It can also form the basis for more detailed analysis (see Section 2), if it is not feasible to split the aggregate interest expense or tax charge between parts of a business.

The published profit and loss account then normally deducts net interest expense, to arrive at profit before tax, and finally charges tax on profits to reach the 'bottom line', profit after tax for the period. (Certain expenses which have to be disclosed separately, such as depreciation, audit fees, directors' remuneration, are normally shown in the notes to the accounts, not in the main profit and loss account itself.)

At one time UK profit and loss accounts deducted dividends paid and proposed from the year's profits at the foot of the profit and loss account. Thus the 'link' between a period's profit and loss account and the end-of-period balance sheet was 'retained profit for the period'. Few other countries followed this practice; and in future, British accounts will add a period's profits directly to shareholders' funds and deduct any dividends actually paid or legally payable therefrom.

BALANCE SHEET CLASSIFICATION

3. How does the balance sheet classify items?

TOTAL ASSETS LESS CURRENT LIABILITIES represents the way in which the company has employed its long-term resources on fixed assets or working capital.

Fixed assets are intended for use on a long-term basis in the company's business. They include tangible assets such as land and buildings, plant and equipment; and intangible assets such as purchased goodwill or brands, and long-term investments.

Current assets are 'current' because as a rule we expect them to turn into cash within twelve months after the balance sheet date (or within the operating cycle of the business, if it is longer). The items usually appear in reverse order of liquidity: first stocks, then debtors, and finally cash itself (the most liquid).

Less: Current liabilities (creditors due within one year). These are due for payment within one year from the balance sheet date, and often much sooner. They include any short-term borrowings, amounts due to suppliers (trade creditors) and current tax payable.

Working capital (net current assets) is the difference between current assets and current liabilities. Even though the various items, as we have just seen, are all 'short term', the net balance of working capital requires long-term capital to finance it.

CAPITAL EMPLOYED is divided between creditors due after one year (long-term liabilities) and capital and reserves (shareholders' funds).

Creditors due after one year mostly represent long-term borrowings (loans, mortgages or debentures) which amount to semi-permanent capital for a company. They are often for fairly long periods, say five to fifteen years. When repayment becomes due, the company may seek to 'refinance' them by more long-term borrowing.

Capital and reserves (shareholders' funds). The called-up share capital, usually in the form of ordinary shares, is the permanent capital of the business. The profit and loss account represents cumulative retained profits, which are legally available to pay dividends to shareholders. In practice, however, dividends are usually paid out of the current year's profits.

CASH FLOW STATEMENT

The third main financial statement in the annual accounts of companies [required by IAS7/FRS1] is the cash flow statement. Its purpose is to show the sources and amounts of cash receipts in the year, from operations, sales of fixed assets, borrowing, issue of shares, and so on, and how the cash has been used in paying tax and dividends, investing in fixed assets, repaying borrowing, and so on. Section 11 deals with cash flows in more detail.

At this stage we can compile a simple cash flow statement for General Trading Limited for the year ended 31 March 2005, by listing the changes in the balance sheet figures between 31 March 2004 and 31 March 2005, which are summarized below. (The Companies Act 1985 requires companies to publish comparative figures for the previous year for both the profit and loss account and the balance sheet.)

To prepare a very simple cash flow statement involves two steps:

1. Calculate balance sheet differences.
2. Classify the sources and uses of cash.

Step 1. Calculate balance sheet differences

GENERAL TRADING LIMITED

| | Balance sheets | | Differences | |
| | 2004 | 2005 | Sources | Uses |
	£'000	£'000	£'000	£'000
Fixed assets	700	800		100
Stocks	270	400		130
Debtors	300	350		50
Cash	80	150		70
Less: (Trade creditors)	(170)	(270)	100	
(Tax)	(20)	(30)	10	
	1 160	1 400		
Loans	140	180	40	
Called up share capital	850	1 000	150	
Profit and loss account	170	220	50	
	1 160	1 400	350	350

Step 2. Classify the sources and uses of cash

One figure of special interest in the cash flow statement is the net flow of cash from operations. In the balance sheet, the profit and loss account balance has increased by £50 000. This is the amount of retained profit for the year: profit after tax £110 000 less dividends paid £60 000. But it is usual to include more detail from the profit and loss account itself. Operating profit before interest and tax is £180 000 (= £110 000 profit after tax + tax charged £50 000 + interest expense £20 000). Tax actually paid is £40 000 (the amount charged of £50 000 less the £10 000 increase in the end-of-year tax payable).

Using the IAS 7 format, the £80 000 net changes in 'working capital' are shown as part of cash flows resulting from operations, as are the separate items for interest, dividends and tax paid. (The FRS 1 format is slightly different.)

GENERAL TRADING LIMITED
Cash flow statement, Year ended 31 March 2005

			£'000
Operating activities			
Operating profit before interest and tax			180
Less:	Increase in stocks	(130)	
	Increase in debtors	(50)	
	Less: Increase in trade creditors	100	
			(80)
			100
Less:	Interest paid	(20)	
	Tax paid	(40)	
	Dividends paid	(60)	
			(120)
			(20)
Investing activities			
Purchases of fixed assets			**(100)**
Net cash outflow before financing			**(120)**
Financing activities			
Ordinary share capital issued		150	
Loans borrowed		40	
			190
Increase in cash			**70**

DISCLOSURE IN ANNUAL REPORTS

Accountants face many problems in reporting complex business transactions in financial statements. How much detail should accounts present and in what form? Most accounting numbers cannot be exactly 'correct' and even if they could, such spurious accuracy would not be useful. Hence larger companies now publish figures to the nearest million pounds only, and the accounts of even quite small UK companies normally go only to the nearest thousand pounds.

A public company's full annual report and accounts must contain at least the following:

- directors' report
- balance sheet
- profit and loss account
- cash flow statement
- notes to the accounts
- auditors' report.

The format and contents of UK companies' accounts must comply with the Companies Act 1985. But the law does not always specify whether certain details should appear in the accounts, in the notes, or elsewhere. The directors' report must deal with certain matters (not all of an accounting nature) unless the annual report includes them somewhere else. The list opposite shows the main items.

Most company chairmen include in the annual report a statement discussing the part year's results and commenting on future prospects. And large companies now publish an Operating and Financial Review together with summary financial statistics covering several past years. Anyone studying a company's performance and financial position should carefully examine all these, as well as the accounts themselves. (Large foreign companies often publish an English version of their accounts.)

The modern trend is to simplify the items shown on the face of the accounts, while extensive notes to the published accounts (see list opposite, below) give many extra details. The notes form *part* of 'the accounts' (sometimes the most important part). They are *not* just an optional extra.

The full annual reports of large companies may now contain around one hundred pages, amounting almost to a small book. There may be fifteen pages reviewing the past year's operations, ten pages on various corporate governance matters, five pages for the accounts and fifty pages of notes to the accounts. The rest may take another twenty pages or more. Many companies send shareholders a short 'Review and Financial Summary'; but for serious analysts this is no adequate substitute for the full 'Directors' Report and Accounts'.

Directors' report (unless shown elsewhere)

1 Names of the directors and details of their shareholdings
2 Main classes of business and any major changes
3 Important changes in fixed assets
4 Research and development activities
5 A fair review of the past year's business and the end-of-year position
6 Likely future developments
7 Any important events since year-end
8 Details of any of its own shares a company has acquired during the year.

Notes to the accounts (not exhaustive)

1 Accounting policies
2 Turnover, profit, net assets – by industrial sector
3 Turnover, profit, net assets – by geographical area
4 Interest payable and receivable
5 Tax on profits
6 Earnings per share
7 Fixed assets: purchases, disposals, depreciation
8 Debtors
9 Creditors
10 Borrowings, short-term and long-term
11 Any shares or debentures issued during the year
12 Transfers to or from reserves
13 The basis on which foreign currencies have been translated
14 Directors' remuneration
15 Number of employees, wages, social security and pension costs
16 Each subsidiary's name and the proportion of shares owned.

MODERN REQUIREMENTS

Requirements for UK company accounts stem from two main sources: Companies Acts (the law) and accounting standards. There is an overriding legal requirement to give 'a true and fair view' of a company's performance and financial position (which we discussed earlier on p. 2).

Company law

Successive post-war Companies Acts have required UK companies to divulge ever more details about their affairs. The 1948 Act required group accounts (see Section 9); the 1967 Act required companies to disclose turnover and to analyse sales and profits between different business segments and between geographical areas. The 1981 Act set out detailed EU Fourth Directive format requirements for accounts (see Appendix 5) and included certain measurement rules for the first time.

Schedule 4 to the Companies Act 1985 currently contains the main legal rules on accounting and audit matters, 187 pages of them. The 1985 Act consolidated several earlier Acts, and the 1989 Act, amending it, gave effect to the EU Seventh Directive on Group Accounts.

A new Companies Act is currently in the pipeline. After the first major review for many years, the Company Law Review Steering Group's Final Report in June 2001 proposed a number of radical changes. But in late 2004 there is no sign when (or whether) its substance will become law.

Accounting standards

Since 1971 UK companies have also been expected to follow 'accounting standards', which deal both with disclosure and with measurement. A similar system operates in the US, where a government agency, the Securities and Exchange Commission [SEC], oversees the US Financial Accounting Standards Board [FASB] more directly.

Between 1971 and 1990, the UK Accounting Standards Committee published twenty-five Statements of Standard Accounting Practice [SSAPs], of which eight survive. Between 1991 and 2004 its successor, the Accounting Standards Board [ASB], issued twenty-seven Financial Reporting Standards [FRSs], many revising earlier SSAPs. Appendix 3 (on page 275) lists all thirty-five UK accounting standards in issue at 1 January 2005, in total comprising more than 1800 pages.

The Foreword claims that compliance with accounting standards will normally be essential for company accounts to give a true and fair view, though ultimately this is for the *courts* to decide. The Companies Act (Schedule 4, section 36A) now requires companies to say whether their accounts follow accounting standards, and if not, to give details and reasons.

The International Accounting Standards Board (IASB) is leading the continuing effort to harmonize accounting standards world-wide. The EU now requires (from 2005) all member-states' listed companies to follow international accounting standards [IASs]. The IASB has published thirty-five general standards (see Appendix 3), comprising over 1000 pages. Most of the IASs are similar to UK standards, and Section 12 discusses the main differences.

Large and small companies

Companies of different sizes must meet varying levels of required disclosure, though similar measurement rules apply to all. Professional managers, who in the UK are rarely also large shareholders, run the major 'stewardship' companies. Their importance may justify extensive disclosure to help protect the interests of their public shareholders (often financial institutions). Companies whose shares are listed on the Stock Exchange must also comply with the Exchange's detailed requirements.

But in small 'proprietorship' companies, a few owners and their families own all or most of the shares, and often act as managers too. Reporting burdens for them must not be too heavy. Thus small- and medium-sized enterprises [SMEs] need not disclose certain details. There is also a special FRS for Smaller Entities [FRSSE], which comprises more than 200 pages. The Companies Act 1985 (as amended) defines 'small' and 'medium' companies as those meeting at least two of the following maximum conditions:

	Small	Medium
Turnover	£5.6 million	£11.2 million
Total assets	£2.8 million	£5.6 million
Number of employees	50	250

Large groups of companies are under continuing pressure to disclose still more. They must consolidate the accounts of the holding company and all its subsidiaries to present the combined affairs of the whole group as if they were the business of a single entity (see Section 9). IAS 22/FRS 3 requires companies to analyse turnover and operating profit between ongoing operations, acquisitions and discontinued operations. They must also disclose details about sales, profits and assets by business and geographical segment [IAS 14/SSAP 22]. Companies must now also give extensive details about directors' remuneration and about corporate governance.

But clearly there must be a limit. Already annual reports of large companies comprise a hundred or more pages – the size of a small book every year. The general principle is that the costs of producing information should not outweigh its likely benefits. But the trouble is that those who might benefit often do not have to bear the costs of ever more disclosure.

AUDITORS' REPORT

An audit is the independent examination by qualified accountants of an enterprises's accounts; but it is the *directors* of a company who are responsible for the accounts on which the auditors report.

The Companies Act 1985 requires all companies above a certain size to have their accounts audited. The auditors report to the shareholders on every balance sheet and profit and loss account laid before the company in general meeting. The auditors' report covers the accounts, including the notes, and (to some extent) also the directors' report.

The long form of auditors' report covers the respective responsibilities of directors and auditors, and the basis of the audit opinion. The standard form of audit opinion itself – the kernel of the report – is as follows:

'In our opinion the accounts give a true and fair view of the state of the company's [or group's] affairs as at the year-end date and of its profit [or loss] for the year then ended, and have been properly prepared in accordance with the Companies Act 1985.'

Auditing standards prescribe the basic principles and essential procedures for the conduct of an audit, under the following main headings:

- responsibility
- planning, controlling and recording
- accounting systems and internal control
- evidence
- using the work of others
- reporting.

Some key principles of auditing are as follows:

- Integrity — Auditors act with integrity, fulfilling their responsibilities with honesty, fairness and truthfulness.
- Independence — Auditors are objective; they express opinions independently of the entity and its directors.
- Competence — Auditors act with professional skill, derived from their qualification, training and practical experience.
- Rigour — Auditors approach their work with thoroughness and with an attitude of professional scepticism.
- Judgement — Auditors apply professional judgement taking account of materiality in the context of what they are reporting on.

Qualifications

Where auditors are unable to report that in their opinion the accounts give a true and fair view, then they must say so ('qualify' their report). This may be due to a limitation in the scope of the audit, where the auditors cannot get sufficient evidence, or to a disagreement between the auditors and a company's directors regarding accounting treatment or disclosure.

In an 'except for' opinion, the auditor can circumscribe the material area of uncertainty or disagreement, but a disclaimer or adverse opinion affects the accounts as a whole. A disclaimer implies something so fundamental or pervasive that the auditors are unable to form an opinion, while an adverse opinion means that the auditors believe the accounts are seriously misleading.

Nature of qualification	Material but not fundamental	Fundamental
UNCERTAINTY	'except for' opinion	disclaimer of opinion
DISAGREEMENT	'except for' opinion	adverse opinion

Circumstances leading to uncertainty may include:

(a) inability to carry out necessary audit procedures, or lack of proper accounting records;
(b) inherent uncertainties, for example in relation to major litigation or long-term contracts, or doubt about the company's ability to continue as a going concern.

Circumstances giving rise to disagreement may include:

(a) failure to follow one or more accounting standards, in which the auditors do not concur;
(b) disagreement as to facts or amounts in the accounts;
(c) disagreement as to the manner or extent of disclosure in the accounts.

Only something important will cause auditors to qualify their report. Since most company directors are anxious to avoid this if at all possible, a qualified audit report should *always* be a matter of concern to readers of accounts. They should try to assess carefully what every word in the audit report means. Even serious qualifications sometimes use what may seem to be highly technical language, but it would be foolish to assume that an auditors' qualification is a mere technicality.

SECTION 1 SUMMARY

This section has briefly reviewed the progress of accounting from the personal finite venture of a sole trader to complex worldwide business empires lasting for generations. The basic 'double-entry' bookkeeping approach to accounts remains, and so does the essential requirement to show 'a true and fair view'. Accounts still emphasize four 'fundamental accounting concepts': going concern, accruals, consistency and prudence. These reflect the practical wisdom of centuries.

The three main accounting statements are the profit and loss account, balance sheet and cash flow statement. Problems arise in preparing annual accounts for ongoing businesses, since many transactions are incomplete at the balance sheet date. Goods may be only partly-finished, assets may be partly worn out, and sales and purchases may not yet have been paid for in cash. But accountants must attach values (often 'costs') to assets, and try to 'match' expenditures against revenues in the relevant accounting period.

The profit and loss account (income statement) shows a firm's revenues and classifies the expenses for a period (often one year). The 'bottom line', profit after tax for the period, represents the *link* with the balance sheet.

The balance sheet (statement of financial position) is a classified summary at a specific date showing fixed assets and net current assets, together with sources of finance. The normal UK format deducts current liabilities from current assets, to present a figure for net current assets (working capital). Thus the balance sheet shows uses of funds (total assets less current liabilities) and sources of funds (borrowings plus shareholders' funds).

The cash flow statement classifies total receipts and payments of cash during a period. One can prepare a simple cash flow statement from differences between the opening and closing balance sheets. The usual format shows three main activities: operations, investment and financing.

The annual report and accounts of the largest companies now comprises up to a hundred pages or even more. The directors' report must deal with certain items, if not shown elsewhere; and the notes form *part* of the accounts and cover a wide range of details.

Company law requires extensive disclosure, but less from a small 'proprietorship' limited (ltd) company than from a large 'stewardship' public limited company (plc). In addition, accounting standards, on both measurement and disclosure, represent detailed rules for companies to follow. Attempts at international harmonization aim to produce a single set of standards worldwide.

Finally we considered the auditors' report, its standard form of wording, and the nature of possible 'qualifications' to an audit opinion.

Although the core of accounting is in many ways remarkably stable, practices have been changing over recent decades to meet new needs, especially for larger public companies. They will surely continue to evolve.

PROBLEMS

We have now finished the first of the fourteen sections of 'text' in this workbook. Each such section of text in the book is followed by a number of pages of 'problems'.

Section 1 has discussed the background to company accounts, and the structure of the three main financial statements: the balance sheet, profit and loss account and cash flow statement. The next sections of text go on to consider how to use accounts to appraise a company's performance and financial position.

Before moving on to Section 2, however, we expect that most readers will wish to attempt some or all of the problems on the next few pages (pages 11 to 18). We believe that working through problems is extremely helpful to most readers in consolidating their learning.

In particular, we strongly recommend that you work the first problem following each section of text. We ask you to take the trouble to *write down* your own attempt at each of ten 'definitions' in the space provided (or, if you prefer, on a separate sheet of paper) *before* going on to look at our version over the page.

The remaining problems after each section of text gradually become more complex and difficult. The first few problems leave space in the book for you to write your answer (sometimes simply by amending a set of accounts in writing); and our solution then appears on the next page overleaf. You may prefer to use pencil (rather than ink) to fill in your attempts at answers in the book to this first set of problems.

For the second set of somewhat harder problems, we ask you to use your own paper for your answers. It would take up too much space for us to provide room for these in the book itself. You can then compare your answers with ours at the end of the book (starting on page 291).

Finally in each section there are a few problems for which we do not publish solutions. You may like to attempt answers for your own satisfaction; or, if you are using the book as part of a formal training course, this third group of problems may, in part or in total, serve for class assignments. (Teachers in a recognized institution may receive answers to this third group of problems on request – see Preface, page viii).

In addition to these problems set out after the end of the pages of text, in most of the later sections of the book there are one or two exercises which we ask you, the reader, to work through *in the text itself*. We strongly recommend you to take the trouble to work through these problems as you come across them. They mostly deal with basic accounting matters, and if you have read the preceding pages of text you should be able to cope. If, however, they give you trouble, then re-reading the relevant portion of text may be helpful.

1.1 Definitions

Please write down, in the space provided, your definition of the terms below. Then compare your answers with the definitions shown overleaf.

(a) Balance sheet

(b) Profit and loss account

(c) Fixed assets

(d) Creditors due within one year

(e) Capital and reserves

(f) Current assets

(g) Working capital

(h) 'A true and fair view'

(i) Cash flow statement

(j) Ordinary dividends

1.1 Definitions

(a) Balance sheet – Statement of financial position which shows at a given date (i) the cumulative sources of funds which shareholders lenders and others have provided to a business and (ii) how the business has used those funds to invest in fixed assets and working capital (= total assets less current liabilities).

(b) Profit and loss account – Income statement which shows the turnover (sales revenue), expenses and operating profit for the financial year. It then charges interest expense and tax on profits, to show the profit after tax (net income) for the year. Thus profit may be defined as sales revenue less total expenses.

(c) Fixed assets are intended for use in the business. There are three kinds of fixed assets, normally shown at cost less amounts written off: intangible (for example trade marks, goodwill), tangible (for example buildings, equipment) and investments (for example long-term securities, either equity or loans).

(d) Creditors due within one year – current liabilities. Amounts which the business owes to others, due within twelve months from the balance sheet date; for example, short-term borrowing, trade creditors, current tax payable. 'Trade creditors' (= accounts payable) are persons or businesses to whom amounts are due for goods or services purchased on credit.

(e) Capital and reserves – shareholders' funds, owners' equity. The three main components are: called up (issued) share capital, cumulative retained profits and other reserves. These amounts represent the interests of the company's owners and ultimately 'belong' to shareholders. They are not 'liabilities' like other sources of funds, since they are not normally payable (to shareholders) until the company ceases to exist (is 'wound up' or 'liquidated'). Shareholders' funds = total assets less external liabilities. It is thus a *residual* amount, depending on the book value of a company's assets (which will normally differ from their current market value).

(f) Current assets are all assets other than fixed assets (see (c) opposite). Either cash, or assets likely soon to be turned into cash or consumed within the business. For example, stocks (= inventories), both for resale and for use, debtors (= accounts receivable), prepaid expenses. Some industries (for example whisky distilling, tobacco, construction) have a normal operating cycle longer than twelve months.

(g) Working capital is current assets minus current liabilities. The vertical balance sheet format reveals working capital (= net current assets) as a sub-total. (See Format 1, item F in Appendix 5 on page 278.) Although each constituent item is 'current' (that is, short-term), the net balance of working capital may need a long-term source of finance. (It may, however, be *negative*, if current liabilities exceed current assets.)

(h) A true and fair view is now required of all company accounts in the European Union. Its meaning is not easy to state precisely, and may indeed vary somewhat between countries. In the UK three 'definitions' are common:

- appropriate measurement, classification and disclosure of items
- the consistent application of generally accepted accounting principles
- compliance with official accounting standards.

(i) A cash flow statement is a statement of sources and uses of cash during the financial year. It shows, in suitably classified format, the sources of cash and the ways in which the business has used cash during the year. The three main headings relate to operating, investing and financing.

(j) Ordinary dividends are the amount of profit paid out to the equity shareholders, the owners of a company's share capital. A company's directors decide how much of the profits the company should distribute in dividends and they ask the shareholders to approve the amount of the 'final' dividend at the annual general meeting. (Companies may also pay 'interim' dividends during the year without needing to get shareholders' agreement.)

1.2 Classification of balance sheet and profit and loss account items

For each item shown below, place a cross in the appropriate column. (Some items may appear in more than one column; and at least one of the items is not explicitly shown in the accounts.)

When you have completed the exercise, please compare your answers with those shown over the page.

	Balance sheet					Profit and loss account	
	Capital and reserves	Creditors due after one year	Creditors due within one year	Fixed assets	Current assets	Before operating profit	After operating profit
(a) Stocks (inventories)							
(b) Trade creditors (accounts payable)							
(c) Taxation							
(d) Called up share capital							
(e) Auditors' report							
(f) Cash							
(g) Fixtures and equipment							
(h) Loan interest							
(i) Turnover (sales revenue)							
(j) Employees							
(k) Debtors (accounts receivable)							
(l) Long-term borrowing							

1.2 Classification of balance sheet and profit and loss account items

Solution

	Balance sheet					Profit and loss account	
	Capital and reserves	Creditors due after one year	Creditors due within one year	Fixed assets	Current assets	Before operating profit	After operating profit
(a) Stocks (inventories)					x		
(b) Trade creditors (accounts payable)			x				
(c) Taxation			x liability				x expense
(d) Called up share capital	x						
(e) Auditors' report							
(f) Cash					x		
(g) Fixtures and equipment				x			
(h) Loan interest			?				x
(i) Turnover (sales revenue)						x	
(j) Employees							
(k) Debtors (accounts receivable)					x		
(l) Long-term borrowing		x					

Notes: Item (h), 'Loan interest', may appear as 'Creditors due within one year', to the extent that it is wholly or partly outstanding at the balance sheet date. Items (e) and (j) do not appear in the accounts.

The following problems involve the construction of company accounts. They range from the simple to the more complex.

A suggested answer to each of the two problems on this page appears overleaf. You are *strongly urged not to look at them* until you have written out your own answers in the spaces provided.

1.3 The Corner Shop Limited

Compile the balance sheet of The Corner Shop Limited at 30 June 2005 from the following information:

	£
Called up share capital	10 000
Leasehold shop	6 000
Cash	4 000
Profit and loss account	4 000
Trade creditors	3 000
Stock	7 000

THE CORNER SHOP LIMITED

£

Fixed asset

Current assets

Less: **Creditors due within one year**

Capital and reserves

1.4 Peterson Equipment Limited

Compile the balance sheet of Peterson Equipment Limited at 30 April 2005 from the following information:

	£'000
Land and buildings	156
Plant and machinery, net	114
Tax payable	14
Cash	17
Cumulative retained profits	107
Debtors	45
Long-term borrowing	80
Stock	38
Called up share capital	140
Trade creditors	29

PETERSON EQUIPMENT LIMITED

£'000

Fixed assets

Current assets

Less: **Creditors due within one year**

Total assets less current liabilities

Less: **Creditors due after one year**

Capital and reserves

15

1.3 The Corner Shop Limited

Solution

THE CORNER SHOP LIMITED
Balance sheet at 30 June 2005

		£
Fixed asset		
Leasehold shop		6 000
Current assets		
Stock	7 000	
Cash	4 000	
	11 000	
Less: **Creditors due within one year**		
Trade creditors	3 000	
Net current assets		8 000
		14 000
Capital and reserves		
Called up share capital		10 000
Profit and loss account		4 000
		14 000

Notes
1 The heading of the balance sheet shows:
   (a) the name of the company
   (b) the balance sheet date.
2 Current assets are shown in order of liquidity, with the least liquid assets at the top.
3 Creditors due within one year are deducted from current assets. The balance (£8 000) is called 'net current assets' (or 'working capital').

1.4 Peterson Equipment Limited

Solution

PETERSON EQUIPMENT LIMITED
Balance sheet at 30 April 2005

		£'000
Fixed assets		
Land and buildings		156
Plant and machinery, net		114
		270
Current assets		
Stock	38	
Debtors	45	
Cash	17	
	100	
Less: **Creditors due within one year**		
Trade creditors	29	
Tax payable	14	
	43	
Net current assets		57
Total assets less current liabilities		327
Less: **Creditors due after one year**		
Long-term borrowing		80
Capital and reserves		
Called up share capital	140	
Profit and loss account	107	
		247

Notes
1 Rounding to the nearest thousand pounds is normal for a company this size.
2 Each main item has a separate subtotal.
3 The subtotal 'Net current assets' (£57 000) may be entitled 'Working capital'.
4 The subtotal of capital and reserves is shown separately, and may be entitled 'Shareholders' funds'.

Please use a separate sheet of paper for your answers to each of the following problems. Solutions to these problems are shown at the end of the book, starting on page 291.

1.5 The Acme Company Limited

The Acme Company Limited prepares accounts to 30 June. From the following information compile the 2005 balance sheet.

	£'000
Cash	20
Current tax payable	20
Fixtures and fittings	30
Trade creditors	30
Profit and loss account	50
Called up share capital	200
Stock	60
Freehold shop	150
Debtors	40

1.6 General Contractors Limited

Prepare the profit and loss account for General Contractors Limited for the year ended 31 December 2004 from the following information:

	£'000
Trading profit before depreciation and interest	200
Tax on the profit for the year	40
Interest payable	10
Invoiced sales in the year	1 250
Cost of sales	1 050
Depreciation on plant and equipment*	50*

* = not included in cost of sales.

1.7 The Marvel Trading Company Limited

The Marvel Trading Company Limited prepares annual accounts to 30 June each year. The company made a trading profit of £100 000 in 2005 after deduction of all charges including depreciation, but before charging interest payable of £8 000. Income from investments during the year amounted to £12 000, and the estimated tax charge on the profit for the year was £26 000. Sales turnover in the year amounted to £1 200 000.

You are asked to prepare the company's profit and loss account for the year ended 30 June 2005.

1.8 The Fine Fare Catering Company Limited

The accounts of the Fine Fare Catering Company Limited for its first year, ended 31 March 2005, contain the following items. Compile the balance sheet and profit and loss account.

	£'000
Turnover	150
Called up share capital	70
Fixtures and fittings	10
Cash	10
Trade creditors	10
Leasehold restaurant	70
Stock	20
Tax due on profit for the year	10
Trading profit after depreciation	30

1.9 Andrew Hunt Limited

Andrew Hunt Limited's first accounts, for the nine months ended 30 September 2004, contain the following items. Prepare the balance sheet and profit and loss account.

	£'000
Cash	200
Trade creditors	320
10% Debenture 2008	400
Debtors	470
Depreciation charge for plant and machinery	50
Leasehold factory	600
Plant and machinery net (after deducting depreciation for the period)	450
Turnover	3 400
Called up share capital	750
Stock	330
Tax on profit	145
Cost of sales (excluding depreciation)	2 740
Interest paid	30

No answers are published for the following problems. Teachers in recognized institutions may send for an Instructor's Guide containing suggested solutions (see p. ix).

1.10 Allen and Faber Limited

Allen and Faber Limited has been trading for many years. Its accounts for the year ended 31 December 2004 contain the following items. You are required to prepare, in suitably classified format, the balance sheet and profit and loss account for 2004.

	£'000
Called up share capital	1 500
15% Debentures 2008	600
Cumulative retained profits, 1 January 2004	1 040
Stock	700
Plant and equipment, at cost	1 730
Debtors	510
Cost of sales (excluding depreciation)	4 250
Debenture interest paid	90
Cumulative depreciation on plant	890
Trade creditors	380
Freehold land and buildings	2 140
Tax on profit for the period	190
Cash	170
Trading profit before interest	790
Tax liability	330
Turnover	5 210
Depreciation for the period	170

1.11 Developing negatives

Could the items below ever be negative? If so, under what circumstances? How would you show each item on the balance sheet?

(a) Retained profit for the year
(b) Corporation tax payable
(c) Working capital
(d) Work-in-progress

1.12 The missing balance sheet

On 3 May 2005 a burglary took place at the head office of Swanton Publishing Limited. Among the items stolen was the only copy of the draft balance sheet at 31 March 2005, and the books of account used to prepare it.

Fortunately, Mr Edgerton, the company's assistant chief accountant, had noted on a separate piece of paper a number of balance sheet items and relationships.

See if you can reproduce the company's balance sheet at 31 March 2005 from Mr Edgerton's notes, which are shown below:

(a) Long-term liabilities = $1\frac{1}{2}$ times working capital
(b) Debtors = Current liabilities
(c) Authorized share capital = £180 000
(d) Cash = $\frac{1}{2}$ stock
(e) Net fixed assets = Total liabilities + £100 000
(f) Called up share capital = 2/3 x shareholders' funds
(g) Liquid assets = Reserves
(h) Shares issued (50p each) = 280 000 out of 360 000 authorized
(i) Acid test ratio = 1.40

The acid test ratio represents $\dfrac{\text{debtors plus cash (= liquid assets)}}{\text{current liabilities}}$

1.13 Sultan Chemicals Limited

From the following information draw up the profit and loss account of Sultan Chemicals Limited for the year ended 30 April 2004.

	£'000
Administrative expenses	450
Cost of sales	3 700
Distribution costs	1 300
Dividends payable	300
Interest expense	200
Profit after tax for the year	(balancing item)
Share of profits of associated undertakings	100
Taxation	200
Turnover	6 000

Section 2
Analysing performance

INTRODUCTION

In Section 1, we studied the structure of the profit and loss account, the balance sheet and the cash flow statement and noted the links between them.

In Section 4 we shall see in more detail how the books of account summarize transactions and events; and in Sections 5, 6 and 7 we shall deal with the accounting rules for measuring profit or loss and for valuing stock and fixed assets.

But first we look at a company's accounts as a whole. In this section and the next, we consider how to extract information useful for analysing performance (Section 2) and financial position (Section 3).

Published accounts may relate to a single company or to a group of companies under common control (see Section 9). The information disclosed will reveal:

- the level of sales (turnover), expenses and profit (or loss);
- earnings per share and dividends;
- different kinds of assets and how they have been financed;
- the relationship between borrowing and shareholders' funds.

We can split the process of analysing financial statements into four main steps:

- overview
- ratio analysis
- cash flow
- business segments.

We deal with the overview in this section, and with ratio analysis in Sections 2 and 3. We discuss cash flows in Section 11, and business segments in Sections 5 and 12. Finally in Section 14 we return to complete analysis and interpretation of the meaning of company accounts.

OVERVIEW

A company's main accounts refer only to the current and previous year. But to establish the context we must look over a longer period at the trends in key figures, such as:

- turnover (sales)
- total assets less current liabilities
- operating profit
- earnings per share.

Over a five-year period, we can calculate the annual percentage changes in each key figure, and compare them with an index of general price changes such as the UK Retail Prices Index [RPI]. For a public company listed on the stock exchange we can also compare changes in share price with the market index or a suitable industry index.

To illustrate, we show below figures for Tesco plc, the leading UK food retailer. In each year, growth in turnover and profit easily outstripped inflation. The average share price has not done quite so well, due mainly to wider stock market movements.

A five-year trend summary will often also provide some financial ratios, though we may prefer to postpone ratio analysis until the second stage. Companies publish the figures in their own five-year summaries on a consistent basis; but outside analysts may often wish to make certain adjustments. (For instance, Tesco calculates its return on equity ratio on a before-tax basis, whereas we prefer to use after-tax profits.)

TESCO PLC: OVERVIEW 2000–2004

52 weeks ended February	2000	2001	2002	2003	2004*
Key figures					
Turnover (£ billion)	18.6	20.8	23.4	26.0	30.8
Operating profit (£ million)	1 030	1 166	1 322	1 484	1 735
Total assets less CL (£ billion)	6.4	7.3	8.7	11.1	12.9
Earnings per share (pence)	10.36	10.87	12.33	14.10	16.45
'Average' share price (pence)	173	217	258	207	210
Annual rate of change (%)					
Turnover	9.6	11.7	12.5	11.1	18.5
Operating profit	8.1	12.6	13.5	13.3	21.4
Total assets less CL	13.5	15.1	19.1	27.2	16.3
Earnings per share	8.0	4.9	13.4	14.4	16.7
'Average' share price	0	25	19	(20)	1
Retail Prices Index (average)	1.1	3.0	2.1	1.4	3.0

* 53 weeks

RETURN ON INVESTMENT

Capital is scarce, so the concept of 'return on investment' [ROI] is paramount in the world of business. People with funds to invest will want a return on their money.

Investors who want a stream of assured income may choose government stocks paying regular half-yearly interest. But equity returns are likely to be riskier, since they involve investing money today in the hope of benefits in the uncertain future. Even so, taking capital growth into account as well as dividends, the expected return on a company's equity shares may be higher than on 'risk-free' government ('gilt-edged') securities.

The capital market tries to adjust the 'required' rate of return according to the degree of risk, but this is not easy to assess. The chart below shows a trade-off between perceived risk and the required rate of return. The slope of the line represents the 'price of risk' ('risk premium'): as the risk grows, so does the required return. The intercept A on the vertical axis represents the 'required' (minimum) rate of return for an 'average-risk' investment.

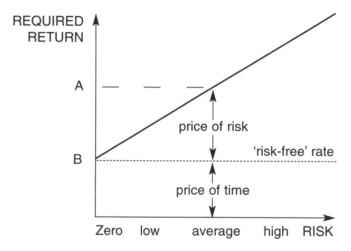

Notice that even a zero-risk investment (the intercept B on the vertical axis) shows a small positive required rate of return. This 'risk-free' rate of interest represents the 'price of time' ('pure time-preference'). It may also include an 'inflation premium', if it is in nominal money terms. Of course, like any market prices, interest rates and risk premiums may fluctuate as conditions change.

In analysing accounts it is important to remember that a company's type of business and its financial structure can both affect its level of risk. Thus we may distinguish between 'business risk' and 'financial risk'. These in turn may affect the level of returns which an investor can hope to obtain. Two main measures of performance are 'return on equity' and 'return on net assets', which we consider next.

Return on net assets

The main operating 'return on investment' ratio is return on net assets. It deals with operating profit before tax and before financing charges, and it looks at (total) net assets (= total assets less current liabilities).

The return on net assets ratio for ABC Trading Limited for 2004 is thus as follows:

$$\frac{\text{Return}}{\text{Net assets}} = \frac{\text{Profit before interest and tax*}}{\text{Net assets}} = \frac{440}{2\,200} = 20.0\%$$

(*This unwieldy expression is shortened to PBIT.)

This measure indicates the performance achieved regardless of the method of financing. As we shall see in Section 8, a company's capital structure (its financial 'gearing') can affect its return on equity; but it makes no difference to return on net assets. Since it is often difficult in practice to split the capital employed in *part* of a business between 'debt' and 'equity', the return on net assets ratio can be useful in measuring the operating performance of divisions within a company.

Return on equity

Return on ordinary shareholders' funds (= return on equity) is a comprehensive measure of the performance of a company and its management for a period – from the *shareholders'* point of view. It takes into account both operating and financing aspects.

Using the figures for ABC Trading Limited for the year ended 30 June 2005 (shown on the right), the ratio is calculated as follows:

$$\frac{\text{Return}}{\text{Equity}} = \frac{\text{Profit after tax}}{\text{Shareholders' funds}} = \frac{240}{1\,600} = 15.0\%$$

The two return on investment measures are linked as shown below:

RETURN ON NET ASSETS	=	Profit before interest and tax	÷ Debt + equity
adjust for		*Interest and tax* *Debt*	
RETURN ON EQUITY	=	Profit after tax	÷ Equity

Profit and loss account for the year ended 30 June 2005

	£'000
Turnover	4 000
Operating profit	440
Interest expense	80
Profit before tax	360
Taxation	120
Profit after tax	240

Balance sheet at 30 June 2005

		£'000
Tangible fixed assets		1 400
Net current assets		800
Total assets less current liabilities		2 200
Less: Long-term loans		(600)
Capital and reserves		
Called up share capital	900	
Profit and loss account	700	
		1 600

The vertical balance sheet format lists fixed assets, then current assets less current liabilities (= net current assets or 'working capital'), to give a sub-total 'total assets less current liabilities'. It then deducts borrowing (long-term liabilities or 'debt'), to leave shareholders' funds (= 'capital and reserves' or 'equity').

In our ratio analysis we sometimes use the terms 'net assets' and 'capital employed':

Net assets:	Capital employed:
Fixed assets + net current assets	Borrowings + shareholders' funds
Total assets less current liabilities	Debt + equity

In addition, we count short-term borrowing as 'debt'. Thus where relevant we exclude short-term borrowing from current liabilities (in effect, increasing 'working capital'). See the example set out in Section 3, on p. 47.

PYRAMID OF RATIOS

Return on net assets is a useful measure for internal management control purposes because it readily splits into a number of elements.

The first level of division is into two basic parts:

Return on Net Assets = Profit Margin x Net Asset Turnover

This means:

$$\frac{\text{Profit}}{\text{Net Assets}} = \frac{\text{Profit}}{\text{Sales}} \times \frac{\text{Sales}}{\text{Net Assets}}$$

'Profit' here is the 'profit before interest payable and tax' (PBIT). Using the figures for ABC Trading Limited, the breakdown is:

$$\frac{440}{2\,200} = \frac{440}{4\,000} \times \frac{4000}{2\,200}$$

$$20.0\% = 11.0\% \times 1.82$$

The 11.0 per cent profit margin on sales is a common measure of performance. The concept of 'net asset turnover' may be less familiar, but it is a useful way of thinking about the use of capital. The number '1.82' can be thought of as the number of times that capital is being turned over in sales revenue in a period. Perhaps more concretely, it is the number of pounds' worth of sales that each pound of investment generates on average in a year.

The basic division of return on net assets into profit margin and net asset turnover can go further to form a 'pyramid' of ratios, as shown on the right. Changes in higher level ratios are 'explained' (or analysed) in terms of changes in a number of lower level ratios.

Thus, for example, one can split the ratio 'Operating Expenses as a percentage of Sales' between the various different kinds of operating expenses; or any given ratio for the whole company (say, gross profit margin on sales) can be split between various divisions or product lines of the company.

This is where the special potential of the return on net assets 'pyramid of ratios' as a management control tool arises. It enables one to study a company's results in ever greater detail:

- by refining the accounting ratios (as in the diagram);
- by analysing ratios between different parts of an enterprise;
- by splitting annual ratios into shorter time periods.

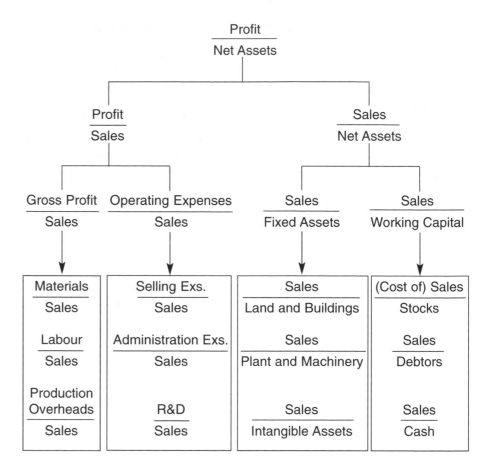

Improving performance

A modified version of the pyramid of ratios appears on the right. The diagram shows how a company could try to increase its return on investment either by increasing the profit ('return') or by reducing the assets employed ('investment'). The essence of a commercial outlook is not merely to look for technical efficiency (a 'better' machine), but for *economic* effectiveness (a better machine *that is worth the extra cost*).

How can a business increase its profit, assuming no change in investment? Either by increasing sales revenue or by reducing expenses.

Increasing sales revenue can mean increasing either the *volume* of sales or the average *price* per unit. Increasing the volume of sales requires the capacity to produce more. It also means increasing customer *demand*. Several product attributes may help towards this end, which may also enable the firm to charge a 'premium' price and thus increase profit margins too. Among them are: novelty, design, quality, packaging, as well as the maker's general 'reputation' comprising the value of the 'brand'.

Reducing expenses means reducing either the *quantity* of certain expense items or their *cost*. For example, careful production may reduce the waste of materials, while efficient purchasing may reduce their average cost. And most firms could improve their use of labour, even if wage rates may not be easy to reduce. Where cause and effect is hard to assess, cutting out certain expenses may not impair the business; for example, some research or advertising. And, reducing the quality of purchases may be judged worthwhile; for example, travelling economy rather than business class.

Accounting can help in assessing trading performance (both past and future), but firms clearly need to combine many other important business skills in order to earn maximum profits. Understanding accounting does not preclude possession of these other skills!

We can apply a similar approach to reducing assets for a given level of sales revenue, looking in turn at fixed assets and current assets. (In times of inflation, this may mean increasing investment in assets *less than in proportion to* an increase in sales revenue.)

Firms can reduce investment in fixed assets per £ of sales revenue in various ways: better building location or layout, more intensive use of facilities, proper maintenance allowing later replacement, efficient management of new capital projects.

As for current assets, reducing investment for a given level of sales revenue may involve: stock control, managing customer credit and efficient treasury management. In many companies, stocks and debtors comprise about half the total assets. So efficient management of these important items can make a big difference.

It may also be possible to use other ratios which we shall not examine further. In some businesses one can analyse sales, expenses, investment and profit on a 'per employee' basis, or 'per £ of employee costs'. And different industries may have their own ratios. Retailers may look at sales and expenses on a 'per square foot' basis; universities look at library costs 'per student', and so on.

MANAGEMENT ACTION TO IMPROVE PERFORMANCE

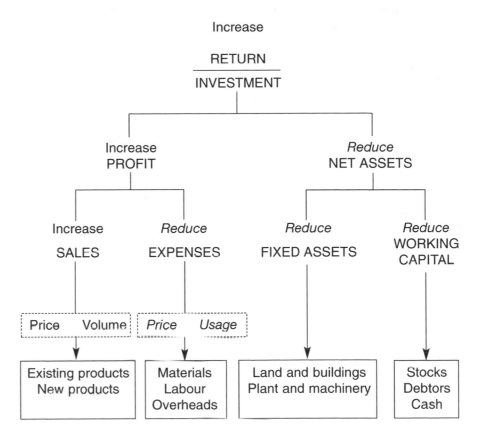

RATIO CALCULATION

After you have studied the diagram showing the 'pyramid' of ratios, and noted the links between various parts, the next step is to calculate a set of financial ratios for yourself.

When approaching the detailed ratio analysis of a company's accounts, it is helpful to group the ratios under three broad headings to measure different facets of the business:

- performance ratios
- financial status ratios
- stock market ratios.

We deal with performance ratios in this section, and with the other ratios in Section 3. The full list of performance ratios which we shall define and use in this section is set out below:

Profitability	**Asset turnover**
Return on net assets (%)	Net asset turnover
Profit margin (%)	Fixed asset turnover
Return on equity (%)	Stock turnover
Tax ratio (%)	Debtor turnover

The first four ratios above relate to profitability, and the second four relate to sales divided by assets. These two kinds of measures are intended to help show how well a business is being run.

The accounts of Precision Locks Limited for the year ended 30 June 2005 are set out on the right (together with comparative figures for 2004). You are asked to study the profit and loss account and balance sheet, and then to calculate the first four performance ratios listed.

At each stage in the analysis you will be asked to calculate the appropriate ratios, and then to compare your answers with those set out on the pages immediately following. In each case the ratios for 2004 have already been calculated, and are set out alongside.

Please now study the Precision Locks accounts, then turn to the next page and begin the detailed analysis of the 2005 results.

PRECISION LOCKS LIMITED

Profit and loss account

for the year ended 30 June	2005 £'000	2004 £'000
Turnover (sales)	1 200	1 000
Cost of sales	800	700
Gross profit	400	300
Administrative expenses	238	195
Operating profit	162	105
Loan interest	22	15
Profit before tax	140	90
Tax	50	30
Profit after tax	90	60

Balance sheet at 30 June		2005 £'000		2004 £'000
Fixed assets		210		200
Current assets				
Stock	350		290	
Debtors	200		150	
Cash	40		60	
	590		500	
Less: **Creditors due within one year** (current liabilities)	250		200	
		340		300
Total assets less current liabilities		550		500
Less: **Creditors due after one year**				
Long-term loan		100		100
Capital and reserves				
Called up £1 share capital	300		300	
Profit and loss account*	150*		100	
		450		400

* A dividend of 40 was paid in the year.

PERFORMANCE RATIOS (Profitability)

Using the appropriate figures from Precision Locks Limited's 2005 accounts set out on the previous page, please calculate the following four profitability ratios for 2005. When you have completed the calculations, compare your answers with those shown overleaf, together with comments.

			2005	2004

Return on net assets

$$\frac{\text{Profit before interest and tax}}{\text{Net assets}} \quad = \quad \rule{3cm}{0.4pt} \quad = \quad 21.0\%$$

Profit margin

$$\frac{\text{Profit before interest and tax}}{\text{Sales (Turnover)}} \quad = \quad \rule{3cm}{0.4pt} \quad = \quad 10.5\%$$

Return on equity

$$\frac{\text{Profit after tax}}{\text{Shareholders' funds}} \quad = \quad \rule{3cm}{0.4pt} \quad = \quad 15.0\%$$

Tax ratio

$$\frac{\text{Tax}}{\text{Profit before tax}} \quad = \quad \rule{3cm}{0.4pt} \quad = \quad 33.3\%$$

The Use of Ratios

One piece of information on its own may not mean much. A 'ratio' is simply a method of *comparing* one number with another: it may *divide* one number by another or express it as a *percentage* of another. An accounting ratio has meaning only if there is some reason to expect a definite relationship between the two, such as between profit and sales or between depreciation and fixed assets. (If we were to divide tax by stocks, the result would be meaningless. There is no reason to expect the two amounts to be related.) Using ratios can help to compare results with a given standard (see page 29). It can also make it easier to compare firms of different size.

For accounting ratios we normally use end-of-year balance sheet numbers and we shall nearly always do so in this book. One might, however, sometimes wish to 'average' opening and closing balance sheet amounts (for example, to get a weighted average of the number of shares in issue in a period), especially if there has been a big change during the period.

Profitability

Return on net assets [RONA]

$$\frac{\text{Profit before interest and tax}}{\text{Net assets}} = \frac{162}{550} = 29.4\% \quad (2004: 21.0\%)$$

This key measure of operating performance ignores both tax and the company's method of financing. (It is thus suitable to use as a basis for analysis of divisions within a company – via the Pyramid of Ratios which we saw on p. 22.)

The ratio calculates the return (before charging interest and tax) on all the 'net assets' (= total assets less current liabilities), whether financed by debt or by equity. This basic 'return on investment' [ROI] ratio is sometimes also called either ROCE (Return on Capital Employed) or ROFE (Return on Funds Employed).

The rather unwieldy term 'Profit Before Interest payable and Tax' is often shortened to PBIT (or to EBIT = Earnings Before Interest payable and Tax).

As we have seen, the return on net assets ratio can be analysed into: profit margin x net asset turnover. Thus in Precision Locks Limited:

in 2005	29.4%	=	13.4%	x	2.18
in 2004	21.0%	=	10.5%	x	2.00.

Profit margin

$$\frac{\text{Profit before interest and tax}}{\text{Sales}} = \frac{162}{1\,200} = 13.5\% \quad (2004: 10.5\%)$$

Analysts may also wish to calculate the percentage to sales of various kinds of expenses (such as cost of goods sold or selling and administration expenses). Changes in such percentages over time can indicate changes in the business.

In most companies some expenses vary (more or less) in proportion to sales, whereas others are (more or less) 'fixed' (at least in the short term). So the net profit margin percentage does not represent the proportion of any *increase* in sales turnover that would come through (to the 'bottom line') as *extra* profit.

If one distinguishes 'variable' expenses from 'fixed' expenses, one can think of the path from sales revenue to profit as follows:

	2005 £'000	2004 £'000
Sales revenue	1 200	1 000
Less: Variable expenses	720	600
= 'Variable profit' ('contribution')	480	400
Less: Fixed expenses	318	295
= Operating profit (PBIT)	162	105

Of course, in the long run even so-called 'fixed' expenses vary, presumably (in the long run) more or less in line with sales. But for Precision Locks Limited, sales in 2005 increased by 20 per cent (over 2004), while fixed expenses rose by only about 8 per cent. As a result, operating profit rose by more than 50 per cent between the two years.

Return on equity

$$\frac{\text{Profit after tax}}{\text{Shareholders' funds}} = \frac{90}{450} = 20.0\% \quad (2004: 15.0\%)$$

This key measure of performance takes into account not only the results of operations, but also the effect of financing and the impact of tax (as set out on the foot of page 21, left).

Tax ratio

$$\frac{\text{Tax expense}}{\text{Profit before tax}} = \frac{50}{140} = 35.7\% \quad (2004: 33.3\%)$$

This ratio indicates the corporation tax charge as a proportion of profit. Comparing the ratio over time, and with other companies in the same industry, may show whether tax is being well managed (though, of course, taxpayers cannot always affect the amount they have to pay).

There are several reasons why the tax ratio above may not be exactly equal to the current UK rate of corporation tax, including overseas profits taxed at a different rate and certain expenses which may not be allowable for tax purposes (see Section 10).

PERFORMANCE RATIOS (Asset turnover)

Please refer back to Precision Locks Limited's 2005 accounts (on page 24) in order to calculate the remaining four performance ratios, concerned with rates of asset turnover, set out below. When you have completed your answers, please compare them with the answers overleaf, and study the comments thereon.

		2005	2004

Net asset turnover

$$\frac{\text{Sales}}{\text{Net assets}} = \underline{\hspace{8cm}} = \qquad\qquad 2.0 \text{ times}$$

Fixed asset turnover

$$\frac{\text{Sales}}{\text{(Tangible) fixed assets}} = \underline{\hspace{8cm}} = \qquad\qquad 5.0 \text{ times}$$

Stock turnover

$$\frac{\text{Cost of sales}}{\text{Stock}} = \underline{\hspace{8cm}} = \qquad\qquad 2.4 \text{ times}$$

Debtor turnover

$$\frac{\text{Sales}}{\text{Debtors}} = \underline{\hspace{8cm}} = \qquad\qquad 6.7 \text{ times}$$

Problems in using ratios

Accounting ratios can be useful in suggesting questions to look into, but they are unlikely on their own to provide complete *answers*. Some of the main problems in using ratios to interpret company accounts are as follows:

(a) Comparisons over time
1. Inflation may need to be allowed for (see Section 13). Its compound effect may be surprisingly large.
2. If accounting policies or product groupings change, figures on the new basis may not be available for earlier periods.

(b) Inter-firm comparisons
1. Defining an 'industry' is often not easy. And even within an industry, firms may differ in product mix, cost structure, size, as well as in business objectives and strategies.
2. Accounting methods and definitions may vary, especially between different countries.
3. Financial periods may end on different dates.

(c) General
1. Accounts record only matters that can be recorded in financial terms. This may exclude vital business information, such as some intangible asssets. Hence it is often important to use other sources of information as well as accounts wherever possible.
2. Not all relevant information is published. Sales revenue comprises volume times price, but published accounts (unlike internal budgets) rarely provide a detailed split.
3. Most accounting numbers are not precisely 'correct'; they usually include an element of *judgement*. And different people may not always agree.

Asset turnover

Net asset turnover

$$\frac{\text{Sales}}{\text{Net assets}} = \frac{1\,200}{550} = 2.18 \text{ times (2004: 2.0 times)}$$

The net asset turnover ratio is one measure of how well a company has used its productive assets. It can be useful to split this overall ratio into its main parts – fixed assets and stocks and debtors (two of the key elements of working capital).

Fixed asset turnover

$$\frac{\text{Sales}}{\text{(Tangible) fixed assets}} = \frac{1\,200}{210} = 5.7 \text{ times (2004: 5.0 times)}$$

This ratio is a measure of how well a company is using its fixed assets (excluding intangibles and investments). It may need care to interpret it where there have been major changes in capacity during a period.

The fixed asset turnover ratio shows how many £s in annual sales each £1 of investment in tangible fixed assets has generated. (But, as we shall see in Section 7, page 140, some UK companies may have revalued their land and buildings above cost.)

Stock turnover

$$\frac{\text{Cost of sales}}{\text{Stock}} = \frac{800}{350} = 2.3 \text{ times (2004: 2.4 times)}$$

This ratio indicates how quickly goods move through the business. Usually the quicker the better, though a high turnover rate may suggest a risk of running out of some goods. (Remember all these ratios from published accounts are looking at aggregates.) Internally one might want to calculate separate ratios for each product line.

Where possible stock turnover should compare stock (which accounts normally value at cost, as we shall see in Section 6) with *cost* of sales. But accounts may not always disclose a separate figure for cost of sales (see profit and loss account formats 2 and 4 in Appendix 5, on pages 280 and 281). In that case, the only option may be to divide sales (at selling prices) by stock:

$$\frac{\text{Sales}}{\text{Stock}} = \frac{1\,200}{350} = 3.5 \text{ times (2004: 3.5 times)}$$

This method of calculation is not ideal, but changes in the ratio over time can still indicate real changes in the business.

Closing stock, of course, may not be the same as average stock during the year, so the apparent 'stock turnover' ratio using end-of-year stock may not represent the real rate of turnover on average. (Moreover, if there are seasonal changes in stock levels, merely averaging the opening and closing year-end figures will not reveal average stock levels during the year.)

Another way to compute this 'turnover' ratio is to express closing stock in terms of the 'number of days' of cost of sales held, by dividing closing stock by average daily cost of sales:

$$\frac{350 \times 365}{800} = 160 \text{ days (2004: 151 days)}$$

An increase in stock levels (causing a fall in apparent stock turnover) may result from stocks piling up because of falling sales during the year. Or it may represent a deliberate building-up of stocks to meet planned sales growth in future. In controlling production and stocks, therefore, forecasting the future level of sales volume plays a vital role.

Debtor turnover

$$\frac{\text{Sales}}{\text{Debtors}} = \frac{1\,200}{200} = 6.0 \text{ times (2004: 6.7 times)}$$

Where companies sell for cash as well as on credit, only credit sales should be included in the ratio to compare with trade debtors. As with stock turnover, if there are seasonal variations in sales, the ratio may need to be interpreted carefully. Only trade debtors should be included (not prepayments and miscellaneous other amounts receivable).

As with stock, it is possible (and some analysts prefer) to calculate the 'number of days' sales' represented by closing trade debtors:

$$\frac{200 \times 365}{1\,200} = 61 \text{ days (2004: 55 days)}$$

Because of Value Added Tax complications, the above calculation may not be literally correct (see page 192). But (as with Sales/Stock above) changes in the number over time may still indicate real changes.

Summary of results: Precision Locks Limited

Please now enter in the 2005 column below the figures that you have calculated; and enter also the 2004 ratios which were set out in the earlier pages. Then summarize briefly below the main comments which occur to you in appraising the company's 2005 performance compared with the results for the previous year.

When you have completed your summary of the performance ratios, and written out your comments, please turn to the suggested answer on the next page.

	2005	2004
PERFORMANCE RATIOS		
Profitability		
Return on net assets　　%		
Profit margin　　　　　%		
Return on equity　　　 %		
Tax ratio　　　　　　　%		
Asset turnover		
Net asset turnover		
Fixed asset turnover		
Stock turnover		
Debtor turnover		

Comments

STANDARDS FOR COMPARISON

Figures for a single accounting period may not be much use on their own. The results are far more revealing when compared with some kind of 'standard'. Similar ratios for earlier periods can indicate trends, budget ratios can show how well a company is achieving its business objectives, or the results of other companies in the same industry can provide an external standard.

(a) Past periods' results

Figures for past periods are likely to be available on a consistent basis and may therefore permit fair comparison with the current period (subject to changed conditions). But an improvement over last year's performance may still be a bad result, just as a worse result than last year's may still be good. Suitable comparisons over time enable us to detect trends, though we should not assume that the future need be like the past. In other words, trends go on until they stop!

(b) Internal budgets

Budgets show planned performance, so actual results in line with budget may well represent an adequate outcome. The more care taken in preparing budgets, the more reliable they are likely to be as standards. Changed conditions since the budget was prepared may call for explicit revisions to budgets, otherwise they will cause unavoidable 'variances'. External analysts rarely have access to a company's own budgets and requiring their publication would surely distort the budgeting process.

In the context of comparing budgets with actual results, 'variance analysis' involves calculating the extent of differences (either positive or negative) – often distinguishing between differences due to changes in *quantity* and those due to differences in *price*. Appropriate management action may vary, depending on the reason for each variance.

(c) Results of other companies

Where suitably detailed figures are available, industry results can provide a useful external standard. Recent attempts to reduce the range of acceptable accounting policies have met with some success. Even so, some of the figures may need adjustment to bring two sets of accounts on to a common basis. Even if analysts possess enough detailed information to do this (which they usually won't), great care is still needed in comparing the adjusted figures.

If other companies in the same industry can do much better than us, we would like to know *why*. This is probably the main value of the various 'league tables' one sees so frequently nowadays. They do not enable an outsider to say with any confidence that School A is better than School B. But, they can help the managers of Hospital C to ask: 'Why does Hospital D – which we know is generally similar to us – come out so much better in certain aspects of the league tables? What could we do to improve?'

It is important for people who use accounting figures to understand what those figures really mean. They should know how companies record transactions and summarize them in accounts, and they should recognize the various possible ways to value assets and to measure profit or loss. Later sections aim to provide such understanding.

Summary of results: Precision Locks Limited

	2005	2004
PERFORMANCE RATIOS		
Profitability		
Return on net assets	29.4%	21.0%
Profit margin	13.5%	10.5%
Return on equity	20.0%	15.0%
Tax ratio	35.7%	33.3%
Asset turnover		
Net asset turnover	2.18 times	2.0 times
Fixed asset turnover	5.7 times	5.0 times
Stock turnover	2.3 times	2.4 times
Debtor turnover	6.0 times	6.7 times

Comments

1 2005's performance is better than 2004's, with return on net assets and return on equity both up by about one third.

2 Sales (turnover) rose by 20 per cent, and the profit margin increased from 10.5 to 13.5 per cent, leading to a 54 per cent increase in profit before interest.

3 The tax ratio in 2005 was similar to 2004, so profit after tax also increased by 50 per cent.

4 Fixed asset utilization improved as sales increased faster than the net investment in fixed assets.

5 Stocks again seem rather high relative to sales volume (and even higher relative to cost of goods sold). But to suggest a 'correct' stock level we would need to know more about the nature of the company's business.

6 The average credit period taken by debtors has increased by 10 per cent. Combined with a higher sales volume, this has meant a 33 per cent rise in debtors. If credit policy has not changed, perhaps the administration of credit control needs looking at.

COMPARING DIFFERENT COMPANIES' RESULTS

To introduce some of the issues that we deal with later, we compare below two companies in the same industry, Brown Limited and Green Limited. To keep it simple, assume that at 30 June 2005 the two companies' accounts looked exactly the same on the surface. But we shall find that even accounting figures which seem identical may reflect very different facts underneath. Subjective opinion and judgement can greatly affect a company's balance sheet and reported profit; and we shall see how misleading the unthinking use of financial statements can be.

The original accounts of Brown Limited and Green Limited are set out on the next page with certain items of further information.

Analysis of results

An initial study of the accounts of Brown Limited and Green Limited would, of course, yield identical results. For example, the operating performance of each company might be summarized as follows:

$$\text{Return on net assets} = \frac{\text{Operating profit}}{\text{Net assets}} = \frac{200}{500} = 40.0\%$$

$$\text{Profit margin} = \frac{\text{Operating profit}}{\text{Sales}} = \frac{200}{1\,200} = 16.7\%$$

$$\text{Net asset turnover} = \frac{\text{Sales}}{\text{Net assets}} = \frac{1\,200}{500} = 2.4 \text{ times}$$

But the further information shown on the right modifies this first impression. On page 32 we take it into account and show adjusted accounts for Brown Limited and Green Limited. Before you turn over the page, we suggest it would be a useful exercise for you to do the same. Please now attempt to produce adjusted accounts yourself for each of the two companies, in the light of the further information presented opposite. Use a separate sheet of paper.

To highlight the changes, please also recalculate the three performance ratios above, and see how much difference your adjustments have made to them. Make all the adjustments you think desirable, then compare your results with ours on page 32.

Please note that our answers are not the only possible set of adjusted accounts. The point of the example is precisely to illustrate that accounts inevitably depend to a large extent on *opinion*; and reasonable, experienced business people may often hold different views about the best accounting treatment of particular items. The range of permissible acounting treatments is not unlimited, but it can often be significant.

BROWN LIMITED
GREEN LIMITED

Profit and loss account for the year ended 30 June 2005

	£'000
Turnover	1 200
Cost of sales	820
	380
Operating expenses	180
Operating profit	200
Tax @ 20 per cent	40
Profit after tax	160

Balance sheet at 30 June 2005

Tangible fixed assets			£'000
Freehold factory at cost			150
Machinery at cost	480		
Less: Accumulated depreciation	180		
			300
			450
Current assets			
Stock		150	
Debtors		180	
Cash		20	
		350	
Less: Creditors due within one year		300	
			50
Total assets less current liabilities			500
Capital and reserves			
Called up share capital			100
Profit and loss account			400
			500

Further information

(a) Freehold factory

Brown acquired its freehold factory in 1990; expert valuers reckon its current market value is £300 000. The current market value of Green's factory, which was bought in 1998, is about the same as the purchase price.

(b) Depreciation of machinery

Brown expects most of its machines to last for some twelve years, and charges to cost of sales each year one-twelfth of the cost. Green reckons the life of similar machines to be eight years, and writes off one-eighth of the cost annually. The result is that Green charges £20 000 a year more depreciation than Brown.

(c) Stock valuation

Brown's policy is to write down stock which has not moved for twelve months to 50 per cent of cost. At 30 June 2005 the balance sheet included at £20 000 stock which cost £40 000. Green writes off the entire cost of stock which has not moved for a year, and charged £40 000 to cost of sales in 2005 in that respect.

(d) Debtors

Much of Brown's business is with a few large customers, one of which (Black Limited) is in financial trouble. Of the £50 000 which Black owed Brown at 30 June 2005, it seems unlikely that more than £40 000 will be recovered. Brown has made no provision for the possible loss, believing (perhaps optimistically) that Black will resolve its troubles and eventually pay the debt in full.

Green trades with a large number of smaller customers, and has provided an amount equal to 2 per cent of debts outstanding at the year-end. In previous years only 1 per cent was provided, which matched the actual average bad debt loss over a number of years. Green increased the level of provision for bad debts in 2005, feeling (perhaps pessimistically) that the coming months might find a number of customers in financial difficulty.

(e) Development costs

Both companies spent £90 000 on developing new products in the year. Brown carries forward as an asset £30 000 spent on one particular project, which is expected to generate revenue in the following year. Thus Brown charges only £60 000 for development costs in the current year; but plans to write off the remaining £30 000 next year. Green writes off all development costs in the year in which they are actually incurred, regardless of which period (if any) is expected to benefit.

Please now attempt your own adjustments to the figures, before turning over the page.

Adjusted results

Clearly the different circumstances for the two companies make it difficult to compare their published accounts directly. The two companies' level of performance is *not* the same, as the original ratios suggested it was.

It is possible, using the further information provided, to adjust the two companies' accounts to bring them more closely on to the same basis. Our own adjusted figures appear on the right; but we emphasize that the 'further information' listed would also permit different adjustments. Moreover, there may still be other facts which are relevant but unknown. We have assumed that all the adjustments affect the tax charge.

Choosing between one basis of accounting and another means exercising judgement. There is no way to avoid subjective opinions affecting accounts. Who can tell for certain how long a particular asset will last, at what price stock will be sold, or whether an outstanding debt will ever be collected?

Our own adjusted accounts give rise to the following performance ratios, which we compare below with the original ratios:

	Original	Brown adjusted	Green adjusted
Return on net assets	$\frac{200}{500} = 40.0\%$	$\frac{140}{602} = 23.3\%$	$\frac{220}{516} = 42.6\%$
Profit margin	$\frac{200}{1\,200} = 16.7\%$	$\frac{140}{1\,200} = 11.7\%$	$\frac{220}{1\,200} = 18.3\%$
Net asset turnover	$\frac{1\,200}{500} = 2.40$	$\frac{1\,200}{602} = 1.99$	$\frac{1\,200}{516} = 2.33$

The adjusted figures, especially Brown's, are now very different. Brown's return on net assets is nearly halved, profit margin on sales has fallen by nearly one-third, and asset turnover by one-sixth. The comparison with Green, whose return on net assets and profit margin have both improved slightly, now shows significant differences. But the ratios based on the published accounts were identical.

So readers of accounts should be cautious about making sweeping interpretations. Often the kind of ratio analysis we have worked through in this section does more to suggest particular *questions* the analyst should ask, than it does to provide definitive *answers*.

BROWN LIMITED
GREEN LIMITED

	Original		BROWN Adjusted		GREEN Adjusted
Profit and loss account					
Year ended 30 June 2005	£'000		£'000		£'000
Turnover	1 200		1 200		1 200
Cost of sales	820	b + 20 e + 30	870	c − 20	800
Operating profit	380		330		400
Operating expenses	180	d + 10	190		180
Profit before tax	200		140		220
Tax @ 20 per cent	40		28		44
Profit after tax	160		112		176
Balance sheet					
at 30 June 2005	£'000		£'000		£'000
Tangible fixed assets					
Freehold factory	150	a + 150	300		150
Machinery, net	300	b − 20	280		300
	450		580		450
Net current assets					
Stock	150	e − 30	120	c + 20	170
Debtors	180	d − 10	170		180
Cash	20		20		20
Less: Creditors	(300)	Tax − 12	(288)	Tax + 4	(304)
	50		22		66
	500		602		516
Capital and reserves					
Share capital	100		100		100
Revaluation reserve	–	a + 150	150		–
Profit and loss account	400		352		416
	500		602		516

Comments on Brown and Green adjusted results

The point of this example is to illustrate that accounting figures which look the same may reflect very different facts underneath the surface. It may be helpful to explain what lies behind the adjustments we have chosen to make, set out on the left. We do emphasize again that these are in no sense 'correct', nor the only possible adjustments one could have made.

(a) We have shown Brown's freehold factory at its estimated current value of £300 000, an increase of £150 000 over cost. The increase goes to 'revaluation reserve' under 'Capital and reserves'. Revaluation is permitted in UK accounting, though not in some other countries which stick more thoroughly to 'historical cost'.

(b) We have brought Brown's depreciation charge on machinery, originally based on an estimated average life of twelve years, into line with Green's depreciation charge, based on a life of eight years. Thus we charge an extra £20 000 to Brown's cost of sales, and reduce the net book value of Brown's machinery by £20 000 to £280 000. (Conceivably a small part of this extra £20 000 should be added to the cost of Brown's closing stock.)

(c) We have adjusted Green's ultra-prudent policy of writing off the entire cost of stock which has not moved for a year into line with Brown's policy of only writing off half the cost of such slow-moving stock. Thus we increase Green's stock value by £20 000 and reduce Green's cost of sales by £20 000.

(d) We have adjusted Brown's accounts to provide for £10 000 bad debt in respect of Black's account of £50 000. Thus Brown's debtors fall by £10 000, and bad debts expense (operating expenses) increase by £10 000.

(e) We change Brown's treatment of development costs in line with the more prudent approach taken by Green. Thus we reduce Brown's asset for stock by £30 000 (we assume that 'stock' includes the development costs carried forward), and increase Brown's cost of sales by £30 000.

Thus in respect of items (b), (d) and (e), we change Brown's accounts in the direction of more prudence, reducing the current period's profit in total by £60 000 and reducing three asset accounts (machinery, stock and debtors) in total by £60 000. In respect of item (c) we change Green's accounts in the direction of less prudence. The adjustment in (a) doesn't affect Brown's profit and loss account, but increases assets by £150 000. In later years this might affect the profit and loss account by increasing the amount of the depreciation charge.

We also assume that all changes to the profit and loss account (including depreciation, for simplicity – but see p. 193) have an impact on the 20 per cent tax charge.

THE NEED FOR CAUTION

In appraising the accounts of Precision Locks Limited, we compared the 2005 results with 2004's. This form of comparison assumes that the two years' figures have been prepared on a consistent basis, and can yield results both for external analysts and for managers within a company.

It is a legal requirement to disclose any material change in the basis of accounting which might impair consistent presentation and, where the accounting treatment has changed, to adjust the comparative figures as well as the current year's. So one might reasonably expect to be able to rely on comparison of one year's accounts with another's.

One might assume, for example, that if two sets of accounts show the same totals for particular items such as fixed assets or stocks, the financial meaning of each item must be the same. But this need not be so. The totals appearing in financial statements usually summarize a whole series of transactions, or combine separate asset and liability balances, the nature and mixture of which can vary from one period to another. (We have already mentioned possible changes in the mix of cash and credit sales, and the problems that they can give rise to in computing trade debtor turnover.)

Nor can one assume that accounting measures of performance are exact, or that the same transactions would always lead to the same financial result whenever they occurred or whoever measured them. We shall see many examples in later sections, when we look more closely at the complex problems of income measurement.

In accounts for periods less than a year, seasonal factors may need special attention. They may complicate comparison of one period with another. And even with annual accounts, the balance sheet position may not be typical: for example, liquidity may seem very good if the balance sheet date occurs when stocks are extremely low, just after a heavy selling period.

In comparisons over time within a company, it can be hard to judge how adequate a level of performance earlier results represent. And business conditions may have changed.

The original published accounts of Brown Limited and Green Limited were identical; but when we examined further information in detail, we found that in some respects the two companies had prepared their accounts on very different bases. We were able to produce adjusted figures which (perhaps) allowed a more useful comparison, but such further information may not always be available.

Nor should we expect too much from computing a few simple financial ratios. The complex far-flung affairs of modern business groups are not so easy to sum up. Still, the sort of analysis introduced in this section and the next can be valuable in focusing attention on key aspects of companies' performance and financial position. In conjunction with relevant standards, ratio analysis can give useful clues about suitable questions for an external analyst to pose. But we can hardly expect it to give all the answers.

DIFFERENT VIEWPOINTS

Accounting controversies often stem from implicit differences of viewpoint. Their existence reminds us that there may be more than one approach to interpreting the meaning of company accounts.

One distinction is between the 'proprietary' view and the 'entity' view. The traditional *'proprietary' view* regards as paramount the interests of shareholders, the ultimate owners of a company. Supporters of this view tend to focus on profit after tax in the profit and loss account and on shareholders' funds (capital and reserves) in the balance sheet.

The *'entity' view*, in contrast, makes the company itself the centre of attention. Proponents see company managements as having to deal with various 'stakeholders' such as customers, employees, lenders, owners, suppliers, and so on. They emphasize operating profit and total assets employed. They also welcome the 'value-added statement', which deducts from sales turnover the costs of 'bought-in' goods and services (other than employees' wages). One can then analyse the 'value added' by a business between various groups of 'stakeholders': employees (wages), loan creditors (interest), government (tax), shareholders (dividends), and so on.

A related distinction is between 'accounting profit', which is probably more suitable for accounting to outside investors for stewardship, and 'economic profit', relevant for decision-making within the business. Historical money cost accounting charges only (an estimate of) the actual expenses incurred; so, for example, *accounting profit* charges only actual interest payable on debt capital, but *economic profit*, which is sales turnover minus the current 'opportunity cost' of goods and services consumed, charges interest on total capital employed (including notional interest on equity capital).

One important difference relates to the purpose of accounts. The traditional view is that annual accounts enable the directors to provide an account of their past *stewardship* to the company's owners (the current shareholders). A more recent view, which most accounting standard-setters seem to accept, is the *'decision-usefulness'* model. This supposes that the purpose of accounts is to help investors (both actual and potential) and others to make decisions about their future actions.

Another difference in viewpoint concerns the relative functions and significance of the *profit and loss account* (income statement) and the *balance sheet*. If the main focus is on the profit (or earnings per share) for the current period, then the matching concept may be important. This may be of special interest to shareholders; and has been apparent in countries like the US and the UK, where capital markets developed early. If, however, the emphasis is on financial soundness, as displayed by the balance sheet, then the concept of prudence may tend to prevail, which may be more relevant for creditors. This has tended to be the position in countries like Germany and France.

SECTION 2 SUMMARY

After outlining the main steps in a full financial analysis of company accounts, this section has dealt with two of them: an overview to give perspective and to detect trends in key figures over a period of several years; and a detailed review of performance ratios. Section 3 deals in detail with financial status ratios and stock market ratios, and later sections cover cash flows (Section 11) and business segments (Sections 5 and 12).

The basic concept of 'return on investment' relates 'risk' and (required) 'return', and there are also links between return on net assets and return on equity.

One can divide the return on net assets ratio into a 'pyramid of ratios'; and this approach can be extremely useful as a tool of internal management control.

The section considered in some detail how to analyse company accounts by means of financial ratios. The accounts of Precision Locks Limited yielded various performance ratios relating to profitability and to asset turnover.

There is a need for *standards* with which to compare a company's financial ratios. Possible standards include previous year(s) (as for Precision Locks); internal budgets; other companies in the same industry; and external industry averages.

In trying to compare the results of two different companies, Brown Limited and Green Limited, it was apparent how important judgement can be in measuring profit or loss, and in attaching values to assets in a going concern.

There is more than one angle from which to look at accounts. For example, the 'entity' viewpoint looks at a company as a whole, while the 'proprietary' viewpoint looks at the interests of the owners (shareholders).

Finally there are several reasons for caution in analysing company accounts. Later sections will look in more detail at many of the matters touched on only briefly here.

PROBLEMS

2.1 Definitions

Please write down, in the spaces provided below your definitions of the ratios listed. Then compare your definitions with those set out overleaf. *Please do take the trouble to actually write down your own attempt at definitions, otherwise you are likely to miss much of the potential learning.*

(a)   Return on net assets

(f)   Stock turnover

(b)   Net asset turnover

(g)   Days' sales in debtors

(c)   Profit margin

(h)   Fixed asset turnover

(d)   Return on equity

(i)   Overview

(e)   Tax ratio

(j)   Required rate of return

2.1 Definitions

(a) **Return on net assets** (RONA) is profit before interest and tax (PBIT) divided by net assets. It is useful at the apex of the 'pyramid of ratios' because it uses operating profit *before* charging interest expense and tax. It can thus help to analyse the performance of *divisions* of companies (whose funds, in effect, all come from the centre). Since 'net assets' (= total assets less current liabilities) is equivalent to 'capital employed' (= borrowings plus shareholders' funds), this ratio is sometimes referred to as 'return on capital employed' (ROCE).

(b) **Net asset turnover** is sales (turnover) divided by net assets. This ratio can vary widely between industries, but changes over time within a business would raise questions. Some companies try to discourage managers from investing 'too much' capital in net assets by charging notional *interest* thereon. The aim is to keep net asset turnover high.

(c) **Profit margin** is profit divided by sales (turnover). Margins can vary widely between industries. The measure of 'profit' used here is 'profit before interest and tax' (PBIT), the same as in the return on net assets ratio. This leads to the equation: Return on net assets = Profit margin x Net asset turnover.

(d) **Return on equity** is profit after tax divided by shareholders' funds. It is not solely the result of operations, since the level of the tax charge and interest on debt can also affect it. We shall see in later sections that the basis for valuing assets in the balance sheet can make a big difference to the amount of 'shareholders' funds' (and hence to the accounting rate of return on equity).

(e) The **tax ratio** is the tax expense divided by profit before tax. ('Tax' here refers only to taxation on company profits, whether called 'corporation tax', 'income tax', or 'profits tax'.) We discuss this topic at more length in Section 10; companies can 'manage' it only to a limited extent.

(f) **Stock turnover** is cost of sales divided by closing stock (inventory). Because stock is normally valued at cost (see Section 6), it makes sense to calculate this ratio by using the *cost* of sales, rather than sales revenue itself (which, of course, is at selling prices). But if the accounts do not reveal the cost of sales, then analysts have to use sales turnover (which can still show trends over time).

(g) **Days' sales in debtors** is debtors (accounts receivable) divided by average daily sales. Like the stock turnover ratio above, seasonal factors can affect it. (Sales may not occur evenly throughout the year.) Value Added Tax also complicates the ratio, since debtors include VAT but sales revenue does not.

(h) **Fixed asset turnover** is sales divided by fixed assets (normally tangible only). Purchases of fixed assets during a year may distort this ratio, if they have not yet generated a full year's sales. Any revaluation of fixed assets upwards (see Section 7) also affects the ratio.

(i) **Overview** is the process of getting an overall impression of a company's performance over recent years to provide context before beginning detailed ratio analysis. Key aspects are the rate of growth in sales, profits and assets, and many analysts will also want to see how the share price has moved. Probably five years is the best period to use: not too short, yet not containing too many out-of-date years.

(j) **Required rate of return** consists of three components:

- pure time-preference (the 'price of time')
- an inflation premium (where the return is in money not in 'real' terms)
- a risk premium (the 'price of risk'), which in practice is not easy to quantify.

The total represents a *minimum* 'required rate of return' (or 'hurdle rate') for investors. Companies, of course, aim to make a higher rate of return than that.

2.2 James Smith Limited (A): performance ratios

The accounts of James Smith Limited for the year 2004 are set out on the right. You are asked to complete the descriptions of each of the profitability and asset turnover ratios set out below; and to calculate each one. (The first ratio has already been calculated for you.)

PROFITABILITY

(a) Return on equity $= \dfrac{\text{Profit after tax}}{\text{Shareholders' funds}} = \dfrac{140}{350} = 40.0\%$

(b) Tax ratio $=$ $=$

(c) Return on net assets $=$ $=$

(d) Profit margin $=$ $=$

ASSET TURNOVER

(e) Net asset turnover $=$ $=$

(f) Fixed asset turnover $=$ $=$

(g) Stock turnover $=$ $=$

(h) Debtor turnover $=$ $=$

You may prefer to go straight on to Problem 2.3 *before* checking the answers overleaf.

2.3 James Smith Limited (B): pyramid of ratios

Please now set out the various necessary ratios, on a separate sheet of paper, in a 'pyramid of ratios' like that on page 24.

Cost of sales comprises:
    Materials 290, Labour 130, Overheads 410.
Operating expenses comprise:
    R&D 50, Selling exs. 140, Admin. 260.

When you have finished, please compare your answers with those overleaf.

JAMES SMITH LIMITED

Profit and loss account, year ended 30 September 2004

	£'000
Turnover	1 500
Cost of sales	830
Gross profit	670
Operating expenses	450
Operating profit	220
Interest	20
Profit before tax	200
Tax	60
Profit after tax	140

Balance sheet at 30 September 2004

		£'000
Tangible fixed assets		
Land and buildings	180	
Plant and equipment	220	
		400
Current assets		
Stocks	300	
Debtors	200	
Cash	50	
	550	
Less: **Creditors due within one year**	350	
		200
Total assets less current liabilities		600
Less: **Creditors due after one year**		250
Capital and reserves		
Called up 50p share capital	200	
Profit and loss account	150	
		350

2.2 James Smith Limited (A)

Solution

PROFITABILITY

£'000

(a) Return on equity $= \dfrac{\text{Profit after tax}}{\text{Shareholders' funds}} = \dfrac{140}{350} = 40.0\%$

(b) Tax ratio $= \dfrac{\text{Tax}}{\text{Profit before tax}} = \dfrac{60}{200} = 30.0\%$

(c) Return on net assets $= \dfrac{\text{Profit before interest and tax}}{\text{Capital employed}} = \dfrac{220}{600} = 36.7\%$

(d) Profit margin $= \dfrac{\text{Profit before interest and tax}}{\text{Sales}} = \dfrac{220}{1\,500} = 14.7\%$

ASSET TURNOVER

(e) Net asset turnover $= \dfrac{\text{Sales}}{\text{Net assets}} = \dfrac{1\,500}{600} = 2.50$ times

(f) Fixed asset turnover $= \dfrac{\text{Sales}}{\text{Fixed assets}} = \dfrac{1\,500}{400} = 3.75$ times

(g) Stock turnover $= \dfrac{\text{Cost of sales}}{\text{Stock}} = \dfrac{830}{300} = 2.77$ times

(h) Debtor turnover $= \dfrac{\text{Sales}}{\text{Debtors}} = \dfrac{1\,500}{200} = 7.50$ times

2.3 James Smith Limited (B)

Solution

Return on net assets
36.7%

Profit margin
14.7%

Net asset turnover
2.50 times

Gross margin 44.7% Operating expenses 30.0% Fixed asset turnover 3.75 times Working capital t/o 7.50 times

Materials	19.3
Labour	8.7
Overheads	27.3
	55.3

R&D	3.3
Selling exs.	9.3
Admin. exs.	17.4
	30.0

| Land & bldg | 8.3x |
| Plant & eqpt | 6.8x |

Stock (cost)	2.8x
Debtors	7.5x
Cash	30x

WORLDCHEM PLC

Consolidated profit and loss account year ended 31 March 2005

		2005 £m	2004 £m
Turnover		1 028	923
Operating costs		889	773
Operating profit		139	150
Interest	(1)	2	6
Profit before taxation		137	144
Taxation		46	48
Profit after taxation		91	96
Dividends		41	33
Profit retained		50	63

Consolidated balance sheet at 31 March

	2005 £m		2004 £m
Tangible fixed assets			
Land and buildings		237	205
Plant and machinery		152	127
		389	332
Current assets			
Stocks	205		178
Debtors and prepayments	211		182
Liquid resources	115		176
	531		536
Less: **Creditors due within one year (2)**	239		230
Net current assets (working capital)		292	306
Total assets less current liabilities		681	638
Less: **Creditors due after one year**			
Loans		161	148
Capital and reserves			
Called up share capital (25p shares)		163	163
Reserves		357	327
		520	490

2.4 Worldchem plc (A): performance ratios

A summary of Worldchem plc's 2005 accounts is shown on the left opposite, with comparative figures for the previous year. Two extracts from the notes are as follows:

	2005 £m	2004 £m
1 Interest payable	15	14
Less: interest receivable	(13)	(8)
	2	6
2 Including short-term borrowing	16	26

You are asked, on a separate sheet of paper:

1. to calculate each of the main profitability and asset turnover ratios for the two years,
2. to compare the two years' results and write down any appropriate comments.

A solution is shown at the end of the book, on p. 293.

No answers are published for the following two problems.

2.5 The Secret Seven

Set out opposite (right) are 'balance sheet percentages' calculated from the accounts of seven UK companies in different industries. The percentages shown relate each item to 'total assets less current liabilities' (but excluding short-term borrowing from current liabilities). In each case goodwill previously written off against reserves has been added back to intangible fixed assets and to shareholders' funds. Below the balance sheet other percentages are shown relating to sales turnover and operating profit.

Can you identify each column of figures with a particular industry? (It will probably be useful to write down the reasons for your answers.) The seven industries represented are (in alphabetical order of industry): aerospace and defence manufacturer; airline; food retailer; pharmaceuticals; property; telecommunications; tobacco.

Two special details, relating to the industry represented by columns A and B:

a   stocks 8 = contract balances 40 less progress payments (32).
b   tangible fixed assets 74, of which 50 = finance leases and hire purchase arrangements.

THE SECRET SEVEN

	A	B	C	D	E	F	G
Fixed assets							
Tangible: cost (or valuation*)	41*	128*	54	126	190	35	98
Cumulative depreciation	23	44	26	28	111	18	1
Net book value	18	84	28	98	79	17	97
Of which: land and buildings	11*	10*	12	83	3	5	96*
plant etc.	7	74b	16	15	76	12	1
Intangibles**	63	6	35	12	3	61	–
Fixed asset investments***	18	5	13	2	2	5	3
	99	95	76	112	84	83	100
Current assets							
Stocks	8a	1	9	8	–	17	1
Debtors****	37	10	30	6	26	17	4
Cash etc.	17	16	16	8	27	15	3
	62	27	55	22	53	49	8
Short-term borrowing*****	8	7	6	5	6	10	8
Other current liabilities	61	22	31	34	37	32	8
Net working capital	(7)	(2)	18	(17)	10	7	(8)
Total assets less CL*****	92	93	94	95	94	90	92
Long-term borrowing	21	50	16	30	63	39	22
Other long-term creditors	5	3	1	–	–	1	1
Provisions	10	12	13	4	13	10	2
Shareholders' funds**	56	26	61	60	18	38	67
Minority interests	–	2	3	1	–	2	–
Sales turnover	88	73	93	232	111	68	n/a
Operating profit	5	4	30	13	(3)	15	7
Goodwill added back**	–	5	27	5	2	9	–
Including own shares***	–	–	12	–	–	1	–
Debtors over one year****	10	–	9	1	6	3	3

Notes to balance sheet percentages:

*   Some land and buildings are shown at valuation, not cost.
**   Goodwill previously written off against reserves has been added back, both to intangible fixed assets and to shareholders' funds.
*** Including own shares.
**** Some debtors, included in current assets, not due for more than one year.
*****100% = total assets less current liabilities, adding back short-term borrowing.

2.6 Hamilton Pumps Limited (A): performance ratios

Below and on the right are shown the accounts of Hamilton Pumps Limited for the year ended 31 December 2004, together with comparative figures for the previous year.

You are asked to calculate the main profitability and asset turnover ratios for the two years, and to make appropriate comments (in writing) on your results. Please also identify the main *questions* you would wish to ask the company's senior management.

HAMILTON PUMPS LIMITED

Profit and loss account year ended 31 December 2004

	2004 £'000	2003 £'000
Turnover	6 750	6 500
Cost of sales	4 820	4 440
Selling and administrative expenses	1 205	1 110
Operating profit*	725*	950
Interest expense	175	75
Profit before tax	550	875
Taxation	200	300
Profit after tax	350	575

*after charging depreciation £375 000 (2003: £250 000)

Note:

Ordinary dividends:				
	Interim	1.25p (1.25p)	50	50
	Final	1.25p (2.50p)	50	100
Retained profit for the year			250	425

HAMILTON PUMPS LIMITED

Balance sheet at 31 December 2004

		2004 £'000		2003 £'000
Fixed assets				
Freehold property		750		600
Plant and equipment		2 250		1 350
		3 000		1 950
Current assets				
Stocks	1 350		1 050	
Debtors	1 850		1 300	
Cash	100		250	
	3 300		2 600	
Less: **Current liabilities**				
Bank overdraft	900		–	
Creditors	1 650		1 550	
Taxation	200		300	
	2 750		1 850	
Net working capital		550		750
Total assets less current liabilities		3 550		2 700
Less: **Long-term liabilities**				
Mortgage debenture	500		500	
Other loans	600		–	
		1 100		500
Shareholders funds				
Issued ordinary 25p shares	1 000		1 000	
Retained profits	1 450		1 200	
		2 450		2 200

Section 3
Financial and stock market ratios

INTRODUCTION

In the last section we looked at performance ratios, dealing with profitability and asset turnover. We now turn to two other kinds of ratios, those dealing with financial status (gearing and liquidity) and with share prices (earnings and dividends).

There may often be some conflict between profitability and gearing, that is between return and risk. We briefly discussed this in the last section, and we shall revisit the subject in Section 8.

There may also be differences between profitability and liquidity, that is between profit and cash. We shall be looking further at these, both in Section 5 which covers accrual accounting, and in Section 11 which deals with cash flows.

Performance ratios and financial status ratios are relevant to nearly all kinds of businesses; but stock market ratios (especially those using market prices) apply mainly to public companies whose shares are 'listed' (quoted) and can be traded on a stock exchange.

Stock market ratios focus on the relationships between share prices and earnings and dividends. In one leading company's recent annual report, the chairman started his report to shareholders by noting four criteria 'which are most commonly used to measure company performance':

- rate of growth in earnings per share
- free cash flow before dividends
- dividend cover
- debt and interest cover.

We shall be discussing cash flows in Section 11; this section defines and discusses the other three measures. It was typical of many UK companies that there was no direct mention of the share price itself – which many shareholders might regard as even more important than accounting measures. In contrast, the annual reports of most large US companies have long included figures and charts relating to share prices over a number of past years.

RATIO CALCULATION

In the last section we looked at performance ratios, and we now consider the two other kinds of ratios needed to give an overall assessment of the position of a business – financial status ratios and stock market ratios.

Financial status ratios

Financial status ratios indicate a company's financial position: they distinguish between solvency and liquidity, between long-term and short-term capacity to meet liabilities. The four ratios we shall define and use are:

Debt/Capital employed (%)
Interest cover
Current ratio
Acid test

Stock market ratios

Stock market ratios relate earnings (profits) and dividends to the number of ordinary shares in issue and to stock market prices. The four ratios we shall look at are:

Earnings per share (pence)
Price/earnings ratio
Dividend yield (%)
Dividend cover

PRECISION LOCKS LIMITED

Profit and loss account

for the year ended 30 June	2005	2004
	£'000	£'000
Turnover (sales)	1 200	1 000
Cost of sales	800	700
Gross profit	400	300
Administrative expenses	238	195
Operating profit	162	105
Loan interest	22	15
Profit before tax	140	90
Tax	50	30
Profit after tax	90	60

Balance sheet at 30 June

		2005		2004
		£'000		£'000
Fixed assets				
Factory and machinery at cost		350		300
Less: Accumulated depreciation		140		100
		210		200
Current assets				
Stock	350		290	
Debtors	200		150	
Cash	40		60	
	590		500	
Less: **Creditors due within one year** (current liabilities)	250		200	
		340		300
Total assets less current liabilities		550		500
Less: **Creditors due after one year**				
Long-term loan		100		100
Capital and reserves				
Called up £1 share capital	300		300	
Profit and loss account*	150*		100	
		450		400

* Dividend of 40 paid in 2005 (30 in 2004)

FINANCIAL STATUS RATIOS

Ratios of financial status measure a company's ability to meet its liabilities. They can be divided between:

Solvency ratios – dealing with long-term liabilities.
Liquidity ratios – dealing with short-term liabilities.

Please refer again to the 2005 accounts of Precision Locks Limited (opposite, left) and calculate the following financial status ratios. Then turn to the next page, and compare your answers with the ratios shown there.

As you calculate the ratios, consider what they mean and how they contribute to your appraisal of the company's financial status.

SOLVENCY RATIOS	2005	2004

Debt ratio

$$\frac{\text{Debt}}{\text{Capital employed}} = \underline{\hspace{4cm}} = \qquad\qquad 20.0\%$$

Interest cover

$$\frac{\text{Profit before interest and tax}}{\text{Loan interest}} = \underline{\hspace{4cm}} = \qquad\qquad 7.0 \text{ times}$$

LIQUIDITY RATIOS

Current ratio

$$\frac{\text{Current assets}}{\text{Current liabilities}} = \underline{\hspace{4cm}} = \qquad\qquad 2.5 \text{ times}$$

Acid test

$$\frac{\text{Liquid assets (debtors + cash)}}{\text{Current liabilities}} = \underline{\hspace{4cm}} = \qquad\qquad 1.05 \text{ times}$$

SOLVENCY RATIOS

Debt ratio: $$\frac{\text{Debt}}{\text{Capital employed}} = \frac{\text{Debt}}{\text{Debt} + \text{Equity}} = \frac{100}{550} = 18.2\%$$

Debt is 18 per cent of the capital employed, which means (in this simple case) that equity is the other 82 per cent. This relatively low debt ratio ('gearing') gives lenders a fairly high level of safety ('equity cushion').

Another way of measuring the same thing is the 'debt/equity' ratio:

$$\frac{\text{Debt}}{\text{Shareholders' funds}} = \frac{\text{Debt}}{\text{Equity}} = \frac{100}{450} = 22.2\%$$

Both these gearing ratios are common, so it is important not to confuse them.

Bank overdrafts are legally repayable 'on demand', and appear under 'Creditors due within one year'. But both bank overdrafts and any current portions of long-term debt represent negotiated interest-bearing finance. They may best be regarded as part of a company's interest-bearing capital employed. They contrast with 'spontaneous' sources of funds, normally *not* bearing interest, such as trade credit or tax payable. The net debt ratio uses 'debt less cash', in this case $100 - 40 = 60$.

Interest cover: $$\frac{\text{Profit before interest and tax}}{\text{Interest payable}} = \frac{162}{22} = 7.4 \text{ times}$$

The 'interest cover' ratio relates profit before interest and tax (PBIT) to (before-tax) interest, which normally includes both short-term and long-term interest.

Interest receivable, which represents the 'return' on liquid assets, should *not* normally be netted off against interest payable, in calculating interest cover.

This ratio shows the relative safety of loan interest, in the same way that the debt ratio aims to measure the loan capital cover. One ratio derives from the profit and loss account, the other from the balance sheet. Section 8, dealing with capital structure, considers these two ratios from another point of view.

LIQUIDITY RATIOS

Current ratio: $$\frac{\text{Current assets}}{\text{Current liabilities}} = \frac{590}{250} = 2.4 \text{ times}$$

This ratio indicates to what extent short-term assets are adequate to settle short-term liabilities. ('Current' in accounting implies turning assets into cash, or paying creditors, within twelve months from the balance sheet date.) Should the ratio be less than 1.0, current assets would not fully cover short-term creditors. This would be all right in a company with a strong daily cash flow, such as a retailer. But for a manufacturing company it would suggest looking closely at the acid test ratio (see below), because short-term financial problems might be developing.

A 'normal' current ratio in a manufacturing business might be between 1.5 and 2.0. Too *low* a current ratio may mean liquidity problems, but a current ratio can also be too *high*. Funds tied up in working capital can be costly to finance.

Acid Test: $$\frac{\text{Liquid assets (debtors + cash)}}{\text{Current liabilities}} = \frac{240}{250} = 0.96 \text{ times}$$

The acid test (sometimes called the 'quick ratio') is a strict test of liquidity. In measuring the resources available to meet current liabilities, it excludes stock which may take several months to turn into cash.

On the other hand, not all creditors need be due within a few months. Thus many companies might fairly safely have an acid test ratio of somewhat less than the 'norm' of 1.0.

A more accurate way to estimate cash sufficiency would be to forecast expected payments and receipts in detail month by month for the near future. A company would normally do this as part of its own cash management; but an external analyst will lack the information needed to complete such a forecast.

Many analysts prefer to treat interest-bearing short-term borrowings as part of 'capital employed' in calculating the debt ratio. We ourselves prefer this approach. But cautious analysts should still treat them as 'short term' for calculating the liquidity ratios. After all, bank overdrafts are usually repayable on demand. (See also page 47.)

STOCK MARKET RATIOS

The following stock market ratios are used extensively in the financial markets in referring to the performance of a company. Please calculate the ratios for 2005, by referring back to the Precision Locks accounts on page 42. Assume that the company's share price was 200p on 30 June 2004, and 360p on 30 June 2005. Then compare your solutions with those shown overleaf.

	2005	2004

Earnings per share

$$\frac{\text{Profit after tax}}{\text{Number of ordinary shares in issue}} = \underline{\hspace{4cm}} = \quad 20.0p$$

Price/earnings ratio

$$\frac{\text{Market price per share}}{\text{Earnings per share}} = \frac{360p}{\underline{\hspace{3cm}}} = \frac{200p}{20p} = 10.0$$

Dividend yield (net)

$$\frac{\text{Dividend per share (net)}}{\text{Market price per share}} = \frac{\underline{\hspace{3cm}}}{360p} = \frac{10p}{200p} = 5.0\%$$

Dividend cover

$$\frac{\text{Earnings per share}}{\text{Dividend per share}} = \underline{\hspace{4cm}} = \quad 2.0 \text{ times}$$

STOCK MARKET RATIOS

Earnings per share:
$$\frac{\text{Profit after tax}}{\text{Number of ordinary shares}} = \frac{90}{300} = 30.0\text{p}$$

The earnings (= profit) figure here is the same 'profit after tax' figure that we used to calculate return on equity. In more complex cases we should strictly use 'earnings attributable to ordinary shareholders' – this would be after preference dividends (see Section 8) and after 'minority interests' (see Section 9).

The earnings per share figure (EPS) is widely used in measuring changes in profit from year to year. 'Per share' figures relate to the number of ordinary shares *in issue*, not the number *authorized*. (If shares have been issued during a period, use a weighted average [FRS14/IAS33].)

Profit after tax (earnings) figures are often volatile, partly because of the uncertain nature of business and partly for technical accounting reasons. For purposes of investment appraisal, therefore, it is often sensible not to use an earnings per share figure for a single year (either last year or an estimate for the current year). Instead it may be better to take an average of the last three or five past years, to smooth out ups and downs. When doing so, 'bottom line' earnings should normally be used, *after* all 'exceptional' items.

Price/earnings ratio:
$$\frac{\text{Market price per share}}{\text{Earnings per share}} = \frac{360\text{p}}{30\text{p}} = 12.0 \text{ times}$$

The price/earnings (P/E) 'ratio' is simply a multiple. Thus Precision Locks Limited 'has a P/E ratio of 12.0'.

The market price (MP) of the equity shares does not appear in the published accounts, and it can fluctuate from day to day. The market price takes account of expected *future* profits, whereas the earnings per share figure is based (like the 'return on investment' ratios) on reported *past* profits.

If a company makes a loss, earnings per share will be *negative*. (A loss is simply a negative profit.) But since the shares will still have a positive value in the stock market, the P/E ratio itself will also be negative. So this ratio requires caution!

Dividend yield (net):
$$\frac{\text{Dividend per share}}{\text{Market price per share}} = \frac{13.3\text{p}}{360\text{p}} = 3.7\%$$

Published accounts disclose dividend per share in the notes, but for Precision Locks we have to calculate it: 40/300 = 13.3p. The dividend per share is shown *net* of tax.

Dividend yield indicates an investor's current income yield in relation to the share's *current* market price. This is unlikely to be the same as the amount *paid* for the shares (the market price on the date the investor bought them).

This ratio deals only with the part of current earnings paid out to shareholders in dividends. (The company 'retains' the rest.) Thus it represents only part of a shareholder's possible total 'return', since it does not include any 'capital gain' arising if the share price goes up.

Dividend cover:
$$\frac{\text{Earnings per share}}{\text{Dividend per share}} = \frac{30.0\text{p}}{13.3\text{p}} = 2.25 \text{ times}$$

This ratio measures the number of times that the actual dividend could have been paid out of the current year's earnings. The higher the dividend cover, the 'safer' the dividend.

The ratio is sometimes expressed the other way round, as the 'dividend payout ratio':

$$\frac{\text{Dividend per share}}{\text{Earnings per share}} = \frac{13.3\text{p}}{30.0\text{p}} = 44.3\%$$

There are, of course, many other influences on the price of a company's shares in the market besides the dividend yield and dividend cover. As a rule, investors expect some dividends each year. However, shareholders' returns come from dividends *plus* capital gains. If a company can use retained earnings profitably enough, shareholders may be willing to forgo dividends. The share price should then tend to rise, to reflect the internally financed growth.

The four stock market ratios discussed here are linked as follows:

Net Dividend Yield		Dividend Cover		Net Earnings Yield		P/E Reciprocal
$\dfrac{\text{DPS}}{\text{MP}}$	x	$\dfrac{\text{EPS}}{\text{DPS}}$	=	$\dfrac{\text{EPS}}{\text{MP}}$	=	$\dfrac{1}{\text{P/E Ratio}}$
3.7%	x	2.25	=	$\dfrac{30.0}{360} = 8.3\%$	=	$\dfrac{1}{12.0}$

Summary of results: Precision Locks Limited

Please now enter the figures which you have calculated, in the 2005 column below. Please also enter the 2004 ratios which were set out in the earlier pages; and then summarize briefly the main comments which you think should be made in appraising the 2005 results compared with the previous year.

When you have completed your summary of the ratios, and written out your comments in the space provided below, please turn to the next page, where suggested answers are shown.

		2005	2004
Financial status ratios			
Debt ratio	%		
Interest cover			
Current ratio			
Acid test			
Stock market ratios			
Earnings per share	pence		
Price/earnings ratio			
Dividend yield (net)	%		
Dividend cover			

Comments

DEBT: SHORT-TERM OR LONG-TERM?

In our earlier discussion of financial status ratios (page 44), we suggested including short-term interest-bearing borrowings as 'debt' in computing the debt ratio. At the same time, we calculate the liquidity ratios including short-term borrowings as *current* liabilities. In each case, in judging the soundness of a company's financial position, we want to see the position 'at its worst'.

To show how much difference it can make, let us reconsider the various ratios for Precision Locks Limited on the new assumption that the current liabilities of £250 000 include £100 000 of short-term bank overdraft. (We assume, however, that interest expense already included bank overdraft interest of £12 000.)

The table below summarizes the accounts, treating the bank overdraft as a current liability (left) and as semi-permanent long-term financing (right). We show selected ratios in each case, with an asterisk against the treatment we prefer. We would treat short-term borrowings as part of 'capital employed' – by *excluding* them from current liabilities. Thus we would take Precision Locks Limited's 'net assets' as £650 000.

PRECISION LOCKS LIMITED
Summarized balance sheet 30 June 2005

	£100 000 overdraft shown as	
	Current liability	Long-term financing
	£'000	£'000
Fixed assets, net	210	210
Current assets (stock 350)	590	590
Less: Current liabilities	(250)	(150)
Total assets less current liabilities	550	650
Less: Debt finance	(100)	(200)
Shareholders' funds	450	450

Selected ratios

Return on net assets (%)	162/550 = 29.5	**162/650 = 24.9***
Debt ratio (%)	100/550 = 18.2	**200/650 = 30.8***
Current ratio (times)	**590/250 = 2.36***	590/150 = 3.93
Acid test (times)	**240/250 = 0.96***	240/150 = 1.60

* preferred treatment

Summary of results: Precision Locks Limited

	2005	2004
Financial status ratios		
Debt ratio	18.2%	20.0%
Interest cover	7.4 times	7.0 times
Current ratio	2.4 times	2.5 times
Acid test	0.96 times	1.05 times
Stock market ratios		
Earnings per share	30.0p	20.0p
Price/earnings ratio	12.0	10.0
Dividend yield (net)	3.7%	5.0%
Dividend cover	2.25 times	2.0 times

Comments

1   Both debt ratio and interest cover indicate only a moderate level of gearing with no apparent cause for concern.

2   As trading activity grows the company will need more funds. With the acid test ratio just below 1.0 the cash position will have to be watched carefully. There seems to be room for more long-term borrowing if necessary.

3   The ordinary dividend rose by one third, so (with profit up by 50 per cent) the dividend cover and the retained profits both increased.

4   The price/earnings ratio has increased from 10.0 to 12.0, as the market price per share rose from 200p to 360p (up 80 per cent),while earnings per share rose by 50 per cent. But general market trends will have affected the share price, as well as Precision Locks Limited's own results.

SECTION 3 SUMMARY

The previous section looked at performance ratios; this one has considered financial status ratios, which are likely to be relevant to all companies, and stock market ratios, which apply to companies whose shares are listed on a Stock Exchange.

Financial status ratios are of two kinds: long-term solvency ratios (debt ratio and interest cover), and short-term liquidity ratios (current ratio and acid test). If liquidity ratios are too low, a firm may be unable to pay its bills; if they are too high, a firm may not be making a high enough rate of return on investment.

With respect to stock market ratios, dividends represent only part of the *total* return to shareholders, which comprises dividends plus capital gains. Market prices of shares are forward-looking, in contrast with earnings per share figures which normally relate to the past. Hence it may not be easy to interpret the meaning of the 'price/earnings ratio'.

It can make a big difference whether one treats bank overdrafts and current instalments of longer-term debt as current liabilities (hence reducing net working capital) or as long-term liabilities (hence forming part of 'capital employed'). We prefer the former in computing liquidity ratios, the latter in looking at performance. There may be a distinction between a debt that is *legally* repayable 'on demand' and one which in fact is unlikely to clear within twelve months from the balance sheet date.

We have been using a set of accounts for Precision Locks Limited to take an overall look at performance, financial status and stock market standing. Now we must look more closely at how a company *records* transactions to enable it to prepare a set of financial statements at the end of the year. It is to this aspect of accounting that we turn in Section 4.

PROBLEMS

3.1 Definitions

Please write out in the spaces provided below your definitions of the ratios listed. Then compare your definitions with those set out overleaf.

(a) Debt ratio

(b) Earnings per share

(c) Price/earnings ratio

(d) Current ratio

(e) Earnings yield

(f) Dividend yield

(g) Acid test

(h) Interest cover

(i) Capital gain

(j) Dividend cover

3.1 Definitions

(a) **Debt ratio** is usually defined as 'total negotiated interest-bearing borrowings' (that is, long-term plus short-term borrowings) divided by 'capital employed' (that is, debt plus equity). It is prudent to include all short-term borrowings as part of 'debt'. Some analysts prefer to use the debt/equity ratio, that is, total debt (as above) divided by equity (shareholders' funds). Others may use *net* debt (total debt less cash). An acceptable level of debt ratio ('financial risk') depends on perceived business risk, which can vary widely between industries and between companies.

(b) **Earnings per share** (EPS) is profit after tax divided by the number of ordinary shares in issue (weighted if necessary for issues during the year). FRS14/IAS33 requires companies to calculate EPS after any 'exceptional' (non-recurring) items, but some companies also publish another version of EPS excluding such items. ('Diluted' EPS is discussed in Section 8.) The absolute level of EPS is not important (see Section 8); but the rate of growth in EPS is widely used as an important measure of performance.

(c) **Price/earnings ratio** (P/E ratio or 'multiple') is market price per ordinary share divided by earnings per share (EPS) for the most recent year (or an average of a number of recent years). A 'high' P/E ratio may imply either high growth or low risk (or both) expected in future. Or it may simply mean that the most recent year's earnings per share figure was abnormally small.

(d) **Current ratio** is current assets divided by creditors due within one year (current liabilities). Most industries would expect a ratio exceeding 1.0. (But note that in Problem 2.5 The Secret Seven (on page 39) several of the companies had *negative* working capital, which means that current liabilities *exceeded* current assets.) A current ratio exceeding 2.0 times might look rather 'high', implying an unprofitable level of liquidity.

(e) **Earnings yield** is earning per share (EPS) divided by market price per share. Where the ratio is net of tax, as it normally would be, it represents the reciprocal of the price/earnings ratio. Thus where the share price is 'high' (relative to EPS), the earnings yield will be low.

(f) **Dividend yield** is total annual dividends per ordinary share divided by market price per share. This may not represent a shareholder's total return from owning ordinary shares in a company, since it excludes any possible increase in share price ('capital gain'). New companies (needing all the cash they can get) or companies making losses may pay no dividends.

(g) **Acid test** (the 'quick ratio') is liquid assets divided by current liabilities (creditors due within one year). 'Liquid assets' normally means cash plus short-term investments plus debtors, but it excludes long-term debtors (if any) and it excludes stocks (inventories). Industries vary, but an acid test ratio of more than 1.0 would indicate abundant liquidity.

(h) **Interest cover** is profit before interest expense and before tax (PBIT) divided by interest expense. For this purpose, 'interest expense' should *include* any interest capitalized (see Section 7). It is normally more prudent to use gross interest expense, *not* to net off any interest income received. Interest cover above, say, 5.0 times would normally be regarded as fairly 'safe'.

(i) **Capital gain** is the excess of sales proceeds from selling shares (or other assets) over their purchase cost. A shareholder's total 'return' is equal to dividends received plus capital gain (or less capital loss). The total return is likely to vary from year to year as share prices fluctuate.

(j) **Dividend cover** is profit after tax (and after preference dividends and minority interests, if any – see Sections 8 and 9) divided by total net ordinary dividends for the year. This is equivalent to EPS divided by DPS: in other words, the ratio can be computed either in aggregate or on a 'per share' basis. The higher the dividend cover, the 'safer' the dividend.

3.2 James Smith Limited (C): Basic financial status and stock market ratios

Please refer back to the 2004 accounts of James Smith Limited on page 37. You are asked to complete the definition of each ratio and to calculate each ratio set out below. Assume the share price at 30 September 2004 was 450p. Net dividends totalled £90 000. When you have finished, please compare your answers with those overleaf.

	Definition	Ratio

Financial status ratios

(a) Debt ratio $\quad = \dfrac{\text{Debt}}{\text{Debt + Equity}} \quad = \rule{1cm}{0.4pt} \quad = \%$

(b) Interest cover $\quad = \rule{2cm}{0.4pt} \quad = \rule{1cm}{0.4pt} \quad = \text{times}$

(c) Current ratio $\quad = \rule{2cm}{0.4pt} \quad = \rule{1cm}{0.4pt} \quad = \text{times}$

(d) Acid test $\quad = \rule{2cm}{0.4pt} \quad = \rule{1cm}{0.4pt} \quad = \text{times}$

Stock market ratios

(e) Earnings per share $\quad = \rule{2cm}{0.4pt} \quad = \rule{1cm}{0.4pt} \quad = \text{pence}$

(f) Price/earnings ratio $\quad = \rule{2cm}{0.4pt} \quad = \rule{1cm}{0.4pt} \quad = \text{times}$

(g) Dividend yield (net) $\quad = \rule{2cm}{0.4pt} \quad = \rule{1cm}{0.4pt} \quad = \%$

(h) Dividend cover $\quad = \rule{2cm}{0.4pt} \quad = \rule{1cm}{0.4pt} \quad = \text{times}$

3.3 James Smith Limited (D) : short-term borrowing

The balance sheet at 30 September 2004 (set out on page 37) contained 'Creditors due within one year' at £350 000. Suppose this total included short-term borrowing of £80 000. Specifically how, if at all, would this new information affect the calculation in James Smith Limited (C) of:

(a) current ratio
(b) interest cover
(c) debt ratio
(d) acid test
(e) return on net assets.

The solution to this problem is shown overleaf.

3.4 GlaxoSmithKline plc: stock market statistics

On 11 April 2004 the following details appeared in the Pharmaceuticals section of the London share prices statistics of *Business*:

	Mkt. val. £m	Price	2003/4 high	low	% Yield	P/E
GlaxoSmithKline	65 755	1108 xd	1299	1060	3.7	14.4

Questions:

1 What was last year's earnings per share?
2 What was the dividend cover?
3 How many 25p ordinary shares were outstanding?
4 How much was last year's profit after tax?

The solution to this problem is shown overleaf.

3.2 James Smith Limited (C)

Solution

Financial status ratios		**Definition**		**Ratio**	

Financial status ratios

(a) Debt ratio $= \dfrac{\text{Debt}}{\text{Debt} + \text{Equity}}$ $= \dfrac{250}{250 + 350} = 41.7\%$

(b) Interest cover $= \dfrac{\text{Profit before interest and tax}}{\text{Interest payable}}$ $= \dfrac{220}{20} = 11.0$ times

(c) Current ratio $= \dfrac{\text{Current assets}}{\text{Current liabilities}}$ $= \dfrac{550}{350} = 1.57$ times

(d) Acid test $= \dfrac{\text{Liquid assets}}{\text{Current liabilities}}$ $= \dfrac{200 + 50}{350} = 0.71$ times

Stock market ratios

(e) Earnings per share $= \dfrac{\text{Profit after tax}}{\text{No. of ordinary shares in issue}}$ $= \dfrac{140}{(200 \times 2)} = 35.0$ pence

(f) Price/earnings ratio $= \dfrac{\text{Market price}}{\text{Earnings per share}}$ $= \dfrac{450}{35.0} = 12.9$ times

(g) Dividend yield (net) $= \dfrac{\text{Dividend per share (net)}}{\text{Market price}}$ $= \dfrac{(90 \div 400)}{450} = 5.0\%$ (net)

(h) Dividend cover $= \dfrac{\text{Earnings per share}}{\text{Dividend per share}}$ $= \dfrac{35.0}{22.5} = 1.56$ times

---

3.3 James Smith Limited (D)

Solution

(a) Current ratio. Unchanged.
(b) Interest cover. Unchanged.
(c) Debt ratio. Up from 250/600 (= 41.7%) to 330/680 (= 48.5%).
(d) Acid test. Unchanged.
(e) Return on net assets. Down from 220/600 (= 36.7%) to 220/680 (= 32.4%).

3.4 GlaxoSmithKline plc

Solution

1 Earnings per share: 1108/14.4 = 76.9p. (Actual: 77.2p)
2 Dividend per share: 1108 x 3.7% = 41.0p DPS (Actual: 41.0p)
   Hence dividend cover: EPS/DPS = 76.9/41.0 = 1.88 times. (Actual: 1.89)
3 25p shares outstanding: 65 755/1108 = 5 934.6 million. (Actual: 5 949 million)
4 Profit after tax: 76.9p x 65 755 million = £4 564 million. (Actual: £4 484 million)

Note: It is not unusual to find the 'calculated' answers slightly different from the 'actual' statistics. There may be complications in calculating earnings per share and more shares may have been issued since the most recent year-end.

3.5 Tarrant and Fisher plc: financial and stock market ratios

A simplified summary of Tarrant and Fisher plc's group balance sheet at 31 March 2005 is set out below:

		£m
Fixed assets		530
Current assets (inc. 60 cash)	320	
Less: Current liabilities (inc. 20 ST debt)	(240)	80
Total assets less current liabilities		610
Less: Long-term debt		260
Capital and reserves:		
Called up 10p shares	7	
Reserves	343	
		350

Notes:
1 Profit after tax was £28 million.
2 Dividend cover was 1.25 times.

Questions
1 What is the debt ratio:
   (a) based on debt/capital employed?
   (b) based on debt/equity?
   (c) based on *net* debt/capital employed?

2 What is the earnings per share?

3 If the share price is £12:
   (a) what is the dividend yield?
   (b) what is the price/earnings ratio?
   (c) what is the market value of the equity?

4 What is the current ratio?

The solution to this problem is shown overleaf.

3.6 Cochran & Company plc: financial and stock market ratios

A simplified summary of Cochran & Company plc's group balance sheet at 30 June 2005 is set out below:

		£ million
Total assets		**436**
Current liabilities		
Short-term borrowings	59	
Other creditors	93	152
Creditors due after one year		
Borrowings	67	
Other creditors and provisions	27	94
Shareholders' funds		
Called up 25p shares	12	
Other reserves	66	
Retained profits	112	190
		436

Questions
1 What is the debt ratio?
2 If the profit after tax was £25 million, what was the earnings per share?
3 If the dividend cover was 2.1 times, what was the dividend per share?
4 If the dividend yield was 3.0 per cent, what was:
   (a) the market price per share?
   (b) the price/earnings ratio?
   (c) market value of the equity?

The solution to this problem is shown overleaf.

3.7 Worldchem plc (B): financial and stock market ratios

Please refer back to the 2005 accounts of Worldchem plc with comparative figures for 2004 (which were set out on page 38).

You are asked, on a separate sheet of paper, to calculate the financial status ratios and the stock market ratios for the two years ended 31 March 2005. Use 142p and 136p respectively as the market price per 25p ordinary share for 2004 and 2005.

After calculating the ratios, please compare the detailed results for 2005 with those for the previous year. *Write down* any appropriate comments on a separate sheet of paper.

When you have completed your answer, please compare it with the solution shown at the back of the book.

3.5 Tarrant and Fisher plc

Solution

1 Debt ratio:
   (a) debt/capital employed: 280/630 = 44.4%
   (b) debt/equity: 280/350 = 80.0%
   (c) net debt/capital employed 220/570 = 38.6%

2 Earnings per share: 28/70   = 40.0p

3 Dividend per share: 40/1.25 = 32.0p
   (a) Hence dividend yield: 32/1200 = 2.7%
   (b) Price/earnings ratio: 1200/40 = 30 times
   (c) Market value of equity: 12 x 70 = £840 million

4 Current ratio: 320/240 = 1.33 times

3.6 Cochran & Company plc

Solution

1 Debt ratio: (67 + 59) / (190 + 94 + 59) = 126/343 = 36.7%

2 Earnings per share: 25 / (12 x 4) = 52.1p

3 Dividend per share: 52.1p / 2.1 = 24.8p

4 (a) Market price per share: 24.8 x 100/3.0 = 827p
   (b) Price/earnings ratio: 827/52.1 = 15.9 times
   (c) Market value of equity: (12 x 4) x 827p = £397 million

No answers are published to the following questions.

3.8 Hamilton Pumps Limited (B) : financial status and stock market ratios

Please refer back to the 2004 accounts of Hamilton Pumps Limited, with comparative figures for the previous year (which were set out on page 40).

You are asked to calculate, on a separate sheet of paper, the financial status ratios and the stock market ratios for the two years ended 31 December 2004. The market price per share at the end of 2003 was 150p, and at the end of 2004 it was 50p.

After calculating the ratios, please compare the detailed results for 2004 with those for the previous year. Write down, on a separate sheet of paper, any appropriate comments. Please also identify any questions about these ratios that you would wish to ask the company's senior management.

3.9 Liquid miscellany

Under what circumstances might:

(a) Some of Company A's stocks be *less* liquid than Company B's fixed assets?
(b) Some of Company C's stocks be *more* liquid than Company D's debtors?
(c) Company E's debt ratio indicate *high* borrowing, while the same company's interest cover indicates *low* borrowing?
(d) Company F's debt ratio indicate *low* borrowing, while the same company's interest cover indicates *high* borrowing?

3.10 What's going on?

(a) Why might a group with total assets on the balance sheet of £24 billion show cash and liquid investments of £3.5 billion at the same time as having total borrowings of £5.0 billion (including short-term borrowings of £1.5 billion)?
(b) Why might a company's market capitalization exceed the book value of shareholders' funds?
(c) Why might a perfectly sound company have an acid test ratio of only 0.25?

Section 4
Recording business transactions

BASIC TRANSACTIONS AND COMPANY ACCOUNTS

A company's accounts are summary statements embracing a wide range of transactions. They include only those items which we can express in financial terms. But what is the link between business events and published financial statements? How do separate transactions get included in accounts?

Anyone who uses accounting statements needs to understand how specific transactions affect them. Managers, for example, should be able to foresee how the company's financial statements will reflect actions that they are planning. So should investors.

To secure this knowledge, and to provide the accounting 'language' skills which are needed to comprehend accounting processes, we shall consider in this section:

1 the impact of transactions on company balance sheets (and profit and loss accounts);
2 their recording in the books (of account);
3 the link between the books of account and published financial statements.

In subsequent sections of the book we shall consider in some detail:

● rules for valuing fixed and current assets;
● procedures for preparing more complex sets of 'group' accounts.

Finally, in Section 14, we shall be able to look in detail at examples of published accounts, knowing what they represent and how they have been prepared. By that stage we shall have made substantial advances in our understanding of the meaning of company accounts.

Readers who want to gain a quick general idea of how business events affect accounts may prefer to skim the later pages of this section. From page 61 they deal in more detail with the accounting records, with the flows of information in recording multiple transactions and with double-entry accounting.

To begin with, on pages 56–60, we look at the impact of a number of separate transactions on the balance sheet of IE Limited (Initial Enterprises).

IMPACT OF TRANSACTIONS ON ACCOUNTS

The changes which occur to accounting statements when a company records transactions can be illustrated most clearly in a simple example. So let us look at a new company, IE Limited, which is just starting business. We shall consider how its accounts change to reflect the transactions in the first three months of its existence.

We shall group these transactions into six stages:

1 Issuing ordinary shares for cash.
2 Buying fixed and current assets for cash.
3 Selling goods for cash at a profit.
4 Buying stock, both for cash and on credit.
5 Selling goods on credit.
6 Further transactions.

In seeing how IE Limited's accounts reflect the above transactions, we shall look at the balance sheet (and profit and loss account) after each stage. The notes underneath each set of accounts explain various matters of interest. To ensure that you understand the procedures, we shall ask you to complete the adjustments for one of the later stages.

Stage 1   The issue of ordinary shares for cash

On 1 April 2005 a number of investors subscribed £50 000 to set up a small trading company, IE Limited (the letters I and E standing for Initial Enterprises). Here is how the balance sheet then looks:

IE LIMITED
Balance sheet at 1 April 2005
ASSETS (Use of funds)

Current asset
Cash   £50 000

LIABILITIES (Source of funds)

Capital and reserves
Called up share capital   £50 000

Notes

1   *The company is separate from its shareholders*
Setting up ('incorporating') IE Limited establishes it as a legal body quite distinct from its shareholders (owners). Ultimate control belongs to a company's *shareholders*, but they elect *directors* to exercise day-to-day control.

2   *The company views shareholders' capital as a potential ultimate 'liability'*
The company is normally assumed to be a 'going concern'. There is no intention that it will ever repay its shareholders the £50 000 they subscribed in exchange for shares in IE Limited. This would only happen when a company ceases to exist (is 'wound up' or 'liquidated'). From the company's point of view, however, such 'permanent' capital is still a potential – though very long-term – 'liability'.

3   *Holding cash is a 'use' of funds*
At this early stage in its existence, IE Limited holds its funds in the form of cash. It is important to note that holding cash is a *use* of funds, for it emphasizes that resources are always employed *somehow*.

4   *Total assets equal total liabilities*
IE Limited's balance sheet balances because in total the company's assets equal its liabilities (including shareholders' funds as such). They must do so, because uses of funds necessarily equal sources of funds. This is simply another way of expressing double-entry accounting.

Stage 2   Buying fixed and current assets for cash

During April the company takes steps to set up business:

(a) It buys a small freehold shop for £20 000 cash.
(b) It buys stock (to resell later) for £20 000 cash in total.

At the end of April the balance sheet reflects these changes. The letters against certain items refer to these two transactions.

IE LIMITED
Balance sheet at 30 April 2005
ASSETS (Use of funds)

		£
Fixed asset		
Freehold shop		20 000
Current assets		
Stock	20 000	
Cash (50 000 − 20 000^a		
− 20 000^b)	10 000	
		30 000
		50 000
LIABILITIES (Source of funds)		
Capital and reserves		
Called up share capital		50 000

Notes

1   The balance sheet still balances. Uses of funds still equal sources, in total.
2   IE Limited has introduced no new source of funds. The nature of its assets has changed, though the total remains the same.

	£	£
Cash	−40 000	
Freehold shop		+20 000
Stock		+20 000
	−40 000	+40 000

3   The balance sheet shows the assets at what they cost the company.

Stage 3   Selling goods for cash at a profit

IE Limited begins to trade, and during May:

(a) sells stock for £6 000 in cash
(b) that cost £5 000.

IE LIMITED
Balance sheet at 31 May 2005
ASSETS

			£'000
Fixed asset			
Freehold shop			20
Current assets			
Stock	20 − 5^b	15	
Cash	10 + 6^a	16	
			31
			51
LIABILITIES			
Capital and reserves			
Called up share capital			50
Profit and loss account			1
Turnover		6^a	
Less: Cost of sales		5^b	
			51

Notes

1   To keep things simple, the accounts now show figures only in thousands of pounds.
2   The profit and loss account shows sales (turnover) as a source of revenue.
3   Physical stock has fallen, so the balance sheet figure also reduces. The profit and loss account deducts the £5 000 *cost* of stock sold from the £6 000 sales revenue, to show the £1 000 profit on the transaction.
4   The profit is a new source of capital, and appears as part of 'capital and reserves', under the heading (balance on) 'profit and loss account'.

Stage 4 Buying stock, both for cash and on credit
In the first week of June IE Limited:

(a) buys stock costing £10 000 for cash
(b) buys stock costing £5 000 on credit.

IE LIMITED

Balance sheet at 5 June 2005			£'000
ASSETS			
Fixed asset			
Freehold shop			20
Current assets			
Stock	$15 - 10^a - 5^b$	30	
Cash	$16 - 10^a$	6	
		36	
			56
LIABILITIES			
Capital and reserves			
Called up share capital			50
Profit and loss account			1
Turnover		6	
Less: Cost of sales		5	
Shareholders' funds			51
Creditors due within one year			
Trade creditor			5
			56

Notes

1 The balance sheet now includes a subtotal 'Shareholders' funds £51 000'. This means the same as 'Capital and reserves'.
2 As in Stage 2, no profit (or loss) arises on the above two transactions. A profit normally arises only when a business *sells* goods or services.
3 The business has gained a further source of funds, from short-term trade credit from suppliers. Throughout the IE example, all creditors appear under liabilities (which are not deducted from current assets).

Stage 5 Selling goods on credit
In the second week of June, IE Limited:

(a) sells for £12 000 cash stock which had cost £10 000
(b) sells on credit for £6 000 stock which had cost £5 000.

IE LIMITED

Balance sheet at 12 June 2005			£'000
ASSETS			
Fixed asset			
Freehold shop			20
Current assets			
Stock	$30 - 10^a - 5^b$	15	
Debtors	$0 + 6^b$	6	
Cash	$6 + 12^a$	18	
		39	
			59
LIABILITIES			
Capital and reserves			
Called up share capital			50
Profit and loss account			4
Turnover	$6 + 12^a + 6^b$	24	
Less: Cost of sales	$5 + 10^a + 5^b$	20	
Shareholders' funds			54
Creditors due within one year			
Trade creditor			5
			59

Notes

1 Sales (turnover) of £6 000 on credit, rather than for cash, involves a new item in current assets – debtors (or 'accounts receivable'). When the customers pay, this will turn into cash.
2 The profit has now risen by £3 000 (sales £18 000 less cost of sales £15 000), so the cumulative total profit has now become £4 000.

Stage 6 Further transactions

In the remainder of the month the company buys further stock, makes some payments, and borrows a long-term loan.

(a) Buys stock for cash £10 000
(b) Buys stock on credit £3 000
(c) Pays existing creditor £5 000
(d) Pays £2 000 operating expenses for the quarter
(e) Borrows £10 000 on 30 June at interest of 10 per cent a year.

At this stage, you should be able to make the necessary adjustments to record the above transactions. Please alter the figures in the balance sheet at 12 June 2005 (shown on the right). Check that after you have made all the changes your amended balance sheet balances! Notice that we have shown the profit and loss account on the right as a separate subsidiary financial statement. But the final balance still appears in the balance sheet under 'Capital and reserves'.

When you have finished, compare your solution with that shown overleaf.

IE LIMITED
Balance sheet at 12 June 2005 £'000
ASSETS
Fixed asset
Freehold shop 20

Current assets

Stock	15	
Debtors	6	
Cash	<u>18</u>	
		<u>39</u>
		<u><u>59</u></u>

LIABILITIES
Capital and reserves

Called up share capital	50
Profit and loss account	<u>4</u>
Shareholders' funds	54

Creditors due within one year

Trade creditor	<u>5</u>
	<u><u>59</u></u>

IE LIMITED
Profit and loss account for the period ended 12 June 2005

£'000

Turnover	24
Less: Cost of goods sold	<u>20</u>
Profit	4

IE LIMITED *30* (*working copy*)
Balance sheet at ~~12~~ June 2005 *Amended draft* £'000
ASSETS
Fixed asset
Freehold shop 20

Current assets

Stock	$+10a + 3b + 15 = 28$	
Debtors	$6 = 6$	
Cash	$-10a - 5c + \underline{18} = 11$	
	$-2d + 10e$	

45

~~59~~ 65

LIABILITIES
Capital and reserves
Called up share capital 50

Profit and loss account $-2d$ ~~4~~ 2

Shareholders' funds ~~54~~ 52

Creditor due after one year
10% loan $+10e$ 10

Creditor due within one year
Trade creditor $5 + 3b - 5c$ ~~5~~ 3

~~59~~ 65

Notes

1 Paying a creditor reduces the amount due within one year (trade creditor) and current assets (cash) by the same amount (£5 000).
2 Notice that the two stages of a credit purchase amount, in the end, to the same thing as a cash purchase:

	Liabilities	*Assets*
Cash purchase		Stock up
		Cash down
Credit purchase		
(i) Purchase	Creditor up	Stock up
(ii) Payment	Creditor down	Cash down

60

IE LIMITED
Balance sheet, 30 June 2005: Final version £'000
ASSETS
Fixed asset
Freehold shop 20

Current assets
Stock	28
Debtors	6
Cash	11

45

65

LIABILITIES
Share capital
Called up share capital 50

Profit and loss account 2

Shareholders' funds 52

Creditors due after one year
10% loan 10

Creditor due within one year
Trade creditor 3

65

IE LIMITED
Profit and loss account for the three months ended 30 June 2005

	£'000
Turnover	24
Less: Cost of goods sold	20
Gross profit	4
Less: Operating expenses	2
Operating profit	2

BALANCE SHEET CHANGES: COLUMNAR ANALYSIS

So far we have been content to record, one by one, the effect of each transaction on the profit and loss account and balance sheet. Clearly, such an approach could not handle the numerous transactions which affect even quite small companies in the course of a year.

What the accountant needs is a way to collect together transactions of a similar kind, to summarize them, and then to enter them in aggregate in the financial statements. Such a system is still referred to as 'bookkeeping', even though today the records may not be in the form of 'books', but may be held on disk, tape, or other forms of electronic computer storage.

Before looking at the contents of the 'books of account', it will be helpful to establish more clearly the links between transactions and financial statements.

We can extend our ability to analyse transactions by using columnar worksheets, rather than simply altering the financial statements directly. Set out on the right is a worksheet which shows the figures for IE Limited at Stage 6:

1   *Opening balances* (the top row)

2   Transactions.

  ● buy stock for cash £10 000
  ● buy stock on credit £3 000
  ● pay existing creditor £5 000
  ● pay £2 000 operating expenses
  ● borrow £10 000 long-term loan.

3   *Closing balances* (the final row)

IE LIMITED – Stage 6

Shop	Stock	Debtors	Cash		Share capital	P & L	Creditors	Loan
20	15	6	18	*Opening balances*	50	4	5	
	10		(10)	Buy stock for cash				
	3			Buy stock on credit			3	
			(5)	Pay creditor			(5)	
			(2)	Pay operating expenses		(2)		
			10	Borrow long-term loan				10
20	28	6	11	*Closing balances*	50	2	3	10

You will see that the closing figures are those needed to compile the balance sheet for IE Limited at the end of Stage 6. The columnar worksheet provides a flexible way of dealing with transactions which form the link between the opening and closing balance sheet figures. The system can be extended by using more columns, so that it can deal with many transactions.

You can test this for yourself now by preparing the 2004 accounts for Cheviot Industries Limited from the information given overleaf.

Please now prepare the balance sheet and profit and loss account for Cheviot Industries Limited for the year ended 31 December 2004, in the spaces provided on the right (on this page).

The figures in the (opening) balance sheet at 1 January 2004 are set out in the top line of the columnar worksheet on the opposite page. You are asked to do three things:

(a) Record in the columnar analysis worksheet the transactions set out below.
(b) Add up each column and compile the closing balance for each 'account'.
(c) Extract the necessary figures to complete the outline financial statements shown on the right (on this page).

The transactions during 2004 which are to be recorded in the columnar worksheet are as follows:

		£
1	Sell on credit goods for	2 500 (already entered)
2	The goods had cost	1 200
3	Pay expenses in cash	500
4	Purchase stock on credit	1 400
5	Receive cash from customers	2 400
6	Pay cash to suppliers	1 100
7	Purchase additional fixed assets for cash	600

When you have completed all three stages, please compare your answer with that shown on page 64.

CHEVIOT INDUSTRIES LIMITED

Balance sheet at 31 December 2004

£

Fixed asset
Plant and machinery

Current assets
Stock
Debtors
Cash   _____

                                                        _____

Capital and reserves   ══════
Called up share capital
Profit and loss account   _____

Creditors due within one year
Creditors   _____

                                                        ══════

Profit and loss account
Year ended 31 December 2004

£

Turnover
Cost of sales   _____

Gross profit
Expenses   _____

Profit for the year   ══════

CHEVIOT INDUSTRIES LIMITED
Columnar analysis – 2004

Plant and machinery	Stock	Debtors	Cash		Share capital	Profit and loss account	Creditors
2 500	1 300	200	650	*Opening balances*	4 500	–	150
		2 500		Sold goods on credit		2 500	
				Cost of goods sold			
				Closing balances			

CHEVIOT INDUSTRIES LIMITED
Columnar analysis – 2004

Plant and machinery	Stock	Debtors	Cash		Share capital	Profit and loss account	Creditors
2 500	1 300	200	650	Opening balances	4 500	–	150
		2 500		Sold goods on credit		2 500	
	(1 200)			Cost of goods sold		(1 200)	
			(500)	Expenses		(500)	
	1 400			Purchases on credit			1 400
		(2 400)	2 400	Cash received from customers			
			(1 100)	Cash paid to suppliers			(1 100)
600			(600)	Fixed assets purchased			
3 100	1 500	300	850	Closing balances	4 500	800	450

Balance sheet at 31 December 2004

	£
Fixed assets	
Plant and machinery	3 100
Current assets	
Stock	1 500
Debtors	300
Cash	850
	2 650
	5 750
Capital and reserves	
Called up share capital	4 500
Profit and loss account	800
	5 300
Creditors due within one year	
Creditors	450
	5 750

Profit and loss account
Year ended 31 December 2004

	£
Turnover	2 500
Cost of sales	1 200
Gross profit	1 300
Expenses	500
Profit for the year	800

Split columns

A longer list of transactions might cause problems in adding up the columns, since plus and minus figures appear together. We can avoid this by dividing each column into two, and showing pluses and minuses on opposite sides of the dividing line within each column. This is the system which companies in fact use to record transactions in ledger accounts.

Using this approach for Cheviot Industries, we show asset balances on the left of each column and liability balances on the right. When we enter each transaction, it may add to, or reduce, the opening balances. We can then determine the closing balances by adding up the two sides (plus or minus) of each column as shown below.

CHEVIOT INDUSTRIES LIMITED
Columnar analysis – 2004

Plant and machinery		Stock		Debtors		Cash			Share capital		Profit and loss account		Creditors	
+	−	+	−	+	−	+	−		−	+	−	+	−	+
2 500		1 300		200		650		Opening balances		4 500				150
		2 500						Sold goods on credit				2 500		
			1 200					Cost of goods sold			1 200			
							500	Expenses			500			
		1 400						Purchases on credit						1 400
					2 400	2 400		Cash received from customers						
							1 100	Cash paid to suppliers					1 100	
600							600	Fixed assets purchased						
3 100	−	2 700 −1 200	1 200	2 700 −2 400	2 400	3 050 −2 200	2 200			4 500	1 700	2 500 −1 700	1 100	1 550 −1 100
3 100		1 500		300		850		Closing balances		4 500		800		450

65

BOOKS OF ACCOUNT: CASH AND LEDGER ACCOUNTS

Columnar worksheets are more flexible than a system of altering figures on the face of the balance sheet and profit and loss account. But still not flexible enough. The number of columns which can be recorded across a page is clearly limited; but even a small company will need many different headings – for different revenue and expense items as well as different asset and liability accounts.

As accounting evolved each column became a 'ledger account' in the 'books of account' to give separate accounts for each kind of asset, liability, income and expense. The asset and expense balances are shown on the left of each account, and the liability and income balances on the right. Thus:

Assets	+ on left	– on right
Liabilities	– on left	+ on right
Income	– on left	+ on right
Expenses	+ on left	– on right

The separate accounts can be listed underneath each other, as shown opposite. In total the books of account 'balance' when the opening balances have been entered on each account. This can be checked by taking out a 'Trial Balance', which is a test listing of all the balances in the books of account to see whether they *do* balance.

CHEVIOT INDUSTRIES LIMITED
Trial balance at 1 January 2004

	£	£
Cash	650	
Fixed asset	2 500	
Stock	1 300	
Debtors	200	
Share capital		4 500
Profit and loss		–
Creditors		150
	4 650	4 650

On the next page the transactions for Cheviot Industries Limited have been entered in the ledger accounts. The cash account has been separated from the other accounts, and has been described as the 'Cash Book'. The other accounts are grouped together and referred to as 'Ledger Accounts' (sometimes referred to as 'T-accounts').

CHEVIOT INDUSTRIES LIMITED
Separate accounts at 1 January 2004

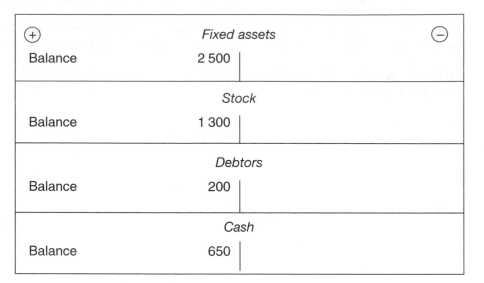

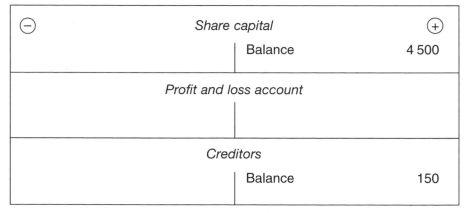

Recording transactions in the books of account

The opening balances have been entered in the cash book (containing the cash account) and the ledger (containing other accounts). The various transactions have then been entered. At each stage the balances on each side of the central line still balance, because an entry has been made on each side. This is the *double-entry* system of accounting.

Looking at each transaction in turn, note that each entry in the accounts cross-refers to the account which contains the other side of the entry.

1 Sell goods on credit   2 500
   + Profit & loss (sale)
   + Debtors
   The entries are on opposite sides of the central line, and both are +. Liabilities increase. Assets increase.

2 The goods sold had cost   1 200
   – Stock
   – Profit & loss (increase 'cost of goods sold')

3 Pay expenses in cash   500
   – Cash
   – Profit & loss (increase expenses)

4 Purchase stock on credit   1 400
   + Stock
   + Creditors

5 Receive cash from customers   2 400
   + Cash
   – Debtors

6 Pay cash to suppliers   1 100
   – Cash
   – Creditors

7 Purchase more fixed assets   600
   – Cash
   + Fixed assets

Once all the transactions have been entered, the accounts can be 'balanced'; and the balance 'carried down' (c/d) to the next period, into which it is 'brought down' (b/d). All the balances brought down appear in the closing balance sheet.

You may like to check that the books as a whole still 'balance' after entering the transactions, by listing all the balances on the various accounts and taking out a closing trial balance.

CHEVIOT INDUSTRIES LIMITED   Accounts – 2004

Cash book

(+)			(−)		
Balance	650		3	Profit & loss account =	
5 Debtors	2 400			Expenses	500
			6	Creditors	1 100
			7	Fixed assets	600
				Balance c/d	850
	3 050				3 050
Balance b/d	850				

Ledger

(−)			(+)		

Share capital

				Balance	4 500

Profit and loss

2 Cost of stock sold	1 200		1 Credit sales	2 500
3 Cash – expenses	500			
Balance c/d	800			
	2 500			2 500
			Balance b/d	800

Creditors

6 Cash	1 100		Balance	150
Balance c/d	450		4 Stock	1 400
	1 550			1 550
			Balance b/d	450

Fixed assets

(+)			(−)		
Balance	2 500		Balance c/d	3 100
7 Cash	600			
	3 100			3 100
Balance b/d	3 100			

Stock

Balance	1 300		2 Profit & loss a/c	1 200
4 Creditors	1 400		Balance c/d	1 500
	2 700			2 700
Balance b/d	1 500			

Debtors

Balance	200		5 Cash	2 400
1 Sale	2 500		Balance c/d	300
	2 700			2 700
Balance b/d	300			

THE ACCOUNTING RECORDS AND DOUBLE-ENTRY BOOKKEEPING

We have noted already that the principal elements in the accounting records are the cash book and the ledger. The other subsidiary records which make the system work are 'day books' ('journals').

Cash book

The cash book is in effect, the 'ledger account for cash'. It shows receipts and payments of cash. The example below shows typical details. (They come from Problem 4.10: Plumridge Engineering Limited.)

Cash receipts are entered on the left-hand side (increases in an asset account), and cash payments on the right-hand side. Accountants refer to the left-hand side as the 'debit' side (abbreviated to Dr), and call the right-hand side the 'credit' side (Cr).

In addition to the date and amount of each cash transaction, the cash book also shows the ledger account in which the *other* side of the transaction has been entered as part of the double-entry system (for example: Loan – Fo(lio) 10). The word 'Folio' means 'page', and each ledger account will have a page or folio reference number. It does not matter whether the accounting records are kept in actual books, or in computer files: the bookkeeping system is essentially the same.

The cash book records all receipts and payments of cash in the order in which they occur, and is thus a 'day book' (or 'journal') record. It is also, as we have seen, in effect a 'ledger account for Cash' – though for convenience it is invariably maintained as a separate record.

Ledger

The ledger is the record which contains the separate ledger accounts, both for the various liabilities and assets, and also for the various items of income and expenses. The later two sets of balances are transferred, at the end of each accounting period, to the profit and loss account.

A typical ledger account (for debtors) is shown below. Again you will see a reference to the account in which the *opposite* side of each transaction can be found. Thus the two sides of the transaction 'receipt of £50 000 cash from debtors' have been recorded. In bookkeeping terms the £50 000 receipt would first be entered in the cash book. It would later be 'posted' to (entered in) the debtors ledger account.

It is usual for accounts to appear in the (nominal) ledger in some sort of classified sequence such as the following. (Gaps may be left in the sequence, to allow for new ledger accounts as required: for example Fo 42 Motor vehicles, Fo 82 Royalty income.)

Shareholders' funds
1   Share capital
2   Capital reserves
3   Profit and loss account

Liabilities
10   Loans
11   Trade creditors

Assets
40   Land and buildings
41   Machinery

50   Trade debtors

Revenue
80   Sales
81   Investment income

Expenses
90   Wages
91   Pensions

etc.

Dr			**Cash book**		CB Fo 10		Cr	
Date	Description	Fo	Amount	Date	Description	Fo	Amount	
			Dr.				Cr.	
1.7.04	Balance	b/d	30 000	1.2.05	Machine	40	80 000	
1.11.04	Sale	80	50 000	8.6.05	Wages	90	30 000	
31.12.04	Loan	10	100 000	20.6.05	Creditors	11	40 000	
7.6.05	Debtors	50	50 000					
				30.6.05	Balance	c/d	80 000	
			230 000				230 000	
1.7.05	Balance	b/d	80 000					

Dr			**Debtors**		Ledger Fo 50		Cr	
Date	Description	Fo	Amount	Date	Description	Fo	Amount	
			Dr.				Cr.	
1.7.04	Balance	b/d	40 000	7.6.05	Cash	CB10	50 000	
				30.6.05	Balance	c/d	30 000	
30.11.04	Sale	80	40 000					
			80 000				80 000	
1.7.05	Balance	b/d	30 000					

Overall bookkeeping system

Even a small company may need hundreds of different ledger accounts. The principal asset and liability accounts may be few but the company could easily have fifty or more suppliers and hundreds of credit customers. Each supplier (creditor) and credit customer (debtor) will have a separate ledger account, to record his or her position with the company. Obviously, the ledger could soon become very large. Another reason for numerous ledger accounts is the need to analyse expenditure in some detail. Depending on the degree of analysis required for management purposes, there could easily be fifty or more separate expense accounts. The analysis of income normally requires fewer ledger accounts.

It is usual to divide the ledger into a number of parts, as illustrated opposite:

	containing accounts for
Creditors (or purchase or bought) ledger	individual suppliers
Debtors (or sales or sold) ledger	individual customers
Nominal ledger	income and expenses
Private ledger	{ liabilities and assets also 'control' accounts for other parts of the ledger

The use of 'control' accounts makes the private ledger, together with the cash book, a self-balancing system. The control accounts will contain the totals of all the detailed entries in the other parts of the ledger. Thus the debtors control account entries will be the totals of all credit sales and all cash receipts from credit customers which have been entered in the individual customer accounts. At any date, therefore, the balance on the debtors control account should equal the sum of all the separate balances in the individual customers' accounts in the debtors ledger.

With this system, any number of accounts can be maintained, and any number of transactions can be dealt with. By suitable classification of the various accounts, and subdivision for more extensive analysis where appropriate, the ledger accounts in the 'books of account' become almost infinitely flexible.

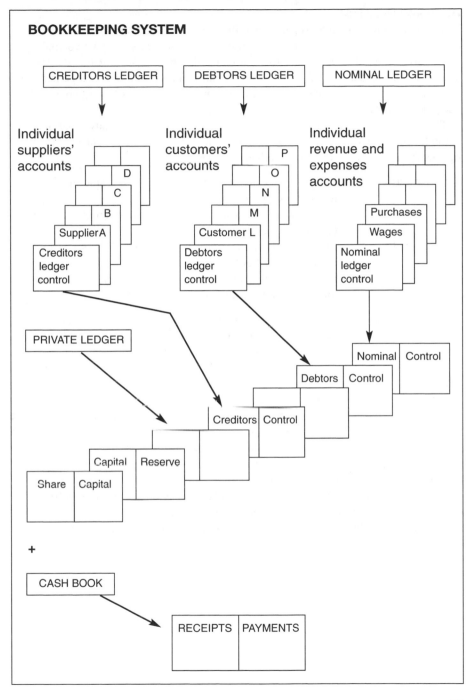

Day books (journals)

To prevent the need to enter separate details of every single transaction in the ledger, day books (journals) are used which summarize transactions. The two main day books, the 'Sales day book' and the 'Purchase day book', are illustrated opposite. They contain details of the individual customers or suppliers, together with references to the prime document – copy sales invoice or goods inward note – which underlie each transaction.

The day books are not part of the ledger: they summarize information before entry in the ledger. (The day books are sometimes called 'books of prime entry'.) 'Posting' figures from the day books to the ledger involves:

Sales ledger:
– Entry in individual customers' accounts of amounts invoiced to them (debit entries)
– Entry in the sales account of the *total* amounts invoiced (credit entry).

Purchase ledger:
– Entry in individual suppliers' accounts of amounts invoiced by them (credit entries).
– Entry in the purchase account (or other expense accounts) in total of all the amounts invoiced (debit entries).

The format of the day books can vary. They may be in the form of a bound book, loose-leaf sheets, or often merely batches of copy invoices or copy goods inwards notes fixed together with an attached listing to give the total.

The final record which we need to mention is the 'Journal' (or 'Private Journal'), which records any entries for which there is no other day book. The bookkeeping system aims to ensure that some record exists outside the ledger for all amounts which are entered in the ledger. Most entries come from the cash books, sales and purchase day books, wages records, and so on. Sometimes, however, there is no other record of prime entry, and the journal is used: for example, where amounts have been posted to the wrong accounts, or adjusting entries where amounts relate to more than one accounting period.

As with the other day books, the journal is *not* part of the ledger. Two entries (one on each side) have to be made in the ledger to post the journal entries. The format of the journal can be anything from a bound book to a file of journal vouchers.

Sales day book

Date	Customer	Invoice No.	DL Fo	Invoice amount £
1 March	A Brown	013672	B 12	125
1 March	B Cook	013673	C 8	60
2 March	Jones & Co	013674	J 17	420
				–
				–
				–
				–
	Total			£2 600

Posted to the *debit* of individual debtors' accounts in the debtors' ledger.

Posted in total to the *credit* of the sales account in the ledger.

Purchase day book

Date	Supplier	Good inwards note	CL Fo	Invoice amount £
1 March	T Lawson & Co	732105	L 9	261
2 March	E Thompson Ltd	732106	T 7	481
3 March	Electrix Ltd	732107	E 11	160
				–
				–
				–
	Total (for week)			£1 900

Posted to the *credit* of individual creditors' accounts in the creditors' ledger.

Posted in total to the *debit* of the purchases account in the ledger.

Journal

Date		Fo	Debit	Credit
30 June	Land and buildings	39	27 000	
	To capital reserve	2		27 000
	Being revaluation of land and buildings from cost £83 000 to £110 000			

INFORMATION FLOWS

We have considered the various parts of the total accounting system. Set out below is a diagram representing the complete system.

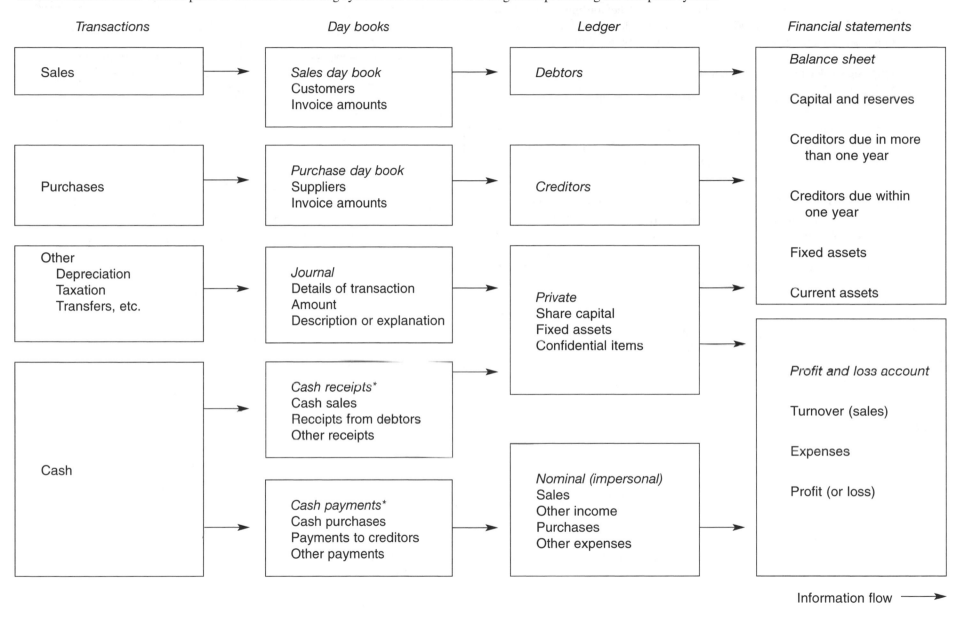

*The cash book constitutes the ledger account for cash, as well as a book of prime entry.

DOUBLE-ENTRY BOOKKEEPING

We have seen that accountants refer to the left-hand side of an account as the 'debit' side, and the right-hand side as the 'credit' side. Thus, for Cheviot Industries, which sold stock for £2 500 on credit, instead of saying: 'Plus Sales, Plus Debtors' (as we did earlier on page 65), in practice one would say: 'Credit Sales, Debit Debtors with £2 500'.

The double-entry rules in summary are as follows:

1 Debits are on the left of a ledger account, credits on the right.
2 For every debit entry there must be a matching credit.
3 In total the debit entries must equal the credit entries.
4 Accounts which normally have DEBIT balances are: assets, expenses, losses.
5 Accounts which normally have CREDIT balances are: liabilities, income, profits.

The diagram opposite may be helpful. The ledger is a way to analyse cash (and credit) transactions. Cash receipts and payments are recorded in the ledger as liability, asset, income, and expense items. Working from a cash entry, therefore, it is easy to tell whether the corresponding ledger entry must be a debit or a credit.

In learning to use the accounting terms we can start by thinking simply that cash is paid with the RIGHT hand (right-hand side of the cash book) and received with the LEFT hand (left-hand side of the cash book).

Cash payments or CREDITS (shown on the right-hand side of the cash book) are recorded on the *opposite* side of the ledger, so the entries in the ledger accounts must be DEBITS (on the left-hand side) – for example purchases of assets, payment to creditors, payment of expenses.

Cash receipts or DEBITS (shown on the left-hand side of the cash book) are recorded on the *opposite* side of the ledger so the entries in the ledger accounts must be CREDITS (on the right-hand side) – for example issuing share capital, sales, receipts from customers.

Familiarity with the terms comes only with use; but starting from *cash* transactions wherever possible should help you to handle most of the commonest transactions without much trouble.

At first, the use of the neutral accounting terms 'debit' and 'credit' sometimes confuses non-accountants, who tend to attach emotional values to them. Debit is thought to be 'bad', and credit 'good', so that it becomes difficult to think of an asset balance as a debit. It is essential to regard the words merely as technical terms, with no connotation whatever of 'good' or 'bad'. Simply, a debit balance or entry is on the left, a credit on the right.

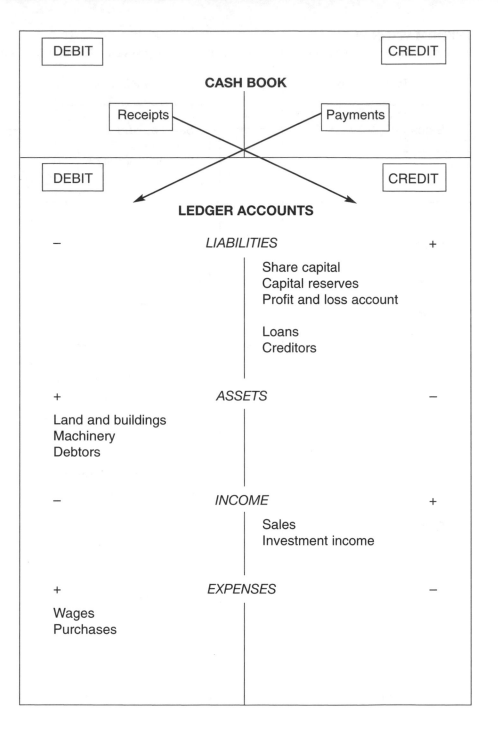

STAGES IN PREPARING PUBLISHED ACCOUNTS

One of the requirements of the Companies Act 1985 is that published accounts must agree with the books of account. It may be helpful now to summarize the process by which:

- business transactions are recorded in the books of account;
- published accounts are prepared from the books of account.

The major sequence of steps is as follows:

1 Record all transactions for a period in the books of account by means of the double-entry system, either in the cash book and ledger accounts, or in one of the day books and the ledger accounts.

2 Total the entries for a period in the cash book and in each ledger account, and determine the 'balance' at the end of the period on each account (including 'cash').

3 Extract a 'trial balance', by listing all the debit and credit balances at the end of the period on the ledger accounts and on the cash book. If the double-entry process has been followed correctly, the total of the debit balances should always equal the total of the credit balances.

4 Make any necessary adjustments to the trial balance schedule (we shall be describing these in Section 5). We show opposite the *format* of a 'trial balance schedule', using the figures for Initial Enterprises Limited at Stage 6 as an example (page 60), but with no entries in the 'Adjustments' columns.

5 Draw up the profit and loss account for the period, and the balance sheet at the end of the period, in suitably classified formats. After all necessary 'adjustments' in the trial balance schedule have been entered in the books of account, every ledger account balance should appear in the balance sheet; either separately, or combined with other balances for similar items. (Income and expense account totals will have been transferred, 'closed off', to the profit and loss account for the period.)

IE LIMITED
Trial balance at 30 June 2005

Folio	Trial balance Dr £	Trial balance Cr £	Adjustments Dr £	Adjustments Cr £	Profit and loss Dr £	Profit and loss Cr £	Balance sheet Dr £	Balance sheet Cr £
1 Share capital		50 000						50 000
4 10% Loan		10 000						10 000
8 Trade creditors		3 000						3 000
10 Freehold shop	20 000						20 000	
20 Stock	28 000						28 000	
21 Debtors	6 000						6 000	
50 Sales		24 000				24 000		
60 Cost of sales	20 000				20 000			
70 Operating expenses	2 000				2 000			
CB Cash	11 000						11 000	
					22 000	24 000		
Profit and loss					2 000			2 000
	87 000	87 000			24 000	24 000	65 000	65 000

Note

The credit entries in the profit and loss column (£24 000) exceed the debit entries (£22 000), so there is a 'credit balance' of £2 000. This is included as such in the balance sheet. In the ledger account for 'profit and loss', the £2 000 would be entered on the debit side as 'balance carried down' in the old period; and it would then be 'brought down' as a credit balance at the opening of the new period.

SECTION 4 SUMMARY

In this section we have considered three methods of recording the effect of business transactions on company accounts.

The simplest method, which we used in looking at Initial Enterprises, is to enter each transaction directly on to the face of the balance sheet and profit and loss account. This is a convenient way to demonstrate the basic notion of double-entry, but it is clearly not feasible for any real business.

The second method, which we adopted for Cheviot Industries, is to use columnar analysis to show how individual transactions combine to link the opening balances with the closing balances for a period. Although this is more flexible, and helps to show the logic of double-entry in terms of 'plus' and 'minus' in the various asset and liability accounts, again it is not practicable for any but the very smallest business.

The third method – 'double-entry accounting' – is the system actually used in business. It consists of entering all transactions first in day books (or journals), and thence into 'ledger accounts'. The possibility of indefinite extension, subdivision, and classification makes this system highly flexible and practical. The development of sophisticated computers in recent years has not affected the underlying principles of double-entry bookkeeping – though, of course, it has substantially changed the physical nature of the 'books of account'.

We saw how the cash book and ledger accounts together form a self-balancing system, because each transaction requires a *double* entry – both a debit entry and a credit entry. Thus the books and any balance sheet prepared from them should always balance. We also briefly considered how preparing financial statements from the books of account involves preparing a 'trial balance', and then making any necessary adjustments.

We shall not repeat here the summary of the rules of double-entry bookkeeping (on page 72), or the description (on page 73) of the sequence of steps from recording business transactions in the books of account to preparing the financial statements.

Those readers who wish to consolidate their understanding of basic accounting procedures should now turn to the problems (and worked solutions), which will give some practice in working through bookkeeping exercises.

PROBLEMS

4.1 Definitions
Please write down below your definitions of each of the terms shown. Then compare your answers with those shown overleaf.

(a) A credit entry

(b) The cash book

(c) A journal entry

(d) Ledger posting

(e) The 'balance' on a ledger account

(f) A trial balance

(g) Debtors' control account

(h) Double-entry accounting

(i) Debit

(j) Write-off

4.1 Definitions

(a) **A credit entry** is an entry on the right-hand side of a ledger account (or cash book). (A debit entry is one on the left-hand side.) It may increase a credit balance on a liability or income account, or decrease a debit balance on an asset or expense account. In accounting, the word 'credit' carries no favourable meaning.

(b) **The cash book** is the accounting 'book' (or other record) in which firms enter all cash receipts and payments (either individually or in summary). The cash book represents the 'ledger account' for cash; it is thus part of the double-entry system. It also represents a 'day book' ('journal'). Thus a firm which pays out £2 500 cash for wages records a credit entry of £2 500 in the cash book, and a debit entry of £2 500 in the ledger account for 'wages'.

(c) **A journal entry** sets out the debit and credit entries to be made in ledger accounts in respect of a business transaction. It describes its nature, which may be somewhat unusual. A journal entry always 'balances', in that the sum of debit entries always equals that of credit entries. Where many transactions of a similar kind occur, it is usual to enter them in a 'day book' ('journal'). They are then 'posted' to the ledger in total, rather than as separate journal entries.

(d) **Ledger posting** is the process of making entries in ledger accounts either from day books or from the cash book. There are no 'negative' entries; to *reduce* a debit entry, simply make a credit entry in that account.

(e) **The 'balance' on a ledger account** is the difference, if any, between the total amount of the credit entries and the total of the debits. Where the former are greater, there is a 'credit balance'. From time to time balances are 'carried down' (c/d) from an earlier period (and 'brought down' (b/d) to the later period). This simply tidies up the ledger account, as part of regular accounting. (Balances are said to be brought 'down' when they appear lower on the same page, and brought 'forward' when they appear at the top of the next page.)

(f) **A trial balance** is a list of all the debit and credit balances on all the ledger accounts (including cash). It forms the basis for preparing published accounts. The sum of debit entries in ledger accounts (including cash) should always equal the sum of the credit entries. So the total of the debit balances on ledger accounts should equal the total of credit balances at any time. If not, there is an error somewhere – either in posting items to the ledger accounts, or in extracting and listing the balances.

(g) **Debtors' control account** is a ledger account in the nominal ledger in which appear (in total) all items posted to the accounts of individual debtors in the sales ledger. The balance on the control account (or 'total' account) should equal the total of all the separate balances.

(h) **Double-entry accounting** is a system of recording business transactions which recognizes that in total the sources of funds must always equal uses of funds. Thus the total amount of debit entries in ledger accounts must equal the total amount of the credit entries in ledger accounts; and the total of all ledger account debit balances (including cash) must equal the total of all credit balances.

(i) **Debit** may be a *noun* (= 'a debit entry'), which is the opposite of a credit entry, and which means an entry on the left-hand side of a ledger account. It carries no unfavourable meaning (for instance, assets are debits). Or, 'debit' may be a *verb*, meaning 'to make a debit entry in a ledger account'.

(j) **Write-off** means charging an amount as an expense in the profit and loss account. A 'write-off' means an amount so treated. This seems to be a rare example of an accounting term carrying a similar meaning to everyday language. 'All the money we spent on pure research turned out to be a complete write-off.'

4.2 Abacus Book Shop Limited (A): Balance sheet

The balances appearing in the books of the Abacus Book Shop Limited at 1 January 2005 were as follows. You are asked to draw up a balance sheet as at that date. Use the Asset/Liability format used in this chapter.

	£
Cash	2 000
Trade creditors	1 000
Debtors	2 000
Called up share capital	3 000
Profit and loss account	4 000
Stock	4 000

The answer is shown on the next page (left).

ABACUS BOOK SHOP LIMITED
Balance sheet, 1 January 2005

4.3 Broadhurst Timber Limited: Balance sheet preparation

Here are the balances in the ledger of Broadhurst Timber Limited at 30 September 2004. Please prepare the company's balance sheet at that date. Use the Asset:Liability format used in this chapter. You may prefer to use a separate sheet of paper for your answer.

	£'000
Bank overdraft	17
Cash	4
Trade creditors	46
Debtors	38
Dividend	6
Leasehold property	74
Long-term loan	35
Plant and equipment	133
Reserves	83
Share capital	100
Stocks and work-in-progress	49
Tax payable	11

The answer is shown on the next page (right).

4.2 Abacus Book Shop Limited (A)

Solution

ABACUS BOOK SHOP LIMITED
Balance sheet at 1 January 2005

ASSETS		£
Current assets		
Stock	4 000	
Debtors	2 000	
Cash	2 000	
	8 000	
		8 000
LIABILITIES		
Capital and reserves		
Called up share capital	3 000	
Profit and loss account	4 000	
	7 000	
Creditors due within one year		
Trade creditors	1 000	
	8 000	

Notes

1 Did you remember to include the correct headings?:
Current assets
Capital and reserves
Creditors due within one year
2 Did you insert a subtotal to show the total shareholders' funds? (This is not always explicitly named on the face of the balance sheet.)

4.3 Broadhurst Timber Limited

Solution

BROADHURST TIMBER LIMITED
Balance sheet at 30 September 2004

ASSETS		£'000
Fixed assets		
Leasehold property		74
Plant and equipment		133
		207
Current assets		
Stocks and work-in-progress	49	
Debtors	38	
Cash	4	
		91
		298
LIABILITIES		
Capital and reserves		
Called up share capital		100
Reserves		83
		183
Creditors due after one year		
Long-term loan		35
Creditors due within one year		
Bank overdraft	17	
Creditors	46	
Tax payable	11	
Dividend	6	
		80
		298

4.4 Abacus Book Shop Limited (B): Amending balance sheet

The balance sheet of the Abacus Book Shop Limited on 1 January 2005 is set out below.

During the month of January, the company:

(a) received £1 000 cash from credit customers
(b) bought new books for £4 000 in cash
(c) sold for £3 000 cash, books which had cost £2 000.

You are asked to amend the balance sheet to show the position at 31 January 2005. When you have done so, please compare your answer with that shown overleaf.

ABACUS BOOK SHOP LIMITED
Balance sheet at 1 January 2005

ASSETS		£
Current assets		
Stock	4 000	
Debtors	2 000	
Cash	2 000	
	8 000	
		8 000
LIABILITIES		
Capital and reserves		
Called up share capital	3 000	
Profit and loss account	4 000	
		7 000
Creditors due within one year		
Trade creditors		1 000
		8 000

The answer to this next problem is shown at the end of the book.

4.5 Chemical Products Company Limited (A): Amending the balance sheet

During August 2004 the Chemical Products Company Limited:

(a) bought for cash new plant costing £10 000
(b) received £8 000 from debtors
(c) paid creditors £5 000
(c) sold on credit for £15 000 goods which had cost £18 000.

You are asked to amend the balance sheet as at 31 July 2004 shown below (*Note:* For simplicity, all figures are shown in thousands.)

CHEMICAL PRODUCTS COMPANY LIMITED
Balance sheet at 31 July 2004

ASSETS		£'000
Fixed assets		
Plant at cost		28
Current assets		
Stock	25	
Debtors	15	
Cash	12	
		52
		80
LIABILITIES		
Capital and reserves		
Called up share capital		50
Profit and loss account		20
		70
Creditors due within one year		
Trade creditors		10
		80

4.4 Abacus Book Shop Limited (B)

Solution

The amended balance sheet of Abacus Book Shop Limited at 31 January 2005 is shown below. The final balance sheet is shown opposite.

ABACUS BOOK SHOP LIMITED (*working copy*)
Balance sheet at 31 January 2005

ASSETS £
Current assets
Stock	+ 4000b – 2000c	6000	4 000
Debtors	– 1000a	1000	2 000
Cash	+ 1000a – 4000b + 3000c	2000	2 000
		9000	8 000
		9000	8 000

LIABILITIES
Capital and reserves
Called up share capital		3 000	
Profit and loss account	+ 1000c	5000	4 000
		8000	7 000

Creditors due within one year
Trade creditors		1 000
	9000	8 000

ABACUS BOOK SHOP LIMITED (*final statement*)
Balance sheet at 31 January 2005

ASSETS £
Current assets
Stock	6 000	
Debtors	1 000	
Cash	2 000	
		9 000
		9 000

LIABILITIES
Capital and reserves
Called up share capital	3 000	
Profit and loss account	5 000	
		8 000

Creditors due within one year
Trade creditors	1 000
	9 000

Notes

1 Did you remember to alter the *date* of the balance sheet?
2 It may help to identify each transaction with the appropriate letter of the alphabet.

Double-entry bookkeeping exercises

4.6   Identifying debit and credit balances

Indicate for each of the items shown below whether it would normally appear in the ledger as a debit balance or as a credit balance.

When you have entered the amounts in the correct column on the right, please compare your answers with those overleaf.

Note

The twelve items listed are only *some* of the ledger balances: there are others not listed, so that the twelve items in their correct columns will not necessarily 'balance'.

		£	Dr £	Cr £
1	Cash	1 000		
2	Payment of telephone expenses	200		
3	Called up share capital	50 000		
4	Debtors	5 000		
5	Cash received on sale of fixed assets	2 000		
6	Stock held for resale	8 000		
7	Received from debtors	1 000		
8	Trade creditors	7 000		
9	Purchase of motor car	5 100		
10	Share premium account	10 000		
11	Paid to suppliers (creditors)	3 000		
12	Repayment of bank loan	1 000		

A solution to this problem is shown overleaf.

4.7   Midmarsh Golf Club: Trial balance errors

The bookkeeper of the Midmarsh Golf Club has been trying for some time to draw up the accounts of the Club for the year ended 31 March 2005. As a preliminary step before making certain final adjustments, he has taken out a 'trial balance' from his ledger accounts and cash book – but it does not balance!

You are asked to examine the results of his efforts, and, on the basis of what you would normally expect, to alter his list to make the two sides balance.

	Bookkeeper's trial balance		Correct trial balance	
	Dr £	Cr £	Dr £	Cr £
Subscription income		3 000		
Cash in hand	200			
Bar stock		950		
Sports equipment for resale	450			
Subscriptions due not received		100		
Electricity bills paid	250			
Staff wages		2 300		
Profit on annual dance		400		
Creditors	300			
Fixtures and fittings	1 400			
Profit on bar sales	500			
Surplus, start of year	2 500			
Repair bills paid		450		
Cleaning expenses	600			
	6 200	7 200		

A solution to this problem is shown overleaf.

4.6 Identifying debit and credit balances

Solution

		£	Dr £	Cr £
1	Cash	1 000	1 000	
2	Payment of telephone expenses	200	200	
3	Called up share capital	50 000		50 000
4	Debtors	5 000	5 000	
5	Cash received on sale of fixed assets	2 000		2 000
6	Stock held for resale	8 000	8 000	
7	Received from debtors	1 000		1 000
8	Trade creditors	7 000		7 000
9	Purchase of motor car	5 100	5 100	
10	Share premium account	10 000		10 000
11	Paid to suppliers (creditors)	3 000	3 000	
12	Repayment of bank loan	1 000	1 000	

Notes

1	Asset	Cash previously received
2	Expense	Opposite to cash payment
3	Liability	Opposite to cash receipt
4	Asset	Opposite to sale, which is a credit
5	Reduction of asset	Opposite to cash receipt
6	Asset	Opposite to cash payment or creditor
7	Reduction in asset	Opposite to cash receipt
8	Liabilities	Opposite to expenses or assets
9	Asset	Opposite to cash payment
10	Liability	Opposite to cash receipt
11	Reduction in liability	Opposite to cash payment
12	Reduction in liability	Opposite to cash payment

Once you remember that a cash receipt is a debit in the cash book (and a cash payment a credit), it is obvious that the 'other side' of the transaction in a ledger account must be a credit (or a debit for a cash payment). That automatically solves most of the problems.

4.7 Midmarsh Golf Club

Solution

	Bookkeeper's trial balance		Correct trial balance	
	Dr £	Cr £	Dr £	Cr £
Subscription income		3 000		3 000
Cash in hand	200		200	
Bar stock		950*	950	
Sports equipment for resale	450		450	
Subscriptions due not received		100*	100	
Electricity bills paid	250		250	
Staff wages		2 300*	2 300	
Profit on annual dance		400		400
Creditors	300*			300
Fixtures and fittings	1 400		1 400	
Profit on bar sales	500*			500
Surplus, start of year	2 500*			2 500
Repair bills paid		450*	450	
Cleaning expenses	600		600	
	6 200	7 200	6 700	6 700

Note

Errors are marked with an asterisk (*). Three balances which should be credits are shown as debits (300 + 500 + 2 500), totalling £3 300. And four balances which should be debits are shown as credits (950 + 100 + 2 300 + 450), totalling £3 800. Hence the net effect of correcting the errors is to increase the total of the debit balances by £500 and to reduce the total of the credit balances by the same amount. When a trial balance fails to 'balance', one obvious possible error is that a balance (or balances) amounting to *half* the difference has been listed on the wrong side.

Answers to these next two problems are shown at the end of the book.

4.8 Abacus Book Shop Limited (C): Amending balance sheet

In February, the Abacus Book Shop Limited was given the opportunity to buy a long lease on the shop for £6 000. It decided to do so, and to borrow £5 000 on the security of the lease. It also carried out the following transactions in February. You are asked to amend the balance sheet shown below to reflect these transactions.

		£
(a)	Receipt of loan at 10 per cent per year	5 000
(b)	Payment for lease	6 000
(c)	Sales for cash of books which had cost £2 000	3 000
(d)	Sales on credit of books which had cost £1 000	2 000
(e)	Purchases of books for cash	3 000
(f)	Purchases of books on credit	2 000

ABACUS BOOK SHOP LIMITED
Balance sheet at 31 January 2005

ASSETS		£
Current assets		
Stock	6 000	
Debtors	1 000	
Cash	2 000	
	9 000	
		9 000

LIABILITIES		
Capital and reserves		
Called up share capital	3 000	
Profit and loss account	5 000	
		8 000
Creditors due within one year		
Trade creditors		1 000
		9 000

4.9 Whitewash Laundry Limited: Preparing accounts

The transactions of the Whitewash Laundry Limited in the quarter ended 31 March 2005 were as follows:

		£'000
(a)	Total invoiced sales in quarter	60
(b)	Cash payments for supplies used in laundry	6
(c)	Cash received from credit customers	55
(d)	Operating costs: wages, fuel, etc. paid in cash	30
(e)	Selling and administrative costs paid in cash	15

The balance sheet at 1 January 2005 is shown below. You are asked to compile a profit and loss account for the quarter to 31 March 2005 (on a separate sheet of paper), and to prepare the balance sheet at the end of the quarter.

WHITEWASH LAUNDRY LIMITED
Balance sheet at 1 January 2005

ASSETS		£'000
Fixed assets		
Laundry and equipment		50
Current assets		
Debtors	30	
Cash	10	
		40
		90

LIABILITIES		
Capital and reserves		
Called up share capital		75
Profit and loss account		15
		90

4.10 Plumridge Engineering Limited: Transaction analysis

The opening balances of Plumridge Engineering Limited on 1 July 2004 were:

	£'000
Share capital	300
Trade creditors	50
Plant and machinery	200
Stock	80
Debtors	40
Cash	30

These have already been entered in the columnar analysis sheet and ledger accounts shown on the next page.

You are asked to enter the details of the company's transactions in the year ended 30 June 2005 which are set out below, both in the columnar analysis sheet and in the ledger accounts. When you have done this, please transfer the balances to the profit and loss account and balance sheet outline shown on the right-hand side of this page. Since you will be entering the same figures in both, the balances on the ledger accounts should be the same as those shown on the columnar analysis sheet.

Transactions in the year to 30 June 2005 were as follows:

		£'000
(a)	Sold stock for cash	50
(b)	The stock had cost	30
(c)	Borrowed from bank	100
(d)	Bought new machine for cash	80
(e)	Sold stock on credit	40
(f)	The stock had cost	20
(g)	Paid wages and other expenses	30
(h)	Paid suppliers (creditors)	40
(i)	Received from customers (debtors)	50

Note

To simplify your workings, we suggest you enter figures only in thousands of pounds. Ignore depreciation of fixed assets.

The solution to this problem is shown on pages 86 and 87.

PLUMRIDGE ENGINEERING LIMITED

Profit and loss account for year ended 30 June 2005

	£'000
Turnover	
Cost of sales	———
Wages and other expenses	———
Net profit for the year	═══

Balance sheet at 30 June 2005

£'000

ASSETS
Fixed assets
Plant and machinery

Current assets
Stock
Debtors
Cash

LIABILITIES
Capital and reserves
Called up share capital
Profit and loss account

Creditors due after one year
Loan

Creditors due within one year
Trade creditors

4.10 Plumridge Engineering Limited

Columnar analysis

Plant etc.		Stock		Debtors		Cash		£'000	Share capital		Profit and loss		Loan		Creditors	
+	−	+	−	+	−	+	−		−	+	−	+	−	+	−	+
200		80		40		30		Opening balances		300						50

T-accounts (ledger accounts)

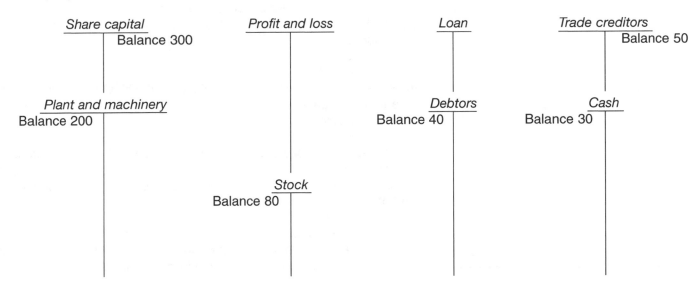

4.10 Plumridge Engineering Limited

Solution

PLUMRIDGE ENGINEERING LIMITED

Profit and loss account for year ended 30 June 2005

	£'000
Turnover	90
Cost of sales	50
	40
Wages and other expenses	30
Trading profit	10

Balance sheet at 30 June 2005

		£'000
ASSETS		
Fixed assets		
Plant and machinery		280
Current assets		
Stock	30	
Debtors	30	
Cash	80	
		140
		420
LIABILITIES		
Capital and reserves		
Called up share capital		300
Profit and loss account		10
		310
Creditors due after one year		
Loan		100
Creditors due within one year		
Trade creditors		10
		420

Transaction analysis

The link between the opening balances, the transactions and closing balances is clear in the columnar worksheets.

(a) Sold stock for cash £50 000. Income has increased and so has cash.
   + Profit and loss account (sale)
   + Cash

(b) The stock had cost £30 000. An asset account has been reduced and so has profit.
   – Stock
   – Profit and loss account (cost of sales)

(c) Borrowed from bank £100 000. An asset has increased. A corresponding liability has arisen.
   + Cash
   + Loan

(d) Bought new machine for cash £80 000. One asset goes up, another down.
   + Plant etc.
   – Cash

(e) Sold stock on credit £40 000. Income has increased and so have debtors.
   + Profit and loss account (sale)
   + Debtors

(f) The stock had cost £20 000.
   As in (b).

(g) Paid wages and other expenses £30 000. Cash has decreased and so has profit.
   – Cash
   – Profit and loss account (expenses)

(h) Paid suppliers (creditors) £40 000. An asset and a liability have been reduced.
   – Cash
   – Creditors

(i) Received from customers (debtors) £50 000. One asset is reduced, another increased.
   – Debtors
   + Cash

The same transactions appear in the 'T' accounts. We have grouped all the income and expense items in a single profit and loss account. Normal practice in the bookkeeping system would be to open separate 'T' accounts for each kind of income and expense. The balances on the separate accounts would then be transferred at the end of the period to the profit and loss account.

Note how the balances are calculated. They are then transferred to the balance sheet. The detailed entries shown in the profit and loss 'T' account are shown separately in the profit and loss account statement.

4.10 Plumridge Engineering Limited

Solution

Columnar analysis

Plant etc. +	Plant etc. −	Stock +	Stock −	Debtors +	Debtors −	Cash +	Cash −	£'000	Share capital −	Share capital +	Profit and loss −	Profit and loss +	Loan −	Loan +	Creditors −	Creditors +
200		80		40		30		Opening balances		300						50
						50		(a) Sold stock for cash				50				
			30					(b) Cost of sale			30					
						100		(c) Borrowed from bank						100		
80							80	(d) Bought machine								
				40				(e) Sale on credit				40				
			20					(f) Cost of sale			20					
							30	(g) Paid wages & expenses			30					
							40	(h) Paid creditors							40	
					50	50		(i) Rec'd from customers								
280	−	80	50	80	50	230	150		−	300	80	90		100	40	50
		−50		−50		−150					−80					−40
280		30		30		80		Closing balances		300		10		100		10

T-accounts

Share capital

		Balance	300

Profit and loss

Stock	30[b]	Cash sale	50[a]
"	20[f]	Credit sale	40[e]
Wages etc.	30[g]		90
	80		
Balance c/d	10		
	90		90
		Balance b/d	10

Loan

		Cash	100[c]

Trade creditors

Cash	40[h]	Balance	50
Balance c/d	10		
	50		50
		Balance b/d	10

Plant and machinery

Balance	200	
Cash	80[d]	
	280	

Stock

Balance	80	Cost of sale	30[b]
		" " "	20[f]
			50
		Balance c/d	30
	80		80
Balance b/d	30		

Debtors

Balance	40	Cash	50[i]
Sale	40[e]	Balance c/d	30
	80		80
Balance b/d	30		

Cash

Balance	30	Machine	80[d]
Sale	50[a]	Wages etc.	30[g]
Loan	100[c]	Creditors	40[h]
Debtors	50[i]		150
	230	Balance c/d	80
			230
Balance b/d	80		

Answers to the next two problems are shown at the end of the book.

4.11 A Green Limited

The balance sheet of A Green Limited (vegetable wholesalers) at 31 March 2005 is shown below. In the three-month period to 30 June the following transactions took place:

		£
(a)	Purchases of vegetables on credit	16 000
(b)	Sales for cash of vegetables which had cost £12 000	15 000
(c)	Sales on credit of vegetables which had cost £4 000	5 000
(d)	Operating expenses paid in cash – wages, vans etc.	2 000
(e)	Cash payments to suppliers	14 000
(f)	Cash receipts from debtors	3 000

You are asked (on separate paper) to:
1. Open up cash book and ledger accounts and enter the opening balances (shown in the 31 March balance sheet).
2. Record the transactions shown above, and balance the accounts.
3. Extract a trial balance.
4. Prepare a profit and loss account for the three months ended 30 June 2005, and a balance sheet as at that date.

A GREEN LIMITED
Balance sheet at 31 March 2005

ASSETS

Fixed assets

		£
Van		4 000
Current assets		
Debtors	1 000	
Cash	3 000	
		4 000
		8 000

LIABILITIES

Capital and reserves

Called up share capital		3 000
Profit and loss account		2 000
		5 000

Creditors due within one year

Trade creditors		3 000
		8 000

4.12 Joseph Sillen Limited

The balance sheet and profit and loss account of Joseph Sillen Limited for the half-year ended 30 June 2004 are set out below. During the second half of 2004 the following transactions occurred:

		£'000	
(a)	Sales for cash	350	(cost £250)
(b)	Sales on credit	150	(cost £110)
(c)	Purchases of goods for cash	250	
(d)	Purchases of goods on credit	80	

Additional cash payments:

(e)	Expenses	100
(f)	Payments to creditors	90

Additional cash receipts:

(g)	Receipts from debtors	130

Required: On separate paper, open up a cash book and ledger accounts incorporating balances at 30 June 2004. Then:
1. Record the transactions in the books of account for the second half of 2004 and balance the accounts as necessary (work in £'000).
2. Extract a trial balance.
3. Prepare a profit and loss account for the year ended 31 December 2004 and a balance sheet at that date. (Leave the tax expense at £10 000.)

JOSEPH SILLEN LIMITED
Balance sheet at 30 June 2004

	£'000	
Fixed assets		
Factory and machinery		250
Current assets		
Stock	200	
Debtors	60	
Cash	40	
	300	
		550
Capital and reserves		
Called up share capital		300
Profit and loss account		150
		450
Creditors due within one year		
Trade creditors		100
		550

Profit and loss account
for half-year to 30 June 2004

	£'000
Turnover	400
Cost of sales	300
Gross profit	100
Expenses	70
Profit before tax	30
Tax expense	10
Profit after tax	20

Answers to the following three problems are not published.

4.13 Stamford Manufacturing Company Limited
On the basis of the information below you are asked to prepare:
(a) the balance sheet at 31 December 2004
(b) the profit and loss account for the year ended 31 December 2004.

A On 1 January 2004 the Stamford Manufacturing Company Limited was formed to make and sell widgets:
1 Ordinary shares were sold to provide £200 000 capital.
2 £160 000 was borrowed short-term from a bank at 10 per cent a year interest.
B During 2004 the following cash payments were made:
1 Premises rented for £12 000 (Commercial expense).
2 Machines purchased for £240 000 (Fixed assets).
3 6 000 widget castings bought for £10 each (Stocks) – £48 000 cash paid, £12 000 still owing at year-end.
4 Operator's wages of £12 000 (Stocks). During 2000 all 6 000 widget castings were machined by the operator into finished widgets.
5 Manager's salary £24 000 (General expense).
C Depreciation on the machines is charged at 10 per cent a year (Stocks).
D During 2004 5 000 finished widgets were sold at £40 each – £180 000 cash received, £20 000 still receivable at year-end.
E At the end of 2004 the bank loan was repaid, plus £16 000 interest.
F Tax for 2004 was assessed at £10 000. £4 000 was paid in cash during the year, and £6 000 remained payable at the year-end.
G A dividend of £16 000 was paid in cash to shareholders during 2004.

Please prepare the 2004 accounts by filling in the *pro forma* balance sheet and profit and loss account shown.

STAMFORD MANUFACTURING COMPANY LTD
Balance sheet at 31 December 2004

	£'000	£'000
Net Fixed Assets		
Fixed assets, at cost		
Less: accumulated depreciation	____	
Current Assets		
Stocks (inventory)		
Debtors (accounts receivable)		
Cash	____	
		____
		≡≡≡
Current Liabilities		
Bank Loan		
Creditors (accounts payable)		
Taxation payable	____	
Capital and Reserves		
Called up Share Capital		
Retained Earnings	____	____
		≡≡≡

STAMFORD MANUFACTURING COMPANY LTD
Profit and loss account for the year 2004

	£'000
Sales	
Cost of Sales	____
Gross Profit	
Commercial Expenses	____
Operating Profit	
Interest Expense	____
Profit Before Tax	
Taxation Expense	____
Net Profit After Tax	____

4.14 Basil Trading Limited: Preparing accounts

There has been a small fire in the offices of Basil Trading Limited in which you have been working. You have managed to recover the following data for the year ended 31 December 2004.

	DR £m	CR £m
Wages	18.4	
Issued Share Capital		7.0
Accumulated depreciation (at 1.1.04)		6.0
Sales		72.0
Rent and rates expense	3.6	
Cash	2.5	
Dividend	4.0	
Audit fee expense	0.2	
Stock (at 1.1.04)	6.0	
Debtors	8.0	
Salaries expenses	3.4	
Plant and machinery	17.0	
Land and buildings	13.0	
Creditors		5.6
Accumulated Profit (at 1.1.04)		10.0
Purchases expense	32.0	
Lighting and heating expense	2.0	
Loan payable		10.0
Loan interest expense	0.5	
	110.6	110.6

In addition the figures above need adjustment for the following items:

Closing stock is to be valued at £4 million.

Loan interest of £300 000 is payable but has not been allowed for in the accounts.

Depreciation of £1.5 million is chargeable for 2004.

Tax is to be charged on the profits for the year at 30%.

Provision of £600 000 is to be made against debtors.

£1 000 000 of the loan is repayable on 1 July 2005.

The task now is to prepare:

(a) a profit and loss account for 2004.

(b) a balance sheet as at 31 December 2004.

4.15 Kaleidoscope plc: chaotic balance sheet

The following balance sheet of Kaleidoscope plc at 31 January 2005 seems to have been badly affected by a glitch in the computer, even though it appears to 'balance'! Assuming the *amounts* shown against each item are correct (though the plus or minus signs may be wrong), prepare a 'correct' version. You may wish to combine certain items where many details have been given.

KALEIDOSCOPE PLC
Balance sheet at 31 January 2005

		£m
Tangible fixed assets		
Cumulative depreciation	(154)	
At cost or valuation	366	
		212
Current liabilities		
Taxation	25	
Prepayments	10	
Provisions for doubtful debts	2	
Other creditors	199	
		(236)
Long-term assets		
Provisions and contingencies	61	
Marketable securities	12	
Intangible fixed assets	25	
Revaluation reserve	22	
Long-term debtors	3	
Minority interests	(23)	
		100
Current assets		
Stocks	118	
Debtors	165	
Cash	37	
FA Investments	87	
		407
		483
Long-term liabilities		
Borrowings: Long-term	76	
Short-term	100	
Other long-term creditors	6	
		182
Shareholders' funds		
Capital and reserves	128	
Less: Proposed dividend	(27)	
		101
		483

Section 5
Measuring profit or loss

PROFIT MEASUREMENT

Measuring profit or loss involves two stages: businesses first 'recognize' the sales revenues they have earned in an accounting period; then determine what expenses to set against those revenues. The difference is profit for the period (or loss, if expenses exceed revenues).

Readers of company accounts want to get a clear idea of what the profit or loss figures mean, how they have been arrived at and what is the margin of error; for published accounts can never be entirely accurate. The larger the number of incomplete transactions, the longer their time-span, and the greater their size, the wider will be the range of possible figures for profit or loss.

In practice there are many accounting rules ('standards') to help deal with the problems that can make measurement difficult. Even so, those preparing accounts often have to make judgements or estimates. As a result, for most businesses a given period's reported profit is subject to a wide margin of uncertainty.

Many of the problems in accounting stem from the 'chopping up' of a business's whole life into a series of much shorter (usually one-year) accounting periods.

...	Year 7	Year 8	Year 9	Year 10	Year 11	Year 12	...

Ongoing life of business

Companies are normally 'going' concerns. To calculate their profit requires, in effect, 'freezing' their financial position at regular intervals. But this is an *artificial* 'snapshot'. We cannot expect to get accurate 'valuations' at balance sheet dates for partially-used assets or for partially finished products, since in most cases there is no available 'market' to provide them.

In this section we shall look at 'accrual accounting' in general, at measuring sales revenue and at how to determine the amount and timing of expenses. We shall be concerned mostly with matters relating to *measurement* and hardly at all with precise details of *disclosure*. Section 6 looks at valuing stock and long-term contracts in progress. Then Section 7 considers fixed assets and provisions for depreciation.

Measuring transactions which are incomplete at the accounting date presents unavoidable problems. Their nature may become clearer by looking at two simple examples over the page. In the first, all transactions are completed within a single accounting period, but the second example involves *incomplete* transactions.

Profit measurement: All items complete within one accounting period

A. Green runs a wholesale greengrocery business. In the year ended 31 December 2004 his cash transactions were:

	£'000
Sales	1 000
Purchases of goods	800
Operating expenses	120

There were no other transactions; and there was no opening or closing stock.

The revenue and expenses figures are known amounts which clearly relate to 2004, and the net profit before tax is £80 000.

	£'000
Sales	1 000
Cost of sales (purchases)	800
Gross profit	200
Operating expenses	120
Net profit before tax	80

Profit measurement: Incomplete transactions

Now suppose that *in addition* to the facts in the above example:

1   Mr Green sold further goods for £10 000 on credit to a customer in financial difficulties who seems unlikely to be able to pay the full amount.
2   At the year-end Mr Green had goods left in stock which had cost £20 000 in cash. Half the goods were highly perishable and would become worthless if not sold next day. The rest would keep for up to a week.

Now there is more than one possible figure for Mr Green's 2004 profit:

Version A		£'000	Version B		£'000
Sales		1 010	Sales		1 010
Purchases	800		*Less:* Bad debt		10
Less: Closing stock	20				1 000
		780	Purchases		800
Gross profit		230	Gross profit		200
Operating expenses		120	Operating expenses		120
Net profit		110	Net profit		80

The difference between the two profit figures results from different views about the outstanding debtor of £10 000 and the stock costing £20 000. Both views depend on *assumptions about uncertain future events*.

Version A assumes that Mr Green will collect the whole £10 000 debt and (in due course) sell all the remaining stock. Thus the 2004 profit is £110 000. If the debt proves to be bad and the stock is not sold, then under Version A, writing off these amounts in 2005 will reduce profits in that year by £30 000.

Version B takes a gloomy view about both matters and reports 2004 profits of only £80 000. If in the end Mr Green does manage to collect the debt and sell the stock, then under Version B the accounts for 2005 will show an extra profit of £30 000.

The 2004 profit varies between £80 000 and £110 000, depending on views about the debtor and the stock at the year-end. Notice that such judgements affect the reported profits of *two* periods, not just one. And *profit* for a period need not be the same as the *cash inflow* from operations. (We discuss cash flows in Section 11.)

Profit measurement: A valuation process ?

The way we define profit for a period – 'sales revenue minus expenses' – has long been widely accepted. Later in this section we discuss how to measure both sales revenue and expenses.

Given the double-entry framework, one can also think of 'profit' for a period as being (a) any dividends paid out to shareholders *plus* (b) the balance sheet increase in shareholders' funds. (The latter amount will normally comprise the increase in cumulative retained profits plus or minus any change in share capital.) That is true as a matter of arithmetic, but in practice firms do not actually calculate their profit for a period by 'deducting' one balance sheet from another.

Assets in balance sheets normally represent estimates not of value but of recoverable cost. If a firm changes the balance sheet amount of tangible fixed assets (by providing for depreciation), or of stocks (by reducing cost to net realizable value), or of debtors (by providing for bad debts), that reduces profits for the period to the same extent. These changes in profits and in book values of assets are two aspects of the same process dealing with incomplete transactions.

Thus the example on the next page shows Millpond Limited's after-tax profit of £100. This represents sales of £1 200 less expenses totalling £1 100. It also happens to be equal to closing shareholders' funds of £550 less opening shareholders' funds of £450. (Of course, this would not be so if there had been any dividends paid or any capital changes during the year.)

MILLPOND LIMITED

Profit and loss account for the year ended 31 December 2004

	2004 £'000	2003 £'000
Sales	1 200	1 000
Cost of sales	900	800
Gross profit	300	200
Other expenses	150	120
Profit before tax	150	80
Taxation	50	30
Profit after tax	100	50

Balance sheet at 31 December 2004 (summary)

	2004 £'000	2003 £'000
Fixed assets	250	200
Net current assets	300	250
Net assets	550	450
Share capital	300	300
Profit and loss account	250	150
Shareholders' funds	550	450

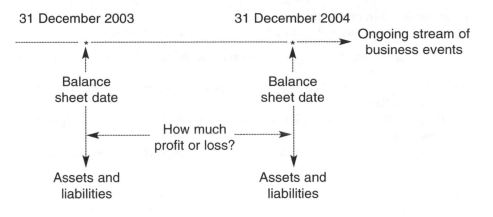

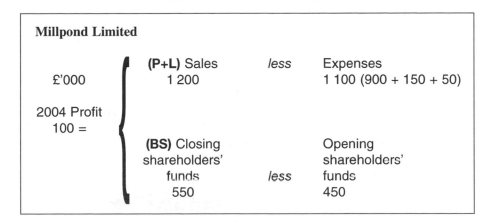

ACCRUAL ACCOUNTING

Accrual accounting recognizes income and expenses when they accrue due, not when cash receipts or payments actually occur. It is therefore important to distinguish between cash receipts and 'income', and between cash payments and 'expenses'.

In analysing the accounts of a small property company for the year ended 31 December 2004, for example, one might find the income and expense adjustments as set out on the following pages. These illustrate the differences between cash amounts received and paid in a period and those amounts reported as accounting income and expenses. In this example, relative precision is quite easy, since all rents receivable and payable accrue on a time basis, day by day. (But even here, for simplicity, we assume months of equal length.)

Cash receipts and accounting income

A number of transactions of Top Flat Limited are illustrated below:

(a) In July 2003, Top Flat receives in advance annual rent of £1 000, half of which relates to 2004.

(b) In January 2004, Top Flat receives in advance annual rent of £500, all of which relates to 2004.

(c) In April 2004, Top Flat receives in advance annual rent of £800, one quarter of which relates to 2005.

(d) In March 2005, Top Flat receives in arrear half-yearly rent of £600, half of which relates to 2004.

Note that accounts prepared on an accrual basis allocate income to the period to which it *relates* as opposed to that in which *cash is received*. Thus Top Flat's 'rent income' for 2004 is £1 900, although the company actually received only £1 300 cash in 2004.

2004 income

		£	
Cash received in 2004		1 300	
Add: (a) received in 2003 relating to 2004		+500	(= liability* at December 2003)
(d) receivable in 2005 relating to 2004		+300	(= asset** at December 2004)
		2 100	
Less: (c) received in 2004 relating to 2005		−200	(= liability* at December 2004)
= 'Rent income' in 2004 =		1 900	

* income received in advance
** income receivable

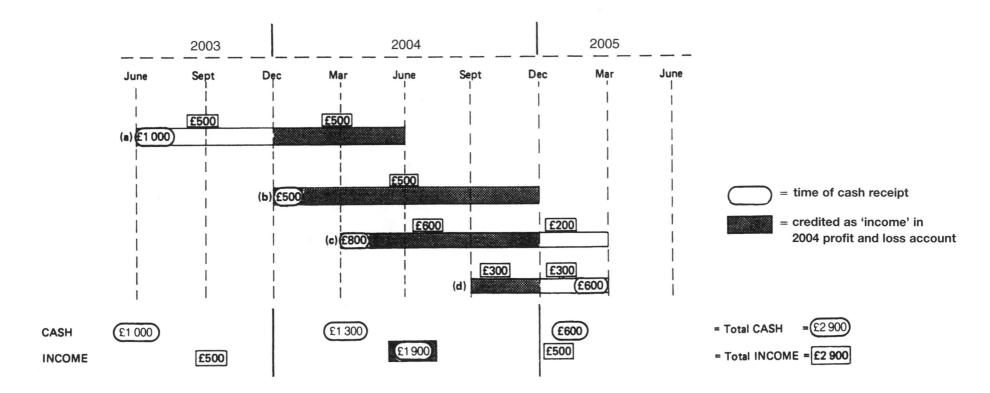

Cash payments and accounting expense

A number of transactions of Top Flat Limited are illustrated below:

(e) In October 2003, Top Flat pays in advance annual rent of £800, three-quarters of which relates to 2004.

(f) In October 2004, Top Flat pays in advance half-yearly rent of £600, half of which relates to 2005.

(g) In December 2004, Top Flat pays in arrear annual rent of £500, all of which relates to 2004.

(h) In June 2005, Top Flat pays in arrear annual rent of £400, half of which relates to 2004.

Note that an accrual accounting system charges rent payable in the period to which it *relates*, not in the period in which *cash is paid*. Thus Top Flat's 'rent expense' for 2004 is £1 600 although the company actually paid only £1 100 cash in 2004.

2004 expense

	£	
Cash paid in 2004	1 100	
Add: (e) paid in 2003 relating to 2004	+600	(= asset* at December 2003)
(h) payable in 2005 relating to 2004	+200	(= liability** at December 2004)
	1 900	
Less: (f) paid in 2004 relating to 2005	−300	(= asset at December 2004)
= 'Rent expense' in 2004 =	1 600	

* prepayment
** accrued charge

On the next page are shown the entries in the books of account to record the rent items receivable and payable.

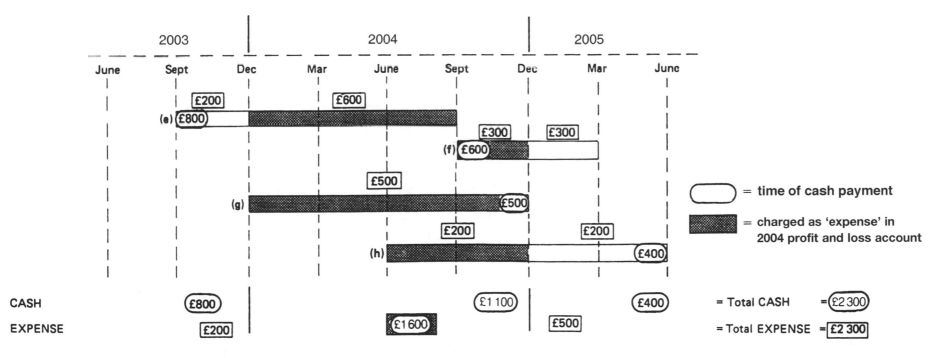

95

TOP FLAT LIMITED

ENTRIES IN THE BOOKS OF ACCOUNT

Receipts and income		Payments and expense	

Cash

2004	£		£
Jan (b) Rent received	500		
Apr (c) Rent received	800		
	1 300		

Cash

	£	2004	£
		Oct (f) Rent paid	600
		Dec (g) Rent paid	500
			1 100

Rents receivable

2004	£	2004	£
Dec Profit and loss account:		Jan Balance b/d	500 (a)
2004 'income'	1 900	Jan Cash	500 (b)
Dec Balance c/d	200 (c)	Apr Cash	800 (c)
		Dec Balance c/d	300 (d)
	2 100		2 100
2005		2005	
Jan Balance b/d	300 (d)	Jan Balance b/d	200 (c)
'Income receivable'		'Income received in advance'	

Rents payable

2004	£	2004	£
Jan Balance b/d	600 (e)	Dec Profit and loss account:	
Oct Cash	600 (f)	2004 'expense'	1 600
Dec Cash	500 (g)	Dec Balance c/d	300 (f)
Dec Balance c/d	200 (h)		
	1 900		1 900
2005		2005	
Jan Balance b/d	300 (f)	Jan Balance b/d	200 (h)
'Prepayment'		'Accrued charge'	

Rentwell Limited: Accrual accounting adjustments

Rentwell Limited's bookkeeper had drawn up the profit and loss account and balance sheet shown on the right. (Tax is ignored to simplify the example.)

The company's auditor found that adjustments were required to cover the following transactions:

(a) Annual rent received of £40 000 for one property, relating to the year ending in September, had all been included in the accounts to 30 June.

(b) No adjustment had been made in the accounts for rent payable by Rentwell on Blackacre. This property was held on a long lease at £20 000 per annum, with rent payable six-monthly in arrears on 31 March and 30 September.

(c) Rates of £4 000 per annum on another property had been paid for a year in advance on 1 April. No allowance had been made for the amount paid in advance at 30 June.

(d) Repair work for which Rentwell was liable on one of the company's properties was in progress at 30 June. The work, which would cost about £2 000 in total, was estimated to be half finished at 30 June.

You are asked to amend the draft profit and loss account and balance sheet opposite to show the correct final figures for the year ended 30 June 2005. Strike out any figures which need changing and insert the correct ones. The answer is shown overleaf.

RENTWELL LIMITED

Profit and loss account for the year ended 30 June 2005

		£'000
Rents receivable		600
Less: Rents payable	400	
Rates	50	
Other expenses	40	
		490
Net profit		110

Balance sheet at 30 June 2005

		£'000
Fixed assets		
Leasehold properties		450
Current assets		
Debtors and prepayments	50	
Cash	10	
	60	
Less: **Creditors due within one year**		
Creditors and accrued charges	10	
		50
Total assets less current liabilities		500
Capital and reserves		
Called up share capital		300
Profit and loss account		200
		500

RENTWELL LIMITED – Working paper

Profit and loss account for the year ended 30 June 2005

					£'000
Rent receivable	−10a			590	~~600~~
Less: Rents payable	+5b	405	~~400~~		
Rates	−3c	47	~~50~~		
Other expenses	+1d	41	~~40~~	493	~~490~~
Net profit				97	~~110~~

Balance sheet at 30 June 2005

					£'000
Fixed assets					
Leasehold Properties					450
Current assets					
Debtors and prepayments	+3c		53	~~50~~	
Cash				10	
			63	~~60~~	
Less: **Creditors due within one year**					
Creditors and accrued charges	+5b +1d		16	~~10~~	
Amount received in advance	+10a		10	—	
			26	37	~~50~~
Total assets less current liabilities				~~487~~	~~500~~
Capital and reserves					
Called up share capital					300
Profit and loss account				187	~~200~~
				~~487~~	~~500~~

```
        90      B/F  =   90
       110     −13  =   97
     = 200             187
```

RENTWELL LIMITED – Final accounts

Profit and loss account for the year ended 30 June 2005

		£'000
Rents receivable		590
Less: Rents payable	405	
Rates	47	
Other expenses	41	493
Net profit		97

Balance sheet at 30 June 2005

		£'000
Fixed assets		
Leasehold Properties		450
Current assets		
Debtors and prepayments	53	
Cash	10	
	63	
Less: **Creditors due within one year**		
Creditors and accrued charges	16	
Amount received in advance	10	
	26	
		37
Total assets less current liabilities		487
Capital and reserves		
Called up share capital		300
Profit and loss account		187
		487

Rentwell Limited: Adjusted trial balance

This case illustrates how adjustments can affect both the profit and loss account and the balance sheet. Obviously the changes would not normally be made on the face of the accounts. In working papers one would use the 'adjustments' column we saw in the trial balance in Section 4. The adjustments would then be incorporated in the books of account when the 'final' accounts had been completed.

The entries would appear on Rentwell's trial balance schedule as follows:

	Trial balance		Adjustments		Profit and loss		Balance sheet	
	Dr	Cr	Dr	Cr	Dr	Cr	Dr	Cr
	£'000	£'000	£'000	£'000	£'000	£'000	£'000	£'000
Called up share capital		300						300
Profit and loss, balance b/f		90[1]						90[1]
Leasehold properties	450						450	
Debtors and prepayments	50		3c				53	
Cash	10						10	
Creditors		10		5b / 1d				16
Received in advance				10a				10
Rents receivable		600	10a			590		
Rents payable	400		5b		405			
Rates	50			3c	47			
Other expenses	40		1d		41			
					493			
Profit for the year[2]					97[2]			97[2]
	1 000	1 000	19[3]	19[3]	590	590	513	513

1 £90 000 is the opening balance. The items which make up the £110 000 original net profit for the year are shown individually.

2 The final profit for the year, £97 000, is added to the balance brought forward on the profit and loss account, £90 000, to give the figure carried forward on the balance sheet, £187 000.

3 Notice that the adjustments 'balance', since they follow the double-entry principle.

Accrual accounting: A summary

We have seen the need to distinguish cash receipts from income, and cash expenditure from expense. Accounts recognize income and expense when they accrue due, not when they are actually received or paid in cash. Amounts paid or received in advance or in arrears are the subject of adjustments in preparing accounts, and give rise to current asset or current liability balances in the balance sheet.

Merely because a company has made a profit does not imply that it has the same amount of cash on hand. The profit may result from credit sales for which it has not yet received cash; or it may already have spent the cash, for example on investment in fixed assets or in dividends.

It is sometimes possible to apportion income and expense on a time basis, thus including amounts in the period to which they relate.

Another basis for making adjustments, which we consider later in this section, is to charge an expense in the accounting period in which related revenue is recognized. Thus the balance sheet may carry forward expenditure from the period in which it is incurred to 'match' it in a later period against the revenue which it has helped to generate. Here there are much greater problems, for this kind of 'revenue investment' may sometimes represent an 'asset' of dubious value. How can anyone tell, for example, whether a film costing £20 million is ever going to recover its cost? Yet a judgement must be made for accounting purposes, which will affect the results of more than one accounting period.

We should emphasize that not all expenses *can* be directly matched against specific revenue. Against which sales, for instance, should the audit fee be matched? Or what about the cost of a flight to Brazil in an (unsuccessful) attempt to win a large sales order? Even so, the only basis for carrying forward costs (as assets) on the balance sheet is a reasonable expectation either of sufficient *future* revenues against which to match them or of ultimate recovery of cash on disposal.

Summary of accrual accounting adjustments

We can distinguish seven different kinds of expenditure/expense (or receipt/income) mix, as shown below, of which five relate in some way to this year.

EXPENDITURE	'EXPENSE'		
1 Last year	Last year	=	Last year
2 Last year	This year	=	Asset start of year[A]
3 This year	Last year	=	Liability start of year[B]
4 This year	This year	=	This year
5 This year	Next year	=	Asset end of year[A]
6 Next year	This year	=	Liability end of year[B]
7 Next year	Next year	=	Next year

[A] Prepayment
[B] Accrued charge

RECEIPTS	'INCOME'		
1 Last year	Last year	=	Last year
2 Last year	This year	=	Liability start of year[C]
3 This year	Last year	=	Asset start of year[D]
4 This year	This year	=	This year
5 This year	Next year	=	Liability end of year[C]
6 Next year	This year	=	Asset end of year[D]
7 Next year	Next year	=	Next year

[C] Income received in advance
[D] Income receivable

MEASURING AND RECOGNIZING SALES REVENUE (TURNOVER)

The sales (turnover) figure is crucial in measuring profit for a period. Until the moment accounts 'recognize' sales revenue, they treat any costs incurred in providing goods for sale as 'stock', and carry them forward as a current asset in the balance sheet. Only when accounts recognize sales revenue does 'cost of goods sold' become an expense. Until that point there can be no profit. (Following the convention of prudence, however, accounts may recognize *losses* sooner.)

The diagram below represents events in a manufacturing business. The business purchases raw materials, and then uses labour and capital equipment to convert them into finished goods stock (point A). When the business sells the finished goods on credit and delivers them, legal title passes to the purchaser (point B), who becomes a debtor. Finally the customer pays cash (point C) to settle the account.

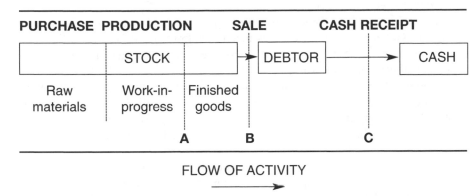

FLOW OF ACTIVITY

Accounts could possibly recognize sales revenue at any of the three points A, B or C in the diagram. Purchasing raw materials begins the process of adding value; but it is hard to tell how much of the ultimate sales value the business has really earned, either at this stage or later (where there is work in progress), when the manufacturing process has begun but not yet ended.

Production of the goods is complete at point A, but prudence forbids accounts to recognize any profit yet. Merely because a company has produced goods does not usually mean it will be able to sell them, or at least not for more than cost. (Exceptions might be certain commodities with stable market prices.)

When the selling company *delivers* the goods, it *invoices* the buyer, and *legal title* passes. These three things often happen more or less at the same time. It is at this stage (point B) that accounts in fact recognize sales revenue [IAS 18] and hence profit. Sales revenue for a period thus represents the total value (excluding VAT [SSAP 5]) of goods and services a business has invoiced to customers.

Accrual accounting does not wait until a business actually receives cash (point C) before treating sales as income. That would be *too* conservative, since customers who fail to pay without good reason legally owe the full sales price, and sellers can provide separately for possible bad debts (see below). Likewise accounts would recognize sales revenue even if some obligation remained, such as after-sales service or warranties, for which sellers could make separate provision.

Where goods are *made to order*, the sale occurs before production, so the moment to recognize sales revenue is on completion of production (or on delivery). This often applies in respect of *services*. Sometimes (as with magazine subscriptions or school fees) cash receipts too precede the provision of services. The earning of revenue (and thus of profit) then accrues over the period of provision. Any balance of cash received not yet treated as sales revenue appears as 'deferred income'. (The *amount* of the current liability is the total revenue not yet earned (pro rata), not the marginal 'cost' of fulfilling the order, which might be very low.)

Types of sale

With *instalment sales* firms normally recognize profit on the sale at once, since title to the goods passes straight away. But finance charges on outstanding instalments are spread over the contract period.

With *hire-purchase sales* however, where title does not pass at the beginning, companies spread profit over time, and only recognize part on the signing of the contract.

Where goods are delivered '*on approval*' or '*on sale or return*', legal ownership does not pass. The 'selling' company's accounts must continue to show the goods as stock (at cost), and not yet record any profit until the sale is final.

Where customers, by agreement, return goods after a genuine sale, the selling company's accounts deduct any such *cancelled sales* from total turnover. Those goods go back into stock at cost (thus eliminating any profit), or even less if necessary.

Discounts

A *trade* discount is a percentage reduction (often large) in the selling price, normally depending on the status of the buyer.

A *quantity* discount is a percentage reduction in the unit price, depending on how many units are being bought.

Accounts treat both 'trade discounts' and 'quantity discounts' as reductions of the selling price (if granted) or of cost (if received)

A *cash* discount is a (usually small) percentage reduction in the amount payable in respect of a credit sale if cash is paid within a certain time (perhaps within ten days from the date of sale). Accounts regard it as a finance-related item and the profit and loss account shows 'cash discounts' as separate items of expense (if granted) or of income (if received).

Analysing sales revenue

Sales turnover is a key sign of business activity. SSAP 25 [IAS 14] requires accounts to analyse turnover (and profit and net assets) between separate classes of business and between geographical areas (see Section 12).

Example

HENKEL GROUP 2003 (in €million)	Sales	Profits	Assets
Laundry and home care	3 074	287	867
Cosmetics/toiletries	2 086	194	767
Adhesives	1 313	141	663
Henkel Technologies	2 666	194	1 961
Corporate	297	(110)	148
Group	**9 436**	**706**	**4 406**

Of course, sales volume may not match production volume, in which case the physical level of stocks must be changing. Even if stock levels remain constant, a change in sales revenue (turnover) in accounts may not reflect physical volume, since selling *prices* may have changed.

A change in 'sales mix' in a multi-product company can be hard to interpret. Profit margins on each item may have *fallen*, but total profit (and the apparent average profit margin) can still *increase* over the previous period if more of a high-profit item is sold and less of a low-profit item. The example below illustrates.

	Last year			This year		
	Margin	Weight		Margin	Weight	
Product A	18.0%	x 1/6	= 3.0	16.0%	x 1/2	= 8.0
Product B	13.5%	x 1/3	= 4.5	12.0%	x 1/3	= 4.0
Product C	7.0%	x 1/2	= 3.5	6.0%	x 1/6	= 1.0
Average			11.0%			13.0%

Bad debts

Accounts recognize revenue from credit sales when a firm performs services or when legal title to goods passes (which is normally when suppliers invoice customers). But if a customer fails to pay the full amount due, in the end the seller has to charge the 'bad debt' as an expense against profit. ('Bad debts' are separate expenses: they do not simply reduce gross sales turnover.) There are three ways to do this: writing off specific bad debts; providing for specific 'doubtful' debts; or making general provisions.

A bad debt may occur because a customer cannot pay, or because of some dispute (for example, if the goods never arrived, or were faulty). As soon as it becomes evident that a specific debt is bad, for whatever reason, there must at once be a complete write-off against profit. 'Writing off' a bad debt also removes the amount from 'debtors' in the balance sheet.

But what happens if a debtor is just slow to pay, or if his financial position begins to worsen? Or what if it is not clear how much a bankrupt debtor's assets will realize for the creditors to share? Here is another area where management's subjective views can affect a period's profit.

The books of account will continue to include in 'debtors' the total amount legally due; but the business may wish to provide for possible specific bad debts ('doubtful debts'). It does so by charging 'bad debts' expense in the profit and loss account, and setting up a 'provision for bad debts' liability account. This will be deducted from total debtors in the balance sheet.

Or a company may make a *general* provision for bad debts, on the basis of past average experience. For example, a company may maintain a provision amounting to 1 per cent of domestic debtors and 2 per cent of overseas debtors. In addition to any specific write-offs and provisions, it would then charge against profit each year the sum needed to adjust the general provision to those percentages of outstanding end-year debtors.

If a company over-provides for bad debts, it must 'write back' the excess in a future period. This means deducting the excess provision from the bad debt expense (and thus increasing profit) in that period. So again we see that errors in accounting estimates – which must sometimes happen – may affect *two* periods' accounts, not just one.

TREATMENT OF EXPENDITURES

We have defined profit as (sales) revenue minus expenses; and we have seen that the point at which accounts recognize revenue is critical in measuring profit. In order to complete the process, we now need to consider in more detail how to measure expenses.

This involves looking at the treatment of expenditures, by which we mean purchases of some kind (not mere payments of cash). We need to look at two kinds of expenditures: those incurred in earlier periods (and brought forward as assets in the opening balance sheet), and those incurred in the current period.

Accounts may carry expenditures forward as assets in the closing balance sheet, in order to match their cost against future revenues (or the proceeds of future disposals). (Thus the 'matching process', which is really a part of the 'accrual' concept (see page 2), relates to the *balance sheet* rather than (solely) to the profit and loss account.) Or else accounts may charge them against profit as expenses in the current period.

Expenses can be of several kinds:

1 They may be 'product costs' being 'matched' against current revenues. Example: direct costs of goods sold, such as materials.
2 They may be 'period costs' or 'overheads'. Even if these do not directly relate to current revenues, they may still belong in the current period's profit and loss account. Examples: office rent; depreciation of many fixed assets.
3 They may be 'revenue investments' – items of expenditure that may partly benefit future periods, but which, as a matter of prudence, accounts usually write off as expenses in the current period. Examples: research or brand promotion.
4 They may simply be losses or 'unmatchable' expenses. Examples: the costs of a (failed) promotion campaign or a (failed) attempt to develop a new product.

EXPENDITURES

Brought forward from <u>previous</u> period	*plus* incurred in <u>current</u> period	*less* carried forward to <u>future</u> period

equals
EXPENSES IN CURRENT PERIOD

Product costs	+Period costs	+Revenue investments	+Unmatchable items
matched with *revenue*	matched with *period*	not matched	not matched

MEASURING 'REVENUE INVESTMENTS'

Let us now consider certain kinds of costs that can be hard to allocate between accounting periods. These are 'revenue investments' – items of expenditure which may partly benefit future periods. Often the question is whether prudence requires writing the amount off as an expense in the current period or whether matching requires carrying the amount forward as an asset, to set against future sales revenue.

We shall consider in turn:

(a) research and development (R & D) costs
(b) personnel costs
(c) marketing costs.

(a) Research and development costs

Many companies invest large sums of money in basic and applied research and in developing new products. Writing off regular fairly small amounts of R&D spending as and when it occurs may cause few problems. But what if large investments in product development arise at infrequent intervals? Or what if a company is growing? Recording expenses in one period and related revenues in later periods could then affect the company's profit pattern. In some industries – pharmaceuticals, for instance – the benefits can arrive (if at all) ten or more years after the related cash outflow.

Although the dividing line may not always be very clear, there are three broad types of research and development:

● Basic (or 'pure') research, for general or scientific or technical knowledge.
● Applied research, to exploit basic research.
● Product development, to introduce or improve specific products or processes.

SSAP 13 [IAS 38] treats investment in basic and applied research as normal spending to maintain a company's business position. No specific period will benefit, so it is best to write these research costs off as expenses as they occur. (But firms capitalize spending on R&D *fixed assets* and write it off over their useful lives.) Companies must disclose the total amount charged as R&D expense in each period.

Many development projects have uncertain future benefits, so firms will write off their costs at once. However companies following IAS 38 must carry forward development spending as an intangible fixed asset and amortize it over the periods expected to benefit, if it satisfies all the following conditions:

● There is a clearly defined project with separate costs.
● The project is technically feasible and commercially viable.
● The firm intends to produce and market, or use, the product or process.
● The firm expects sufficient future benefits to cover all the costs.

(b) Personnel costs

Most wages and salaries are current expenses, paid for labour services during the current period. One exception may be direct labour costs related to production of goods: companies carry them forward where appropriate in the total cost of closing stock in the balance sheet (see Section 6).

Costs of management development and staff training are written off at once as expenses, even though they may, at least partly, benefit future periods. The prudence concept may cover not only the limited and uncertain duration and extent of any such benefits, but also the potential mobility of staff. (There may be a definite conflict between training specific to the employer's business and *general* training which will also make the employee more useful to other employers.)

Football clubs capitalize the transfer fees paid for players they acquire from other clubs, and amortize the cost over the contract period. But this practice, required by FRS 10 [IAS 38], raises problems of its own. For example, what about 'home-grown' players? What about transfer fees *received*? What about team managers?

Other 'people-based' businesses, of which there are many as modern economies continue to switch away from manufacturing towards various kinds of services, face similar problems. For example, advertising agencies, consultancies and universities may also find it hard to account sensibly for their 'investment' in personnel.

In many companies, senior executives' remuneration consists in part of stock options. These are exercisable only after some time and subject to certain restrictions. Because they are personal, they are not directly tradeable, and valuing them is not easy.

FRS 20/IFRS 2 says these options represent a cost to the company and should be charged as an expense in the profit and loss account at the time they are granted. Warren Buffett shares this view. He asks three pertinent questions: 'If executive stock options are not compensation, what are they? If compensation is not an expense, what is it? If an expense does not belong in the (profit and loss account), where does it belong?'

Others say the effect of charging executive stock options as an expense would be disastrous. It would severely inhibit their use, which might be extremely damaging, especially to new or small high-technology companies. Many people also argue that measuring their value is virtually impossible.

Pensions

Most companies operate pension schemes, which often require employees to contribute to them. Pension schemes can be either funded or unfunded.

Unfunded pension schemes are of two kinds. Under *terminal funding*, when each employee leaves, the company pays into an external fund an amount sufficient to finance the retiring employee's pension. Under the *pay-as-you-go* method, the company pays pensioners directly during their retirement. In either case the employing company provides for pensions year by year as the liability accrues. If a company goes bankrupt, pensioners in unfunded schemes may lose part of their pensions, though they will at least rank as creditors ahead of shareholders.

Funded pension schemes may also be of two kinds. With *defined contribution* schemes, each year the company charges the contribution as pension expense. The pensioners eventually get whatever their contributions have earned in the fund, with no extra liability falling on the employer company.

With *defined benefit* schemes, however, the amount in the fund at any time may differ from the employer company's actuarial liability for future pensions. This depends on salary changes, mortality rates, retirements, interest rates, and so on, and is normally re-calculated every three years.

Accounting standards [FRS 17/IAS 19] regard pensions as deferred pay. Under the accruals concept, therefore, companies now match the cost of pensions against the benefit from employees' services over their working lives. Previously, they had simply expensed the annual pension *contributions* to defined benefit schemes. That sometimes gave rise to large fluctuations, as over-funding resulted in 'pension holidays' (or even refunds of pension fund surpluses). Inadequate disclosure often made things worse.

FRS 17/IAS 19 requires balance sheets to show companies' total pension 'liabilities' (discounted) and the corresponding total pension fund assets, revalued at current market values each year. As a result there could be large swings in the annual charge for net pensions 'expense'.

c) Marketing costs

The treatment of selling expenses is generally straightforward, the amount incurred in a year being charged as an expense in that same year. One obvious example is sales commission which directly relates to specific items of revenue.

Future selling expenses do not, of course, increase the 'cost' of finished goods in stock, as they have not yet occurred. But future expenses of selling stock *are* deducted in estimating whether the expected ultimate 'net realizable value' of stock is lower than cost (see Section 6).

Market research costs – like technical research – are normally written off as current expenses when they occur. But certain promotion costs may raise similar problems to product development costs. Suppose a company launches a major new product every third year, when it updates the previous model. The company's year ends on 31 December. Between September and December 2004 it spends £20 million on media advertising for a product launch due in February 2005. In which period should it charge the £20 million as an expense?

The general rule is to charge costs as an expense in the year in which they occur, but that would fail to 'match' the costs against any related sales revenues. How much if anything should the company carry forward as an asset in the balance sheet at 31 December 2004? A wide range of answers is possible, which illustrates once again how subjective measuring profit or loss can be. In practice, the concept of 'prudence' would normally override that of 'matching' in this context; and few companies would carry forward any such costs as an asset.

A specific example of capitalizing marketing costs arises with respect to brands (see Section 9). To what extent does expenditure on brands contribute to sales of the product in the current period; and to what extent does it represent an asset which will assist sales in future periods? If one could determine the answer, that would establish the basis on which, perhaps, to capitalize some of the costs. Since, however, it is almost impossible to do so with any precision, prudent accountants normally write off the entire costs of 'internal' brand support as an expense in the period in which it is incurred.

Failure to maintain spending on brands could increase current profits without any adverse effects in the accounts, even though it may damage the 'value' of the brands (which the balance sheet does not usually show as an asset).

MORE COMPLEX ASPECTS OF MEASURING PROFIT

Income-smoothing

Income-smoothing attempts to make an entity's profit performance seem less volatile than it 'really' is. When the focus is on profit rather than financial position, excessive 'prudence' can be almost as dangerous as excessive imprudence. In the extreme it can mislead shareholders (and others), by failing to disclose poor current performance through drawing secretly on hidden reserves which a company established through understating profits in previous periods.

Income-smoothing spreads income between accounting periods, often by adjusting expenses (in the same way as depreciation of fixed assets, though less transparently). If in some years it understates 'real' profit, in other years it overstates it. Income-smoothing, however, may also represent a way for managers to try to present a more accurate *trend* of results over a period of years. Examples are providing for deferred tax ('tax equalization') [FRS19/IAS12], using the percentage completion method for long-term contracts [SSAP9/IAS11], and pensions adjustments spread out over the remaining working lives of existing employees [IAS19].

So strong are the incentives for managers to avoid volatility in reporting results that banning income-smoothing altogether might even tempt some companies to do things (to affect reported results) that they wouldn't otherwise do. Income-smoothing might be much less tempting if companies were still able to report 'extraordinary' items of profit or loss 'below the line' (as they could before FRS3/IAS8).

Provisions

A provision is a liability of uncertain timing or amount [FRS12/IAS37]. The question is whether, on grounds both of prudence and matching, to provide *ahead of time* for intermittent expenditures – such as long-term maintenance – which are likely to arise from time to time, but less often than annually. The alternative is to wait until actually incurring such expenditure before charging any expense. (We are not here discussing pensions or deferred tax (Section 10).)

There is no doubt that the effect of making an annual provision in advance is to 'smooth' income; it is also prudent. This may be important if management has the discretion to delay such spending for one or more years.

Another way of looking at it is to regard infrequent lumpy write-offs of infrequent lumpy expenditure as injecting 'volatility' into reporting of profits. But if the real world *is* volatile, many people would argue that companies should report it as such. One solution would be to 'capitalize' such occasional expenditure, on the grounds that its benefits would last for several years, and simply amortize it over time, like other fixed assets – thus 'smoothing', but in arrear not in advance.

Discounting liabilities

Interest-bearing debt already appears in balance sheets at a discounted value, though using *past*, not current, interest rates. Discounting trade creditors, tax or other *current* items for a few months would normally make little difference. So the question whether or not to discount future liabilities concerns mainly non-interest-bearing long-term provisions, such as for pensions or deferred tax.

IAS 37/FRS 12 normally requires companies to discount provisions. With respect to pensions, actuarial calculations already allow for changes in interest rates. Some people argue that failing to discount long-term provisions would mean overstating them on the balance sheet, which amounts to creating hidden (secret) reserves.

Those against discounting believe any choice of interest rate would be arbitrary; and that calculations for deferred tax would be extremely complex. IAS 12 forbids discounting for deferred tax, which FRS 19 permits but does not require. (Some people advocate the 'flow-through' method, which obviates the problem – see Section 10.)

Capitalizing borrowing costs

When a company borrows money to finance the construction of fixed assets, should it capitalize the interest cost during construction (add it to the cost of the fixed asset), or write it off at once as an expense? (There would normally be no effect on tax.) FRS 15 says either capitalize all such borrowing costs or none; while IAS 23 prefers expensing, but permits capitalization.

Those who prefer capitalization believe that writing interest off as an expense by way of depreciation over the fixed asset's life results in more accurate matching. They say that the cost of interest is just as much as part of the total cost as the cost of materials or direct labour. They argue that if a company purchased the asset externally, the quoted price would automatically include any finance cost.

Those who prefer to expense all debt interest at once say that most companies, in effect, operate with a 'pool' of funds, so one cannot usually tell whether a particular asset was financed by debt or by equity. (The latter, of course, carries no interest in accounts.) They also feel in practice it is often an arbitrary choice between an average interest rate and a marginal one. They claim the analogy with an outside purchase proves too much, because such an outside purchase would include a finance cost even if the alternative were an equity-financed purchase. Further they argue it is not logical to *stop* capitalizing interest on the means of financing fixed assets at the moment when they come into use.

SECTION 5 SUMMARY

At the beginning of this section we pointed out that 'the larger the number of incomplete transactions, the longer their timespan and the greater their size, the wider will be the range of possible figures for profit or loss'. The force of this statement should now be obvious.

Business transactions may be incomplete at the balance sheet date either because the production process is not yet finished or because certain fixed assets are not yet worn out, or because other aspects of transactions remain to be settled (such as credit customers paying). In all these cases, preparers of accounts have to make the best estimates they can about the uncertain future.

Accrual accounting distinguishes cash receipts from 'income' and cash payments from 'expenditures'. Accounts recognize income and expenses in the relevant period when they accrue, not when the firm happens to receive or pay cash.

The sales (turnover) figure is critical in measuring profit. As a rule, companies recognize sales revenues when they *deliver* the goods or services.

Expenses may be of several kinds:

- 'Product costs' being matched directly against current revenues.
- 'Period costs' which (mostly) belong in the current period's profit and loss account.
- 'Revenue investments', such as research, training, advertising, which may partly benefit future periods, but where 'prudence' dominates 'matching'.
- Unmatchable expenses or losses.

Indeed the 'matching' concept relates as much to the balance sheet as to the current profit and loss account. Firms 'carry forward' expenditures as assets in the closing balance sheet only if they have good reason to expect to recover the (unamortized) cost, either from future sales revenues or from the ultimate proceeds of disposal.

In looking at more complex aspects of measuring profit, we discussed income-smoothing, provisions for liabilities which are uncertain in timing or amount, capitalizing borrowing costs and discounting long-term non-interest-bearing provisions, such as deferred tax. We do not discuss accounting for derivatives in this book.

Throughout this section we have emphasized that the process of measuring profit or loss usually contains an important element of judgement. This is not a criticism, it is a fact. The requirement to show 'a true and fair view' in accounts is over-riding, but it would be quite wrong to suppose that most reported profit or loss figures are in any sense uniquely 'correct'. They are really only 'best guesses', tempered by consistency of treatment over time as well as by a degree of prudence.

PROBLEMS

5.1 Definitions
Write down on this page your definitions of the terms shown. Then compare your answers with the definitions overleaf.

(a) Matching

(f) Provision

(b) An accrued charge

(g) Expense

(c) Turnover

(h) Bad debts

(d) Sales mix

(i) Prudence

(e) Expenditure

(j) Prepayment

5.1 Definitions

(a) **Matching** is the process of charging expenses in the same period in which the accounts recognize related revenue. Expenses which cannot be 'matched' are written off at once. Thus companies carry forward expenditure as an asset in the balance sheet only when it is likely to be recoverable in future, either by matching against related revenues in later periods or by sales proceeds on ultimate disposal.

(b) **Accrued charges** are expenses in a period which have not yet been invoiced or paid. They often relate to periods of time, for example rent payable, but may also relate to usage of utilities, etc.

(c) **Turnover** means sales revenue in a period. It is the term required by all four permitted UK profit and loss account formats [see pp. 280/1]. Turnover includes both cash and credit sales of goods and services, but does not include Value Added Tax. (Nor, of course, does it include sales of fixed assets.)

(d) **Sales mix** describes, in a multi-product company, the combination of all the company's different products in a period's total sales revenues. The mix can change over time even if total sales revenue remains more or less constant. Because companies, even in the same industry, can have very different sales mixes, comparing the accounts of one company with another can often be difficult and only very approximate.

(e) **Expenditure** simply means a purchase. It need not involve spending money (to begin with), since it may be on credit. Some expenditures will be treated as expenses in the profit and loss account, others as assets in the balance sheet.

(f) A **provision** is a liability of uncertain timing or amount. It involves charging an amount as an expense in the profit and loss account and showing the same amount as a liability in the balance sheet. (This may be, but need not be, under the heading Provision for Liabilities and Charges'.

(g) An **expense** is an amount charged against profit in the profit and loss account. It is not the same as 'expenditure', which may represent an asset. An expense may stem from a cash payment, a purchase on credit, or a provision either for a liability or to reduce an asset.

(h) **Bad debts** are amounts owing to a business which will never be paid in full, either because the debtor *cannot* pay (for example, through bankruptcy) or *will not* pay (for example, due to some dispute over quality or delivery or price). It may be hard to tell when accounts should recognize bad debts, and to what extent. Provision may be either for specific debts or by way of a 'general' provision, probably based on past experience.

(i) **Prudence**, which used to be known as 'conservatism', in practice means two things in accounting: (1) do not recognize sales revenues (and therefore profits) until there is fair certainty – that is, 'Don't count your chickens until they are hatched'; (2) Provide for all known liabilities, even if you have to estimate their amount. The 'prudence' concept can clash with the 'matching' concept in several areas, for example, the treatment of research, training and advertising.

(j) A **prepayment** is almost the opposite of an accrued charge. As the name implies, it means paying cash 'in advance' of an expense which the business has not yet incurred. Examples might be insurance premiums, magazine subscriptions, rents payable, tuition fees. Balance sheets often combine prepayments with debtors under 'current assets', but the Notes to the Accounts will disclose separate details.

5.2 Hermes Travel Limited: Accruals and prepayments

Hermes Travel Limited started business as a travel agency on 1 November 2004. The company's first accounting period ended on 31 October 2005 by which time £38 000 had been paid in cash in respect of telephone expense. This amount was made up as follows:

Rent	£
2 months to 31 December 2004	800
3 months to 31 March 2005	1 200
3 months to 30 June 2005	1 200
3 months to 30 September 2005	1 200
Calls	
2 months to 31 December 2004	6 400
3 months to 31 March 2005	15 200
3 months to 30 June 2005	12 000
Total cash paid	38 000

At 31 October 2005, there was an unpaid account for £16 000 in respect of calls for the three months to 30 September 2005 (£14 800) and rent for the three months to 31 December 2005 (£1 200). Calls for the months of October 2005 were estimated to have amounted to £5 400.

Calculate how much should be charged as telephone expense for the year ended 31 October 2005, and show a summary of the ledger account for the year. The answer is shown on the next page.

5.3 Urban Properties Limited: Year-end adjustments

The draft accounts of Urban Properties Limited for the year ended 30 June 2005 are set out opposite. The following items are to be taken into account:

(a) No adjustment has been made in respect of business rates for the year to 31 March 2006 paid in advance, amounting to £16 000 a year.
(b) Rent receivable of £3 000 for the June quarter has not been included.
(c) Rent received for the half-year to 30 September 2005 (£8 000) has all been included in the accounts to 30 June 2005.
(d) No rent has been paid on one disputed property since £6 000 was paid in advance in respect of the quarter to December 2004. As from the end of 2004 only half the level of rent previously payable is expected.

Please amend the draft accounts opposite to incorporate any necessary adjustments. To avoid complexity, we show current liabilities below capital and reserves. Alter the tax charge to 30 per cent of your amended profit. Work in £'000. The answer is shown on the next page.

URBAN PROPERTIES LIMITED

Draft profit and loss account
Year ended 30 June 2005

		£'000
Rent receivable		286
Other income		28
		314
Rent payable	64	
Business rates payable	41	
Other expenses	31	
		136
Profit before tax		178
Tax (@ 30 per cent)		54
Profit after tax		124

Draft balance sheet at 30 June 2005

		£'000
Fixed assets		
Properties		660
Current assets		
Debtors	6	
Cash	127	
		133
		793
Capital and reserves		
Called up share capital		500
Reserves		230
Shareholders' funds		730
Current liabilities		
Creditors	9	
Tax	54	63
		793

5.2 Hermes Travel Limited

Solution

In addition to the £38 000 cash paid, the following amounts should also be included in telephone expense for the year ended 31 October 2005.

	£
Rent October 2005	400
Calls 3 months to 30 September 2005	14 800
October 2005	5 400
'Accrued charges' at 31 October 2005	20 600

Thus total telephone expense for the year ended 31 October 2005 is £58 600.

Ledger account (summary)

Telephone expense

Year 2004/05	£	Year 2004/05	£
Cash	38 000	Profit and loss account	58 600
Accrued charges c/d	20 600		
	58 600		58 600
		Year 2005/06	
		Accrued charges b/d	20 600

Notice how the £20 600 accrued charges are brought down as a credit in year 2005/06. The effect will be to reduce the expense in 2005/06 (the year in which the amounts concerned will actually be paid).

5.3 Urban Properties Limited

Solution

URBAN PROPERTIES LIMITED

Profit and loss account for the year ended 30 June 2005

			£'000	
Rent receivable	+3b	−4c	~~286~~	285
Other income			28	
			~~314~~	313
Rent payable	+6d		70 ~~64~~	
Business rates payable	−12a		29 ~~41~~	
Other expenses			31	
			~~136~~	130
Profit before tax			~~178~~	183
Tax (@ 30 per cent)			~~54~~	55
Profit after tax			~~124~~	128

Balance sheet at 30 June 2005

Fixed assets — £'000

Properties			660	

Current assets

Debtors	+3b		9 ~~6~~	
Prepayment	+12a		12	
Cash			127	
			~~133~~	148
			~~793~~	808

Capital and reserves

Called up share capital		500	
Reserves	(+4 − see P&L)	~~230~~	234
Shareholders' funds		~~730~~	734

Current liabilities

Creditors	+4c +6d	~~9~~	19
Tax	(+1)	~~54~~	55
		~~63~~	74
		~~793~~	808

5.4 Wheeler Limited (A): Adjusting trial balance

The trial balance of Wheeler Limited extracted from the books at the end of the year ended 31 March 2005 is shown below.

The following items have not been taken into account:

(a) An audit fee (administrative expenses) of £5 000 is to be provided for.

(b) Loan interest is payable half yearly at 30 June and 31 December. The last payment was on 31 December 2004.

(c) Finished goods stock in the books at £12 000 is obsolete, and is to be written off as cost of goods sold in the current year.

(d) Tax of £95 000 is to be provided for.

You are asked to make the necessary adjustments in the adjustments column of the trial balance schedule, and extend the figures into the profit and loss account and balance sheet columns. Each pair of columns should balance.

The answer is shown on the next page.

	Trial balance		Adjustments		Profit and loss		Balance sheet	
	Dr £'000	Cr £'000	Dr £'000	Cr £'000	Dr £'000	Cr £'000	Dr £'000	Cr £'000
Cash book	201							
Ordinary £1 share capital		200						
Profit and loss account 1 April 2004		283						
12% loan		300						
Fixed assets: cost	942							
Fixed assets: accumulated depreciation		347						
Sales ledger control	183							
Stock	141							
Purchase ledger control		39						
Accrued charges								
Tax liability								
Sales		1 442						
Cost of goods sold	818							
Selling and administrative expenses	299							
Loan interest	27							
Tax expense								
Profit for year retained								
	2 611	2 611						

5.4 Wheeler Limited (A)

Solution

	Trial balance Dr £'000	Trial balance Cr £'000	Adjustments Dr £'000	Adjustments Cr £'000	Profit and loss Dr £'000	Profit and loss Cr £'000	Balance sheet Dr £'000	Balance sheet Cr £'000
Cash book	201						201	
Ordinary share capital (£1 shares)		200						200
Profit and loss account b/f		283						283
12% loan		300						300
Fixed assets: cost	942						942	
Fixed assets: accumulated depreciation		347						347
Sales ledger control	183						183	
Stock	141			(c) 12			129	
Purchase ledger control		39		(a) 5				39
Accrued charges				(b) 9				14
Tax payable				(d) 95				95
Sales		1 442				1 442		
Cost of goods sold	818		(c) 12		830			
Selling and administrative expenses	299		(a) 5		304			
Loan interest	27		(b) 9		36			
Tax expense			(d) 95		95			
					1 265			
Profit for year					177			177*
	2 611	2 611	121	121	1 442	1 442	1 455	1 455

Notes on trial balance schedule solution

1 Notice that *two* accounts have been opened for tax: one for 'tax expense', which appears in the profit and loss account as an expense; and the other for 'tax payable', which appears in the balance sheet as a current liability. An accountant could easily deal with all the necessary entries on a single account, but it may be simpler for anyone else to set up *two* tax accounts, one for the expense and the other for the liability. In the same way, it may be best to have *separate* accounts for 'depreciation expense' and 'accumulated depreciation'.

2 Notice how the profit for the year in the trial balance schedule (£177)* is the excess of the total credits in the profit and loss account columns over the total debits. It is therefore added to the debits, to 'balance' the columns and the credit balance is extended into the balance sheet columns. The new accumulated balance on the profit and loss account now becomes £460 (= £283 + £177).

5.5 Wheeler Limited (B): Preparing final accounts

From the trial balance schedule as adjusted (see 5.4 Wheeler Limited (A)), please now prepare in final form the profit and loss account and balance sheet of Wheeler Limited for the year ended 31 March 2005. Use a separate sheet of paper.

The answer is shown on the next page.

5.6 Dover Trading Limited: Sale of stock

Dover Trading Limited buys and sells pictures. A view of the entrance to the Channel Tunnel, which had been purchased for £300, is sold for £700 on credit. Describe in words how this transaction would affect the company's accounts. Remember the double-entry principle!

The answer is shown on the next page.

5.7 Tiptop Office Supplies: Bad debts

Tiptop Office Supplies sold to many small customers who, in total, owed £420 000 at 30 September 2005 (not including £17 000 bad debts which had been written off during the year). Tiptop's policy was to provide 4 per cent of outstanding debtors at the year-end in respect of anticipated bad debts. Credit policy in 2005, however, had been somewhat laxer than in previous years, in an attempt to boost sales volume, so Tiptop decided to provide 5 per cent in respect of debtors at 30 September 2005.

The provision for bad debts account had a balance of £10 000 brought forward at 1 October 2004. This represented 4 per cent of £250 000, the total amount of debtors outstanding at 30 September 2004.

(a) What should the provision for bad debts be at 30 September 2005?
(b) How much will the 2005 charge for bad debts expense be?
(c) Write up ledger accounts for 2005 (i) for provision for bad debts, and (ii) for bad debts expense.

Work in £'000. The answer is shown on the next page.

Answers to the following four problems are not published.

5.8 What do you think? ...

(a) Would you change current accounting practice in respect of 'revenue investments', such as expenditure on 'research' (not 'development')? Why or why not?
(b) Why may 'income-smoothing' be dangerous in accounting? What are the arguments, if any, in its favour?
(c) Should accounts discount provisions for deferred taxation?
(d) Should accounts capitalize interest on money borrowed to finance the construction of fixed assets? Why or why not? What do you see as the main arguments of those who take the opposite view? How would you seek to persuade them to change their mind?

5.9 Rolling five-year accounts

Suppose that companies produced every year not annual accounts for a twelve-month period, but rolling five-year accounts. Thus a company with a calendar year-end would produce early in 2005 a set of accounts for the five-year period 2000–2004 inclusive; then early in 2006 a set of accounts for the five-year period 2001–2005 inclusive; and so on.

What do you see as the major differences between such a system and the existing annual publication of accounts covering a twelve-month period? (You may prefer to leave this question until you have covered some of the later sections.)

5.10 TOAD Magazine: Subscriptions in advance

TOAD, a new monthly magazine, attracts a large number of annual subscriptions by advertising. The company's first accounting period ends on 30 June 2005: but before that date many subscriptions have been received entitling subscribers to issues of TOAD as far ahead (in some cases) as June 2006. How should such 'advance subscriptions' be treated?

(a) Included in sales, on the grounds that *selling* the magazine is the critical event, and that marginal (editorial and paper) costs are very low?
(b) Omitted from sales and from cash, on the grounds that the subscriptions relate to post-balance sheet events?
(c) Shown as a current liability on the balance sheet, on the grounds that the publishers 'owe' these subscribers not money, but future issues of TOAD?
(d) Shown as a current liability to the extent of the marginal cost of producing TOAD each month, with the balance included in the current period's sales revenue?

5.11 Morris and Hyde: Change in shareholders' funds

At 31 December 2004, shareholders' funds in Morris and Hyde Limited's balance sheet totalled £387 000 (including 200 000 £1 ordinary shares issued). At 31 December 2005, shareholders' funds in the company totalled £724 000 (including 280 000 £1 shares issued). During the year the following transactions had taken place. You are asked to calculate the company's profit after tax for 2005.

1. Obsolete stock of £36 000 was written off as an exceptional expense.
2. Tangible fixed assets were increased by land and buildings being revalued upwards from a net book value of £437 000 to £620 000. (The increase is not treated as profit.)
3. 80 000 £1 ordinary shares were issued at a premium of 50p each.
4. Deferred tax of £21 000 was provided for in the profit and loss account.
5. The 2005 cash flow statement showed net dividend paid totalling £30 000. This was made up as follows:

   Final dividend of 8.0p per share for 2004, on 200 000 shares = £16 000.
   Interim dividend of 5.0p per share for 2005, on 280 000 shares = £14 000.

6. A final dividend of 10.0p per share is proposed in respect of 2005. Goodwill of £80 000 arising on the purchase of a new subsidiary was amortized over ten years.

This question covers matters discussed in the next six sections (6 to 11). You may wish to attempt it now; or you may prefer to leave it until you have worked through the later sections.

5.5 Wheeler Limited (B) *Solution*

WHEELER LIMITED

Profit and loss account for the year ended 31 March 2005   £'000

Turnover	1 442
Cost of goods sold	830
Selling and administrative expenses	304
Operating profit	308
Interest expense	36
Profit before tax	272
Tax	95
Profit after tax	177

Balance sheet at 31 March 2005

Fixed assets

At cost		942
Less: accumulated depreciation		(347)
		595

Current assets

Stock	129	
Debtors	183	
Cash	201	
	513	

Less: **Creditors due within one year**

Creditors and accrued charges	(53)	
Tax	(95)	
	(148)	
Net current assets		365
Total assets less current liabilities		960

Less: **Creditors due within one year**

12% Loan		(300)

Share capital and reserves

Ordinary share capital	200	
Profit and loss account	460	
		660

5.6 Dover Trading Limited

Solution

The picture which was in stock as a current asset valued at cost of £300 is transformed, by the sale, into a debtor (also a current asset) of £700.

In the profit and loss account, turnover increases by £700, and cost of sales by £300. As a result, profit increases by £400. (For simplicity we ignore tax.)

Hence *cumulative* retained profits under shareholders' funds in the balance sheet will also increase by £400, thus balancing the £400 increase in current assets.

In formal double-entry terms:	Dr	Cr
Debtor	£700	
Turnover		£700
Cost of sales	£300	
Stock		£300

5.7 Tiptop Office Supplies

Solution (all amounts in £'000)

Provision for bad debts at 30 September 2005 is 5% x £420 = £21. (This *credit* balance is deducted on the balance sheet from debtors, which will appear simply as £399 at 30 September 2005.)

Bad debt expense = £28. This is the amount of specific bad debts written off, plus the increase of £11 in the general provision.

Provision for bad debts				
Sept 05 Balance c/d	21	Oct 04	Balance b/f	10
		Sept 05	Bad debts	11
	21			21
		Oct 05	Balance b/d	21

Bad debts expense				
Sept 05 Debtors	17	Sept 05	Profit & loss a/c	28
Sept 05 Provision for bad debts	11			
	28			28

Section 6
Valuing stock

STOCK IN ACCOUNTS

There are three main types of stocks (inventories), which companies need to disclose separately in the notes [SSAP 9/IAS 2]:

- raw materials and consumable services
- work-in-progress
- finished goods for resale.

Under the matching convention, accounts normally carry forward the *cost* of stocks on hand at the end of a period as a current asset in the balance sheet, to expense against the related sales revenue in a future period. Thus any change in stock value will affect *two* accounting periods, not just one: the closing stock at the end of the first period and the opening stock at the start of the next.

In a manufacturing business the 'cost' of work-in-progress and finished goods comprises costs of purchase and conversion and other costs (including production overheads) incurred in bringing the stocks to their present location and condition. Any payments received on account should be deducted from stocks.

Accounts do not include in the cost of stocks, but recognize as expenses in the period in which they are incurred:

- abnormal amounts of material, labour or other production costs
- storage costs, unless necessary before a further production stage
- selling costs.

Being consistent in the approach to valuing stock is important. It is worth noting that if a company makes an operating profit of 10 per cent a year on net assets, and if stocks represent 25 per cent of net assets, then a change of 4 per cent in stock value will mean a 10 per cent change in profit.

Net realizable value

Sometimes a business may expect not to recover the entire cost of stocks on hand, perhaps due to damage or obsolescence, or a fall in selling prices, or increased costs of completion. In such cases, the prudence convention requires that where a business expects the net realizable value of stocks to be less than cost, it should recognize the resulting loss at once by writing off the difference as part of the current period's 'cost of sales' expense. Such a write-down may be reversed later.

Hence the basis for valuing stocks is 'the *lower* of cost or net realizable value', since this will represent the best estimate of *recoverable* cost. This rule applies to individual items of stock, or groups of similar items, not merely to the overall aggregates. 'Net realizable value' means the anticipated selling price, less any further costs to completion and less any related selling and distribution costs.

Because net realizable value will usually be higher than cost, to value stocks at (higher) net realizable value would normally mean recognizing profit before selling the goods. That would not be prudent.

TRADING STOCK

A trading company's 'cost of goods sold' includes all expenses which 'bring the goods into a saleable condition'. This covers the cost of purchasing the goods, together with transport inwards, warehousing, etc.

The other main heading 'operating expenses' includes all expenses needed to sell the goods and run the business, such as advertising, distribution, office rent, selling and administrative salaries, and so on.

Where a trading company sells identifiable separate items of stock, such as cars or furniture, the 'cost of goods sold' figure is simply the cost of all the items the firm has sold. Any items left in stock at the end of a period are valued at what they cost, and (subject to adjustments) this total amount appears as a current asset in the balance sheet.

Where, however, the goods sold are too numerous or too small to keep records showing the cost of each item (as, for example, in a grocery store), the firm must calculate a 'cost of sales' figure *indirectly*. It can do this because the cost of goods sold in any period equals the cost of all goods *available* for sale in a period (opening stock plus purchases), less the cost of any goods unsold at the end.

Example

The accountant of Self Service Stores Limited is preparing the annual accounts to 31 March 2005 and wants to determine the cost of sales figure. He knows the opening stock figure was £310 000, based on a stock check carried out on 31 March 2004. The purchases figure for the year, according to the books of account, was £4 730k. From stock sheets prepared on 31 March 2005, he reckons the closing stock on that date was £350k.

He can now calculate that the cost of goods sold for the year was £4 690k:

	£'000
Opening stock, 31 March 2004	310
Add: Purchases in year	4 730
Available for sale	5 040
Less: Closing stock, 31 March 2005	350
= Cost of goods sold in year	4 690

Thus cost of goods sold equals purchases (£4 730k) *less* the *increase* in stock during the period (£350k – £310k = £40k) – or *plus* any *decrease* in stock. Opening stock and purchases appear in the books of account, but to obtain a figure for closing stock may require a physical stock check. This involves:

1 Locating and counting each item of stock.
2 Valuing each item (normally at the lower of cost or net realizable value).

Possible errors

Stock checking can be tedious and time-consuming. As a result, many businesses take a physical stock check only once or twice a year, probably at a time when stocks are at a seasonal low. Instead of checking all items in stock at a single date, a firm may keep 'perpetual' stock records. It can check these physically against actual stock throughout the year, though not all at the same time. Such records can then supply 'closing stock' figures at the end of any accounting period.

Clearly the 'cost of sales' figure (and hence reported profit) may be heavily dependent on the opening and closing stock valuations, which are subject to various possible errors:

- *omission or double counting* of physical stock items
- *errors in pricing* items,
- *errors in the arithmetic* of computing stock values, or in adding totals.

Hence audit checks will lay heavy emphasis on verifying the stock amounts. The figure of £4 690k for Self Service Stores Limited aims to represent the cost of goods actually sold, but this total will also include the cost of any stock losses through theft or wastage, since these too will reduce the amount of closing stock. It may be possible to control separately items of stock which are large or of high value. Otherwise one needs to compare the calculated cost of sales figure, based on a stock check, with some standard, in order to discover significant stock losses.

Where the company's pricing policy is to add a fixed percentage mark-up to the purchase cost of goods, it may be possible to measure the accuracy of the cost of sales figure based on the stock check.

Example

Self Service Stores Limited adds a 25 per cent mark-up on cost in setting selling prices. In the year to 31 March 2005, sales were £5 500k.

	£'000
Cost of sales, based on stock check	4 690
Cost of sales 'should be' 100/125 x £5 500k	4 400
Unexplained stock loss	290

On the basis of this variance, it looks as if Self Service Stores Limited may have a shoplifting problem!

Since few companies maintain the same level of mark-up on all goods, however, it is seldom so easy to arrive at an accurate standard. It may often be best to use a cost of sales percentage based on past average experience. But if conditions change (for example, if the sales mix varies) it may not be clear whether it is the standard or the stock check amount which is 'wrong'. Still, such a check can signal substantial errors or losses to look into.

Obsolescent and slow-moving stock

The accounting rule is that balance sheets should show stock 'at the *lower* of cost or net realizable value'. Where the stock exists in good condition, but is moving slowly or becoming out of date, how much, if anything, needs to be written off? Here is a difficult area of decision, involving a commercial judgement about the likely market demand for the stock in future periods.

Example

Bargain Motors Limited started business on 1 January 2004 buying and selling cars. Retained profit in the first year amounted to £100 000 and stock at the end of 2004 amounted to £400 000. During 2005 the company bought cars costing £5 000 000; and it sold for £6 400 000 cars which had cost £4 800 000. Operating expenses (ignoring tax) were £1 400 000. The left-hand column opposite sets out summaries of the draft profit and loss account and balance sheet for 2005 showing a profit of £200 000 and net assets of £1 300 000.

The balance sheet stock figure was calculated as follows:

	£'000
Opening stock at cost	400
Add: Purchases at cost	5 000
	5 400
Less: Cost of cars sold	4 800
Calculated closing stock, at cost	600

A detailed review of the items remaining in stock revealed that:

1 The stock included a number of discontinued items, which had cost £200 000, but which could now be sold for only 20 per cent of cost.
2 Cars which had cost £120 000 had been damaged and were now thought to be worth only about £70 000.

The right-hand column opposite sets out revised accounts for 2005 incorporating the necessary stock adjustments. Notice that these affect both the profit and loss account and the balance sheet.

BARGAIN MOTORS LIMITED

Profit and loss account summary for 2005

	Draft £'000	Revised £'000
Turnover	6 400	6 400
Cost of sales	4 800	5 010
Gross profit	1 600	1 390
Operating expenses	1 400	1 400
Net profit (loss)	200	(10)

Balance sheet summary at 31 December 2005

	Draft £'000	Revised £'000
Stock	600	390
Other net assets	700	700
Net assets	1 300	1 090
Share capital	1 000	1 000
Profit and loss	300	90
Capital employed	1 300	1 090

Note:

£210 000 has been written off the cost of stock in the revised accounts (right-hand column above). This increases the cost of sales, and therefore reduces profit for the period. As a result, the balance sheet amount for (cumulative) retained profit falls by £210 000 to balance the decline in stocks.

FLOW OF GOODS ASSUMPTIONS

Companies keep records showing the invoice price of each item purchased, so they may simply use the unit costs on the most recent invoice to value stock. But what if the closing stock level exceeds the quantity of items purchased on the most recent invoice? Or what if the price of an item fluctuates sharply? To deal with these issues a company must establish a policy for valuing stock, which will affect both the balance sheet stock figure and the reported profit or loss.

Example

Glass Bottles Limited buys and sells a standard glass bottle. In the year to 30 September 2004, 12 500 bottles were sold for £100 000. The stock and purchases accounts showed the following figures:

		Units	Unit cost	Total
			£	£
1 October 2004	Opening stock	5 000	4.00	20 000
1 January 2005	Purchases	4 000	5.00	20 000
1 April 2005	Purchases	4 500	6.00	27 000
1 August 2005	Purchases	5 000	7.00	35 000
		18 500		102 000

To determine the cost of sales in the year, we need to know the 'value' of the closing stock of 6 000 bottles at 30 September 2005. But on what (consistent) basis should Glass Bottles Limited value the stock? Two methods are widely used:

- the 'First In First Out' method (FIFO), which may match the physical flow of goods;
- the 'Average Cost' method.

As we shall see, the two methods can give different results. We illustrate first with FIFO (below) and then with Average Cost (on the right). (IAS 2 no longer permits a third method called Last In First Out (LIFO), which used to be common in the USA.)

(a) 'First In First Out' basis (FIFO)

This method assumes that the oldest items are sold first, leaving in stock those items which were purchased most recently. On this basis, the cost of the 12 500 bottles sold and of the 6 000 bottles in closing stock would be:

		Cost of sales			Closing stock
		£			£
5 000	@ £4.00 =	20 000			
4 000	@ £5.00 =	20 000	1 000	@ £6.00 =	6 000
3 500	@ £6.00 =	21 000	5 000	@ £7.00 =	35 000
12 500		61 000	6 000		41 000

(b) 'Average cost' basis

This method assumes that average cost, recalculated regularly or (as below) on every purchase (*), forms the basis for cost of sales and closing stock value. On the dates of the three replenishments during the year stock levels were 3 500, 4 000, and 4 500 bottles.

		Units	Average cost	Total	Cost of sales
			£	£	£
1 October 2004	Stock	5 000	4.00	20 000	
	Issues	(1 500)	4.00	(6 000)	6 000
		3 500	4.00	14 000	
1 January 2005	Purchases	4 000	5.00	20 000	
		7 500	4.53*	34 000	
	Issues	(3 500)	4.53	(15 867)	15 867
		4 000	4.53	18 133	
1 April 2005	Purchases	4 500	6.00	27 000	
		8 500	5.31*	45 133	
	Issues	(4 000)	5.31	(21 239)	21 239
		4 500	5.31	23 894	
1 August 2005	Purchases	5 000	7.00	35 000	
		9 500	6.20*	58 894	
	Issues	(3 500)	6.20	(21 698)	21 698
30 September 2005	Stock	6 000	6.20	37 196	64 804

Hence, using the average cost method, Glass Bottles Limited's cost of sales would be £64 804, the gross profit would be £35 196, and the closing stock value at 'cost' would be £37 196.

Notice that whatever the method of valuing closing stock, that amount plus cost of sales in the period equals £102 000 – which is the 'cost of goods available for sale': opening stock £20 000 plus (cost of) purchases £82 000.

	Cost of sales	+	Closing stock	=	Goods available
	£		£		£
FIFO	61 000		41 000	=	102 000
Average cost	64 804		37 196		

MANUFACTURING STOCK

We have seen that problems can arise in valuing a trading company's stock if purchase prices change during a year, but at least purchase invoices do show the actual cost of an item at certain points in time. But what is the 'cost' of an item which a company makes itself? Varying quantities of stock usually remain in various stages of completion at the end of each period, so one needs to value 'work-in-progress' as well as stocks of raw materials and finished goods.

All that we can attempt here is a general look at one widely used system – batch costing. From this we can see the kind of problems which will arise under any system used to calculate total cost. There are two kinds of cost:

Direct material and direct labour costs can be identified with specific batches of products. Dividing total batch costs by the number of units produced gives unit costs.

Factory indirect costs include the costs of supervision, depreciation and maintenance of equipment, factory rent, light and heat, and so on. In capital-intensive industries the indirect costs ('overheads'), may be difficult to allocate to specific batches. They may also be much higher in total than the direct costs. Most labour costs in modern automated plants may be indirect.

Apportioning indirect costs

The cost records will usually show the 'prime costs' (material and direct labour), but it can be hard to tell how much of the total indirect costs relate to a particular product. Who can say how to apportion the works manager's time or the factory rent over all the products made in a period?

Example

Timber Box Limited makes wooden boxes and owns a small factory and some machines. It employs a works manager and other staff, some of whom work directly on making boxes, while others deal with purchases, stores, maintenance, cleaning, and so on. On 31 December 2004 the following balances appeared in the company's books:

	£'000
Sales	14 000
Direct material	6 000
Direct labour	1 500
Factory overheads	4 500
Administrative expenses	2 500

At the end of the year the company had in stock finished boxes for which the direct costs (in £ thousands) were: material 700, direct labour 200. At what amount should the accounts show the finished stock?

Absorption (full) costing

One common method is to add factory overheads as a *percentage of direct labour costs*. Timber Box's overhead rate would then be 300 per cent:

$$\frac{\text{Overheads} = £4\,500}{\text{Direct labour} = £1\,500} = 300\%$$

This absorption (or 'full') costing method would value finished stock ('at cost') as follows:

	£'000
Direct material	700
Direct labour	200
Factory overheads (300% x direct labour £200 000)	600
Finished goods stock	1 500

In practice, Timber Box Limited would normally determine overhead absorption rates *in advance*. Dividing forecast overhead costs by forecast (normal) production volume would give the overhead absorption (or 'recovery') rate for the ensuing period.

So total indirect costs 'absorbed' by products could differ from actual indirect costs incurred for two reasons:

1 Actual overheads could differ from forecast overheads (spending variance).
2 Actual production could differ from forecast volume (volume variance).

Any overheads 'underabsorbed' (or 'overabsorbed') will have to be written off as a variance in the current period's profit and loss account – reducing (or increasing) reported profit.

If no variance arises under either heading, the products manufactured will exactly 'absorb' the actual total indirect costs. But even then a problem will arise if the *level of stock* varies. For example, if Timber Box Limited had no stock at the beginning of 2004, only £3.9 million overheads will be charged as an expense in 2004, even though actual overheads totalled £4.5 million.

The remaining £600 000 of overheads incurred in 2004 have been added to the value of closing stock, and will presumably be charged against profit as part of the cost of goods sold next year, in 2005. This accounting treatment can lead to a temptation to continue with a rate of production exceeding the current level of sales, which would, of course, increase the level of stock. It might also have the effect of *increasing reported profit* in the current period, by attributing a larger proportion of the current period's (probably largely fixed) indirect overheads to the value of closing stock. (See the Walters Supplies Exercise on page 121.)

Direct (marginal) costing

Some accountants argue that fixed production overhead costs represent the basic provision of capacity to produce, and regard them as 'period costs', incurred on a time basis, and not as 'product costs' (as absorption costing implies). On this 'direct' (or 'marginal') costing basis, Timber Box Limited's finished stock value would be only £900 000 (direct material £700 000 plus direct labour £200 000).

The table below summarizes the treatment of costs of stock:

	Product costs	Period costs
Expense (P&L)	In period when product sold	If related to current period
Asset (BS)	Product unsold end of period	If related to future period

Direct costing avoids arbitrary allocations of overheads to products. It also avoids the sharp fluctuations in reported profit which can occur under absorption costing if stock levels vary, and which many managers find hard to understand. Under direct (marginal) costing, profit tends to vary with sales not with production, which some people think makes more sense. One might also regard direct (marginal) costing as more prudent because it shows *lower* stock values (and profits).

The contrary argument is that it would understate stock values to include nothing for the use of equipment and for indirect labour costs needed to convert raw materials into finished products. One must allocate some indirect production overheads to closing stock values to do a proper job of matching.

Accounting standards [SSAP 9/IAS 2] accept the latter argument and require absorption (full) costing. Accounts must value stock and work-in-progress at 'the lower of cost and net realizable value' of the separate items of stock, where 'cost' *includes* production overheads based on a normal level of activity.

Timber Box Limited's 2004 profit and loss accounts, summarized on both bases, appear on the right (top). The two methods of valuing stock lead to very different results. The first method takes all indirect overhead costs into account (absorption costing), while the second ignores them all (direct costing). In some businesses the ratio of indirect to direct costs might be higher, and the difference in profit even greater.

Clearly two managements using different methods (if they were allowed to do so) could arrive at very different stock valuations, and hence profit or loss figures, especially where stock levels fluctuate. Comparisons between different companies can be hazardous in the absence of detailed information about methods of valuing stock.

Profit and loss accounts (summarized) for the year 2004

TIMBER BOX LIMITED

	Absorption costing £'000		Direct costing £'000
Sales		14 000	14 000
Direct material	6 000		6 000
Direct labour	1 500		1 500
Factory overheads	4 500		4 500
	12 000		12 000
Less: Closing stock	1 500		900
		10 500	11 100
Gross profit		3 500	2 900
Administrative expenses		2 500	2 500
Profit before tax		1 000	400
Closing stock in balance sheet		1 500	900

The chart below shows the flow of material through the manufacturing production process:

FLOW OF MATERIAL THROUGH PRODUCTION PROCESS

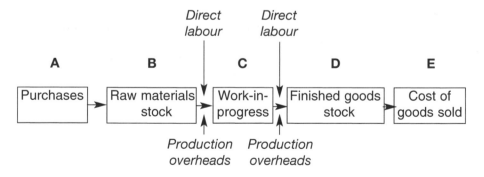

A and B: Value at the cost of material

C, D and E: Value at the cost of material and direct labour (= direct cost) plus allocated production overheads (= absorption cost).

LONG-TERM CONTRACTS

'Long-term' contracts involve two or more accounting periods. We have seen that when a transaction covers more than one period, firms must decide when to recognize sales revenue and charge expenses. It is rather obvious that not all the profit on a long-term contract arises on the day the firm signs the contract, nor on the final day of work. We need some other basis to spread the total profit 'fairly' over the contract period.

SSAP 9/IAS 11 requires the balance sheet to include work on long-term contracts:

- at cost
- *plus* attributable profit
- *less* foreseeable losses
- (and less any progress payments already received).

'Attributable profit' is the profit fairly relating to work done at the balance sheet date. 'Foreseeable losses' are losses expected to arise over the whole duration of the contract.

Example

Alpha Construction Limited agrees to build an office block for Omega Property Limited for £15 million. Alpha estimates that the project will cost £12 million and that construction will take three years. At the end of the first year the job is one quarter over and costs so far, at £5 million, are on target.

What profit (if any) has Alpha made in the first year? How should the company split the expected total profit over the three years?

With a further two years of construction to go, prudence may well cause Alpha to report zero profit in year 1. Much could still go wrong. The total costs may exceed £12 million, to complete construction may take more than two further years, and so on.

But what if Alpha is showing a loss on its other transactions? What if this contract involves a different kind of work from normal? How might these factors affect the accounting decision?

The scope open to the directors of companies such as Alpha is evident. The company's auditors can at least try to ensure that the firm adopts a consistent accounting basis from one year to another. But the directors are in the best position to make commercial judgements and unless their conclusions seem clearly unreasonable, it may be hard for the auditors to disagree with them.

Under these conditions, measuring profit or loss can only be approximate. Accounting measures indicate a range within which profits probably fall, but do not define an exact figure. Where the element of uncertainty is substantial, judgements are crucial. The point is that even honest and competent judgements will sometimes prove wrong.

Variable production

Walters Supplies makes baths. Production capacity is 20 000 units a year, variable costs are £40 per unit and the fixed costs of the factory are £1.0 million a year. Sales at £120 per unit were running at capacity in 2004 and closing stock was 2 000 units.

The company is expecting sales volume to decline sharply in 2005 to only 15 000 units, but hopes for a recovery in the market in 2006. The question is whether to cut back production in 2005 to 15 000 units, which would leave closing stock at 2 000 units, or to continue producing at capacity in 2005, which would build up stocks to 7 000 units by the year end.

Using (i) the full (absorption) costing basis and (ii) the marginal (direct) costing basis, please calculate (a) the closing stock values (using FIFO) and (b) the gross profit for 2005 under each of the two production plans for 2005. Please also write down on a separate sheet of paper your explanation of any difference

2005 Projection	15 000	units	20 000	units
	Total £'000	Per Unit £	Total £'000	Per Unit £
Variable costs	600	40.00	800	40.00
Fixed costs	1 000	66.67	1 000	50.00
Total production costs	1 600	106.67	1 800	90.00

(i) Profit and loss summary 2005 – full (absorption) costing

Opening stock (@ £ per unit)		
Cost of units manufactured	1 600	1 800
= Goods available		
(a) *Less:* Closing stock (FIFO)	_____	_____
= Cost of goods sold		
Sales: 15 000 units @ £120	1 800	1 800
(b) Gross profit (or loss)	_____	_____

(ii) Profit and loss summary 2005 – marginal (direct) costing

Opening stock (@ £ per unit)		
Cost of units manufactured	1 600	1 800
= Goods available		
(a) *Less:* Closing stock (FIFO)	_____	_____
= Cost of goods sold		
Sales: 15 000 units @ £120	1 800	1 800
(b) Gross profit (or loss)	_____	_____

Varying production: Answer

(i) Profit and loss summary 2005 – full (absorption) costing

Opening stock (@ £90 per unit)	180	180
Cost of units manufactured	1 600	1 800
= Goods available	1 780	1 980
(a) *Less:* Closing stock (FIFO)	(213[a])	(630[b])
= Cost of goods sold	1 567	1 350
Sales: 15 000 units @ £120	1 800	1 800
(b) Gross profit (or loss)	233	450

(ii) Profit and loss summary 2005 – marginal (direct) costing

Opening stock (@ £40 per unit)	80	80
Cost of units manufactured	1 600	1 800
= Goods available	1 680	1 880
(a) *Less:* Closing stock (FIFO[c])	(80[c])	(280[c])
= Cost of goods sold	1 600	1 600
Sales: 15 000 units @ £120	1 800	1 800
(b) Gross profit (or loss)	200	200

Notes:
[a] 2,000 units @ £106.67 = £213 333
[b] 7,000 units @ £90 = £630 000
[c] 2,000 units @ £40 = £80 000; 7 000 units @ £40 = £280 000

Full (absorption) costing

The result of producing 20 000 units instead of 15 000 units is to increase gross profit in 2005 by £216 667 (from £233 333 to £450 000). This happens because the fraction of annual fixed production overheads carried forward in closing stock (and therefore *not* charged as part of cost of goods sold expense in 2005) increases:

from $2/15 \times £1\,000\,000 = £133\,333$

to $7/20 \times £1\,000\,000 = £350\,000$

Marginal (direct) costing

Of course the profit under this method is the same at different levels of production, since all the difference in (variable) costs is reflected in closing stock valuation and none of the fixed production overheads are carried forward whatever the level of production.

The 'breakeven' level of sales can be calculated as follows:

$$\frac{\text{Annual fixed costs}}{\text{Sales price} - \text{variable costs}} = \frac{1\,000\,000}{120-40} = \frac{1\,000\,000}{80} = 12\,500 \text{ units.}$$

So if sales are 15 000 units a year, the profit is a 'contribution' of £80 per unit on 2 500 units = £200 000.

SECTION 6 SUMMARY

Valuing opening and closing stock can be critical in measuring the cost of sales for a period, and therefore profit or loss. Companies must disclose in the notes the three main kinds of stock: raw materials, work-in-progress and finished goods.

Under the matching convention, accounts normally carry forward the *cost* of stocks on hand at the end of a period as a current asset in the balance sheet, to expense against the related sales revenue in a future period. But the prudence convention means that accounts value stock at the *lower* of 'cost' and 'net realizable value'.

Trading companies purchase goods ready for sale. Most such firms have to calculate their cost of sales indirectly, since they do not identify each item separately. Companies may need to write down obsolete or slow-moving stock by making suitable provisions at the end of each year.

Two methods of measuring the cost of stock on hand at the end of a period imply different assumptions about the physical flow of goods: First In First Out (FIFO) and Average Cost. There can be large differences between these methods when prices change over time.

Direct (marginal) costing treats 'fixed' production overheads as *period* costs in valuing manufacturing stock and thus writes them all off as an expense when incurred. Accounting standards, however, require published accounts to use absorption (full) costing. This attributes a share of indirect production overheads to the cost of end-of-year stock (in effect, as *product* costs). Such treatment may do a better job of 'matching', but it can lead to increases in the current period's reported profit when 'making for stock'.

Finally we looked at how accounting for long-term contracts achieves a balance between prudence and matching. Companies may recognize some profit during the life of a long-term contract, but on a prudent basis making full provision for any expected losses.

PROBLEMS

6.1 Definitions
Write down on this page your definitions of the terms shown. Then compare your answers with the definitions overleaf.

(a) Cost of sales

(b) Foreseeable losses

(c) Absorption (full) costing

(d) Under-absorption

(e) FIFO

(f) Work-in-progress

(g) Direct (marginal) costing

(h) Net realizable value

(i) Attributable profit

(j) Production overheads

6.1 Definitions

(a) **Cost of sales** ('cost of goods sold') is the cost of producing the goods that have been sold in a period. They exclude selling costs. In practice 'cost of sales' comprises the costs which are included in stock values for finished goods: direct materials, direct labour and a share of indirect production overheads.

(b) **Foreseeable losses** are losses expected to arise over the whole duration of a long-term contract. The profit and loss account must recognize them at once.

(c) **Absorption (full) costing** is a method of valuing stock which includes a share of indirect production overheads, in effect treating them as 'product costs'. It is the method which SSAP 9/IAS 2 requires for company accounts.

(d) **Under-absorption** of production overheads (by products) can occur either (i) when actual overhead costs exceed standard costs (spending variance), or (ii) when actual production volume is less than normal volume (volume variance). Any under-absorption must be written off as an expense in the current period.

(e) **FIFO** is the 'First In First Out' method of valuing stock (and thus of measuring cost of sales). FIFO assumes that firms sell goods in the same order as they purchase or make them. (Accounting may use the method even if that assumption is untrue.) FIFO results in balance sheets valuing stock at the most recent costs, while the cost of sales in the profit and loss account consists of somewhat earlier purchases (at slightly out-of-date costs).

(f) **Work-in-progress** (WIP) is a kind of stock comprising products on which work has begun but is not yet complete. In a manufacturing company, if work had not begun the products would still be raw materials, while if it was complete they would be finished goods. Accounts generally value work-in-progress at cost, including a share of production overheads, but with full provision for any expected losses. The aggregate amount is reduced by any advances or progress payments received from customers.

(g) **Direct (marginal) costing** is a method of valuing stock which does not include production overheads, but only direct material costs and direct labour costs. In effect direct costing treats production overheads as 'period costs'. SSAP 9/IAS 2 does not permit direct costing in published accounts, but some companies use it for internal management accounting purposes.

(h) **Net realizable value** (NRV) is the estimated net proceeds of selling stocks after deducting any further costs of completion as well as any selling costs. The prudence convention means that balance sheets show stocks 'at cost' only if the cost is recoverable in full in a future period. If not, that is if net realizable value is *lower* than cost, then the lower figure is used to value stocks and any loss appears in the current accounting period.

(i) **Attributable profit** is the profit fairly relating to the work completed on a long-term contract. The basis might be pro rata to time elapsed, or to planned costs, probably after allowing some deduction for contingencies or a margin of error.

(j) **Production overheads** are added to the value of stocks in published accounts under absorption (full) costing (but are excluded by the direct (marginal) costing method). They include indirect overheads such as: indirect labour, factory rent, lighting and heating, and depreciation of production equipment.

6.2 Joshua Antiques Limited: Stock adjustments

Joshua Antiques Limited ended its financial year on the first Friday after 31 March in each year. Details were available of each antique dealt in, showing date of purchase, name of supplier, and cost; and (when sold) date of sale, name of customer (usually), and proceeds. From these records the manager prepared stock sheets at 1 April 2005 showing items apparently unsold with a total cost of £57 600. This was the figure shown as closing stock in the draft accounts for the 52 weeks ended 1 April 2005.

In the course of audit work the following queries arose. Please identify for each item below what adjustment, if any, is needed to the closing stock figure; and calculate what the total closing stock should be in the final accounts.

(a) Three items of china, with a total cost of £240, were cracked. The manager thought they could be sold for £150 in total, instead of at the normal 100 per cent mark-up on cost.

(b) A picture of Westminster Bridge, which the manager had thought to be by Hogarth, had turned out to be by an unknown artist. Its selling value was accordingly reduced from £4 000 to £500 (which compared with a cost of £1 700).

(c) Offsetting the 'Hogarth' blunder, the firm had in stock a pair of water colours, which together had cost only £100. They were now attributed to Constable; and as a result their selling price had been raised from £250 to £6 000.

(d) A number of items of jewellery, which the records showed to have cost £430 in total, ought to have been in stock according to the records, but no trace could be found of them (nor had they been recorded as sold since 1 April 2005). The manager reckoned the total sales proceeds would have been about £860.

(e) A rather dented silver coffee pot, which had cost £150, had been in stock for over a year. Because of its poor condition, it had been written down to £80 in the 2004 accounts but it appeared on 1 April 2005 in the stock records at £150. Its selling price was currently set at £180, but the manager doubted if he would get more than £90 for it.

(f) A first edition of Ian Fleming's first book (*Casino Royale*) had been purchased for £400. Its estimated selling price had been £1 000. Unfortunately some coffee had subsequently been spilled on the dust-jacket, which it was feared might reduce the price by as much as 25 per cent.

An answer is shown on the next page.

6.3 Canning and Sons Limited: Writing down stock

CANNING AND SONS LIMITED
Balance Sheet at 31 December 2004

		£'000
Fixed assets, net		330
Current assets		
Stock	213	
Debtors	254	
Cash	26	
	493	
Less **Creditors due within one year**		
Trade creditors	152	
Tax	30	
	182	
		311
		641
Capital and reserves		
Called up share capital		400
Profit and loss account (129 B/F + 112)		241
		641

Profit and loss account for the year ended 31 December 2004

	£'000
Turnover	1 127
Cost of sales	871
Gross profit	256
Selling and administrative expenses	113
	143
Tax	31
Profit after tax	112

The 2004 accounts of Canning and Sons Limited, sellers of toys, are shown above as they were prepared for audit. The auditors raised only one significant point, to do with valuing stock. They recommended that a consignment of electric cars which had cost £40 000 and had not sold well over the Christmas period should be written down to 50 per cent of cost.

The company's directors reluctantly felt they had no choice but to accept the auditors' recommendation. You are asked to amend the draft accounts accordingly, making any necessary change to the provision for tax (which is based on a rate of 20 per cent).

An answer is shown on the next page.

6.2 Joshua Antiques Limited

Solution

(a) The china should be shown at £150 (net realizable value) instead of at £240 (cost).

(b) The 'Hogarth' picture should be reduced from £1 700 (cost) to £500 (net realizable value).

(c) The water colours should continue to be shown at cost, £100. (This illustrates the 'prudence' concept: losses tend to be recognized at once, but profits only when actually earned.)

(d) The jewellery items should not be included in the closing stock, which should therefore be reduced by £430. If they had been sold, it seems odd that the sales proceeds had apparently not been matched against the purchase.

(e) The coffee pot should be shown at estimated net realizable value, which appears to be below cost. There is sufficient uncertainty that it might be best to show the item at £80 (the same as last year); even though, if the write-down were being made for the first time in 2005, the estimated sales proceeds of £90 would be the correct figure. Accordingly, a deduction of £70 needs to be made from the total stock figure.

(f) Net realizable value (? £750) is still expected comfortably to exceed cost (£400); so the book should be included in stock at cost £400.

Summary

	£	£
Original closing stock total		57 600
(a)	– 90	
(b)	– 1 200	
(c)	–	
(d)	– 430	
(e)	– 70	
(f)	–	1 790
Revised closing stock		55 810

6.3 Canning and Sons Limited

Solution

CANNING AND SONS LIMITED
Balance sheet at 31 December 2004

		£'000
Fixed assets (net)		330
Current assets		
Stock	193	
Debtors	254	
Cash	26	
	473	
Less **Creditors due within one year**		
Trade creditors	152	
Tax	26	
	178	
		295
		625
Capital and reserves		
Called up share capital		400
Profit and loss account (129 B/F + 96)		225
		625

Profit and loss account for the year ended 31 December 2004

	£'000
Turnover	1 127
Cost of sales	891
Gross profit	236
Selling and administrative expenses	113
	123
Tax	27
Profit after tax	96

6.4   Anderson Tiles Limited: FIFO stock valuation

At 1 April 2004 Anderson Tiles had 3 000 cases of a particular kind of tile in stock. They were shown as costing £4 a case.

In the year to 31 March 2005 three batches of cases were purchased. In June 4 000 cases @ £4.25 per case; in October 2 000 cases @ £4.75; and in December 3 000 cases @ £5.00.

Using the FIFO method of stock valuation, calculate the closing stock valuation at 31 March 2005, when there were 6 000 cases in stock. Then compute the cost of sales for the year. Verify your computation by identifying the volume of tiles and related costs per case assumed to be sold.

6.5   Newport Machines Limited: Absorption and direct costing

In the year ended 30 June 2005, Newport Machines incurred the following factory costs:

	£'000
Direct material	450
Direct labour	300
Overheads	540

At 30 June stock was on hand on which had been incurred £30 000 direct material costs and £20 000 direct labour costs. This meant that if direct costing were adopted, the stock would be valued at £50 000 for accounting purposes.

Calculate the overhead percentage on direct labour, and value the stock on the absorption cost basis.

6.6   Berwick Paper Limited: Average cost stock valuation

Berwick Paper Limited replenished its stock of a certain type of paper at the end of each quarter. For the year 2004 opening stock was 1 200 tonnes. The cost attributable to the opening stock was £21 per tonne. Purchase prices per tonne through the year were £18 (March), £15 (June), £25 (September), and £20 (December).

Quantities purchased and issued each quarter (in tonnes) were as follows:

	Purchases	Issues
March quarter	1 800	900
June quarter	2 400	1 700
September quarter	1 200	1 400
December quarter	1 800	1 900
	7 200	5 900

Thus closing stock amounted to 2 500 tonnes (= opening stock 1 200 tonnes plus purchases 7 200 tonnes less issues in year 5 900 tonnes).

Assuming that purchases are made at the end of each quarter, and that the average cost method of valuing stock is used for issues, calculate the value of closing stock at 31 December 2004, and the cost of paper used during the year.

6.7   Kenton Limited: Overheads in closing stock

Kenton normally produces 6 million square metres of carpets a year. Direct material costs are £8 per m^2 and direct labour costs £4 per m^2. Production overheads amount to £36 million a year.

Immediate prospects for sales are poor. The production manager is worried about warehousing capacity, and proposes to cut production for the last three months of the year from 1½ million to ½ million m^2. He then expects end-of-year stock to amount to 1 million m^2.

The managing director, however, is conscious that senior management bonuses are based largely on annual profits. He wants to know how much difference it would make to gross profits before tax if instead of cutting back as proposed above, production were to continue at the normal level, resulting in closing stock of 2 million m^2.

No answers are given to the following two problems:

6.8   Shiny Snappers Limited: Changing stock levels

Shiny Snappers Limited was formed to produce cameras. Sales were estimated at about 5 000 units per quarter, at an average price of £30 per unit; so production was set at this level. Stocks were planned to build up at the start, since the first quarter's sales were not expected to exceed 3 500 units. But even that sales estimate was too optimistic, and production was accordingly cut back to 2 000 units for the second quarter.

Direct costs of production averaged £20 per unit, and fixed production overheads amounted to £20 000 per quarter. The company sold 2 000 units in the first quarter and 4 000 (at a price reduced by 5 per cent) in the second. When the managing director saw the company's profit and loss accounts (set out below) for the first two quarters, he was astonished to see that profits (on the full cost basis) were the same in each quarter, although unit sales had doubled in the second.

	1st quarter		2nd quarter	
		£'000		£'000
Sales revenue		60		114
Opening stocks	–		72	
Cost of production	120		60	
	120		132	
Less: Closing stocks	72		30	
Cost of goods sold		48		102
Gross profit		12		12

Explain the results for the two quarters. How would it affect profits if marginal costing had been used instead of full costing?

6.9 Roger Ancastle

In April 2005 Roger Ancastle was considering how to value the unsold copies of a book his firm of financial consultants had just published: 2 000 copies of the book had been printed, of which 1 000 copies had been bound. In the year ended 31 March 2005 400 copies had been sold for cash @ £45 each, of which the firm received £30 a copy. Stock on 31 March 2005 was 500 bound copies (plus 1 000 unbound), 100 bound copies having been sent out to reviewers to publicize the book. No other advertising was planned.

The main cost of printing a book is the set-up cost, in this case £20 000. The marginal cost, mainly the cost of paper, was £2 per copy. Thus while printing 2 000 copies had actually cost £24 000, printing 5 000 copies would in total have cost only £30 000. In addition it cost £4 to bind each copy. The firm had decided initially to bind only 1 000 copies of the 2 000 printed, to see if sales justified spending a further £4 000 on binding the second 1 000 copies.

Mr Ancastle's first thought was to value the stock of 1 500 unsold copies of the book at £20 000, as follows:

Method A

			£	
500 bound copies	@ £16	=	8 000	
1 000 unbound copies	@ £12	=	12 000	£20 000

Mr Ancastle was unsure whether it was correct to spread the set-up cost over the total number of copies printed, especially in view of the small marginal cost of printing more copies. He wondered if the firm ought to spread the set-up cost over the first 1 000 copies only, since only that number had been bound. The stock at 31 March 2005 would then be valued at only £15 000.

Method B

		£	
Set-up cost: $\frac{500}{1000}$ x £20 000	=	10 000	
Marginal printing cost: 1 500 @ £2	=	3 000	£15 000
Binding cost: 500 @ £4	=	2 000	

Although Method B would result in showing a small loss of £1 000 on the book in the year ended 31 March 2005 (compared with a profit of £4 000 under Method A), Mr Ancastle thought it might be better accounting practice. The table shows what the stock value at 31 March 2005 would be under both Method A and Method B if the number of copies printed had been: (a) 1 000 copies, (b) 2 000 copies (the actual number), (c) 5 000 copies.

Mr Ancastle thought it strange that printing 5 000 copies rather than 1 000 would show £7 000 profit under Method A instead of £1 000 loss. Method A would produce £8 000 more profit under those circumstances even though the firm would have paid out £8 000 more cash. Method B would show the same £1 000 loss in all three cases.

Table

	1 000 copies £'000	2 000 copies £'000	5 000 copies £'000
Binding 1 000 copies	4	4	4
Cost of printing	22	24	30
Total expenditure	26	28	34
Less: Sales revenue	12	12	12
Net cash out-of-pocket	14	16	22
Method A			
Binding 500 copies @ £4	2	2	2
Unbound copies (proportion)	11	18	27
= Closing stock	13	20	29
Method B			
Binding 500 copies @ £4	2	2	2
500 balance of first 1 000 (printing set-up)	10	10	10
500 balance of first 1 000 (marginal cost)	1	1	1
Excess over 1 000 (marginal cost)	–	2	8
= Closing stock	13	15	21

Questions

1. Assume that in the year ending 31 March 2006 a further 600 copies of the book are sold. Calculate what stock value would be shown at 31 March 2006 under both Method A and Method B; and what profit or loss would be reported in the year ended 31 March 2006.

2. How much profit or loss do you think Roger Ancastle's firm made on the book in the year ended 31 March 2005?

3. How would it affect your answer to (2) if Mr Ancastle's views on future sales after 31 March 2005 were as follows (in April 2005):

   (a) Doubtful if as many as 200 more copies would be sold?
   (b) Confident that at least 800 more copies would be sold?
   (c) No idea how many more copies would be sold?

Section 7
Fixed assets and depreciation

CAPITAL EXPENDITURE

So far our concern has been to allocate 'revenue' expenditure between two accounting periods (with the split affecting *both* periods). Now we must look at 'capital' spending on acquiring fixed assets which have a life stretching over several years. These include intangible assets and investments, but in this section we shall mainly be looking at tangible fixed assets [IAS 16/FRS 15].

Companies use tangible fixed assets on a continuing basis in their business; they are not intended for resale until the end of their life. Typical examples are land, buildings, plant and equipment. Purpose, rather than physical nature, determines whether an item represents capital or revenue and whether it should appear in the balance sheet as a fixed or current asset. Cars, for example, which are fixed assets for many companies, are mostly current assets (stocks) for Ford, which sells cars.

Measuring the cost of tangible fixed assets is often fairly easy. For purchased items, it is the total invoiced cost of acquiring fixed assets and preparing them for use. This includes legal costs of acquiring property and costs of preparing the site, or the costs of delivering and installing equipment, plus any professional fees.

Where a company constructs tangible fixed assets for its own use, the 'cost' may be the outlay for labour and materials, or it may include directly related overheads. The 'cost' may also include interest on finance during the period of production [IAS 23/FRS 15].

Lessees must capitalize 'finance leases' (which transfer substantially all the risks and rewards of ownership), and show them as tangible fixed assets on the balance sheet, with a matching long-term liability [IAS 17/SSAP 21].

Government grants relating to fixed assets are credited to revenue over their useful life [IAS 20/SSAP 4]. Companies:

- show the assets at total gross cost;
- credit the grant to 'deferred income' (which is *not* part of shareholders' funds), and
- release part of the grant to revenue each year, thus setting it off against depreciation.

If substantial repairs merely restore a fixed asset, they are revenue expenses. But to the extent that they 'improve' on an asset's original condition, they are capital and increase that fixed asset's cost. An improvement may: increase an asset's capacity; lengthen its useful life; reduce its running costs; or improve the quality of its output.

Capital commitments are significant amounts of capital spending which a company is contractually bound to pay in the future, or which has been approved (but not actually contracted for) at the balance sheet date.

Much of the remainder of this section now deals with depreciation, the process which allocates the cost of fixed assets to expenses over a number of accounting periods. This is a major example of the difference between cash and profit. Cash is paid at the start of a fixed asset's life, but the charge to expense is spread out over its whole life.

PRESENTATION IN PUBLISHED ACCOUNTS

The Companies Act 1985 requires companies to disclose three different kinds of fixed assets:

1 Intangible assets
2 Tangible assets
3 Investments.

Intangible assets

The permitted balance sheet formats (see pages 278 and 279) list four different kinds of intangible assets:

1 Development costs (see page 103)
2 Concessions, patents, licences, trade marks and similar rights and assets
3 Goodwill (see page 176)
4 Payments on account.

Accounts normally show intangible fixed assets at cost less aggregate amortization (depreciation) to date. Thus if there is no specific 'cost', accounts normally do not show intangible assets on the balance sheet, even if in reality they are significant to the business.

Where a company capitalizes development costs, it must disclose over what period it is writing them off. Where a company purchases goodwill, it must state the amortization period, with reasons.

Investments

The Companies Act 1985 requires balance sheets to disclose the following different kinds of fixed asset investments:

1 Shares in or loans to subsidiary companies
2 Shares in or loans to associated companies
3 Other shares
4 Other loans
5 Own shares.

The accounts must disclose the aggregate market value of listed (quoted) investments, and must provide for and disclose any permanent diminution in an investment's value. (Group accounts would not normally show investments in subsidiaries as such, for reasons explained in Section 9.)

Investments of a short-term nature are current assets.

Tangible fixed assets

The permitted balance sheet formats list four different kinds of tangible fixed assets (though it is usual to combine items 2 and 3):

1 Land and buildings
2 Plant and machinery
3 Fixtures, fittings, tools and equipment
4 Payments on account and assets in the course of construction.

These are the kinds of assets we shall mainly be discussing in this section.

The Companies Act 1985 requires extensive detailed disclosure, so the balance sheet itself normally shows only the total net book value (NBV) of tangible fixed assets: £381m (£353m) in the example below. A note to the accounts then sets out all the remaining details, such as those shown below. It is usual to distinguish between capital expenditure on fixed assets, and those resulting from acquisition of other companies. Also the total net book value may vary as a result of changes in foreign exchange rates.

	Land and buildings £ million	Plant and equipment £ million	Total £ million
Cost			
At start of year, 1.1.04	121	593	714
Acquisitions	6	32	38
Capital expenditure	18	76	94
Disposals	(2)	(12)	(14)
Foreign currency changes	(10)	(53)	(63)
At end of year, 31.12.04	133	636	769
Depreciation			
At start of year, 1.1.04	47	314	361
Acquisitions	2	12	14
Charge for year	5	48	53
Disposals	(1)	(10)	(11)
Foreign currency changes	(4)	(25)	(29)
At end of year, 31.12.04	49	339	388
Net book value, 31.12.04	84	297	381
Net book value, 31.12.03	*74*	*279*	*353*

DEPRECIATION

Most tangible fixed assets are gradually used up in providing goods or services over time. So every period firms charge part of a fixed asset's cost as 'depreciation' expense in the profit and loss account, and reduce the balance sheet NBV by the same amount.

Example

On 1 January 2003, Lance plc purchased a three-year shop lease for £96 000. The company's accounts over the next three years would include the following items:

	2003 £'000	2004 £'000	2005 £'000
Profit and loss account for year			
Lease: depreciation expense	32	32	32
Balance sheet at 31 December			
Lease at cost	96	96	96
Less: Accumulated depreciation	32	64	96
Net book value	64	32	0

In historical cost accounting, a fixed asset's NBV during its life represents the unallocated residue of its original cost *not* its (realizable) market value. The depreciation process allocates cost, it does not 'value' assets. By the time a fixed asset stops being useful, at the end of its 'life', its NBV should have fallen to its residual second-hand or scrap value (which may be zero).

Depreciation spreads a fixed asset's net cost over its expected useful life, to match against related revenue. This implies charging a fraction of a year's depreciation both in the year of purchase and in the year of disposal. The *accounting* purpose is to measure profit or loss. If the accounts charge too little depreciation in any period, they will overstate reported profit.

In contrast, the possible *financial* purpose is (by limiting maximum dividends payable) to amass funds with which to replace a fixed asset at the end of its life. But firms may not always 'replace' fixed assets, or not with identical assets.

We have seen that companies may carry forward as an asset certain 'revenue' spending (for example on stocks) which they expect to benefit future periods. In that sense one could regard a fixed asset's NBV largely as 'prepaid depreciation expense'.

The Inland Revenue has its own rules for computing depreciation for tax purposes (called 'writing-down allowances' or 'capital allowances'). So no company can affect its UK tax charge by altering the depreciation expense in its accounts (see Section 10).

The four variables in depreciation

There are three key variables to measure in computing depreciation of fixed assets:

A Cost
B Residual value } = net cost
C Useful life

More than one *method* of depreciation (D) is then possible in order to write off a fixed asset's net cost over its useful life.

Because both the residual value and the useful life of a fixed asset are usually unknown in advance, as a rule the annual depreciation expense charged in company accounts can only be an *estimate*, not a precisely accurate amount. (Thus, as we have already noted, reported profit itself is usually only an estimate too.)

The diagram below summarizes the position with respect to fixed assets and depreciation.

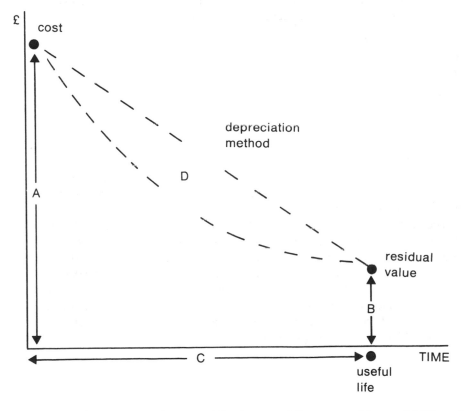

We have already looked at the cost of fixed assets. We next consider useful life and residual value (they go together), and then the various *methods* of depreciation.

USEFUL LIFE AND RESIDUAL VALUE

Let us now look at Furniture Removals Limited, which started to trade on 1 January 2004 and at once purchased vans for £60 000. During the first year, cash sales were £100 000 and cash expenses were £60 000.

The draft accounts for 2004 appear in the left-hand column opposite, before providing for any depreciation on the vans. Clearly they do not reflect the true picture. Without any charge for using the vans, the accounts overstate profit at £40 000; and the balance sheet still shows the vans at their original cost of £60 000 despite one year of use.

How much should the 2004 accounts provide for depreciation? In order to tell, we must answer two questions *in advance*:

1 For how many years will the company use the vans?
2 What will they be worth at the end of that time?

These questions clearly involve subjective estimates by managers. The likely useful life of an asset may be limited, depending on its nature, by:

* the passing of time;
* physical wear and tear, or
* technical or market obsolescence.

In this case the company's manager reckons that:

1 the vans will be used for five years, and
2 they will then be worth £10 000.

Let us call this Assumption A. On this basis, the net cost of the vans to Furniture Removals over their whole useful life will be £50 000: their original cost of £60 000 less their expected ultimate sale proceeds of £10 000. So in total the company must write off £50 000 depreciation over the five years.

The next question is: How much of this to charge in the first year? How much in the second, and so on? There are several possible answers, but let us assume that the company decides to charge an *equal* amount each year (the so-called 'straight line' method). Then the annual depreciation charge will be £10 000 (= £50 000/5).

The 2004 accounts including this expense are shown in the centre column opposite. Notice that charging depreciation *does not change the cash balance*. Compared with the draft accounts in the left-hand column, the vans' net book value is £10 000 less, as is the profit for the year.

FURNITURE REMOVALS LIMITED

Balance sheet at 31 December 2004

	Draft £'000	After depreciation £'000	After dividend £'000
Vans at cost	60	60	60
Less: Accumulated depreciation	–	10	10
Net book value of vans	60	50	50
Cash	40	40	10
	100	90	60
Share capital	60	60	60
Retained profit	40	30	–
	100	90	60

Profit and loss account for 2004

	Draft £'000	After depreciation £'000	After dividend £'000
Turnover	100	100	100
Cash expenses	60	60	60
Depreciation	–	10	10
Profit for the year	40	30	30
Dividend paid	–	–	30
Retained profit	40	30	–

Distribution of profit

Let us now further assume that the directors have decided to distribute all the £30 000 profit as dividends to shareholders. (To keep it simple we ignore tax.) The right-hand column above shows the position after payment of £30 000 dividends in cash during 2004.

The effect of charging depreciation is to reduce the amount of profit available for dividends. Without such a charge, the company might pay out too much in dividends. It might thus by mistake distribute part of its financial capital.

At the end of Year 5, when the fixed assets have been written down to £10 000, depreciation will total £50 000. Other things being equal £50 000 cash will be on hand. Assuming the old vans then realize the predicted amount of £10 000 on disposal, the company will once again have its original money capital of £60 000. (As we discuss in Section 13, this may no longer be enough to buy similar vans in periods of inflation.)

Alternative asset lives and residual values

We were able to complete the 2004 accounts of Furniture Removals Limited by assuming that the vans, which had cost £60 000, would last for five years and have a residual value of £10 000. (We called this Assumption A.)

What difference would it make if the directors were to take another view of the uncertain future? What would be the effect, for example, of (Assumption B) estimating a four-year useful life with a residual value of £16 000? Or (Assumption C) a six-year useful life with a residual value of £6 000?

For each of these two alternative estimates, you are asked to calculate and write down (in the spaces provided on the right, opposite) for each year of the vans' life, figures for:

- the annual depreciation charge;
- the net profit, and
- the balance sheet net book value.

Please complete your entries before looking at the answers over the page. In each year assume that profit before depreciation is £40 000.

You may also wish to consider what happens if the ultimate sales proceeds on disposal of a fixed asset are not exactly the same as its residual net book value at the time of sale. This is a common event.

In effect we normally treat the difference (whether a profit or a loss) simply as an adjustment of the depreciation estimates. Overleaf we look at the accounting result if Furniture Removals actually sells its vans at the end of Year 4 for £18 000.

Assumption B

	£'000
Cost	£60
Estimated residual value	£16
Estimated life	4 years

Annual depreciation _____ =
(£'000)

Profit and loss account

	Depreciation expense £'000	Net profit £'000
Year 1		
Year 2		
Year 3		
Year 4		

Balance sheet

	Cost £'000	Accum. dep'n. £'000	Net book value £'000
Year 1	60		
Year 2			
Year 3			
Year 4			

Assumption C

	£'000
Cost	£60
Estimated residual value	£6
Estimated life	6 years

Annual depreciation _____ =
(£'000)

	Depreciation expense £'000	Net profit £'000
Year 1		
Year 2		
Year 3		
Year 4		
Year 5		
Year 6		

	Cost £'000	Accum. dep'n £'000	Net book value £'000
Year 1	60		
Year 2			
Year 3			
Year 4			
Year 5			
Year 6			

Furniture Removals Limited

Opposite (right) are figures (in £'000) based on the alternative assumptions (B and C) about asset lives and residual values; and assuming a profit of £40 000 before charging depreciation. The profit and loss account and the balance sheet figures are both different – even though the *same* assets in the same business are involved.

Assumption B

	£'000
Cost	£60
Estimated residual value	£16
Estimated life	4 years

Annual depreciation $\dfrac{60-16}{4} = 11$ (£'000)

	Depreciation expense £'000	Net profit £'000	Net book value* £'000
Year 1	11	29	49*
Year 2	11	29	38
Year 3	11	29	27
Year 4	11	29	16

Assumption C

	£'000
Cost	£60
Estimated residual value	£6
Estimated life	6 years

Annual depreciation $\dfrac{60-6}{6} = 9$ (£'000)

	Depreciation expense £'000	Net profit £'000	Net book value* £'000
Year 1	9	31	51*
Year 2	9	31	42
Year 3	9	31	33
Year 4	9	31	24
Year 5	9	31	15
Year 6	9	31	6

*Net book value = Cost less accumulated depreciation (end of year)

Disposal of assets at end of life

Had the vans in fact been sold for £18 000 at the end of Year 4, the entries opposite would have appeared in the profit and loss account in Year 4.

On Assumption B, there is a profit of £2 000 compared with the net book value of £16 000; while on Assumption C there is a loss of £6 000 compared with the net book value of £24 000 at the end of Year 4. But it all comes out in the wash: the total net amount (in £'000) charged over the vans' life in each case is £42 (cost £60 less proceeds £18).

You may care to enter below the result of selling the vans for £18 000 at the end of Year 4 under Assumption A: cost £60 000; residual value £10 000; estimated life: five years. (The answer is shown on the next page, right, foot.)

Year 4 £'000

Profit before depreciation

Less: Depreciation

(Profit)/loss on sale ⎯⎯⎯

⎯⎯⎯

Net profit for year ⎯⎯⎯

Assumption B

Year 4		£'000
Profit before depreciation		40
Less: Depreciation	11	
Profit on sale[b]	(2)	
		9
Net profit for year		31

b: Proceeds £18 less NBV £16

Whole life

4 x £11 per year	=	44
Less: Profit on sale	=	2
Total net charge		42

Assumption C

Year 4		£'000
Profit before depreciation		40
Less: Depreciation	9	
Loss on sale[c]	6	
		15
Net profit for year		25

c: NBV £24 less proceeds £18

Whole life

4 x £9 per year	=	36
Plus: Loss on sale	=	6
Total net charge		42

METHODS OF DEPRECIATION

We have seen that estimates of useful lives and residual values of fixed assets can affect depreciation. So can the choice of *method*. So far we have assumed an equal expense in each year of a fixed asset's life; but this is only one of a number of possible approaches.

Three common methods of providing for depreciation are:

(a) straight line
(b) usage (machine hour)
(c) declining balance.

Less common is (d) the annuity method.

(a) The straight line method

The 'straight line' method is the simplest of all and in the UK it is by far the commonest. It involves writing off an equal charge each year based on estimates of an asset's net cost (original cost less residual value) and useful life.

Furniture Removals Limited used this method (Assumption A):

$$\frac{60\,000 - 10\,000}{5} \quad \begin{aligned} &= £10\,000 \text{ a year depreciation} \\ &= 16.7 \text{ per cent of cost } (= \tfrac{1}{6}\text{th}). \end{aligned}$$

The figure opposite shows the 'straight line' of the falling net book value year by year, and the 'straight line' annual charge. Using the straight line basis, annual depreciation can always be expressed as a constant percentage of original cost. (If there is any residual value, this is *not* the same as $\frac{1}{n} \times$ cost, where n is the useful life.)

(b) Usage (machine hour) method

Under the usage method, depreciation for a period is based on usage (for instance, the total number of hours a machine works).

Example

A company purchased a special processing machine for £55 000. The technical director thought the machine would last for 12 000 hours before it would be worn out, with £7 000 residual value. The company will charge the net cost of £48 000 over the total expected life of 12 000 hours, to give a rate of £4 per hour. Thus depreciation expense will *vary* with production volume: it will not be a fixed 'period' cost. If the company uses the machine for 2 000 hours in the first year and for 3 500 hours in the second, depreciation charges will be £8 000 in Year 1 and £14 000 in Year 2. (A similar approach, based on mileage, can be used for cars; or, based on ore aggregates, for mineral extraction.)

The straight line method

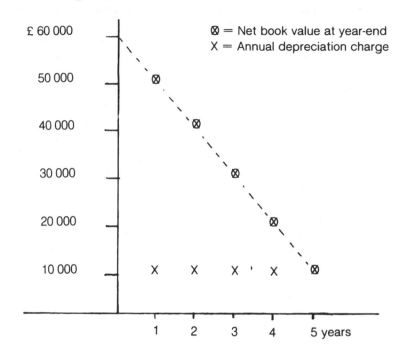

⊗ = Net book value at year-end
X = Annual depreciation charge

	Depreciation expense	Accumulated depreciation	Net book value
	£	£	£
Year 1	1/6 x £60 000 = 10 000	10 000	50 000
Year 2	1/6 x £60 000 = 10 000	20 000	40 000
Year 3	1/6 x £60 000 = 10 000	30 000	30 000
Year 4	1/6 x £60 000 = 10 000	40 000	20 000*
Year 5	1/6 x £60 000 = 10 000	50 000	10 000

* hence sale for £18 000 EOY 4 results in a loss on disposal of £2 000.

(c) The declining balance method

The 'declining balance' ('accelerated') method charges more depreciation in an asset's earlier years than in later years. The annual charge is found by applying a constant percentage to the asset's (declining) net book value each year. This aims – like all the methods – to reduce the asset's net book value to its residual value by the end of its useful life.

The straight line percentage applies to *original* cost, so the declining balance method needs about twice as high a percentage rate to write an asset's cost off in the same time. Clearly the declining balance method will *never* reduce an asset's net book value to zero; but when the net book value gets small enough, it can be entirely written off in a single year.

What if Furniture Removals Limited had used the declining balance method? The required percentage rate to reduce the vans' net book value to their expected residual value of £10 000 at the end of Year 5 would have been about 30 per cent. (The precise formula is shown on page 299.)

The figure opposite shows the net book value and annual depreciation charge year by year. Notice how quickly the asset's net book value falls, and how much the annual charge itself declines after the first year or two.

Another method of accelerated depreciation, called the 'sum of the years' digits' (SYD), is common in the US but rare in the UK. The SYD system calculates the annual charge for an asset with a five-year life by applying the following fractions in succeeding years to the asset's original cost (less residual value): 5/15, 4/15, 3/15, 2/15, and 1/15. The figure 15 used as the denominator is the 'sum of the years' digits'.

(d) The annuity method

The methods which we have looked at so far make no allowance for the return earned by depreciation provisions retained in the business. The (rarely used) annuity method does allow for this. The depreciation charges still equal the asset's total net cost over its useful life, but there is a *lower* charge in the early years (the opposite of accelerated depreciation).

The annuity method does not (as other methods do) tend to show an *increasing* rate of return on investment over an asset's life. It may be suitable where the asset's life is certain and there will be no additions during its life (for example, the lease of an office building).

Annuity depreciation for Furniture Removals Limited's vans, using an interest rate of 10 per cent a year, would be as shown at the foot of the next page. (The formula for calculating it is set out on page 301.)

The declining balance method

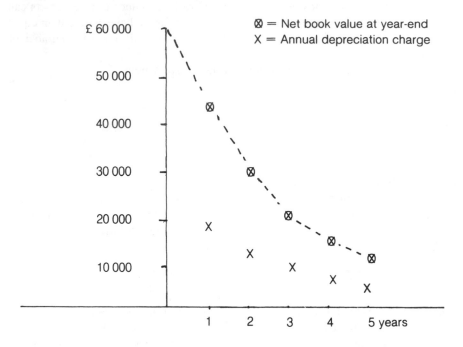

	Depreciation expense	Accumulated depreciation	Net book value
	£	£	£
Year 1	30% x £60 000 = 18 000	18 000	42 000
Year 2	30% x £42 000 = 12 600	30 600	29 400
Year 3	30% x £29 400 = 8 820	39 420	20 580
Year 4	30% x £20 580 = 6 174	45 594	14 406
Year 5	30% x £14 406 = 4 322	49 916	10 084

VARYING DEPRECIATION CHARGES

All depreciation methods aim to write off the same total amount over an asset's useful life, but the pattern of spreading the net cost between years is different.

We have said enough about different methods of depreciation to suggest that great care may be needed in trying to compare the results of two companies. We can emphasize the force of this warning by working through an example with large differences.

Let us take a case where possible technical changes affect the estimates of a fixed asset's likely useful life. While engineers can often forecast physical wear and tear fairly closely, the effects of technical or market obsolescence are much harder to foresee. Depreciation depends on an asset's *economically* useful life, not just its physical life in working order.

Example

Let us assume that two companies, Brown Limited and Green Limited, are in the same type of business, and that they are both making regular profits of £200 000 a year before depreciation. (Ignore tax to simplify the example.) Let us further assume that they both acquire identical machines for use in production, at a cost of £100 000 each.

Brown's technical director regards the machine as being of a standard design. He thinks it will continue in use for at least five years, after which time it should be possible to sell it for about £25 000. The company accepts his estimates, and uses straight line depreciation as usual.

Green's technical director, on the other hand, believes that the machine could soon be replaced by more sophisticated equipment. He proposes that the company should write it off over three years, allowing for a residual value of only £12 500; and use a 50 per cent rate of declining balance depreciation.

Please show the results of applying these technical and commercial judgements in the accounts of Brown Limited and Green Limited. There is space opposite for you to *write in* your answers.

Annuity depreciation for Furniture Removals Limited's vans

	Annual depreciation £	Cumulative depreciation £	10 per cent thereon £	'Net' charge £
Year 1	8 190*	8 190	–	8 190
Year 2	9 009	17 199	819	8 190
Year 3	9 910	27 109	1 720	8 190
Year 4	10 901	38 010	2 711	8 190
Year 5	11 990	50 000	3 800	8 190
	50 000		9 050	40 950

*1 per year compounds @ 10% p.a. to 6.105 in five years; and £50 000/ 6.105 = £8 190.

BROWN LIMITED

Cost of machine:	£100 000
Estimated life:	5 years
Residual value:	£25 000
Depreciation method:	Straight line

	Profit before depreciation £'000	Annual depreciation £'000	Net profit £'000	Accumulated depreciation £'000	Net book value £'000
Year 1	200				
Year 2	200				
Year 3	200				
Year 4	200				
Year 5	200				

GREEN LIMITED

Cost of machine:	£100 000
Estimated life:	3 years
Residual value:	£12 500
Depreciation method:	Declining balance

(Percentage to reduce net book value to £12 500 in 3 years = 50 per cent.)

	Profit before depreciation £'000	Annual depreciation £'000	Net profit £'000	Accumulated depreciation £'000	Net book value £'000
Year 1	200				
Year 2	200				
Year 3	200				

Please now compare your answers with those shown on the next page.

Varying depreciation changes: Answer

This example illustrates the impact of opinion on reported results, for the widely different figures for the two companies represent the same physical facts. When the two companies chose their depreciation methods there was no way to tell which would produce the more 'correct' answer.

If Brown's judgement proved to be correct, then the net book values in Green's accounts in Years 1 to 3 are too low, as are the profits in Years 1 and 2. But if Green's anticipation of swift obsolescence proved true, then Brown would have shown profit figures which were too high in Years 1 to 3. At the end of Year 3, the machine's net book value of £55 000 would be £42 500 higher than the residual value at that time; and Brown would have to write the difference off as an expense in Year 3.

Revising initial estimates

At the beginning of the life of a fixed asset, both its economic life and its ultimate residual value can only be an estimate. Hence there are bound to be errors in the light of events. One way to deal with such errors is simply to record a profit or loss on disposal at the end of the asset's useful life. In effect this represents an adjustment of prior year depreciation charges.

Insignificant differences – small profits or losses on disposal – are usually absorbed in the figure shown for depreciation expense. Substantial profits or losses on disposal, however, may require separate disclosure in the year of sale. Significant regular profits (or regular losses) on disposals of fixed assets may indicate a definite tendency to provide too much (or too little) for depreciation.

It is good practice regularly to revise the original estimates of fixed asset lives (and/or residual values). Imperial Chemical Industries plc's annual report, for example, includes the following statement about accounting policy on depreciation:

'The Group's policy is to write off the book value of each tangible fixed asset evenly over its estimated remaining life. Reviews are made periodically of the estimated remaining lives of individual productive assets, taking account of commercial and technological obsolescence as well as normal wear and tear.'

Where there is a revision of a fixed asset's estimated useful life, the remaining net book value (less any estimated residual value) should normally be expensed over the revised remaining useful life. But if the original estimate of an asset's life was too *short*, a company may find it has completely written off the cost of some fixed assets which continue in productive use. Even though the *net* book value is zero, the original cost is *still included* in the gross total cost of fixed assets and in the accumulated depreciation total. Cost and accumulated depreciation are 'written out' (eliminated) from the books only when a company actually disposes of a fully written-off fixed asset or retires it from active use.

BROWN LIMITED

Cost of machine:	£100 000	
Estimated life:	5 years	
Residual value:	£25 000	
Depreciation method:	Straight line $\dfrac{100-25}{5}=15$	

	Profit before depreciation £'000	Annual depreciation £'000	Net profit £'000	Accumulated depreciation £'000	Net book value £'000
Year 1	200	15	185	15	85
Year 2	200	15	185	30	70
Year 3	200	15	185	45	55
Year 4	200	15	185	60	40
Year 5	200	15	185	75	25

GREEN LIMITED

Cost of machine:	£100 000
Estimated life:	3 years
Residual value:	£12 500
Depreciation method:	Declining balance

(Percentage to reduce net book value to £12 500 in 3 years = 50 per cent.)

	Profit before depreciation £'000	Annual depreciation £'000	Net profit £'000	Accumulated depreciation £'000	Net book value £'000
Year 1	200	50	150	50	50
Year 2	200	25	175	75	25
Year 3	200	12.5	187.5	87.5	12.5

LEASING FIXED ASSETS

Leasing is a way for a lessee to enjoy the use of assets without owning them. In an operating lease the lessee simply charges the lease rentals as an expense in the profit and loss account. No fixed asset appears in the lessee's balance sheet. In an operating lease the lessor (owner) retains most of the risks and rewards of ownership, which a finance lease transfers to the lessee (user).

Under a finance lease, the lessee *controls* the use of an asset without legally *owning* it. Accounting standards [SSAP 21/IAS 17] require reporting according to 'economic substance' rather than 'legal form'. Thus lessees must capitalize finance leases and show them as fixed assets on the balance sheet. The discounted value of the total unpaid finance lease rentals appears as a creditor. The result is much the same as if the lessee had borrowed to purchase the asset outright.

	Operating lease	*Finance lease*
Period	May be very short; far less than the asset's useful life	Nearly all the asset's useful life
Payments	May be very small	The asset's full cost plus interest on the finance provided by the lessor
Commitment	Cancellable	Non-cancellable
Repairs	Done by lessor (owner)	Responsibility of lessee

Most of the annual finance lease rental charge reduces the balance sheet liability, being an instalment of the 'purchase price'. The remainder of the rental charge represents 'interest' expense on the unpaid instalments. Over time, the annual depreciation expense on the fixed asset reduces its net book value in the usual way.

Capitalizing finance leases may have a fairly small effect on profit, since depreciation and interest together may not differ much from the rental charge. But including both a fixed asset and a creditor will affect the balance sheet: it will reduce the apparent rate of return on net assets, and increase the debt ratio (see Section 10). An example appears opposite.

	Operating lease £'000	Finance lease £'000
Balance sheet summary		
Leased assets	–	40
Other fixed assets	100	100
Net current assets	60	60
	160	200
Less: Borrowing	50	90
Shareholders' funds	110	110
Profit and loss account summary		
Depreciation expense	10	14
Lease rental expense	8	–
Profit before interest and tax	32	36
Interest payable	5	9
Profit before tax	27	27
Ratios		
Return on net assets	20.0%	18.0%
Debt ratio	31.3%	45.0%
Interest cover	6.4	4.0

139

REVALUING FIXED ASSETS

The UK differs in one important respect from other countries such as the US, Germany and Japan. The Companies Act 1985 permits UK companies to show tangible fixed assets at more than historical cost. Companies may continue to use cost (less amounts written off), but they may choose to substitute either 'current cost' (see Section 13) or market value instead. (Fixed asset investments may be shown either at market value or at directors' valuation.)

One reason for allowing companies to depart from historical money cost may be the high UK rates of inflation over the past thirty years (see Section 13 and Appendix 4). In any event, some UK companies do revalue certain fixed assets upwards, especially land and buildings, often with a significant effect on the balance sheet. The result is to increase the book value both of net assets and of shareholders' funds. Hence revaluation reduces the reported percentages for (a) return on net assets, (b) return on equity, and (c) debt ratio; and reduces the ratios for net asset turnover and fixed asset turnover.

FRS 15/IAS 16 requires companies to base depreciation on any revalued amount, rather than on cost. But there is often little impact on the profit and loss account. The effect is usually small in respect of buildings, because of their long life. And few UK companies revalue plant and equipment, which might significantly increase depreciation expense and hence reduce reported profit. (But there is *no* impact on tax: see Section 10.)

The current position is that some UK companies continue to use historical cost only, but others have revalued some of their fixed assets at some time in the past. FRS 15/IAS 16 requires companies whose policy is to revalue some fixed assets, to apply the policy to all tangible fixed assets within a class, and to do a full valuation at least every five years. The result is that comparing the accounts of UK companies can be extremely difficult, and even comparisons over time may not be easy.

SECTION 7 SUMMARY

Companies use fixed assets on an ongoing basis in their business, not meaning to resell them. Whether an asset is 'fixed' or 'current' depends on intentions not physical attributes.

The cost of fixed assets includes related legal, installation and other costs, and may include interest on finance during construction.

The three main kinds of fixed assets are intangible, tangible and investments. The section mainly deals with tangible fixed assets.

Once a firm has determined the cost of a tangible fixed asset, there are three main problems in computing the annual depreciation expense:

1 Estimating the fixed asset's useful life. This may depend on the passing of time, wear and tear, or technical or market obsolescence.
2 Estimating residual value (in practice often ignored if small).
3 Choosing a depreciation method, the main ones being (a) straight line, (b) usage, and (c) declining balance.

Depreciation allocates original cost (less ultimate resale value) against profit, in aiming to match expense against related revenue. It is *not* a process of 'valuation' year by year.

Straight line depreciation is the most common in the UK. It writes off a constant percentage of cost each year; while the declining balance method writes off a constant (higher) percentage of the (declining) net book value at the start of each year.

Different methods all write off the same total amount over a fixed asset's life (namely, original cost less ultimate proceeds); but the pattern differs between accounting periods. This affects both reported profits over time and net assets from year to year.

Because the future is uncertain, there are bound to be errors in guessing in advance (a) the useful life and (b) the ultimate resale value of fixed assets. On disposal of a fixed asset, any profit or loss on disposal usually represents, in effect, an adjustment to prior years' depreciation charges.

Lessees (users) must capitalize finance leases which transfer most of the risks and rewards of ownership; and then depreciate the fixed asset in the usual way. The 'balancing' long-term creditor is the discounted liability to pay future rentals.

Many UK companies revalue their land and buildings from time to time (but not normally plant and equipment). The result can affect a number of performance and other financial ratios, and thus make it hard to compare different companies. (It does not, however, affect tax.)

PROBLEMS

7.1 Definitions

Write down your definitions of each of the terms shown. Then compare your answers with those given overleaf.

(a) A tangible fixed asset

(b) Depreciation

(c) Net book value

(d) Residual value

(e) Accelerated depreciation

(f) A finance lease

(g) Revaluation

(h) An 'improvement'

(i) The useful life

(j) Profit (or loss) on sale

7.1 Definitions

(a) **A tangible fixed asset** is a resource acquired at a definite cost, with a useful life spanning more than one year, which an enterprise intends to use in producing goods or services for sale, not to resell in the normal course of business.

(b) **Depreciation** allocates part of the cost (or valuation) of tangible fixed assets to expense in an accounting period, on a systematic basis. (For *intangible* fixed assets it's called 'amortization'.) *Accumulated* depreciation is the total amount provided on fixed assets a company still owns.

(c) **Net book value** (NBV) is the difference between a fixed asset's cost (or valuation) and the accumulated depreciation thereon. It does not normally represent current (realizable) market value, except at the end of a fixed asset's life.

(d) **Residual value** is the amount an enterprise reckons in advance it can sell a tangible fixed asset for at the end of its useful life. Thus depreciation aims to write off its 'net cost' over an asset's life, that is its original cost less its expected residual value (which, for simplicity, is often assumed to be zero).

(e) **Accelerated depreciation** is any method which charges higher amounts in the early year's of a fixed asset's life than in the later years (though the total charge over the whole life is the same under any method). One such method is 'declining balance', which writes off a constant percentage of a fixed asset's declining net book value, while 'sum-of-the-years'-digits' (SYD) is another.

(f) **A finance lease** is a non-cancellable commitment, lasting for most of an asset's useful life, which transfers to the lessee nearly all the risks and rewards of ownership. IAS 17/SSAP 21 requires companies to capitalize finance leases, which means including them as fixed assets together with a long-term liability representing the discounted total of future lease payments. (This contrasts with the treatment of 'operating leases'.)

(g) **Revaluation** of tangible fixed assets is the process of increasing their net book value (and therefore any subsequent depreciation charge). The increase goes to shareholders' funds. Revaluation affects many important financial ratios and makes it difficult to compare the accounts of UK companies with each other.

(h) **An 'improvement'** to a fixed asset 'improves' on an asset's original condition, not merely restores it. An enterprise capitalizes the cost, and then depreciates it over time. For example, 'improvements' might increase an asset's capacity, lengthen its useful life, reduce its running costs, or improve the quality of its output.

(i) **The useful life** of a fixed asset is the period during which the enterprise intends to use it. This need not mean the asset is literally 'useless' at the end of its 'useful life' – as someone else may be happy to buy it second-hand and use it for many more years. Thus two companies might well attribute very different useful lives to identical fixed assets, if their intentions as to use were different.

(j) **Profit (or loss) on sale** of a fixed asset is the surplus (or deficit) of sales proceeds over net book value at the end of a fixed asset's life. It represents an adjustment to total depreciation and reflects the 'error' made in advance in estimating the asset's ultimate sales proceeds. It thus reminds us that depreciation is nearly always only an approximation.

It may be most convenient for you to work in £'000.

7.2 Jonas Limited (A): Straight line depreciation

Jonas Limited buys a fixed asset for £84 000, expects it to last for six years (after which it will have no value) and proposes to write off depreciation on the straight line basis. Calculate the depreciation charge each year, and the net book value at the end of each year.

The solution to this problem is given overleaf.

Space for answer

		£'000
	Cost	
Year 1	Depreciation	
		____
	Net book value, end of year 1	
Year 2	Depreciation	
		____
	Net book value, end of year 2	
Year 3	Depreciation	
		____
	Net book value, end of year 3	
Year 4	Depreciation	
		____
	Net book value, end of year 4	
Year 5	Depreciation	
		____
	Net book value, end of year 5	
Year 6	Depreciation	
		____
	Net book value, end of year 6	

7.3 Potter Press Limited: Changing from straight line to declining balance

Potter Press Limited is considering changing from the straight line method of depreciation to the declining balance method. Neither residual values nor estimated asset lives would change, but the percentage depreciation rate would be doubled. Assuming that Potter Press expects to replace its existing fixed assets fairly regularly over a ten-year cycle without marked fluctuations from year to year, how would you expect such a change to affect the company's accounts?

Please write out your answer on a separate sheet of paper.

A solution to this problem is given overleaf.

7.4 Lawson Limited (A): Profit or loss on disposal

Lawson Limited paid £72 000 for a fixed asset which is expected to last for six years. It is to be written off on the straight line basis, assuming ultimate salvage proceeds of £6 000.

Calculate the depreciation charged each year, and the profit or loss on disposal, if the asset is actually sold for:

(a) £35 000 at the end of year 4
(b) £14 000 at the end of year 5
(c) How would the asset be shown in the balance sheet at the end of year 3?

The solution to this problem is given overleaf.

Space for answer

		(a) £'000	(b) £'000
	Cost		
Year 1	Depreciation	____	____
	Net book value, end of year 1		
Year 2	Depreciation	____	____
	Net book value, end of year 2		
Year 3	Depreciation	____	____
	Net book value, end of year 3		
Year 4	Depreciation	____	____
	Net book value, end of year 4		
Year 5			

(a) profit/loss on disposal, year 4

(b) profit/loss on disposal, year 5

(c) end of year 3 balance sheet

7.2 Jonas Limited (A)

Solution

		£'000
	Cost	84
Year 1	Depreciation	14
	Net book value, end of year 1	70
Year 2	Depreciation	14
	Net book value, end of year 2	56
Year 3	Depreciation	14
	Net book value, end of year 3	42
Year 4	Depreciation	14
	Net book value, end of year 4	28
Year 5	Depreciation	14
	Net book value, end of year 5	14
Year 6	Depreciation	14
	Net book value, end of year 6	–

7.3 Potter Press Limited

Solution

In the first few years after the change, depreciation expense would be higher under the declining balance method and reported profit therefore lower. After about ten years the new total annual depreciation charge should be about the same under both methods; but the extra declining balance depreciation charged in years 1 to 10 after the change will result in higher accumulated depreciation (and therefore lower fixed asset net book values) than under the straight line method.

The immediate effect of the change will be to reduce reported profits and return on investment; but the ultimate effect will be to reduce reported capital employed without affecting profit (much), and thus to *increase* reported return on investment. (It is assumed here that the total cost of fixed assets remains more or less constant over time.) These will have no impact on tax.

7.4 Lawson Limited (A)

Solution

		(a) £'000	(b) £'000
	Cost	72	72
Year 1	Depreciation	11	11
	Net book value, end of year 1	61	61
Year 2	Depreciation	11	11
	Net book value, end of year 2	50	50
Year 3	Depreciation	11	11
	Net book value, end of year 3	39	39
Year 4	Depreciation	11	11
	Net book value, end of year 4	28	28
	Sale proceeds	35	
	Profit on sale	7	
Year 5	Depreciation		11
	Net book value, end of year 5		17
	Sale proceeds		14
	Loss on sale		3

(a) Profit on disposal = £7 000
(b) Loss on disposal = £3 000
(c) End of year 3 balance sheet:

	£'000
Fixed asset at cost	72
Less: Accumulated depreciation	33
Net book value	39

Notes (in £'000)
1 Where a residual value is taken into account in calculating depreciation the straight line method does *not* charge simply one sixth of cost each year (1/6 x £72 = £12). Instead the charge is one sixth of the expected *net* cost (1/6 x £66 = £11).
2 In both case (a) and case (b) the total amount written off over the life of the asset is its total net cost (original cost less residual value):
   (a) £72 – £35 = £37 = (4 x £11) – £7 profit
   (b) £72 – £14 = £58 = (5 x £11) + £3 loss

7.5 Jonas Limited (B): Different lives

Jonas Limited buys a fixed asset for £84 000, expects it to last for six years, and proposes to write off depreciation on the straight line basis. (See 7.2 Jonas Limited (A).)

(a)   What happens if the asset is sold for £20 000 after only four years?
(b)   What happens if the asset lasts for eight years?

Please write your answers in the space below, trying to cover all the important accounting issues involved.

A solution to this problem is given overleaf.

(a)

(b)

Solutions to the next four problems are given overleaf.

7.6 Lawson Limited (B): Early disposal

Lawson Limited paid £72 000 for a fixed asset which is expected to last for six years. It is to be written off on the straight line basis, assuming ultimate salvage proceeds of £6 000 (see 7.4 Lawson Limited (A)).

The asset is actually sold for £35 000 at the end of year 4 (as in part (a) of Lawson Limited (A)).

Please set out the Disposal of fixed assets account (in £'000).

7.7 Whizzo Buses Limited: Usage method

Whizzo Buses Limited decides to depreciate its buses on the basis of miles travelled. A particular vehicle costs £100 000; its residual value is expected to be £20 000; and its expected mileage during its life with Whizzo is expected to be 420 000 miles

How much depreciation should be charged in the first three years of its life if it travels 24 000 miles, 42 000 miles, and 30 000 miles in years 1, 2, and 3 respectively? How will the vehicle be shown in the end of Year 2 balance sheet?

7.8 Dingle Brothers: Government grant

Dingle Brothers installed equipment costing £60 000 in a development zone. The equipment is expected to last six years, and to have no residual value. It is to be written off by the straight line method. Dingle Brothers receive a government grant of £24 000 which they credit to a deferred income account.

What items will appear in the profit and loss account each year in respect of the equipment? What will the balance sheet at the end of year 2 show? What would the end of Year 2 balance sheet show if the government grants were deducted from the cost of the fixed asset?

7.9 Caxton Trains plc: Book versus tax depreciation

Caxton Trains plc acquires a new fixed asset for £1 million. For book purposes it assumes zero residual value, a ten-year life, and uses the straight line method. For tax purposes the same asset is liable to a 'writing-down allowance' (= tax depreciation) calculated at 25 per cent on the declining net balance each year.

(a)   At the end of five years, which will be larger: the net book value or the tax written-down value?
(b)   What will the difference be, to the nearest £ thousand?

7.5 Jonas Limited (B)

Solution (in £'000)

(a) At the end of the fourth year, the £8 difference between the £28 net book value and the £20 sales proceeds will have to be written off as a loss on disposal. This will be treated as an expense in the profit and loss account in year 4, in addition to the normal annual depreciation of £14 in year 4.

Thus over the four-year life of the asset the total amount written off will be:

	£'000
Depreciation = 4 x £14 =	56
Loss on sale =	8
	64

Notice that the £64 total amount written off over the asset's life is exactly equal to the original £84 cost less the £20 sale proceeds.

(b) No depreciation will be charged in years 7 and 8, since the asset has already been completely written off by the end of year 6. Any sales proceeds at the end of year 8 will be treated as a profit on sale.

In the balance sheet at the end of years 6 and 7 the asset will appear as follows:

	£'000
Fixed asset at cost	84
Less: Accumulated depreciation	84
Net book value	–

At the end of year 8, when the asset is taken out of use (and perhaps disposed of) both Cost of fixed assets and Accumulated depreciation will be reduced by £84.

7.6 Lawson Limited (B)

Solution

Disposal of fixed assets

	Dr £'000		Cr £'000
Cost	72	Accumulated depreciation	44
P & L profit on sale	7	Cash received	35
	79		79

7.7 Whizzo Buses Limited

Solution

Depreciation will be charged at £1 per 3 miles (= $\frac{£160\,000 - £20\,000}{420\,000}$). Hence in the first three years depreciation based on usage will be £8 000, £14 000 and £10 000 respectively.

End of year 2 balance sheet:

	£'000
Cost	100
Less: Accumulated depreciation	22
Net book value	78

7.8 Dingle Brothers

Solution (in £'000)

Depreciation charges will amount to £60/6 = £10 a year; but this will be reduced by a credit to the profit and loss account each year of £24/6 = £4 a year. Thus the *net* charge will amount to £6 a year (= (£60 – £24)/6).

At the end of year 2 the balance sheet will show:

		£'000
Fixed asset.	Equipment at cost	60
	Less: Accumulated depreciation	20
	Net book value	40
Deferred income.	Government grant	24
	Less: Credited to profit	8
	Balance	16

If the government grant were deducted from the cost of the fixed asset, the end of Year 2 balance sheet would show:

		£'000
Fixed asset.	Equipment at (net) cost	36
	Less: Accumulated depreciation	12
	Net book value	24

7.9 Caxton Trains plc

(a) The net book value (£500 000) will be larger.
(b) £263 000 (see page 193 in Section 10).

Answers to the following eight problems are given at the end of the book.

7.10 Jonas Limited (C): Changes in net cost

Jonas Limited buys a fixed asset for £84 000, expects it to last for six years, and plans to write off depreciation on the straight line basis. (See 7.2 Jonas Limited (A).)

(a) What difference would it make to the annual depreciation charges and net book values if Jonas Limited wanted to allow for salvage proceeds of £6 000 at the end of year 6 (instead of the original estimate of zero)?

(b) How would you take into account an improvement costing £12 000 at the start of year 4, which is not expected to affect the asset's life or residual value? What would the asset's net book value be at the end of years 4, 5, and 6?

7.11 James Hillier Limited (A): Declining balance

James Hillier Limited buys a fixed asset for £8 000, and expects salvage proceeds of £750 at the end of its anticipated four-year life. The asset is to be written off by the declining balance method, using a 50 per cent rate.

(a) Calculate the depreciation charge and the net book value each year. What profit or loss is expected on disposal?

(b) If expected salvage proceeds at the end of year 4 were £1 300, what declining balance percentage depreciation rate would be appropriate?

7.12 James Hillier Limited (B): Declining balance disposal

The asset (in 7.11(a) James Hillier (A)) actually lasts for six years, at the end of which time it is sold for £600.

(a) Starting with the net book value at the end of year 4 (calculated in James Hillier (A)(a)), complete the depreciation schedule.

(b) Compile journal entries relating to the disposal of the fixed asset in year 6.

(c) Draw up ledger accounts relating to the fixed asset for year 6, starting with the balances brought forward from the end of year 5.

7.13 Gilbert Limited and Sullivan Limited: Different depreciation

Gilbert Limited and Sullivan Limited are identical companies except for their depreciation policies. In respect of a fixed asset costing £72 000, Gilbert estimates a useful life of ten years, a salvage value of £12 000, and proposes to use the straight line method of depreciation. Sullivan estimates a life of six years, no salvage value, and proposes to use one-third as the annual proportion of the declining net book value to be written off each year.

The asset becomes technically obsolete at the end of year 4, and has to be scrapped with salvage proceeds of only £2 000. Calculate for each of the two companies the depreciation charge each year, the net book value at the end of each year, and the profit or loss on disposal.

7.14 Nick Saint plc

Nick Saint plc's group tangible fixed assets at 30 September 2004 were shown as follows in the notes to the accounts:

	Land and buildings £m	Plant and equipment £m
Cost or valuation		
At 1 October 2003	320	785
Additions	39	109
(Disposals)	(3)	(32)
Adjustments for revaluations	4	4
At 30 September 2004	360	866
Depreciation		
At 1 October 2003	32	367
Provided in the year	8	75
(Disposals)	–	(27)
At 30 September 2004	40	415
Net book values		
At 1 October 2003	*288*	*418*
At 30 September 2004	320	451

Questions

1 What was the total net book value of disposals in the year ended 30 September 2004? If the proceeds from disposals were £9m in total, how would the difference be accounted for?

2 If plant and equipment is depreciated on the straight line basis, what is the average useful life implied by the table above? What assumptions have you made?

3 Incorporate the following transactions occurring during the year ended 30 September 2005 in preparing a table of fixed asset details (similar to the one above) as at the end of that year:

(a) Additions: land and buildings £28m; plant and equipment £84m

(b) Disposals: plant and equipment £5m net book value (£21m accumulated depreciation), proceeds £8m

(c) Depreciation average life (straight line): land and buildings 50 years; plant and equipment 12 years.

7.15 Talmen Limited (A): Reduced economic life estimate

Talmen Limited spent £300 000 on 1 January 2000 on machine A, which was expected to last for ten years and to have a residual value of £60 000 on 31 December 2009. Accordingly, for the first three years of its life straight line depreciation of £24 000 per annum was charged.

On 31 December 2002 a routine review reckons the remaining life is now only four years, and the residual value on 31 December 2006 will be only £20 000. What, if anything, should the company do to account for the revised estimate?

7.16 Talmen Limited (B): Increased economic life estimate

On 1 January 2000 Talmen Limited spent £300 000 on machine B, which was expected to last for ten years and to have a residual value of £60 000 on 31 December 2009. As for machine A, therefore, £24 000 a year straight line depreciation was charged for the first three years.

A routine review on 31 December 2002 reckons that machine B still has a remaining life of ten years; and that its residual value on 31 December 2012 will be £100 000. What, if anything, should the company do to account for the revised estimate?

7.17 Annuity depreciation

A company decides to use annuity depreciation for an item of equipment costing £12 000 with a five-year life and zero residual value. The interest rate to be used is 8 per cent a year. What will the depreciation charge be for each of the five years?

No answers are given for the following problems.

7.18 Revaluing plant

Assuming that everything else stayed the same, what would be the effect on a company's return on capital employed of:

(a) revaluing land upwards
(b) revaluing plant and equipment upwards
(c) increasing the estimated remaining lives of fixed assets.

7.19 Negative depreciation?

Greenhouse Monstrosities Limited owns and leases out office buildings in the City of London. As a rule it expects its buildings to last for 50 years; and regards straight line depreciation as less inappropriate than any other method. But since it anticipates that the market value of its buildings will increase over each of the next several years, the company is wondering whether it is really sensible to provide for any depreciation at all in its published historical cost accounts. What should it do, and why?

7.20 Raphael Machines Limited: New fixed assets

Soon after the end of the year to 31 March 2005, Mr Gabriel, an accountant working for Raphael Machines Limited, was preparing the company's final accounts for the year just ended. Among many fixed asset transactions for the year were:

(a) New equipment was installed during the year. The invoice cost had been £250 000, although only £245 000 cash had actually been paid to the suppliers since a 2 per cent cash discount for payment within 15 days had been taken.
(b) In addition to the invoice cost, £9 000 had been paid to have the equipment transported to the factory; and a further £14 000 to have it installed in working order. During its first week of operation, abnormal material scrap amounting to £12 000 was incurred while the new equipment was adjusted to perfect running order.
(c) The firm exchanged one of its used motor vehicles for a new van during the year. The book value of the old vehicle was £4 800 (cost £15 200 less accumulated depreciation £10 400); and the list price of the new van was £20 800. The garage concerned offered a trade-in price of £7 200 for the old van, which it was reckoned could have been sold for £6 000 cash.

Mr Gabriel was not sure how the above transactions should be treated in the accounts. You are required to advise him of the most appropriate treatment in each case, identifying the main alternatives and explaining the reason for your recommendation for each of the items.

7.21 Maintaining improvement

Which of the following items would you capitalize (and depreciate over time), and which would you write off as expenses in the current period? Why?

(a) cost of moving equipment from one factory in the group to another, and installing it
(b) special overhaul costs to bring existing equipment up to recently enacted government safety standards
(c) cost of acquiring newly offered range of accessories for the firm's 400 word processors
(d) raw material wastage due to inevitable 'teething problems' of new equipment
(e) replacement of worn-out principal component of a cutting machine with a modern improved version which costs *less* than the original component did.

Section 8
Capital structure

CAPITAL EMPLOYED

In our approach to company accounts, when looking at *uses* of funds, we have defined 'net assets' (= 'capital employed') as total assets less current liabilities. That is the same as fixed assets plus net working capital (= fixed assets plus current assets less current liabilities.) But there is one important refinement: we 'add back' short-term borrowing. So in effect we treat short-term borrowing as being part of 'capital employed'.

In this section we look more closely at *sources* of funds, at the items comprising 'capital employed':

1 Ordinary shareholders' funds (Equity)
2 Loans, both 'long-term' and 'short-term' (Debt)
3 Preference share capital
4 Provisions for liabilities and charges.

The proportion of debt and equity in the capital structure (the level of financial 'gearing') can vary over time and between companies, even in the same industry. The table below shows the main distinctions between 'debt' (negotiated interest-bearing borrowing) and 'equity' (ordinary share capital and reserves). The main differences relate to cost and risk. (Preference share capital, which is rarely significant, falls between the two.)

Differences between debt and equity

	Debt	Equity
Capital		
Period	Nearly always finite	'Permanent'
Amount	Fixed in money terms	Residual: varies
Priority on liquidation	Before equity	After all others
Income		
Amount	Usually fixed*	Varies
Commitment	Legal liability	Discretionary

*or varies according to an agreed formula

From a company's viewpoint debt capital is cheaper than equity. Interest is tax-deductible but debt is more *risky*, with legally binding commitments as to interest and repayment of capital. The 'cost' of equity capital to a company is really an 'opportunity cost': it is the return that shareholders could have earned in other equivalent-risk investments.

From the investors' viewpoint the reverse is true. To them, ordinary (equity) shares are more risky (and debt is *less* risky, hence requires a smaller risk premium), but the potential profits – either in dividends or in capital gains through increased market value – may be much higher. Any residual profits after tax (and after interest on loans) 'belong' to equity investors.

ORDINARY SHAREHOLDERS' FUNDS

Ordinary shares are shares in the ownership of a company which in total give ultimate rights of control over its affairs. Capital and reserves together ('shareholders' funds') constitute a company's 'equity' capital.

The table below shows details of Tarrant Limited's ordinary shareholders' funds of £10 million. We shall follow the balance sheet order in looking first at called up share capital and then at the various kinds of reserve.

It is important to note that 'reserves' in a balance sheet do *not* indicate money available for spending! Only cash represents that. Reserves merely explain (to some extent) how a company has managed to finance its assets.

TARRANT LIMITED
Capital and reserves

		£'000
Share capital		
(Authorized: £5 million)		
Called up: 16 million ordinary 25p shares		4 000
Reserves		
Share premium account	2 000	
Revaluation reserve	1 000	
Other reserves	500	
Profit and loss account	2 500	
		6 000
		10 000

Called up share capital

A company's articles specify how many shares it is 'authorized' to issue, and the type and nominal amount of each share.

Issued ('called up') ordinary shares represent 'permanent' capital, not normally redeemed during a company's existence. Individual shareholders who want to realize their investment must sell their shares to someone else. This will not directly affect the company itself unless it changes control.

The price which sellers can get for their shares (the market value) varies over time as conditions change. Investors who own the shares of 'listed' ('quoted') companies can trade them on a stock exchange. But the vast majority of companies are 'unlisted'. Their shares are privately owned, often by members of one or two families, and are much less easy to trade.

A successful company may pay high dividends, but when business conditions are poor, ordinary shareholders may get nothing at all. Dividends are payable only out of current or past profits. There is no certainty that a company will make profits and even if it does, there is no legal commitment to pay dividends. A company's directors may choose to retain all the profits in the business.

A company ends its existence by 'winding up'. The company turns all its assets into cash ('liquidates' them) and, if possible, pays all its creditors in full. After that, the shareholders receive anything that is left over.

A company's creditors can look only to the *company's* assets to settle amounts owing. The liability of shareholders is limited to the nominal (or 'par') value of their shares. (Hence the name: '(public) limited company'.) Once the shares are fully paid up, shareholders are not liable for any further payment, even if the company still owes money to creditors. By contrast, in a partnership every full partner bears unlimited personal liability for the firm's debts.

Share premium account

When a company issues ordinary shares for more than the nominal amount per share, the excess goes to the share premium account. In effect, share premiums are permanent capital, which may be used to 'capitalize' reserves in connection with 'bonus issues' (see below).

Revaluation reserve

If a company revalues tangible fixed assets upwards, the balance sheet states the fixed assets at the new higher amount and adds the surplus to shareholders' funds under 'revaluation reserve'. Of course, merely increasing the book value of some of its assets provides no *cash* flows into a company.

Clearly though, the resulting increases in equity and net assets will reduce the apparent 'return on investment' ratios. Revaluing *depreciable* fixed assets will also increase future depreciation expense in the profit and loss account.

A revaluation giving rise to a surplus is shown below. The directors of Land Holdings Limited had the company's leasehold property revalued on 31 December 2004 at £1.5 million, £0.5 million higher than its former book value.

LAND HOLDINGS LIMITED
Balance sheet at 31 December 2004

	Before revaluation £'000	After revaluation £'000
Fixed asset (leasehold property)	1 000[a]	1 500[b]
Net current assets	200	200
Total assets less current liabilities	1 200	1 700
less: **Loans**	(400)	(400)
	800	1 300
Capital and reserves		
Called up share capital	600	600
Revaluation reserve	–	500
Profit and loss account	200	200
	800	1 300

Notes

[a] = at cost
[b] = at valuation

Other reserves

These may include:

- a capital redemption reserve arising on redeeming preference shares (see below) or cancelling ordinary shares;
- amounts resulting from fluctuations in foreign currencies;
- a consolidation reserve or merger reserve (see Section 9).

Profit and loss account

Any profits for a period increase the cumulative balance on profit and loss account. This is the *link* between the profit and loss account for a period and the balance sheet (see page 4). If a company later pays out part of the profits to shareholders in dividends, that reduces the profit and loss account balance on the balance sheet.

ISSUES OF ORDINARY SHARES

A company can increase its ordinary share capital in a number of ways:

1   Issues on acquiring another company.
2   Rights issues for cash.
3   Bonus issues.

On acquisition

Star Trading plc's balance sheet is summarized below. There are no long-term creditors. The company's 3.5 million £1 ordinary shares have a current stock market price of 300p each. The directors decide to issue a further 1 million shares in order to acquire all the assets of another company, valued at £3 million.

STAR TRADING PLC
Balance sheet summary at 30 June 2004

	Before acquisition £'000	After acquisition £'000
Net assets	6 000	9 000
Capital and reserves		
Called up ordinary £1 share capital	3 500	4 500
Share premium account	–	2 000
Profit and loss account	2 500	2 500
Capital employed	6 000	9 000

The £3 million proceeds of the share issue represent:

1   £1 million increase in called up share capital (1 million new ordinary shares with a nominal value of £1 each);
2   £2 million share premium on the issue of 1 million £1 shares at a price of £3 each (that is, 1 million new shares x £2 premium per share).

Rights issues

Star Trading's 4.5 million £1 ordinary shares stand at £3 (300p) in the market. Suppose the company wants to raise £3.3 million more cash to expand its business. It can offer 1.5 million new shares to existing shareholders for 220p cash per share, by means of a '1 for 3 rights issue'. A holder of 300 £1 shares will then have the right to subscribe for 100 new shares at 220p each, paying £220 cash to the company.

Any shareholders who don't want to invest more cash can sell their rights* in the market. Because of this, in theory the *price* at which a rights issue is made makes no difference to shareholders. If any shareholders do nothing, the company will sell their rights in the market on their behalf. The *buyer* of those rights would then subscribe the required 220p per share to acquire the new shares.

The result of a rights issue is equivalent to a new issue of shares at the current market price, combined with a 'bonus issue' (see below) whose precise terms depend on the terms of the rights issue (see Problem 8.11). What happens to the market price of the shares after a rights issue depends on how profitably the company invests the new capital.

The balance sheet of Star Trading before and after the 1 for 3 rights issue appears below. (We assume that the company has retained profits of £0.7 million since 30 June 2004.) The *total* equity capital increases by the £3.3 million new cash raised. The issue of 1.5 million £1.00 shares at 220p each increases the share premium account by £1.8 million (= 1.5 million shares @ 120p premium each).

STAR TRADING PLC
Balance sheet summary at 31 March 2005

	Before rights issue £'000	After rights issue £'000
Net assets	9 700	13 000
Capital and reserves		
Called up ordinary £1 share capital	4 500	6 000
Share premium account	2 000	3 800
Profit and loss account	3 200	3 200
	9 700	13 000

*The 'rights' are worth 80p (300p – 220p) per *old share* held. Three shares (@ 300p) are worth £9.00 in total before the issue; so after a 1 for 3 rights issue @ 220p, *four* shares will be worth £11.20 (= £9.00 + £2.20). This works out at a market price per share *after* the rights issue of 280p per share.

Bonus issues

A bonus (or 'scrip') issue gives more shares (free) to shareholders. Star Trading has 6 million £1 shares in issue. To reduce the market price of 280p per share, the company can convert some of its reserves into called up share capital. If each shareholder gets (say) two bonus shares free for every three shares already held, Star Trading's balance will appear as shown below (centre column), with 10 million shares then in issue.

After the 2 for 3 bonus issue, the share price will fall to three-fifths of its former level. Someone who owned 3 shares @ 280p (= 840p) will now own 5 shares @ 168p. The *total* equity capital remains the same. The only 'real' change is that the £200 000 'capitalized' from the profit and loss account is no longer legally available to cover dividends. (The £3.8 million in the share premium account never was.)

STAR TRADING PLC
Balance sheet summary at 1 April 2005

	Before bonus issue £'000	After bonus issue £'000	After share split £'000
Net assets	13 000	13 000	13 000
Capital and reserves			
Called up ordinary share capital	6 000	10 000[a]	10 000[b]
Share premium account	3 800	–	–
Profit and loss account	3 200	3 000	3 000
	13 000	13 000	13 000

Notes
[a] = 10 million £1 shares
[b] = 40 million 25p shares

Share splits

Share splits aim, like bonus issues, to increase the number of shares in issue and to reduce the market price per share; but they do *not* involve capitalizing reserves. If Star Trading feels that the share price after the 2 for 3 bonus issue is still too high (at 168p), it might split each £1 share into four shares of 25p each (nominal). The total called up share capital will remain at £10 million (see right hand column above), but the number of shares in issue will quadruple, from 10 million £1 shares to 40 million 25p shares; and the market price per share will fall from 168p to 42p.

Notice that a '2 for 3' bonus issue (scrip issue) means two new shares *in addition to* every three old shares held, whereas a '4 for 1' share split means four new shares *in place of* every one old share. Neither raises any new cash, hence total 'capital and reserves' above stays the same throughout.

LOANS

A company that borrows money must pay regular interest on the loan and repay the debt outstanding on the due date. Failure to do either entitles the lender to take legal action to recover the amount owing. If a company goes into liquidation it must pay all debts in full before preference shareholders or ordinary shareholders get anything.

To seek greater protection, lenders may 'secure' their rights by a charge on some of the company's assets. In the event of winding-up, this will entitle them to recover their debt in full before trade and other 'unsecured' creditors can receive anything from the proceeds of sale of the charged assets.

Companies may borrow from banks, insurance companies or other financial institutions, and (for large companies) from the public via the Stock Exchange. For smaller companies, individual shareholders or directors may sometimes advance loans on suitable terms. In measuring a company's total debt, we suggest it is normally best to include both short-term and long-term negotiated interest-bearing loans.

Long-term loans may be for a period of up to fifteen years or more. The rate of interest may be a fixed percentage, or it may vary ('float') as interest rates change. Money interest rates will allow for expected future inflation, depending on the currency. The more risk lenders perceive in making a loan, the higher the interest rate they may require, or the more stringent the other conditions they may insist on.

Convertible loans

Holders of 'convertible' loans can choose to convert them, on pre-arranged terms, into ordinary shares. Otherwise when the option period is over, the conversion rights lapse.

Companies issuing convertible debt normally hope for ultimate conversion. In effect they intend to borrow for a few years against the 'proceeds' of a later equity issue. Prior to conversion, convertible debt combines the safety of debt with the profit potential of equity, but it is still 'debt', not (yet) equity.

Converting debt capital will reduce future interest payments and thus increase profit after tax. But it might add so many extra ordinary shares to those already outstanding that earnings per share would fall (as in the Highways example). Companies must [FRS 14/IAS 33] disclose earnings per share figures computed on *two* bases:

- number of ordinary shares currently in issue;
- potential total ordinary shares if all existing conversion options were exercised.

The example opposite computes the 'fully diluted' earnings per share of Highways Limited after the assumed conversion of £5 million 8 per cent convertible loan stock into 2 million ordinary shares at 250p per share on 31 March 2004.

HIGHWAYS LIMITED

Balance sheet at 31 March 2004	Before conversion £m	After conversion £m
Capital and reserves		
Called up share capital:		
million £1 ordinary shares	6	8
Share premium account	–	3
Profit and loss account	9	9
	15	20
Creditors due after one year		
8% Convertible loan stock	5	–
	20	20

Profit and loss account
year ended 31 March

	2004 £'000	2005 £'000
Operating profit (PBIT)	3 400	3 400 (a)
Interest	400	–
Profit before tax	3 000	3 400
Tax (at 30 per cent)	900	1 020
	2 100	2 380
Number of ordinary shares (million)	6	8
Earnings per share	35.0p	29.75p

Notes

(a) assumed unchanged

GEARING

The proportion of debt relative to equity in a company's capital structure is known as financial 'gearing'. The two main ways to measure it are (1) debt ratio (debt ÷ capital employed, or debt ÷ equity), and (2) interest cover (PBIT ÷ interest payable). A company with a high proportion of debt in its capital structure is said to be highly 'geared' (or 'leveraged'). The higher the financial gearing, the greater the risk for equity owners, but the greater their prospect of profit if all goes well.

Example

Two otherwise identical companies, Brown Limited and Green Limited, have very different debt ratios. In year 1, when each company's return on capital employed (ROCE) is 30 per cent, the highly geared Brown (debt ratio 50 per cent) has a much higher return on equity than Green (debt ratio 10 per cent). But in year 2, when ROCE is much less, only 7.5 per cent, there is nothing left for Brown's highly-geared equity, while Green's shareholders still see a positive return on equity.

	Low gearing GREEN		High gearing BROWN	
	£'000		£'000	
Equity	900		500	
Debt (15% interest)	100		500	
= Capital employed	1 000		1 000	
Debt ratio	10%		50%	
	*	●	*	●
	Year 1	**Year 2**	**Year 1**	**Year 2**
	£'000	£'000	£'000	£'000
Return on capital employed	30.0%	7.5%	30.0%	7.5%
PBIT	300	75	300	75
Interest	15	15	75	75
Profit before tax	285	60	225	–
Tax (at 20%)	57	12	45	–
Profit after tax	228	48	180	–
Return on equity	25.3%	5.3%	36.0%	0.0%
Interest cover	20.0	5.0	4.0	1.0

The diagram below shows how gearing works. When the return on capital employed exceeds 15 per cent (the rate of interest payable on debt), Brown's return on equity is higher than Green's; but the reverse is true when ROCE is less than 15 per cent. The example shows that Brown's return on equity is zero when ROCE is 7.5 per cent. The dotted line in the diagram shows that Green's return on equity is zero when ROCE is 1.5 per cent.

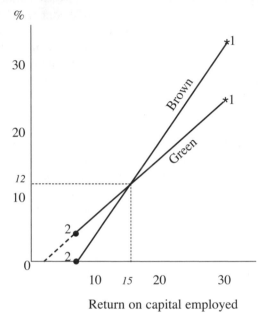

The effect of gearing is to make return on equity more volatile (change more sharply) than return on total capital employed. Of course this works both ways, when profits are falling as well as when they are rising.

As the debt ratio increases, at least beyond a certain level, new capital becomes more expensive as the risk grows, both for lenders of debt capital and for subscribers of equity capital. (Thus the overall weighted average 'cost of capital' (WACC) may be almost flat over a wide range of gearing.)

As well as 'financial gearing', most companies also have some degree of 'operational gearing'. When a large proportion of total expenses is fixed, operational gearing is high. The more stable an industry is, the higher the debt ratio can safely be. In other words, the lower the business risk, the more a company can take on financial risk. The overall riskiness of the equity shares depends on both sorts of gearing.

Gearing: high versus low

Winslow plc and Shepherd plc are otherwise identical companies, but Winslow has low gearing and Shepherd high. Their balance sheets at 30 June 2003 are summarized below:

	Winslow £m	Shepherd £m
Net assets	4 000	4 000
Less: 12% debt	500	3 000
Equity	3 500	1 000
Debt ratio:	12.5%	75.0%

You are asked to complete (opposite) each company's projected profit and loss account for the next two years (assuming no change in debt) if in 2004 profit before interest and tax for each company is £200 million, and in 2005 PBIT for each company is £1 000 million. Assume a tax rate of 30 per cent.

Please also calculate for each company for each year:

(a) Interest cover
(b) Return on capital employed*
(c) Return on equity*

*Use 30 June 2003 figures for equity and capital employed.

You may also wish to calculate on a separate piece of paper at what level of PBIT the two companies would have the same rate of return on equity. (Hint: let the unknown level of PBIT be £x, and express the (equal) rates of return on equity algebraically.)

When you have completed your workings opposite, please turn to the answers over the page.

2004	Winslow £m	Shepherd £m
PBIT	200	200
Interest payable	——	——
Profit before tax		
Tax (@ 30 per cent)	——	——
Profit after tax	——	——

(a) Interest cover

(b) Return on capital employed

(c) Return on equity

2005	Winslow £m	Shepherd £m
PBIT	1 000	1 000
Interest payable	——	——
Profit before tax		
Tax (@ 30 per cent)	——	——
Profit after tax	——	——

(a) Interest cover

(b) Return on capital employed

(c) Return on equity

Return on equity would be the same for each company at a PBIT of £   million.

Please complete your answers above before turning to the next page.

Gearing: high versus low: Answer

2004

	Winslow £m	Shepherd £m
PBIT	200	200
Interest payable	60	360
Profit before tax	140	(160)
Tax (@ 30 per cent)	42	(48)
Profit after tax	98	(112)

(a) Interest cover   3.33   0.56

(b) Return on capital employed 200/4 000 = 5.0%   200/4 000 = 5.0%

(c) Return on equity   98/3 500 = 2.8%   (112)/1 000 = (11.2%)

2005

	Winslow £m	Shepherd £m
PBIT	1 000	1 000
Interest payable	60	360
Profit before tax	940	640
Tax (@ 30 per cent)	282	192
Profit after tax	658	448

(a) Interest cover   16.67   2.78

(b) Return on capital employed 1 000/4 000 = 25.0% 1 000/4 000 = 25.0%

(c) Return on equity   658/3 500 = 18.8%   448/1 000 = 44.8%

Breakeven PBIT

Return on equity would be the same for the two companies at a PBIT level of £480 million. Let the required PBIT level be x. Then:

Winslow	=	Shepherd
$\dfrac{.70\,(x-60)}{3\,500}$	=	$\dfrac{.70\,(x-360)}{1\,000}$
$\dfrac{x-60}{7}$	=	$\dfrac{x-360}{2}$
$2x-120$	=	$7x-2\,520$
$2\,400$	=	$5x$
480	=	x

This can be checked arithmetically as follows:

	Winslow £m	Shepherd £m
PBIT	480	480
Interest payable	60	360
Profit before tax	420	120
Tax (@ 30 per cent)	126	36
Profit after tax	294	84

Return on equity: $\dfrac{294}{3\,500} = 8.4\%$ $\dfrac{84}{1\,000} = 8.4\%$

Return on capital employed: $\dfrac{480}{4\,000} = 12.0\%$ $\dfrac{480}{4\,000} = 12.0\%$

PREFERENCE SHARE CAPITAL

Preference shares come between ordinary shares and debt. Legally they form part of a company's share capital, but with only limited rights to share in profits. Unlike lenders, who can enforce payment of interest (but like ordinary shareholders), preference shareholders receive dividends only if the directors propose them.

In practice however, if there are profits, companies usually have little choice but to pay preference dividends. These are normally 'cumulative', which means that no ordinary dividends are possible until a company has paid all preference dividends due (including any arrears).

The tax rules treat preference dividends as distributions of after-tax profits; whereas debt interest is an *expense* charged before computing taxable profits. So preference capital tends to be an expensive form of finance, at least compared to debt. For this reason, over the years many companies have replaced preference capital with debt (often called 'debentures' or 'loans').

On a winding up, preference shareholders have priority over ordinary shareholders, in the same way that creditors have priority over both. Again, however, their rights are limited. No matter how large a company's remaining surplus is after selling all its assets and paying all its creditors, the preference shareholders will normally receive only the nominal amount of their shares. The ordinary shareholders will get all the rest.

Preference shares may seem to provide companies with an attractive, if expensive, form of capital, combining the finite capital liability of debt with the dividend flexibility of equity. But, as we have seen, companies must pay any preference dividends due in a period if they want to pay any ordinary dividends.

The 'in between' nature of preference capital can pose problems. It certainly forms part of a company's 'permanent' capital employed (even though it may be redeemable). Some analysts normally treat preference capital as similar to debt, but on occasions – for example at a time of financial distress – the unique nature of preference capital might need explicit recognition.

The example opposite shows that the before-tax cost of Tarrant Limited's £5 million 10 per cent debentures is £500 000 per year (£350 000 after 30 per cent tax).

Preference dividends are denominated in terms of the 'net-of-tax' rate of dividend payable. On its £2 million 7 per cent preference capital therefore, Tarrant actually pays £140 000 net per year. (But in order to leave £140 000 available after tax at 30 per cent on profits, the company must earn before-tax profits of £200 000.)

In calculating earnings per ordinary share, preference dividends must be deducted from profits to show the profits 'available for ordinary shareholders'. Hence Tarrant's earnings per share for 2004 is 12.25p.

TARRANT LIMITED

Balance sheet at 31 December 2004

	£'000
Capital and reserves	
Called up ordinary 25p share capital	4 000
Reserves	6 000
Ordinary shareholders' funds	10 000
7% (net) Preference share capital	2 000
10% (gross) Debentures 2008	5 000
Capital employed	17 000

Profit and loss account for the year ended 31 December 2004

	£'000
Operating profit (PBIT)	3 500
Debenture interest payable	500
Profit before tax	3 000
Tax (at 30 per cent)	900
Profit after tax	2 100
Preference dividends	140
Profit available for ordinary shareholders	1 960
Earnings per share (1 960 ÷ 16 000)	12.25p

SECTION 8 SUMMARY

The main kinds of capital employed are:

1 called up ordinary share capital and reserves ('equity')
2 creditors due after one year ('debt').

Debt capital carries regular interest payable as a legal commitment, and must be repaid when due at the end of the loan period. Debt has priority over equity capital in a winding-up. From a company's point of view, debt is cheaper than equity capital, but riskier.

'Capital' reserves (which are not available for distribution as dividends) arise either on issuing new shares at a premium over their nominal ('par') value, or on revaluing fixed assets upwards. 'Revenue' reserves arise through retained profits (the cumulative excess of profits after tax over dividends paid).

A company can increase its share capital in a number of ways:

1 Issues on acquiring another company.
2 Rights issues.
3 Bonus ('scrip') issues.

Rights issues comprise new share issues offered to existing shareholders in return for cash. Bonus issues, in contrast, merely 'capitalize' reserves: they transfer amounts from reserves into called up share capital on the balance sheet, *without* causing any increase in total equity.

Two main ways of measuring a company's debt burden are:

1 debt ratio (capital)
2 interest cover (income).

Companies with a high debt ratio (or a low interest cover) are said to be 'highly geared', or to have high 'financial gearing' ('leverage').

Preference share capital carries rights (usually cumulative) to a fixed dividend payable before any ordinary dividend, and to a fixed money amount on liquidation or redemption. In these respects it is similar to debt (though preference dividends are not mandatory). But preference dividends, being paid out of after-tax profits, tend to be expensive compared to debt interest (which is deductible before tax).

For the sake of completeness it may be helpful to list (for Randall Limited, below) all the categories of capital employed which are likely to be disclosed, including provisions for liabilities and charges.

RANDALL LIMITED: Capital employed

		£'000
Capital and reserves		
Called up ordinary share capital		xxx
Reserves:		
Share premium account	xxx	
Revaluation reserve	xxx	
Other reserves	xxx	
Profit and loss account	xxx	
		xxx
Ordinary shareholders' funds		xxx
Preference share capital		xxx
		xxx
Minority interests (see Section 9)		xx
Creditors due after one year		
Convertible debentures	xxx	
Long-term loans (secured)	xxx	
Long-term loans (unsecured)	xxx	
Finance lease capitalized (see Section 7)	xxx	
		xxx
Provisions for liabilities and charges		
Deferred taxation (see Section 10)	xxx	
Provisions for employee benefits	xxx	
Reorganization costs	xxx	
Other provisions	xxx	
		xxx
Short-term borrowing (see Section 3)		xxx

PROBLEMS

8.1 Definitions

Please write down your definitions of the terms shown. Then compare your answers with those shown on the next page.

(a) Capital employed

(f) Reserves

(b) A highly geared company

(g) Preference share capital

(c) Ordinary shareholders' funds

(h) Share premium

(d) A bonus issue

(i) Fully diluted earnings per share

(e) Convertible loans

(j) A rights issue

8.1 Definitions

(a) **Capital employed** has two main components: equity (called up ordinary share capital and reserves) and debt (negotiated interest-bearing long-term and short-term borrowings). It also includes minority interests (Section 9) and preference share capital.

(b) **A highly geared company** has a high debt ratio (proportion of debt to total capital employed, or debt to equity) or a low interest cover. This is financial gearing. Operating ('business') gearing normally means a high proportion of fixed costs (not varying with sales) to total expenses. High financial gearing normally goes with low operating gearing and vice versa.

(c) **Ordinary shareholders' funds** consist of called up ordinary share capital and reserves ('equity'). A change in the book value of net assets may affect the amount of the reserves, which in effect represent a residual amount.

(d) **A bonus issue** (a 'scrip' issue) is a free issue of ordinary shares (a 'bonus') to existing shareholders pro rata to existing holdings. Such an issue should not affect the *total* market value of the equity, since the value of each existing share will decline in proportion.

(e) **Convertible loans** give the holder an option to 'convert' the loan into ordinary shares, on pre-arranged terms and within a given time period. Unless and until that happens however, they remain as interest-bearing debt.

(f) **Reserves** comprise 'capital' and 'revenue' reserves. Capital reserves normally arise either from share premiums or from revaluing tangible fixed assets and are not available for paying dividends to shareholders. Revenue reserves are cumulative retained profits, legally available for paying as dividends – which also, of course, requires *cash*.

(g) **Preference share capital** has a prior claim over ordinary share capital, both as to dividends and as to capital repayment in a winding up. It normally entitles holders only to fixed dividends each year and to a fixed money amount in a winding up. Unlike debt interest, payment of preference dividends is not legally binding. But most preference dividends are 'cumulative', so that if a company fails to pay ('passes') them in respect of any period, it must make them up in full later before it can pay an ordinary dividend.

(h) **Share premium** is the excess of the proceeds of an issue of ordinary shares over their nominal ('par') value (which is 'called up share capital'). Accounts treat it as a capital reserve, not available for payment as dividends.

(i) **Fully diluted earnings per share** is what earnings per share would have amounted to if holders of all conversion and other options outstanding had exchanged them for ordinary shares (on the agreed terms) at the start of the period under review.

(j) **A rights issue** is an issue of ordinary shares to existing shareholders at a cash price less than the current market price. Companies give 'rights' to take up such shares to existing shareholders in proportion to their existing holdings. Shareholders who do not wish to increase their investment can sell their rights in the market. Their value will depend on the discount between the current share price and the rights issue price.

8.2 Highsight Properties Limited: Revaluation

The balance sheet of Highsight Properties Limited at 31 July 2004 is shown below. It does not include the results of a professional valuation of land and buildings at £5 000 000 as at 31 July 2004.

Please incorporate the revaluation in the accounts by amending the balance sheet where necessary. The answer is shown overleaf.

HIGHSIGHT PROPERTIES LIMITED
Balance sheet at 31 July 2004

	£'000
Fixed assets	
Land and buildings, at cost less accumulated depreciation	3 400
Net current assets	350
	3 750
Less: **Creditors due after one year**	1 500
	2 250
Capital and reserves	
Called up share capital	2 000
Profit and loss account	250
	2 250

8.3 Whittaker Foods Limited: Bonus issue

The summarized balance sheet of Whittaker Foods Limited at 30 April 2005 is shown below. A bonus issue of ordinary shares on terms of '3 for 4' is proposed.

Please amend the balance sheet to show how it would look after the bonus issue. The answer is shown overleaf.

WHITTAKER FOODS LIMITED
Balance sheet at 30 April 2005

	£'000
Fixed assets	4 700
Net current assets	2 300
	7 000
Less: **Creditors due after one year**	1 800
	5 200
Capital and reserves	
Called up share capital:	
9.6 million ordinary 25p shares	2 400
Share premium account	600
Profit and loss account	2 200
	5 200

8.2 Highsight Properties Limited

Solution

HIGHSIGHT PROPERTIES LIMITED
Balance sheet at 31 July 2004

	£'000
Fixed assets	
Land and buildings, at valuation	5 000
Net current assets	350
	5 350
Less: **Creditors due after one year**	1 500
	3 850
Capital and reserves	
Called up share capital	2 000
Revaluation reserve	1 600
Profit and loss account	250
	3 850

Notes

1 Did you remember to change the description of 'Fixed assets' in the balance sheet from 'at cost less accumulated depreciation' to 'at valuation'? (The date of the valuation should be given in a note to the accounts.)

2 Notice that the debt ratio has fallen from 40 per cent to 28 per cent as a result of the revaluation (even though nothing has 'really' changed). What would you expect to happen to: (a) return on net assets? (b) return on equity? (c) interest cover?

8.3 Whittaker Foods Limited

Solution

WHITTAKER FOODS LIMITED
Balance sheet at 30 April 2005

	£'000
Fixed assets	4 700
Net current assets	2 300
	7 000
Less: **Creditors due after one year**	1 800
	5 200
Capital and reserves	
Called up share capital:	
16.8 million ordinary 25p shares	4 200
Profit and loss account	1 000
	5 200

Notes

1 Since there are 9.6 million ordinary shares already in issue, the '3 for 4' bonus issue means issuing a further 7.2 million ordinary 25p shares.

2 Did you remember to change the *number* of ordinary shares in issue, as well as the money amount?

3 Notice that the bonus issue does not affect the total shareholders' funds, which remain at £5.2 million. It merely 'capitalizes' reserves, which already formed part of shareholders' funds.

4 The normal procedure would be to transfer the required amount of £1.8 million (= 7.2 million shares @ 25p each) to issued share capital, first by using capital reserves and then by using the profit and loss account to make up the balance. So here £0.6 million has come from share premium and the balance of £1.2 million from profit and loss account.

8.4 Edwards Limited, Thomas Limited and Charles Limited: Share issues

Each of these three companies has capital and reserves as follows: issued ordinary £1 share capital £1 200 000 plus £700 000 on profit and loss account.

The companies make the following ordinary share issues:

Edwards Limited issues 200 000 new shares for cash at £1.50 each
Thomas Limited makes a 1 for 3 bonus issue
Charles Limited makes a 1 for 4 rights issue at £2.

Please show below:

(a) the appropriate journal entries in each case (including any cash transactions);
(b) the details of capital and reserves after the various issues.

Answers are shown overleaf.

(a) *Journal entries*

	Dr £'000	Cr £'000
Edwards		
Thomas		
Charles		

(b) *Capital and reserves*

	Edwards £'000	**Thomas** £'000	**Charles** £'000
Called up share capital: Ordinary £1 shares			
Reserves:			
	_____	_____	_____

8.5 Debt ratios

The accounts of three companies in the same industry are summarized below.

Please calculate and compare their debt ratios and interest covers. The answers are shown overleaf.

	A £'000	B £'000	C £'000
Fixed assets, net	900	1 500	7 000
Current assets	700	900	6 500
	1 600	2 400	13 500
Called up ordinary share capital	300	600	3 000
Reserves	500	800	2 000
7% Preference share capital	–	–	2 000
Long-term 15% loans*	200	300	4 000
Creditors due within one year	600	700	2 500
	1 600	2 400	13 500
Profit after tax (at 25%)	225	300	1 500

*The loans have all been outstanding throughout the year.

8.4 Edwards Limited, Thomas Limited and Charles Limited

Solution

(a) Journal entries

	Dr £'000	Cr £'000
Edwards		
Cash	300	
To ordinary share capital		200
To share premium		100
Being issue of 200 000 new ordinary £1 shares at £1.50 each		
Thomas		
Profit and loss account	400	
To ordinary share capital		400
Being transfer from retained profits to issued ordinary share capital on bonus issue of 400 000 £1 shares		
Charles		
Cash	600	
To ordinary share capital		300
To share premium		300
Being issue of 300 000 new £1 ordinary shares at £2 each		

(b) Capital and reserves

	Edwards £'000	Thomas £'000	Charles £'000
Called up share capital:			
Ordinary £1 shares	1 400	1 600	1 500
Reserves:			
Share premium	100	–	300
Profit and loss account	700	300	700
	2 200	1 900	2 500

Notes

1 Details would be shown in the notes to the accounts.
2 It may be best to start by considering how much *total* shareholders' funds have been increased by a particular issue (£300, nil and £600 respectively).

8.5 Debt ratios

Solution

	A	B	C
Fixed assets, net	900	1 500	7 000
Current assets	700	900	6 500
Less: Creditors due within one year	600	700	2 500
Net working capital	100	200	4 000
= Net assets	1 000	1 700	11 000
Called up ordinary share capital	300	600	3 000
Reserves	500	800	2 000
Ordinary shareholders' funds	800	1 400	5 000
7% Preference share capital	–	–	2 000
Long-term 15% loans	200	300	4 000
= Capital employed	1 000	1 700	11 000
Profit before interest and tax	330	445	2 600
Interest	30	45	600
Profit before tax	300	400	2 000
Tax (at 25%)	75	100	500
Profit after tax	225	300	1 500
Preference dividends	–	–	140
Debt ratio =	20.0%	17.6%	36.4%
Interest cover =	11.0	9.9	4.3

Notes

1 The layout has been changed. By subtotalling ordinary shareholders' funds and by deducting creditors due within one year from current assets, the balance sheet totals represent capital employed and net assets.
2 Note that the rankings of the debt ratios and the interest covers are not the same (as between A and B).
3 We use debt/capital employed for the debt ratio. The debt/equity ratios would be 25, 21, and 57 per cent respectively.
4 We have not counted C's preference share capital as debt.
5 We assume there is no short-term borrowing in 'creditors due within one year'.

8.6 Rights issue: varying terms

Reynolds plc plans to raise £60 million of new equity by means of a rights issue. There are currently 240 million 25p ordinary shares in issue, and the market price is 150p per share. Among possible alternative terms for the rights issue are:

1 for 5 @ 125p
1 for 1 @ 25p

You are asked to show (below) how Reynolds plc's 'shareholders' funds' in the balance sheet would change as a result of each of the two alternative rights issues. Please also calculate in each case what the market price per share would amount to afterwards.

REYNOLDS PLC
Ordinary shareholders' funds

	NOW	After 1 for 5 @ 125p	After 1 for 1 @ 25p
	£m	£m	£m
Called up ordinary 25p shares	60		
Share premium account	40		
Profit and loss account	200		
Total market value (£m)	360		
Number of shares (million)	240		
Market price per share (p)	150		

8.7 Rights issue: taking up rights or not

You are also asked to show (opposite) for each of the alternative rights issues by Reynolds plc (Problem 8.6):

(a) the position of Andrew Young (AY), who owns 1 000 shares and wants to subscribe for the new shares to which he is entitled; and

(b) the position of Norma Owen (NO), who also owns 1 000 shares; but who wants to sell her rights to the new shares while keeping the 1 000 shares she already owns.

When you have completed your answers to all the questions, please compare them with the answers on the next page.

Position of individual shareholders

1 for 5 @ 125p	AY £	NO £
Opening holding: 1 000 shares @ 150p:	1 500	1 500
Buy shares @ p:		
Sell rights @ p:		
Closing holdings:		
AY: shares @ p:		
NO: shares @ p:		
Difference: shares @ p = £		

Value of rights

	£
5 shares @ 150p =	750
_ share @ p =	
_ shares @ p =	
Rights per share = p	

1 for 1 @ 25p	AY £	NO £
Opening holding: 1 000 shares @ 150p:	1 500	1 500
Buy shares @ p:		
Sell rights @ p:		
Closing holdings:		
AY: shares @ p:		
NO: shares @ p:		
Difference: shares @ p = £		

Value of rights

	£
1 shares @ 150p =	150
_ share @ p =	
_ shares @ p =	
Rights per share = p	

8.6 Rights issue: varying terms

Solution

REYNOLDS PLC
Ordinary shareholders' funds

	NOW	After 1 for 5 @ 125p	After 1 for 1 @ 25p
	£m	£m	£m
Called up ordinary 25p shares	60	72	120
Share premium account	40	88	40
Profit and loss account	200	200	200
	300	360	360
Total market value (£m)	360	420	420
Number of shares (million)	240	288	480
Market price per share (p)	150	145.83	87.5

Notes

1 In each case, total ordinary shareholders' funds has increased by £60 million – the cash proceeds from the rights issue.
2 The 1 for 5 @ 125p rights issue involves issuing a further 48 million shares at a premium (over nominal value of 25p per share) of 100p. Hence the share premium account increases by £48 million.
3 The 1 for 1 @ 25p rights issue involves issuing a further 240 million shares at par (nominal value). Hence there is *no* increase in the share premium account.
4 We assume the total market value of the equity shares increases by the £60 million cash raised, from £360 million to £420 million.
5 The market price after each rights issue is calculated to one or two decimal places to facilitate the other calculations.

8.7 Rights issue: taking up rights or not

Solution

1 for 5 @ 125p	AY £	NO £
Opening holding: 1 000 shares @ 150p:	1 500	1 500
Buy 200 shares @ 125p:	250	
Sell 1 000 rights @ 4.17p:		(41.7)
Closing holdings:		
AY: 1 200 shares @ 145.83p:	1 750	
NO: 1 000 shares @ 145.83p:		1 458.3

Difference: 200 shares @ 145.83p = £291.7.

Value of rights

	£
5 shares @ 150p =	750
1 share @ 125p =	125
6 shares @ 145.83p =	875

Rights per share = 4.17p (150 − 145.83) = 25/6 (25 = 150 − 125)

1 for 1 @ 25p	AY £	NO £
Opening holding: 1 000 shares @ 150p:	1 500	1 500
Buy 1 000 shares @ 25p:	250	
Sell 1 000 rights @ 62.5p:		(625)
Closing holdings:		
AY: 2 000 shares @ 87.5p:	1 750	
NO: 1 000 shares @ 87.5p:		875

Difference: 1 000 shares @ 87.5p = £875.

Value of rights

	£
1 share @ 150p =	150
1 share @ 25p =	25
2 shares @ 87.5p =	175

Rights per share = 62.5p (150 − 87.5) = 125/2 (125 = 150 − 25)

Answers to the following seven problems are shown at the end of the book.

8.8 Kent Traders Limited: Rights issue

The balance sheet of Kent Traders Limited at 30 April 2005 is shown below. You are asked to amend the balance sheet to give effect to a 1 for 4 rights issue on that date at 200p a share.

KENT TRADERS LIMITED
Balance sheet, 30 April 2005

		£'000
Fixed assets, net		750
Current assets		
Stock	260	
Debtors	190	
Cash	70	
	520	
Less: **Creditors due within one year**	240	
		280
		1 030
Less: **Creditors due after one year**		
Long-term loans		270
		760
Capital and reserves		
Called up share capital:		
1 200 000 ordinary 50p shares		600
Profit and loss account		160
Shareholders' funds		760

8.9 Antrobus Lathes Limited: Convertible debt

The 10 per cent convertible loan stock of Antrobus Lathes Limited was all converted in 2004 into ordinary £1 share capital on the basis of 40 ordinary £1 shares for every £100 of 10 per cent loan stock.

You are asked to amend the summarized 2004 accounts shown below to give effect to the conversion of the 10 per cent loan stock at the start of 2005 assuming 2005 PBIT is the same as 2004. Assume all profits are paid out in dividends. Enter the revised numbers in the right hand column.

ANTROBUS LATHES LIMITED
Balance sheet at end of 2004

	Actual £'000	With loan converted £'000
Capital and reserves		**End 2005**
Called up ordinary £1 share capital	2 400	
Reserves	1 100	
Shareholders' funds	3 500	
10% Convertible loan stock	1 500	
8% Loan stock	1 000	
Capital employed	6 000	
Debt ratio	$\dfrac{2\,500}{6\,000} = 42\%$	$\underline{\hspace{1cm}} = \%$
Profit and loss account, 2004		**For 2005**
PBIT	1 430	
Loan interest payable	230	
Profit before tax	1 200	
Tax at 30%	360	
Profit after tax	840	
Earnings per share	$\dfrac{840}{2\,400} = 35.0\text{p}$	$\underline{\hspace{1cm}} = \text{p}$
Interest cover	$\dfrac{1\,430}{230} = 6.2$	$\underline{\hspace{1cm}} =$

8.10 Western Enterprises Limited: Share issues

The balance sheet of Western Enterprises Limited at 1 January 2004 is summarized below. Please amend it to record the following events which occurred during the year to 31 December 2004. Assume that retained profit is reflected in increasing working capital (net current assets). Identify your amendments by the letters (a) to (f).

(a) March 2004. 50 000 ordinary £1 shares issued to employees at £3 each.
(b) June 2004. Land and buildings were revalued at £1 500 000.
(c) September 2004. There was a 2 for 1 bonus issue.
(d) December 2004. Profit for ordinary shareholders for the year was £380 000.
(e) A 12p (net) cash dividend per share was paid in December.
(f) A 1 for 15 bonus issue is proposed, to occur in January 2005.

WESTERN ENTERPRISES LIMITED
Balance sheet, 1 January 2004

	£'000
Fixed assets	
Land and buildings, at cost	700
Plant, net	1 700
	2 400
Net current assets	800
	3 200
Less: **10% Loan stock**	1 200
	2 000
Capital and reserves	
Called up ordinary £1 shares	700
Share premium	350
Profit and loss account	950
Ordinary shareholders' funds	2 000

8.11 Equivalent rights

Can you prove that a rights issue at a discount from the current market price can always be regarded in theory (ignoring transaction costs) as equivalent to an issue of new shares at the current market price combined with a bonus issue on appropriate terms?

8.12 Sadler Limited (A): Interest cover

Sadler Limited has 200 000 £1 ordinary shares in issue, 60 000 3½% cumulative preference shares of £1 each, and £80 000 10% debentures, repayable in 2007. Reserves amount to £60 000. For the year ended 31 December 2004, the company reported a profit of £40 000 before tax. Tax is to be provided for at 20 per cent. An ordinary dividend of 8p (net) is paid in the year. Calculate:

(a) the interest cover
(b) the dividend cover for the ordinary dividend
(c) earnings per share.

8.13 Sadler Limited (B): Capital cover

At 31 December 2004, Sadler Limited's profit and loss account balance is £60 000. There are no other reserves. Other accounts are as in the (A) problem. Calculate:

(a) the debt ratio
(b) the amount per share the preference shareholders would receive if the company were liquidated at 31 December 2004, and the net assets – that is, total assets less current liabilities – realized £125 000
(c) the amount per share that ordinary shareholders would receive if the net assets realized £190 000.

8.14 Bell Limited, Book Limited and Candle Limited: Gearing

The net assets of Bell, Book and Candle are identical, but they have different capital structures in 2004 and 2005 as shown below:

	Bell £'000	Book £'000	Candle £'000
Ordinary £1 shares	150	300	400
Reserves	250	500	600
Equity	400	800	1 000
10% Loans	600	200	–
Capital employed (in both 2004 and 2005)	1 000	1 000	1 000

Assume

(1) Tax rate of 20 per cent.
(2) All 2004 profits after tax are distributed as dividends.
(3) Profit before interest payable and tax is £180 000 in 2004 and £50 000 in 2005.

Please calculate for each company for (a) 2004 and (b) 2005:

(i) return on net assets (= on capital employed) (iii) interest cover
(ii) return on equity (iv) earnings per share

No answers are given for the following four problems.

8.15 Grundy International Limited

The balance sheet of Grundy International Limited at 1 January 2004 is summarized below.

GRUNDY INTERNATIONAL LIMITED
Balance sheet at 1 January 2004 | | £'000

Fixed assets

Land and buildings, net		1 900
Plant and equipment, net		2 500
Net current assets		1 700
		6 100

Creditors due after one year

10% Debentures 2009	1 500	
8% Convertible loan stock	600	
		2 100

Shareholders' funds

Ordinary £1 shares	2 300	
Share premium	500	
Profit and loss account	1 200	
		4 000
		6 100

You are asked to show how the balance sheet would need to be amended to record each of the events shown below, which occurred during the year ended 31 December 2004.

(a) January — The 8% convertible loan stock was converted into ordinary shares at 375p each.

(b) February — Land and buildings were revalued at £2 700 000.

(c) April — There was a 5 for 1 share split.

(d) June — The insured value of plant and equipment was increased to £3 000 000.

(e) July — There was a 2 for 3 bonus issue.

(f) September — There was a fully subscribed rights issue of 1 for 5 at 80p.

(g) November — Employees exercised options to buy 400 000 shares at 50p.

(h) December — The after-tax return on (beginning-of-year) equity for 2004 was 20 per cent. A cash dividend of 1.8p (net) per share was paid. Assume that any retained profit is reflected in increased net current assets.

8.16 Scylla Limited and Charybdis Limited

Scylla Limited and Charybdis Limited each reported profit before interest and tax for the calendar year 2004 of £12 million. Each company had issued £20 million 10 per cent debentures on 1 January 2000, which were redeemable in 2013. Each company had 100 million 25p ordinary shares outstanding throughout 2004.

At the start of 2005 each company invested £15 million in a capital project expected to produce an additional £3 million PBIT in 2005. Scylla Limited financed this project by issuing £15 million 12 per cent debentures on 1 January 2005. Charybdis Limited financed the project by issuing 25 million ordinary shares at 60p each on 1 January 2005.

Assuming (i) a tax rate (on reported profits before tax) of 30 per cent; and (ii) that the capital project did produce in each case the expected additional PBIT in 2005, and that the remaining 2005 PBIT for each company was the same as in 2004:

(a) what would each company's 2005 earnings per share amount to?

(b) ignoring assumption (ii) above, at what identical PBIT level in 2005 would the two companies report identical 2005 earnings per share?

8.17 Auckland and Melbourne

Auckland Limited and Melbourne Limited both have capital employed of £2 million, but with different capital structures. Auckland's debt represents 80 per cent of its capital employed, Melbourne's 20 per cent. All debt carries an interest rate (before tax) of 12 per cent a year. In Year 1 both companies earn 25 per cent (before interest and tax) on capital employed, in Year 2 both earn 5 per cent. Assume a corporation tax rate of 25 per cent; and assume all available profits are paid out in dividends.

Questions

(a) Calculate return on equity for each company for each year.

(b) Calculate interest cover for each company for each year.

(c) Prepare a graph plotting return on equity against return on capital employed for each company. What is the crossover point? Why?

(d) Assuming that all equity capital consists of paid-up £1 ordinary shares, at what level of PBIT will the two companies have identical earnings per share? What will the e.p.s. be at that PBIT?

8.18 M F Hotskin: Fully diluted earnings per share

Below are shown simplified summarized 2004 consolidated accounts for M F Hotskin plc. You are asked to calculate fully diluted earnings per share for the year ended 30 April 2004 on the basis of the following information:

1 The £10 million 10 per cent convertible unsecured loan stock 2011 is convertible into ordinary 5p shares in January in any of the years 2007 to 2011 on the basis of 11 ordinary 5p shares for every £1 of loan stock.
2 The £60 million 5 per cent cumulative convertible redeemable preference share capital, in shares of £1 each, is convertible into ordinary share capital on 30 September in any of the years 2005 to 2019 on the basis of one ordinary share of 5p for every four preference shares of £1. The preference shares are redeemable at par on 30 September 2020.
3 Under executive share option schemes, at 30 April 2004 options are outstanding in respect of a total of 4 million ordinary shares, at prices ranging from 45p to 250p per share.
4 Assume a corporation tax rate of 30 per cent.

M F HOTSKIN plc
Consolidated profit and loss account, year ended 30 April 2004

		£ million
Turnover		200
Profit before interest payable and tax		31
Interest payable on convertible loan stock		1
Profit before tax		30
Tax (at 30 per cent)		9
Profit after tax		21
Dividends: Preference	3	
Ordinary	3	
		6
Retained profit for the year		15
Earnings per share		18.0p

M F HOTSKIN plc
Consolidated balance sheet at 30 April 2004

		£ million
Fixed assets		
Tangible		30
Investments		10
		40
Current assets		
Stock	50	
Debtors	45	
Cash	55	
	150	
Less: **Creditors due within one year**	60	
		90
		130
Less: **Provision for liabilities and charges**	10	
Creditors due after one year		
10% Convertible unsecured loan stock 2011	10	
		20
		110
Capital and reserves		
Called up share capital:		
Ordinary shares of 5p each		5
Reserves		45
Ordinary shareholders' funds		50
5% Cumulative convertible redeemable preference £1 shares		60
		110

Section 9
Group accounts

INVESTMENTS IN EQUITY

So far we have been dealing mainly with independent companies and how they report their financial results. In this section we consider how companies account for holdings of equity shares in other companies. Such investments fall into two main groups: controlling shareholdings and others.

Controlling shareholdings

Controlling shareholdings normally comprise more than 50 per cent of the voting rights in a 'subsidiary' company. Where a company owns 100 per cent of the shares, the subsidiary is 'wholly owned'.

Our main concern in this section is with this kind of 'controlling' equity investment. Where one company controls other companies, the holding company must normally publish group ('consolidated') accounts dealing with the state of affairs and profit or loss of 'the company and its subsidiaries' [FRS 2/IAS 27].

Control of a subsidiary (or 'dominant influence' over it) need not be through holding shares with more than 50 per cent of the voting rights. It may be through an agreement or contract with other parties or with the board of directors.

Other shareholdings

Other kinds of investment in equity shares are as follows:

(a) Shareholdings between 20 per cent and 50 per cent, where the holding company 'influences' the commercial policies of the 'associate'. These include 'joint ventures'.
(b) Other holdings of less than 20 per cent where there is a strong trading link ('trade investments').
(c) Other equity holdings. These are simply equity investments, which may be listed on a stock exchange or unlisted.
(d) In the holding company's own shares, often to do with executive incentive schemes.

'Investments' may also include non-equity investments, such as preference shares or loans, or holdings of government securities. They may be either short-term (current) assets or longer-term (fixed asset) investments.

Investments other than in associates and joint ventures (for which see pages 181/2) will normally appear in the balance sheet at cost, less any amounts written off. Income will consist of dividends or interest received.

GROUP ACCOUNTS

Nearly all medium or large companies have subsidiaries and therefore have to publish group accounts. As a rule all companies in a group use the same accounting policies and have the same financial year-end.

The typical accounts of a holding company with one or more subsidiaries comprise:

1 directors' report
2 group profit and loss account
3 group balance sheet
4 holding company balance sheet
5 group cash flow statement
6 notes to the accounts
7 auditors' report.

Group ('consolidated') accounts for Diageo plc for 2003 are set out (somewhat simplified) on this page and the next. Please note all the new accounting headings (marked *) which we have not met before.

The group profit and loss account

● Adds together the earnings of all the group companies, thus combining the profits (and losses) of the holding ('parent') company with those of all its subsidiaries.
● Includes separately the before-tax share of profits (and losses) of associates.
● Deducts the share of the group's profit after tax which 'belongs' to the outside shareholders ('minority interests') in subsidiaries which are *less* than wholly owned.

Thus Diageo's £76m 'profit for the financial year' is attributable to shareholders in the parent company.

Groups provide a 'segmental' breakdown of their turnover, operating profits and net assets for each main class of business and for each geographical area [SSAP 25/IAS 14]. For Diageo there is only one main class of business ('premium drinks'), but the geographical split is shown on the right.

DIAGEO plc
Consolidated profit and loss account for year ended 30 June 2003

	£ million
Turnover[a]	9 440[a]
Operating costs[b]	7 579[b]
Operating profit[a]	1 861[a]
*Share of associates' profits	457*
	2 318
Loss on disposal of businesses[c]	(1 313)[c]
Interest payable (net)	(351)
Profit before taxation	654
Taxation[c]	(487)[c]
Profit after taxation	167
*Minority interests	(91)*
Profit for the year	76

Notes

[a] including discontinued operations 479 (turnover) and 53 (operating profit)
[b] after exceptional expenses 168
[c] loss on disposal of businesses mostly non-deductible for tax purposes.

SEGMENTAL ANALYSIS

Geographical area by destination

	Turnover £m	Operating profit £m	Fixed assets £m
Great Britain	1 472	220	1 922
Rest of Europe	2 568	458	564
North America	3 159	783	2 862
Asia Pacific	1 008	243	664
Latin America	481	143	45
Rest of World	752	182	205
	9 440	2 029	6 262

The group balance sheet

- Adds together the assets and liabilities of all group companies, those of the holding company and of all its subsidiaries.
- Cancels out inter-company balances.
- Shows purchased 'goodwill' as an intangible fixed asset.
- Shows separately the ('minority') interests of outside shareholders in subsidiaries which are *less* than wholly owned.
- Includes the interests in associates in 'investments'.

The holding company must publish its own ('company') balance sheet as well as the consolidated balance sheet. In the holding company's own balance sheet, the investment in subsidiaries (including any net loans to them) appears as a separate item.

After studying the Diageo accounts, it will be helpful to look a little more closely at how group accounts are prepared, and at the items (marked * opposite) which appear only in group accounts.

In this section we now go on to look in turn at:

- inter-company transactions
- acquisitions
- goodwill and intangible assets
- minority interests
- non-consolidated subsidiaries
- associates and joint ventures.

DIAGEO plc
Consolidated balance sheet at 30 June 2003

	£ million	£ million
Fixed assets		9 743
Intangible assets[a]	4 288[a]	
Tangible assets	1 974	
*Investments in associates	3 034*	
Other investments[b]	447[b]	
Current assets		6 454
Stocks	2 193	
Debtors	3 070	
Cash at bank and liquid resources	1 191	
Creditors – due within one year		(6 846)
Borrowings	(3 563)	
Other creditors	(3 283)	
Net current liabilities		(392)
Total assets less current liabilites		9 351
Creditors – due after one year		(2 999)
Borrowings	(2 981)	
Other creditors	(18)	
Provisions for liabilities and charges		(869)
		5 483
Capital and reserves		
Called up share capital		897
Share premium account	1 327	
Revaluation reserve	120	
Capital redemption reserve	3 046	
Profit and loss account	(436)	
Reserves		4 057
Shareholders' funds		4 954
*Minority interests – equity	186*	
– non-equity	343*	
		529*
		5 483

Notes

[a] net of £1643 cumulative goodwill written off against reserves

[b] including £259 cost of 45 million shares in Diageo plc itself.

INTER-COMPANY TRANSACTIONS

Certain adjustments are needed in practice to eliminate from group accounts two kinds of inter-company transactions:

(a) end-of-year balances
(b) unrealized profits.

(a) Inter-company balances

It is fairly simple on consolidation to exclude inter-company balances (that is, amounts owing to and by companies in a group). For example, suppose that A owns B and C, and details of net current assets at the balance sheet date include the amounts shown below for debtors and creditors due within one year.

	Separate £'000				Consolidation adjustments	Consolidated £'000
	A	B	C	= Total		A Group
Debtors						
A	*	–	23		a – 23	
B	48	*	–		b – 48	
C	–	21	*		c – 21	
Other (external)	174	87	63			= 324
	222	108	86	= 416	– 92	324
Creditors due within one year						
A	*	48	–		b – 48	
B	–	*	21		c – 21	
C	23	–	*		a – 23	
Other (external)	140	54	41			= 235
	163	102	62	= 327	– 92	235
Net excess				+ 89		+89

It is easy to see that £92 000 is owed within the group. The group balance sheet eliminates this amount from total debtors and creditors, leaving only *external* debtors (£324 000) and *external* creditors (£235 000). Exactly the same kind of procedure applies to any long-term inter-company loans and advances. The net excess of debtors over creditors remains, of course, at £89 000.

(b) Unrealized inter-company profits

As a single entity for accounting purposes, a group of companies earns no revenue until it sells to the outside world. This is the realization principle applied to a group. Group accounts must therefore exclude inter-company (intra-group) purchases and sales.

More important, group accounts must exclude any *profits* of group companies on inter-company business until the *group* as a whole has realized them by selling outside. Otherwise the group figures would overstate sales, profits and stock. (It would also be possible to arrange spurious intra-group transactions on purpose to distort the published group accounts.) Best practice is to exclude the *whole* of any unrealized inter-company profits even if there are some minority interests.

The key question is not whether there are inter-company profits, but whether the group has *realized* such profits, at the balance sheet date, by sales to outside customers. Group accounts exclude only *unrealized* profits (and losses). (The adjustments are made on worksheets outside the books of account. They do not affect the permanent accounting records of the various group companies.)

Example

Suppose S, a subsidiary, has sold goods which cost £33 000 to H, its holding company, for £48 000. There are three possibilities.

1 Wholly realized by group

If H has sold all the goods (costing it £48 000) to outside customers for £60 000, H will show a profit of £12 000, S will show a profit of £15 000, and the group profit is £27 000. That is the £60 000 proceeds from (H's) outside customers, less the £33 000 cost from (S's) outside suppliers. No adjustment is needed because the group has realized externally all the £27 000 profit.

2 Wholly unrealized by group

If H has not yet sold any of the goods it purchased from S, H's stock will include them as costing £48 000. But the group accounts must show that stock as costing (the group) only £33 000, the cost S incurred from outside suppliers. Group profits must be reduced by £15 000, to leave out – for the time being – S's profit on the 'internal' sale to H. The group has not yet realized this profit externally. (Notice how these adjustments preserve double-entry: reduce (H's) stock value by £15 000, and reduce (S's) profit by £15 000.)

3 Partly realized by group

If H has sold, say, two-thirds of the goods, and one-third is still in stock, then only one-third of S's £15 000 profit is unrealized by the group. So the group needs to subtract only £5 000 from stock and from profit.

ACQUISITIONS

Let us consider a simple example of an acquisition and subsequent consolidation of accounts. On 31 December 2003, H purchased all the equity shares in S for £150 million cash. The separate balance sheets of H Limited (holding company) and S Limited (its wholly-owned subsidiary) are set out opposite (left).

To prepare the group balance sheet (opposite, right), as a rule we add together ('consolidate') the amounts shown in the separate balance sheets of the holding company and (all) its subsidiaries. (In this case, S is the only one.)

This process eliminates H's £150 million investment in S, and S's £90 million capital and reserves ('equity'). It also shows as purchased 'goodwill' the £60 million excess of the purchase price over the fair value of S's separable net assets.

Fair values of separable net assets

In S's case we assume that the £90 million *book value* of equity is the same as the *fair value* of the net assets. If the fair value were different, we would need to adjust the amounts (book values) in S's balance sheet to the fair values, and to change the book amount of S's equity accordingly [FRS 7/IFRS 3].

Negative goodwill

Goodwill arose because H paid more than £90 million (the 'fair value') for S's equity. Had H paid less than £90 million for 100 per cent of S's equity, the difference would be 'negative goodwill' (which is rare). If it arises, negative goodwill should be recognized (as a profit) at once in the profit and loss account.

Pre-acquisition profits

If H acquired a subsidiary S *during* the year, only S's *post-acquisition* profits would be included in the H group's profits for the year. Any profits S made *before* the acquisition do not relate to the H group. (If S were to pay out pre-acquisition profits to H in dividends, H could not legally distribute them to its own shareholders. Instead H would have to use the dividend to write down – reduce – the cost of its investment in S.)

H LIMITED AND S LIMITED
Balance sheets at 31 December 2003

	Separate £ m		Consolidation adjustments		Group £ m
	H	S			H Group
Fixed assets					
Goodwill			(a) + 150 (b) – 15 (c) – 75		= 60
Plant and machinery	500	70			= 570
Investment in S	150		(a) – 150		
Net current assets	300	60			= 360
	950	130			990
Less: **Long-term creditors**	(250)	(40)			= (290)
	700	90			700
Capital and reserves					
Called up share capital	500	15	(b) – 15		500
Profit and loss account	200	75	(c) – 75		200
	700	90			700

(a) is H's cost of investment in S.
(b) and (c) are H's interest in S's equity (in total, 100% of £90 million);

GOODWILL AND INTANGIBLE ASSETS

We have seen that the group balance sheet shows purchased goodwill, initially 'at cost', under intangible fixed assets. The *amount* is the excess of the price paid over the fair value of the separable net assets acquired.

FRS 10 requires group accounts normally to amortize goodwill and other purchased intangible fixed assets by the straight line method over their expected economic life, up to a normal maximum of twenty years. Some companies distinguish brands from goodwill when they acquire other companies, the effect of which is to reduce the amount of 'goodwill'.

If the acquiring company regards goodwill as having an 'infinite life', then (under FRS 10) it need not amortize it but instead must carry out an annual 'impairment review'. (IFRS 3 requires this treatment for *all* purchased goodwill.) If the review shows that the goodwill has maintained its value, the company does not write it down. (It must, however, then make special reference to the 'true and fair override' (see page 2) to justify departure from the requirement in the Companies Act 1985 [Schedule IV, para. 21] for systematic amortization of goodwill.)

To the extent that the annual review does show 'impairment' (loss of value) of an intangible asset below its current book value, the group must write it off at once as an expense in the profit and loss account.

Most marketing spending on a brand helps to generate the current period's sales, so it is 'matched' against turnover as an expense. It is hard to tell to what extent (if any) it may have increased a brand's 'value', so companies do not, as a rule, capitalize 'homegrown' brand values. They may do so *only* where there is a readily ascertainable market value.

Some companies argue that continued spending on purchased goodwill or brands at least maintains their value. This may often be true, in that if they spent nothing, the value of goodwill or brands would probably fall. Failing to amortize such intangible assets, but instead leaving them on the balance sheet 'at cost', is in effect to *substitute* internally generated value for the asset's declining *original* value (as shown in the diagrams opposite). This is an indirect way of capitalizing a highly subjective amount. (IAS 38 forbids doing so directly.)

IAS 38 allows two different ways of treating intangible assets:

- The 'cost' model requires amortization of assets over their useful life.
- The other approach requires regular revaluations, assuming there is an 'active market' for the asset. Any increase goes directly to equity (under 'revaluation reserve'), while any reduction is charged as an expense to the profit and loss account.

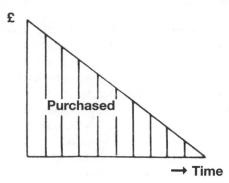

Cost of purchased brand, with notional amortization

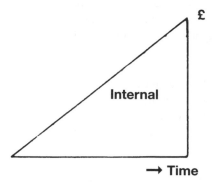

Notional build-up of brand value, 'internally'

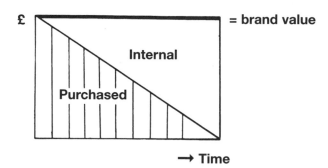

MINORITY INTERESTS

In the example so far, H acquired 100 per cent of S for £150 million on 31 December 2003. Let us now suppose that H acquired for £100 million only *two-thirds* of the equity shares in S. The other one-third represents 'minority interests' in S.

Rather than including only two-thirds of each of S's assets and liabilities ('proportional consolidation'), the H group balance sheet (shown on the right) will include the total net assets it *controls*. So H consolidates 100 per cent of each of S's assets and liabilities, but shows as a separate item under equity – 'minority interests in subsidiaries' – the amount of S's equity it does not own.

So, too, the H group profit and loss account (shown below) includes 100 per cent of each item in S's profit and loss account, eliminates any unrealized inter-company profits, and then deducts separately the one-third share of S's profits after tax relating to the minority interests.

In the group profit and loss account, any dividends which H may have received from S will be eliminated on consolidation.

H LIMITED AND S LIMITED
Profit and loss account summary for the year ended 31 December 2004

	Separate H £m	Separate S £m	Consolidation adjustments £m	Group H Group £m
Turnover	830	120		950
Operating profit (PBIT)	150	25		175
Goodwill[a]				– a
Interest payable	(20)	(5)		(25)
Profit before tax	130	20		150
Taxation	(40)	(5)		(45)
Profit after tax	90	15		105
Minority interests			5[b]	(5)[b]
Profit available for shareholders in H				100

Notes

[a] Goodwill of £40 million is assumed not to be amortized

[b] The one-third 'minority interest' in S's £15 million profit after tax is £5 million

H LIMITED AND S LIMITED
Balance sheets at 31 December

	Separate H £m	Separate S £m	Consolidation adjustments		2003 Group £m	2004 Group £m
Fixed assets			(g)	+ 100		
Goodwill			(c)	– 10	40	40
			(e)	– 50		
Plant and machinery	500	70			570	570
Investment in S	100*		(g)	– 100		
Net current assets	350**	60			410	515[1]
	950	130			1 020	1 125
Less: **Long-term creditors**	(250)	(40)			(290)	(290)
	700	90	– 60		730	835
Capital and reserves						
Called up share capital	500	15	(c)	– 10	500	500
			(d)	– 5		
Profit and loss account	200	75	(e)	– 50	200	300[2]
			(f)	– 25		
	700	90			700	800
Minority interests			(d)	+ 5	30	35[3]
			(f)	+ 25		
	700	90	– 60		730	835

Notes

Separate
*£50m less than before   **£50m more than before

Consolidation adjustments
(c) Two-thirds of £15m plus (e) two-thirds of £75m = £60m H share of S equity.
(d) One-third of £15m plus (f) one-third of £75m = £30m minority interests in S equity.
(g) H's £100m cost of investment in two-thirds of S's equity.

Changes in 2004 group balance sheet
1 Net current assets assumed increased by retained profits for 2004 (H £90m + S £15m).
2 H group profits up by £100m, (£90m + £10m).
3 Minority interest up by one-third share of S £15m profit.

MERGERS

When one company acquires most of the shares in another, it normally accounts for the purchase as an 'acquisition', including the results of the acquired business as from the date of purchase. Any difference between the purchase price and the fair value of the separable net assets acquired represents 'goodwill', which the acquiring group treats as an intangible fixed asset and either amortizes against profit or subjects to a regular impairment review. That is what we have been describing so far in this section.

But where two (or more) sets of shareholders continue their interests on a combined basis, FRS 6 says such business combinations must use 'merger' accounting if, but only if, they meet each of the following criteria:

1 No party is portrayed as either 'acquirer' or 'acquired'.
2 All parties join in managing the new entity.
3 No party dominates the new entity by virtue of its relative size (more than 50 per cent larger than each other party).
4 Each party's equity shareholders receive mainly equity shares in the new entity (not cash or loan stock).
5 No equity shareholders of any of the combining entities retain any material interest in the future performance of only part of the new entity.

Under FRS 6, merger accounting:

- combines the two (or more) companies' assets and liabilities at their *former book value*, so no 'goodwill' arises;
- treats as a *change in reserves* any difference between the holding company's called up share capital and the merging companies' total share capitals;
- includes shares issued at their *nominal* value (despite the Companies Act requirement to include a share premium whenever a company issues shares for more than their nominal value);
- reports as profits of the new group the combined companies' profits for the *entire* accounting period in which the merger occurs, and restates the profits for earlier periods on a combined basis;
- leaves the combined retained profits of the merging companies available for payment as dividends by the new group.

An example showing the difference between acquisition accounting and merger accounting is set out on the right. Clearly the return on investment ratios are likely to be higher under merger accounting: there is no goodwill to amortize and the 'investment' in the group balance sheet is likely to be lower.

But note that IFRS 3 forbids merger accounting.

Example

Company A acquires all company B's 80 million ordinary 25p shares in exchange for 50 million ordinary £1 shares in A worth 500p each. The total cost to A is thus £250 million.

BALANCE SHEET SUMMARIES

Before combining

	A £ million	B £ million
Net assets	100	80
Called up share capital	50	20
Reserves	50	60
	100	80

After combining

	AB Group 'acquisition' accounting £ million	AB Group 'merger' accounting £ million
Goodwill	170 (a)	–
Other net assets	180	180
	350	180
Called up share capital	100 (b)	100 (b)
Share premium account	200 (c)	–
Other reserves	50	80 (d)
	350	180

Notes

(a) The value of A's shares issued £250m less fair value of B's net assets (= equity) acquired £80m (assumed the same as book value).

(b) A's original share capital £50m plus new shares issued for acquisition £50m.

(c) Share premium is issue value £250m less nominal value of shares issued £50m.

(d) A's reserves of £50m plus B's reserves of £60m (= £110m), less excess of *nominal* value of A's shares issued (£50m) over B's shares acquired (£20m) (= £30m); that is £80m.

Comprehensive consolidation

Below and on the right we give an example of the consolidation of a holding company (GIANT) and a subsidiary (Dwarf) for you to work through.

The balance sheets at 31 December 2004, and the profit and loss accounts for the year ended on that date, are set out for GIANT plc and Dwarf Limited. GIANT acquired for £130 million two-thirds of the equity of Dwarf on 31 December 2003, when the cumulative balance on Dwarf's profit and loss account was £27 million.

Use the worksheets below and on the right to prepare the consolidated balance sheet and consolidated profit and loss account for the GIANT group for 2004. Assume that goodwill is being amortized against profit on the straight line method over ten years.

No dividends are proposed for 2004.

When you have completed GIANT's consolidated accounts for 2004, please compare your work with the solution set out over the page.

GIANT and Dwarf
Profit and loss accounts
for the year ended 31 December 2004

	Separate		Adjustments	GIANT
	GIANT	Dwarf		Group
	£m	£m	£m	£m
Turnover	2 200	550		
Operating profit	174	66		
Interest	20	4		
Amortization of goodwill				
Profit before tax	154	62		
Taxation	54	20		
Profit after tax	100	42		
Minority interests				
Profit for the year	100	42		

GIANT and Dwarf
Balance sheets
at 31 December 2004

	Separate		Adjustments	GIANT
	GIANT	Dwarf		Group
	£m	£m	£m	£m
Fixed assets				
Goodwill				
Plant and machinery	500	60		
Investment in Dwarf	130			
Net current assets	420	102		
	1 050	162		
Creditors due after one year	(250)	(45)		
	800	117		
Capital and reserves				
Called up share capital	500	48		
Profit and loss account:				
Brought forward	200	27		
Year 2004	100	42		
	800	117		
Minority interests				
	800	117		

GIANT and Dwarf
Profit and loss accounts
for the year ended 31 December 2004

	Separate GIANT £m	Dwarf £m	Adjustments £m	GIANT Group £m
Turnover	2 200	550		2 750
Operating profit	174	66		240
Interest	20	4		24
Amortization of goodwill			8 (g)	8
Profit before tax	154	62		208
Taxation	54	20		74
Profit after tax	100	42		134
Minority interests			14 (f)	14
Profit for the year	100	42		120

Notes (to balance sheets on right)

(a) Cost of investment in Dwarf £130m.
(b) 2/3 of Dwarf's £48m opening share capital.
(c) 1/3 of Dwarf's £48m opening share capital.
(d) 2/3 of Dwarf's £27m opening retained profits.
(e) 1/3 of Dwarf's £27m opening retained profits.
(f) 1/3 of Dwarf's £42m retained profit for 2004 (leaving 2/3 of £42m = £28m to include in GIANT group's profits for 2004).
(g) 1/10 of £80m cost of goodwill being amortized.

GIANT and Dwarf
Balance sheets
at 31 December 2004

	Separate GIANT £m	Dwarf £m	Adjustments £m	GIANT Group £m
Fixed assets				
			+ 130 (a)	
			− 32 (b)	
Goodwill			− 18 (d)	72
			− 8 (g)	
Plant and machinery	500	60		560
Investment in Dwarf	130		− 130 (a)	
Net current assets	420	102		522
	1 050	162		1 154
Creditors due after one year	(250)	(45)		(295)
	800	117	−58	859
Capital and reserves				
Called up share capital	500	48	−32 (b)	500
			−16 (c)	
Profit and loss account:				
Brought forward	200	27	− 18 (d)	200
			− 9 (e)	
Year 2004	100	42	− 14 (f)	120
			− 8 (g)	
	800	117		820
			+ 16 (c)	
Minority interests			+ 9 (e)	39
			+ 14 (f)	
	800	117	−58	859

NON-CONSOLIDATED SUBSIDIARIES

FRS 2 says a parent company (P) must exclude a subsidiary (N) from consolidation if:

(a) severe *long-term restrictions* substantially hinder the exercise of P's rights over N's assets or management;
(b) P holds its interest solely for *subsequent resale*, and has not previously consolidated N;
(c) N's activities are *so different* from other group undertakings that their inclusion would prevent a true and fair view.

(IAS 27 allows only (b) above as a reason for non-consolidation.)

In such cases the accounting treatment is the 'equity' method. (An example is shown below.) The group profit and loss account includes P's entire share of N's profit or loss for the period. The group balance sheet shows P's investment in N at cost plus P's share of N's post-acquisition retained earnings. Any dividends which N pays to P simply reduce P's investment in N and increase P's cash balance.

Example
P buys 100 per cent of N at 31 March 2004, for £400 000 cash. In the year ended 31 March 2005:

1   P makes a profit of £190 000, but pays no dividend.
2   N makes a profit of £70 000, and pays a dividend (to P) of £20 000.

P treats N as a non-consolidated subsidiary.

P LIMITED
Group balance sheet at 31 March (extract)

	2004 £'000	2005 £'000
Investment in N	400[a]	450[b]
Tangible fixed assets, net	900	900
Net current assets	500	710[c]
Total assets less current liabilities	1 800	2 060

Group profit and loss account, year to 31 March 2005 (extract)

	£'000
Profit of P	190
100% share of N's profit	70
Total group profit	260

Notes

[a] at cost 400
[b] 400 + 50 (N retained earnings = 70 − 20)
[c] 500 + 190 + 20 = 710.

ASSOCIATES

FRS 9/IAS 28 requires companies to use the 'equity' method to account for 'associates'. These are entities which are not controlled (and are therefore not subsidiaries), but where the holding company:

(a) owns at least 20 per cent of the equity shares; and
(b) has a significant influence over strategic policy decisions.

The group *profit and loss account* includes, and shows separately, the group's share of pre-tax profit, tax and retained profit, but not the group's share of turnover. (An example of the layout is shown below.) Unrealized inter-company profits resulting from group transactions with associates should be excluded.

The group's *balance sheet shows* (as a fixed asset investment) the investment in associates at *cost* plus the group's share of the associate's *post-acquisition retained earnings*.

Accounts must include a list of names of associates and of other companies in which at least a 20 per cent stake is held. The investing group must disclose more details where the group's aggregate share in associates exceeds 15 per cent of its gross assets, turnover or profit.

Example

GROUP PROFIT AND LOSS ACCOUNT
Year ended 31 December 2004

	£'000	£'000
Turnover		18 000
Operating profit		3 500
Share of associates' profit before tax		400
Group profit before tax		3 900
Taxation: Group	1 200	
Associates	140	
		1 340
Group profit after tax		2 560
Profit for the year:		
Parent company	1 330	
Subsidiaries	1 170	
Associates	60	

181

JOINT VENTURES

FRS 9 defines a 'joint venture' as an entity in which the reporting entity holds an interest on a long-term basis and which the reporting entity jointly controls with one or more other venturers under a contractual arrangement.

FRS 9 requires group accounts to use the 'gross equity method' for joint ventures, disclosing the share of the joint venture's turnover and gross assets and gross liabilities. IAS 31 distinguishes between three types of 'joint venture':

- jointly controlled operations
- jointly controlled assets
- jointly controlled entities.

For the first two, the 'gross equity method' should be used (as for FRS 9 above).

For jointly controlled entities, IAS 31 permits *either* proportionate consolidation *or* the equity method. Under proportionate consolidation the venturer's share of each of the assets, liabilities, income and expenses of a jointly controlled entity is combined line by line with similar items in the venturer's accounts.

SECTION 9 SUMMARY

Two main kinds of investment in other companies' equity shares can be distinguished: controlling shareholdings and other shareholdings.

A holding (parent) company which controls one or more subsidiaries must normally present consolidated (group) accounts, as if the group were a single entity. The consolidation process cancels out debtor and creditor balances between members of the same group, and excludes intra-group profits which are unrealized (by the group) at the balance sheet date.

When two or more companies combine their businesses, the normal accounting treatment is to use the 'acquisition' method. This aggregates profits and losses from the relevant date, and may give rise to 'goodwill' in the group accounts.

Goodwill is the excess of the purchase price of a subsidiary over the fair value of its separable net assets at the date of acquisition. Group accounts treat both brands and purchased goodwill as intangible fixed assets and either amortize them against profit or subject them to regular impairment reviews.

Where a holding company owns less than 100 per cent of a subsidiary's equity shares, 'minority shareholders' own the rest. Group accounts include 100 per cent of such subsidiaries' net assets and profits. The group balance sheet shows the amount of 'minority interests in subsidiaries' below shareholders' funds; and the group profit and loss account deducts 'minority interests share of profit' from group profit after tax, to leave the 'profit for the year' attributable to shareholders in the holding company.

When two or more companies of similar size combine by means of a shares-for-shares exchange (and meet certain other conditions) FRS 6 says they must use 'merger' accounting. No goodwill arises, and the new group discloses results combined for the *whole year* in which the merger occurs (and for earlier years too). *But IFRS 3 forbids merger accounting*.

Where, for some good reason, a parent company (P) does not consolidate the accounts of a subsidiary (N), P should normally use the 'equity' method of accounting. This means taking credit in the group accounts for P's share of N's profit (not just for dividends received); and showing P's investment in N in the group balance sheet at cost plus P's share of N's post-acquisition retained earnings.

Companies also use the 'equity' method when they own between 20 per cent and 50 per cent of another company's voting shares and influence their 'associate's' commercial decisions.

For joint ventures they use the 'gross equity' method for jointly controlled operations or assets, but for jointly controlled entities IAS 31 permits *either* proportionate consolidation *or* the 'equity method'.

PROBLEMS

9.1 Definitions
Please write down below your definition of the terms shown. Then compare your answers with the definitions overleaf.

(a)   A subsidiary undertaking

(b)   Group accounts

(c)   Minority interests

(d)   Pre-acquisition profits

e)   'Merger' accounting

(f)   An associated undertaking

(g)   Non-consolidated subsidiaries

(h)   The 'equity' method

(i)   Goodwill

(j)   Inter-company profits

9.1 Definitions

(a) **A subsidiary undertaking** is a company which another company controls. The 'holding' company either owns more than 50 per cent of its equity capital, or controls its board of directors or controls through an agreement or contract.

(b) **Group accounts** ('consolidated accounts') comprise the aggregate financial statements of a holding company and its subsidiaries. They aim to present a true and fair view of the financial position and performance of the companies which the holding company controls, as if they were a single enterprise.

(c) **Minority interests** are the equity interests of shareholders other than the holding company in the net assets (and profits or losses) of subsidiaries which the holding company does not wholly own. Group accounts show them separately both in the balance sheet and in the profit and loss account.

(d) **Pre-acquisition profits** are the retained profits of subsidiaries at the date of acquisition, which the holding company itself cannot pay out in dividends. (It must use any dividends it receives therefrom to write down the cost of its investment.)

(e) **'Merger' accounting** ('pooling of interests') adds together the book values of the combining companies' net assets (so no 'goodwill' arises) and aggregates profits for periods *before* the date of the merger (so no pre-acquisition profits arise).

(f) **An associated undertaking** is an enterprise in which another company owns between 20 per cent and 50 per cent of the equity shares and can influence its commercial decisions. The 'equity' method is used to account for it.

(g) **Non-consolidated subsidiaries** are subsidiaries whose accounts the holding company does not consolidate for one of three reasons:

- severe long-term restrictions hinder control;
- its activities are so different that their inclusion would prevent a true and fair view;
- the parent holds its interest solely for subsequent re-sale.

In such cases the accounts must be presented either separately, or in some suitable combination, using the 'equity' method.

(h) **The 'equity' method** is the normal method of accounting for non-consolidated subsidiaries and for associated undertakings. The group balance sheet shows the investment at cost plus the holding company's share of post-acquisition retained profits. The group profit and loss account includes the holding company's share of profits or losses (share of dividends plus share of retained profits).

(i) **Goodwill** is the excess of the purchase price paid by a holding company over the fair value of (its share of) the subsidiary's net assets at the date of acquisition. The holding company includes it as an intangible fixed asset and either amortizes it against profit over its useful life or subjects it to an annual impairment review.

(j) **Inter-company profits** are what one member company of a group earns on sales to another. Group accounts eliminate such profits until they are realized from the group's point of view, by sales to customers outside the group.

9.2 Whale Limited (A): Simple consolidation

Whale Limited acquired all the equity shares in Minnow Limited for £200 000 in cash on 1 January 2005. At 31 December 2004 (*before* the purchase price had been paid), the two companies' balance sheets were summarized as follows:

	Whale £'000	Minnow £'000	Consolidation adjustments £'000	Whale Group £'000
Tangible fixed assets	790	150		
Net current assets	230	40		
	1 020	190		
Less: Long-term debt	(70)	(60)		
	950	130		
Called up share capital	500	80		
Reserves	450	50		
Shareholders' funds	950	130		

Please draw up Whale Limited's consolidated balance sheet immediately after the acquisition, on the assumptions (1) that Minnow Limited is its only subsidiary, and (2) that goodwill is carried forward in the balance sheet as an intangible fixed asset, to be amortized against profit over its useful life.

The answer is shown overleaf.

9.3 Dexter Limited (A): Minority interests

On 1 April 2004 Dexter Limited (which previously had no subsidiaries) acquired 75 per cent of the equity share capital of Close Limited for 50 000 £1 ordinary shares. Dexter Limited's ordinary shares were valued at 180p each. The two companies' summarized balance sheets at 31 March 2004 had been as follows:

	Dexter £'000	Close £'000	Consolidated adjustments £'000	Dexter Group £'000
Tangible fixed assets	251	72		
Net current assets	64	12		
	315	84		
Less: Long-term debt	(78)	(20)		
	237	64		
Called up £1 share capital	150	40		
Reserves	87	24		
Shareholders' funds	237	64		

Please draw up Dexter Limited's group balance sheet straight after the acquisition, assuming that goodwill is capitalized as an intangible fixed asset.

The answer is shown overleaf.

9.2 Whale Limited (A)

Solution

WHALE LIMITED
Group* balance sheet at 1 January 2005

	Whale £'000	Minnow £'000	Consolidation adjustments £'000	Whale Group £'000
Goodwill			(a) + 200 (b) − 130	70(c)
Tangible fixed assets	790	150		= 940
Net current assets	230	40	(a) − 200	70(d)
	1 020	190	− 130	1 080
Less: Long-term debt	(70)	(60)	═══	= (130)
	950	130		950
Called up share capital	500	80	(b) − 80	500
Reserves	450	50	(b) − 50	450
Shareholders' funds	950	130	− 130	950

Notes (£'000)

(a) £200 purchase price
(b) £130 Minnow equity
(c) Goodwill £70 = £200 purchase price − £130 Minnow equity
(d) Whale £230 less £200 purchase price paid (to Minnow's *shareholders*, not to Minnow Limited) = £30 + Minnow £40 = £70.

*There is no significant difference between the headings 'Group accounts' and 'Consolidated accounts'.

9.3 Dexter Limited (A)

Solution

DEXTER LIMITED
Group balance sheet at 1 April 2004

	Dexter £'000	Close £'000	Consolidation adjustments £'000	Dexter Group £'000
Goodwill			(b) + 90 (c) − 30 (e) − 18	(g) 42
Tangible fixed assets	251	72		= 323
Investment in Close			(a) + 90 (b) − 90	—
Net current assets	64	12		= 76
	315	84		441
Less: Long-term debt	(78)	(20)		= (98)
	237	64	+42	343
Called up £1 share capital	150	40	(a) + 50 (c) − 30 (d) − 10	200
Share premium			(a) + 40	40
Reserves	87	24	(e) − 18 (f) − 6	87
Shareholders' funds	237	64		327
Minority interests			(d) + 10 (f) + 6	16
	237	64	+42	343

Notes (£'000): (a) 50 000 new £1 shares issued at 180p = £90 proceeds. £50 is nominal share capital, so the £40 'excess' is share premium; (b) £90 cost of investment in Close; (c) and (e) 75% of Close's equity = (75% x £40) + (75% x £24) = £30 + £18 = £48; (d) and (f) 25% of Close's equity = (25% x £40) + (25% x £24) = £10 + £6 = £16; (g) Cost of investment £90 less 75% of Close's equity £48 = £42 goodwill.

9.4 Whale Limited (B): Consolidating profits

Whale Limited's consolidated ('group') balance sheet at 1 January 2005 is shown on the previous page (left) (see the Solution to Whale Limited (A)).

In the year ended 31 December 2005 Whale Limited made a profit after tax of £150 000, and Minnow Limited made a profit after tax of £40 000. No dividends were paid or proposed by either company.

You are asked to draw up Whale Limited's consolidated balance sheet at 31 December 2005. Please make the following assumptions:

1 The 2005 profits for each company were reflected entirely in net current assets.
2 Long-term debt and the net book value of tangible fixed assets for each company remained unchanged during 2005.
3 Goodwill is being amortized against profit over ten years.

The answer is given overleaf.

WHALE LIMITED
Group balance sheet at 31 December 2005

	Whale £'000	Minnow £'000	Consolidation adjustments £'000	Whale Group £'000
Goodwill				
Tangible fixed assets	790	150		
Investment in subsidiary	200			
Net current assets	180	80		
	1 170	230		
Less: Long-term debt	(70)	(60)		
	1 100	170		
Called up share capital	500	80		
Reserves: Brought forward	450	50		
Year 2005	150	40		
	1 100	170		

9.5 Dexter Limited (B): Pre-acquisition profits

At 31 March 2005 the balance sheets of Dexter Limited and Close Limited were as summarized below. In the year ended 31 March 2005 Dexter made a profit after tax of £40 000, and Close made a profit after tax of £12 000. Neither company paid a dividend in respect of the year.

Dexter Limited had acquired 75 per cent of the equity share capital of Close Limited for 50 000 £1 ordinary shares valued at 180p cash on 1 April 2004, when Close's reserves amounted to £24 000. Goodwill is being amortized over six years.

You are asked to draw up Dexter's group balance sheet at 31 March 2005 in the right hand column below.

The answer is given overleaf.

Balance sheets at 31 March 2005

	Dexter £'000	Close £'000	Consolidation adjustments £'000	Dexter Group £'000
Tangible fixed assets	280	85		
Investment in Close	90			
Net current assets	87	17	—	—
	457	102		
Less: Long-term debt	(90)	(26)	—	—
	367	76	—	—
Called up £1 share capital	200	40		
Share premium	40	—		
Profit and loss account	B/F 87	24		
	Yr 2005 40	12		
Shareholders' funds	367	76	—	—

9.4 Whale Limited (B)

Solution

WHALE LIMITED
Group balance sheet at 31 December 2005

	Whale £'000	Minnow £'000	Consolidation adjustments £'000	Whale Group £'000
Goodwill			(c) + 200 (d) − 80 (e) − 50 (f) − 7	63
Tangible fixed assets	790	150		= 940
Investment in subsidiary	200		(c) − 200	—
Net current assets	180(a)	80		= 260
	1 170	230	− 137	1 263
Less: Long-term debt	(70)	(60)	—	= (130)
	1 100	170	− 137	1 133
Called up share capital	500	80	(d) − 80	500
Reserves { B/F	450	50	(e) − 50	633
{ Year 2005	150(b)	40(b)	(f) − 7	
Shareholders' funds	1 100	170	− 137	1 133

Notes (£'000)

(a) Whale's £230 net current assets at 31 December 2004 were reduced by the £200 cost of the shares in Minnow Limited, making £30 at 1 January 2005. The profits for 2005, £150, are added, to make £180.
(b) Reserves have gone up by £150 and £40 respectively, the profits for the year.
(c) The £200 cost to Whale of all the shares in Minnow goes to goodwill.
(d) The £80 called up share capital in Minnow Limited (entirely owned by Whale) goes to goodwill, as before.
(e) Minnow's pre-acquisition profits (£50) also go to goodwill; but the post-acquisition profits (£40) remain, to be added in as part of the group's distributable reserves.
(f) Goodwill is being written off (amortized) in the group profit and loss account over ten years: 70/10 = 7.

9.5 Dexter Limited (B)

Solution

DEXTER LIMITED
Group balance sheet at 31 March 2005

	Dexter £'000	Close £'000	Consolidation Adjustments £'000	Dexter Group £'000
Goodwill			(a) + 90 (b) − 30 (d) − 18 (f) − 7	35
Tangible fixed assets	280	85		= 365
Investment in Close	90		(a) − 90	–
Net current assets	87	17		= 104
	457	102		504
Less: Long-term debt	(90)	(26)		= (116)
	367	76	− 55	388
Called up £1 share capital	200	40	(b) − 30 (c) − 10	200
Share premium	40			40
Profit and loss account:			(d) − 18	
Brought forward	87 }	24 }	(e) − 6 }	= 87 }
Year 2005	40 }	12 }	(e) − 3 } (f) − 7 }	= 42 }
Shareholders' funds	367	76		369
Minority interests			(c) + 10 } (e) + 9 }	19
	367	76	− 55	388

Notes (£'000)

(a) The original £90 investment in 75% of Close shares goes to goodwill.
(b) 75% of Close's share capital goes to goodwill.
(c) The other 25% of Close's share capital goes to minority interests.
(d) Dexter's 75% share of Close's pre-acquisition retained profits (£24) goes to goodwill. In future years the adjustment will be the same.
(e) 25% of the *whole* of Close's retained profits at 31 March 2005 (£24 + £12) goes to minority interests (i.e. £6 + £3 = £9).
(f) 1/6 of £42 goodwill is amortized in the year (= £7).

Answers to the following five problems are given at the end of the book.

9.6 Barber Limited and Jenkins Limited: Non-consolidated subsidiary

Jenkins Limited purchased all the share capital of Barber Limited at 31 December 2004. Summarized 2005 accounts for holding company and subsidiary are shown below, showing the £400 000 cash payment which Jenkins Limited made on 31 December 2004 for its investment in Barber.

	Jenkins Limited £'000	Barber Limited £'000
Net assets	3 600	280
Investment in Barber Limited	400	–
Total net assets at 31 December 2005	4 000	280
Profit after tax, 2005	500	100
Dividend paid	300	–
Retained profit for 2005	200	100

The holding company proposes *not* to consolidate the accounts of its subsidiary.

(a) You are asked to summarize the relevant parts of the final 2005 group accounts of Jenkins Limited.

(b) What difference would it make to your results if Barber Limited paid a dividend of £75 000 in respect of 2005?

9.7 Woodley Limited and McNab Limited: Mergers

Woodley Limited and McNab Limited agreed to combine their businesses at 1 April 2005. All the FRS 6 criteria for merger accounting were satisfied (see page 178). The two companies' summarized balance sheets at 31 March 2005 are shown below. Neither company had any borrowing.

Summarized balance sheets at 31 March 2005

	Woodley £m	McNab £m
Called up share capital	40	20
Profit and loss account	20	15
Shareholders' funds/net assets	60	35

The arrangement was that Woodley Limited would issue 20 million £1 ordinary shares (valued at 200p each) in exchange for all McNab Limited's shares. How would Woodley Limited's consolidated balance sheet appear at 1 April 2005?

9.8 Triple Enterprises Limited: Multiple consolidation

At 31 March 2005 three companies in the same industrial sector agreed to merge their businesses into a new single company, to be called Triple Enterprises Limited. Their balance sheets at 31 March 2005 before the merger are summarized below:

	Brighton Brands £'000	Corbett Chemicals £'000	Duckham Drugs £'000
Fixed assets, net	260	330	210
Net working capital	280	410	110
	540	740	320
Less: Long-term debt	(150)	(200)	(60)
	390	540	260
Capital and reserves			
Called up share capital	120	200	80
Profit and loss account	270	340	180
Shareholders' funds	390	540	260

For the purposes of the merger, the values of the shares in the three companies were agreed as follows:

Brighton Brands	£500 000
Corbett Chemicals	£600 000
Duckham Drugs	£400 000

Certain fixed assets were revalued upwards accordingly in all three companies; and in addition Corbett's stocks were written down by £30 000. After these adjustments, shareholders' funds in each of the three companies' balance sheets were shown at the agreed valuation figure.

You are asked to prepare the initial consolidated balance sheet of Triple Enterprises Limited on 1 April 2005 using merger accounting assuming that each of the three constituent predecessor companies became wholly owned subsidiaries, and that shareholders in each of the companies received £1 ordinary shares in Triple Enterprises Limited in exchange for their existing shares, in accordance with the agreed valuations at 31 March 2005. If you need any extra information, make (and state) some suitable assumption, and work with that to complete your answer.

9.9 Philip Limited: Inter-company trading

Philip Limited traded with its wholly owned subsidiary Sidney Limited. In the year ended 31 March 2005 Sidney had sold Philip for £80 000 goods which had cost £50 000. At 31 March 2005 Philip still held in stock goods which had been invoiced from Sidney at £20 000.

What, if any, consolidation adjustments are needed? Why?

9.10 Diageo (A) plc

Refer back to the segment analysis on page 172. Calculate return on net assets, profit margin and net asset turnover for each geographical area.

No answer is given to the following two problems.

9.11 Chain Industries Limited: Indirect interests

Chain Industries Limited, an industrial holding company, owns 60 per cent of A Limited's share capital. A owns 60 per cent of B's share capital; B owns 60 per cent of C's; C owns 60 per cent of D's; and D owns 60 per cent of E's share capital. How much of E's share capital does Chain Industries Limited (indirectly) own, if in each case the 40 per cent minority interest is owned by shareholders unconnected with Chain Industries? Would you expect Chain Industries Limited to consolidate E's accounts? Why or why not?

If shareholders' funds in the balance sheets of the various companies at 31 December 2004 are as shown below, and if Chain Industries Limited has no other subsidiaries which are not wholly owned, at what figure would you expect minority interests to stand in the consolidated balance sheet at 31 December 2004?

Shareholders' funds	£'000
Chain Industries Limited	999
A Limited	420
B Limited	300
C Limited	180
D Limited	240
E Limited	100

9.12 Portswood plc

On 1 October 2004, Portswood plc acquired 60 per cent of the share capital of William Kelsey plc, by paying £4.5 million cash. On that date the share capital and reserves of Kelsey amounted to £5.0 million, and the fair value of Kelsey's net assets was equal to their book value. Extracts from the accounts of the two companies for the year ended 30 September 2005 appear opposite.

Separate balance sheets at 30 September 2005

	Portswood £m	William Kelsey £m
Tangible fixed assets, net	9.0	5.0
Investment in William Kelsey plc	4.5	—
Net current assets	4.5	1.4
	18.0	6.4
Less: Loans over one year	(3.2)	(1.0)
	14.8	5.4
Ordinary £1 share capital	10.0	4.0
Revenue reserves	4.8	1.4
	14.8	5.4

Separate P & L accounts for 2005

Profit after taxation	1.5	1.0
Dividends payable	1.0	0.6
Retained profit for the year	0.5	0.4

The Kelsey dividend has *not* been included in Portswood's profit above. Goodwill is to be written off over ten years on the straight line basis.

Questions

1 Prepare a consolidated balance sheet for the Portswood plc Group as at 30 September 2005.
2 Complete the *pro forma* consolidated profit and loss account for the Portswood plc Group for the year ended 30 September 2005. (Hint: As a first step you should incorporate Portswood's share of the Kelsey dividend in Portswood's balance sheet.)

Consolidated profit and loss account
Year ended 30 September 2005
£ m

Profit after taxation
Less: Minority interests
———
Available for ordinary shareholders (in Portswood)
Dividends payable
———
Retained
═══

Section 10
Company taxation

TOTAL TAXATION

The main purpose of taxation is to raise revenue to pay for government spending. In many OECD countries total taxes have increased significantly over the past forty years as a percentage of GDP. Tax on company profits (right-hand column) often raises about *one-tenth* of total tax revenues.

GOVERNMENT TAX REVENUE
(as a percentage of Gross Domestic Product)

	1965 Total	1980 Total	2000 Total	2000 Company tax
Denmark	30	44	49	2.4
France	35	41	45	3.2
Germany	32	38	38	1.8
Italy	26	30	42	3.2
Sweden	35	48	54	4.1
Australia	22	27	32	6.5
Canada	26	31	36	4.0
UK	30	35	37	3.7
US	25	27	30	2.5
Japan	18	25	27	3.6
EU 15 (unweighted)	28	36	42	3.8

UK CORPORATION TAX

While the details vary between countries, many of the basic features of corporation tax are similar to the UK system we discuss in this section. In computing the amount of 'taxable profits', companies adjust their reported 'book' profits before tax to substitute tax capital allowances for book depreciation and to add back disallowed expenditure.

The normal *rate* of UK corporation tax is 30 per cent; though a reduced rate of 19 per cent applies on annual taxable profits below £300 000. If the tax rate changes, profits are split on a time basis to determine which rate to apply.

Companies' *capital gains* are subject to corporation tax at the normal rate. When a business reinvests the proceeds from selling a chargeable asset in another business asset in one of five 'qualifying classes', however, no chargeable gain arises until the second asset is sold. As a result of this 'rollover' relief, most business fixed asset disposals are tax free as long as replacement continues.

Profits earned overseas by UK companies are subject to overseas tax whether or not remitted home. But agreements on double taxation relief mean that only where the UK rate of corporation tax is higher than the overseas rate are overseas profits normally liable to any UK tax. Rules about transfer pricing between subsidiaries in different countries aim to prevent multinational companies seeming to earn most of their taxable profits in relatively low-tax countries.

Losses are computed in a similar way to profits. For tax purposes, UK companies may:

- set off losses against current profits, or
- carry them back to set against taxable profits for the three preceding years, or
- carry them forward to set against future profits (indefinitely).

Losses in one country cannot be offset against profits in another country, hence the average tax ratio for a multinational company with significant unrelieved tax losses in one or two countries can seem high. (But an EU case is pending.)

OTHER TAXES

UK taxes raise about 40 per cent of GDP in total, made up as follows:

UK TAX REVENUE 2004			Per cent of GDP
Income	Income tax	12	
	Corporation tax	3	
	Employees' national insurance	4	
			19
Employment	Employers' national insurance		4
Expenditure	Value Added Tax	6	
	Oil	3	
	Drink and tobacco	2	
	Miscellaneous	2	
			13
Local	Business rates	2	
	Council tax	2	
			4
Capital	Stamp duties	1	
	Capital gains tax	–	
	Inheritance tax	–	
			1
			41

Sole traders and partnerships are liable to personal income tax on their business profits, not to corporation tax (which applies only to limited companies). Taxable profits are computed as for companies.

The basic UK *personal income tax* rate of 22 per cent applies to income as reduced by personal allowances and other deductions. There is a lower rate of 10 per cent on the first £2 000 of income and a higher tax rate of 40 per cent on income above £30 000.

'*Social security*' taxes in the UK are called 'national insurance': they are split roughly equally between employees (a sort of income tax) and employers (in effect, an employment tax).

Value Added Tax, which companies in effect collect from customers on behalf of the government, is not included in turnover (sales revenue) in the profit and loss account [SSAP 5]. But any amounts due from customers under debtors (accounts receivable) in the balance sheet *will* include VAT.

Stamp duty is charged on purchases of shares and houses and other property. The total yield is now about twice as much as that of capital gains tax and inheritance tax combined.

Capital gains tax is charged only on realized gains. Gains of up to £8 000 a year are exempt. Capital gains are calculated by a 'tapering' system (in place of indexation for inflation), which reduces the percentage of the gain chargeable (at marginal income tax rates) from 100 per cent (for assets held for less than one year) to 25 per cent (for assets held for more than ten years).

Inheritance tax is payable at 40 per cent on estates on death exceeding £250 000. Like capital gains tax, it raises virtually no revenue.

ACCOUNTING FOR TAX

A company's *balance sheet* includes all overseas and UK corporation tax owing on taxable profits earned to date, less any payments made on account. These appear as a separate heading under current liabilities. Any provision for deferred tax (see below) appears under 'Provision for liabilities and charges'.

References to 'taxation' in company accounts nearly always mean 'corporation tax' on profits. The balance sheet includes social security and other taxes owing, including deductions from employees' wages, under current liabilities.

In the *cash flow statement*, profit before tax is one of the sources of cash from operating activities and tax actually paid in the year is a separate use of cash. (Thus changes in 'working capital' in a period exclude any change in the current tax owing.)

The *profit and loss account* includes social security and other taxes among operating expenses. The notes analyse the total (corporation) tax expense for the year between:

1   UK corporation tax (with deferred tax noted separately)
2   less: double tax relief
3   overseas tax
4   tax related to income from associates.

IAS 12 also requires companies to explain the link between tax expense and accounting profit by a numerical reconciliation: *either* between tax expense and accounting profit multiplied by the applicable tax rate(s) *or* (as below) between the average effective tax rate and the applicable tax rate.

Here is an example of both from Tesco plc's 2004 accounts:

Note 9 Taxation

(a) Analysis of charge in year

	£ million
Current tax	
UK Corporation tax @ 30.0%	433
Prior year items	(64)
Overseas taxation	33
Share of joint ventures and associates	27
	429
Deferred tax	
Origination and reversal of timing differences	29
Prior year items	41
Share of joint ventures and associates	(1)
	69
Tax on profit on ordinary activities	**498**

(b) Factors affecting the tax charge for the year 2004

	%
Standard rate of corporation tax	**30.0**
Effects of:	
Expenses not deductible for tax purposes*	4.1
Capital allowances in excess of book depreciation	(3.9)
Differences in overseas taxation rates	(0.9)
Timing of tax relief of share-based payments	1.4
Prior year items	(4.0)
Other items	0.1
Effective rate of corporation tax for the year**	**26.8**

Notes

*   Primarily goodwill amortization and non-qualifying depreciation

** £429m ÷ £1 600m

ADJUSTMENTS TO ACCOUNTING PROFITS

The simplest business tax computation begins with reported ('book') profits before tax for a year. Two adjustments then translate accounting profits into taxable profits:

1   Add back book depreciation charged in the accounts, and deduct instead the tax writing-down allowances.
2   Add back any disallowed items of expenditure.

The relevant rate of corporation tax is then applied to 'taxable profit' to determine the *amount* of tax payable.

Writing-down allowances

The UK tax system disallows as a deduction from taxable profits the depreciation of fixed assets charged in company accounts. It deducts tax 'writing-down allowances' (wdas) instead. A company's depreciation policy, therefore, cannot affect its UK tax bill. (The position is different in some other countries.)

All book depreciation is disallowed for tax purposes; but tax writing-down allowances are deductible from taxable profits only where the tax laws expressly say so. It follows that, if there is no provision for them in the tax statutes (whether by accident or design), certain kinds of capital spending attract no tax allowances at all.

Plant and equipment and cars are normally subject to a 25 per cent 'annual allowance', computed on the declining balance basis. New industrial buildings carry an annual allowance of 4 per cent (straight line) on original cost. (In neither case does residual value have to be estimated in advance.) Buildings classified as industrial or agricultural attract writing-down allowances, but other buildings (for example, shops, showrooms and offices) attract *no* writing-down allowances for tax purposes.

Calculation of writing-down allowances

	Plant and equipment 25% on declining balance	Industrial property 4% on cost
	£	£
Cost	1 000	1 000
Year 1 allowance	250	40
	750	960
Year 2 allowance	188	40
	562	920
Year 3 allowance	141	40
	421	880
Year 4 allowance	105	40
	316	840
Year 5 allowance	79	40
Written-down value, EOY 5	237	800

Timing differences

The 25 per cent annual writing-down allowance is computed on the 'pool' basis. Any proceeds from selling a fixed asset are deducted from the tax written-down value of the pool of similar assets. They thus reduce the year's annual allowance (on the declining balance). The result is to *delay* the tax charge (or allowance) on any profit (or loss) on sale. But over the whole life of the business, the total cost of eligible fixed assets, less the total proceeds of sales, is allowed as a deduction from taxable profits.

Sometimes tax officials may regard as 'capital' items which a business has treated as 'revenue' expenditure. The business will not then be allowed to charge the whole of such amounts as expenses against taxable profits in the current year. It will have to 'add back' to book profits the amounts charged in the accounts, and write them off in stages over a number of years. This difference in treatment affects the *timing* of charges against profit, and of tax payments; but it does not change the total amount of tax payable (unless the tax rate changes).

Disallowed expenditure

The law expressly disallows certain items as deductions for tax purposes, such as:

(a) legal expenses in connection with capital transactions;
(b) general reserves for bad debts (but *specific* provisions are allowed);
(c) business entertainment expenses (except a reasonable amount for staff).

Sometimes tax officials may consider an item not to be 'wholly and exclusively for the purposes of the trade'. (The *intention* to make a profit is what matters, not the actual result.) The rules applying to *employees'* expenses are stricter than those applying to businesses and the self-employed. They require expenses to be 'wholly, exclusively *and necessarily* incurred for the purpose of the office or employment'. In practice, though, expenses are sometimes apportioned between allowable and non-allowable.

Business accounts aim to show 'a true and fair view' of the results, whereas tax officials have to enforce the law. Since tax statutes are not always clear (to put it mildly), there is often room for discussion between taxpayers (or their agents) and officials. The Inland Revenue normally accepts consistent business accounting practice as a basis for computing taxable profits. Among the exceptions to this general rule are the LIFO method of valuing stock (see Section 6), and inflation accounting adjustments (see Section 13).

Simple corporation tax computation

		£'000
Reported accounting profit before tax		9 000
Add back: Book depreciation	2 600	
Disallowed expenditure	400	3 000
		12 000
Less: Tax writing-down allowances		4 000
= Taxable profit		8 000

DEFERRED TAX

Over a fixed asset's whole life, tax writing-down allowances (wdas) will in total equal book depreciation. Both will amount to *cost less disposal proceeds*. But the pattern over time may differ. Tax wdas based on declining balance are higher in the early years than straight line book depreciation (and *therefore* lower in the later years).

The amount of tax expense matters because it affects profit after tax, earnings per share, return on equity, and a number of other financial ratios. In theory there are two main ways for accounts to *report* the tax expense; but the accounting treatment does not affect the *actual tax payable*:

1 The 'flow through' method charges as an expense only the *actual* tax payable on the year's taxable profits. As a proportion of reported pre-tax profits, this may often be *less* than the current rate of corporation tax.
2 'Full provision' for 'deferred tax' charges in total what tax payable *would have been* if book depreciation were deducted for tax purposes. Apart from other timing differences, disallowed items and losses (which we ignore here), the tax expense will then equal the current tax rate on reported pre-tax profits. This is the system required by FRS 19/IAS 12.

Example
George Orwell plc reported profit before tax of £80m for the year ended 31 December 2004, after charging book depreciation of £45m. Writing-down allowances amounted to £75m, so taxable profit was £50m; and, with a tax rate of 30 per cent, actual tax payable was £15m.

If George Orwell charged only the actual tax for the year ('flow through' method), while another company with identical operating results (Eric Blair plc) provided in full for deferred tax, their accounts would show different results:

	George Orwell (Actual) £ million	Eric Blair (Deferred) £ million
Profit and loss account, 2004		
Profit before tax	80	80
Corporation tax @ 30 per cent	15	24
Profit after tax	65	56
Balance sheet, end 2004		
Deferred tax provision	–	9

As a result of their different methods of *accounting* for tax in 2004, George Orwell would *report* higher profit after tax (and higher earnings per share) than Eric Blair, even though their *actual* tax bill was the same. Eric Blair's £24m tax expense would exceed the £15m tax actually payable by £9m. This is the 30 per cent tax rate multiplied by the £30m excess of tax wdas (£75m) over book depreciation (£45m). This £9m difference would *increase* the 'deferred tax provision' account in the balance sheet (under long-term 'provision for liabilities and charges').

If in 2005 George Orwell and Eric Blair each had tax wdas of £55m and their financial results were otherwise the same as in 2004, actual tax payable in 2005 would be £21m (= £70m @ 30 per cent). Their 2005 accounts would show the following:

	George Orwell (Actual) £ million	Eric Blair (Deferred) £ million
Profit and loss account, 2005		
Profit before tax	80	80
Corporation tax @ 30 per cent	21	24
Profit after tax	59	56
Balance sheet, end 2005		
Deferred tax provision (cumulative)	–	12

Again George Orwell's reported profit after tax is *higher* than Eric Blair's. The deferred tax provision would *rise* by a further £3m in 2005, to reflect 30 per cent tax on the £10m surplus of tax wdas (£55m) over book depreciation (£45m).

The deferred tax provision represents a *temporary* deferral of tax. In a fixed asset's later years, book depreciation will *exceed* the tax wdas, thus clearing the deferred tax provision in respect of that specific fixed asset. But many companies expand, or at least replace fixed assets (which cost more money in times of inflation). So the *cumulative* balance of deferred tax provision may continue to grow year after year.

There is a question whether deferred tax provisions should be discounted. FRS 19 allows the option, while IAS 12 forbids discounting.

Deferred tax problem

Topaz Limited, a new company, projects profits of £200 a year (before tax and straight line depreciation) for each of the next four years. In Year 1 the company plans to spend £320 on equipment which has a four-year life with no residual value. Topaz Limited plans no capital spending in Years 2, 3 or 4.

The rate of corporation tax is 20 per cent. Assume that for tax purposes Topaz may deduct a first-year writing-down allowance of 100 per cent of the cost of equipment and carry forward any unused allowance to set against taxable profits in future years.

You are asked, in the space below, to set down:

- the corporation tax actually payable for each of the next four years;
- the projected profit and loss account summary for each of the next four years, assuming full provision is made for deferred tax;
- the cumulative provision for deferred tax in the balance sheet each year.

The solution to this problem is shown overleaf.

TOPAZ LIMITED

	Year 1 £	Year 2 £	Year 3 £	Year 4 £
Corporation tax payable				
Profit before depreciation	200	200	200	200
Less: writing-down allowance				
Taxable profit				
Corporation tax @ 20 per cent =				
Profit and loss account summary				
Profit before depreciation	200	200	200	200
Straight line depreciation				
Profit before tax				
Tax expense				
Profit after tax				
End-of-year balance sheet				
Provision for deferred tax (cumulative) =				

Solution

TOPAZ LIMITED

	Year 1 £	Year 2 £	Year 3 £	Year 4 £
Corporation tax payable				
Profit before depreciation	200	200	200	200
Less: writing-down allowance	200*	120*	–	–
Taxable profit	–	80	200	200
Corporation tax @ 20 per cent =	–	16	40	40

*The writing-down allowance is £320; of which £200 is used up in Year 1, and the balance of £120 is carried forward to Year 2.

Profit and loss account summary				
Profit before depreciation	200	200	200	200
Straight line depreciation	80	80	80	80
Profit before tax	120	120	120	120
Tax expense**	24	24	24	24
Profit after tax	96	96	96	96
**Actual tax liability	–	16	40	40
Deferred tax	24	8	(16)	(16)

End-of-year balance sheet				
Provision for deferred tax[a]	24	32	16	–

If no deferred tax ('flow through')				
Profit after tax[b]	120	104	80	80

Notes

[a]In this simple example, the deferred tax balance clears by the end of Year 4.

[b]Profit after tax is higher in the early years if there is *no* provision for deferred tax.

[c]Over the four years, profit before depreciation totals £800; depreciation (= cost of equipment) totals £320; on £480 profit before tax, tax @ 20 per cent amounts to £96, which leaves profit after tax of £384 (= 96 + 96 + 96 + 96 = 120 + 104 + 80 + 80).

SECTION 10 SUMMARY

In many countries total taxation has risen in the past forty years. UK taxes now take about 40 per cent of GDP. Corporation tax yields about one-tenth of total tax revenue.

The UK rate of corporation tax is 30 per cent, but only 19 per cent for companies with 'small' profits.

Individual shareholders with taxable income exceeding about £30 000 a year are subject to higher-rate income tax at 40 per cent. Shareholders with realized capital gains exceeding about £8 000 a year are liable to capital gains tax at marginal income tax rates (but tapered, depending on the holding period).

Company balance sheets combine UK and overseas corporation tax owing as a current liability. Profit and loss accounts (or notes thereto) analyse the total corporation tax expense between UK tax, double tax relief, overseas tax and tax relating to income from associates. Deferred tax is also shown separately.

There is also a requirement to provide a tax reconciliation, explaining the difference between the standard rate of corporation tax and a company's actual effective rate.

A simple company tax computation:

- starts with reported 'book' profits before tax;
- adds back book depreciation charged;
- deducts instead tax writing-down allowances; and
- adds back any disallowed expenses.

This determines taxable profit for the period, to which the relevant rate of corporation tax is applied.

On plant and equipment, tax writing-down allowances are normally 25 per cent a year, on the declining balance basis.

Deferred tax is used for timing differences between accounting profits and taxable profits. The effect is normally to increase tax expense in the profit and loss account above the actual amount of tax currently payable. The balance sheet shows the (cumulative) excess under 'Provisions for liabilities and charges'.

PROBLEMS

10.1 Definitions
Write down on this page your definitions of the terms shown. Then check your answers with those overleaf.

(a)   Disallowed expenditure

(f)   Timing differences

(b)   Writing-down allowances

(g)   Deferred tax

(c)   Taxable profits

(h)   The 'flow through' method

(d)   Overseas tax

(i)   Tax reconciliation

(e)   Double taxation relief

(j)   Withholding taxes

10.1 Definitions

(a) **Disallowed expenditure** is 'added back' to reported profits before tax in computing taxable profits. It may be due to:

- timing (general versus specific provisions for bad debts);
- political acceptability (some kinds of business entertaining); or
- 'oversights' in the legislation (depreciation of office buildings).

The effect is to increase the 'real' rate of tax on profits.

(b) **Writing-down allowances** ('capital allowances') represent 'tax depreciation', often using declining-balance, which some countries substitute for book depreciation, often using straight-line, in computing taxable profits. The total charge is the same over an asset's life, but the timing is different.

(c) **Taxable profits** are reported book profits before tax as adjusted (a) for disallowed expenditure, (b) for writing-down allowances, or (c) for any other special allowances .

(d) **Overseas tax** is tax on profits earned in overseas countries by the parent company or by subsidiaries. It can normally be offset against domestic corporation tax on the same profits. The rate of overseas tax may vary from the domestic rate.

(e) **Double taxation relief** reduces or eliminates a domestic tax liability by offsetting overseas tax paid on the same income.

(f) **Timing differences** may relate to fixed assets, where both book depreciation and tax 'writing-down allowances' write off a fixed asset's original cost less residual proceeds over its useful life, but with a different pattern over time; or to certain other items, such as provision for bad debts. Even ignoring interest, timing differences can affect the total amount of tax payable, if the rate of tax changes.

(g) **Deferred tax** is broadly the difference between the actual tax charge for a period based on tax writing-down allowances and what the (normally higher) charge would have been if only straight-line book depreciation had been deducted for tax purposes. It is charged as an expense in the profit and loss account and the cumulative 'liability' is shown under 'Provision for liabilities and charges'.

(h) **The 'flow through' method** is the system of accounting for tax that charges no deferred tax, but simply charges as an expense the actual tax liability for a period.

(i) **Tax reconciliation** is a detailed explanation of the difference between the actual tax charge for a period and the reported book profit before tax multiplied by the nominal rate of corporation tax (or the equivalent in terms of percentages).

(j) **Withholding taxes** are deducted at source (from interest, dividends, or other items) by the paying agent. They are remitted to the tax authorities, who credit the amounts as tax paid by the ultimate recipients. In the UK the PAYE ('Pay As You Earn') system deducts income tax from employees wages.

Answers to the problems on this page are shown overleaf.

10.2 Modern Services Limited: Business tax computation

Modern Services Limited reported profits before tax of £8.2 million in the year ended 31 March 2005, after charging depreciation of £750 000. Disallowable expenses for tax purposes were £150 000 and tax writing-down allowances were £450 000.

Compute the company's taxable profit for the year and calculate the amount of corporation tax payable.

10.3 Tom, Dick and Harry: Personal income tax rates

Assume that income tax rates are as follows:

Range of taxable income (in £ thousands)	Rate of tax on range
0 – 2	10%
2 to 30	22%
30 and over	40%

In the current year, Tom has an income of £25 000, Dick of £40 000 and Harry of £60 000. Assuming that each is entitled for income tax purposes to personal allowances and deductions totalling £5 000 in the year, calculate for each of the three:

(a) his marginal rate of income tax; and
(b) his average rate of income tax (as a percentage of his total income).

10.4 Blue Sky Speculations Limited: Change in rate of tax

Blue Sky Speculations Limited made taxable profits of £4.0 million in the year ended 30 June 20x4 and £3.0 million in the year ended 30 June 20x5.

What would the company's corporation tax liability amount to in respect of each of those two years if the tax rates for corporation tax (CT) years were as follows:

CT Year 20x3 30%
CT Year 20x4 35%
CT Year 20x5 40%
CT Year 20x6 45%.

CT years begin on 1 April. Thus 'CT Year 20x3' is the year *ending* on 31 March 20x4.

10.5 Graphic Enterprises Limited: Writing-down allowances

At 1 January 2005, Graphic Enterprises Limited showed the following amounts in the books for fixed assets (£'000):

Land £600 (cost)
Factory buildings £280 (cost) less £105 (accumulated depreciation)
Office buildings £106 (cost) less £24 (accumulated depreciation)
Plant and machinery £184 (cost) less £142 (accumulated depreciation)

During the year ended 31 December 2005, there were minor additions to both the factory buildings (costing £20) and to the office building (costing £14). Depreciation on buildings was charged each year at 5 per cent on cost.

New plant costing £22 was acquired during the year, as was second-hand equipment costing £4. Annual depreciation was charged at 10 per cent (straight line) on all plant (ignoring residual value). No fixed assets were sold during the year, and the company charged a full year's depreciation on all fixed assets acquired during a year.

For tax purposes, written-down values at 1 January 2005 of the various classes of fixed asset were as follows (£'000):

Land	£600
Factory buildings	£90
Office buildings	£106
Plant and machinery	£30.

You are asked to calculate for each fixed asset category in respect of the year 2005:

(a) the depreciation that would be charged in the company's books
(b) the net book value at the end of the year
(c) tax writing-down allowances for the year
(d) the tax written-down value at the end of the year.

10.6 Regeneration Limited: Amount of tax

Regeneration Limited's taxable profits in recent periods have been as follows after deducting writing-down allowances:

Year ended 30 June 20x3	£2.0 million
9 months ended 31 March 20x4	£1.5 million
Year ended 31 March 20x5	£2.4 million

Calculate the corporation tax payable in respect of the above if the tax rate is 30 per cent for CT Years 20x2 and 20x3, and 40 per cent for CT years 20x4 and 20x5.

10.2 Modern Services Limited

Solution

	£'000
Reported profit before tax	8 200
Add back: Depreciation charged	750
Disallowed expenses	150
	9 100
Less: Tax writing-down allowances	(450)
= Taxable profit	8 650

Corporation tax payable = 30% x £8 650 000 = £2 595 000.

10.3 Tom, Dick and Harry

Solution

Range (£'000)	Tax rate	Tom £	Dick £	Harry £
Taxable income		*25 000*	*40 000*	*60 000*
0 – 2	10%	200	200	200
2 to 30	22%	3 960	6 160	6 160
30 and over	40%	–	2 000	10 000
Total income tax =		4 160	8 360	16 360
	Marginal	22%	40%	40%
	Average*	16.6%	20.9%	27.3%

* on total income

10.4 Blue Sky Speculations Limited

Solution

Year ended 30 June 20x4
CT Year 20x3: 75% x £4m = £3m @ 30% = £900 000
CT Year 20x4: 25% x £4m = £1m @ 35% = £350 000 } £1 250 000

Year ended 30 June 20x5:
CT Year 20x4: 75% x £3m = £2.25m @ 35% = £787 500
CT Year 20x5: 25% x £3m = £0.75m @ 40% = £300 000 } £1 087 500

10.5 Graphic Enterprises Limited

Solution

	Factory buildings £'000		Office buildings £'000		Plant and machinery £'000
(a)(b) in the books					
Cost b/f	280		106		184
Additions	20		14		26
		300		120	210
Depreciation b/f	105		24		142
Charge for year	15		6		21
		120		30	163
Net book value		180		90	47
(c)(d) For tax purposes					
Written-down value b/f	90		106		30
Additions	20		14		26
		110		120	56
Annual allowances	12		–		14
Written-down value c/f		98		120	42

Notes on annual allowances

1 Annual allowance is 4 per cent on cost of factory buildings (£300).
2 No tax writing-down allowances on office buildings.
3 Annual allowance on plant is 25 per cent of written-down value (£56).
4 No tax writing-down allowances or book depreciation on land (£600).

10.6 Regeneration Limited

Solution

		£'000
CT Year 20x2: 75% x £2.0m = £1.5m @ 30% =		£450
CT Year 20x3: 25% x £2.0m = £0.5m @ 30% =		£150
		£600
CT Year 20x3 (9 months):	£1.5m @ 30% =	£450
CT Year 20x4 (12 months):	£2.4m @ 40% =	£960

10.7 Amethyst Limited: Deferred tax

Amethyst Limited, a new company, projects profits of £600 a year (before tax and straight line depreciation) for each of the next four years. In Year 1 the company is planning to spend £1 280 on equipment which has a four-year life (with no residual value). It has no plans for capital spending in Years 2, 3 or 4.

The tax rate is expected to be 30 per cent of taxable profit. Writing-down allowances of 25 per cent on declining written-down value are available, and the whole remaining written-down value is available as a tax allowance in the final year. Any unused allowances can be carried forward to set against profits in future years (but not back).

Required

(a) Set out the schedule of writing-down allowances over the four years.
(b) Calculate the corporation tax payable in each of the next four years.
(c) Set out each year's projected summary profit and loss account, showing profit before and after tax. Assume full deferred taxation.
(d) Set out the amount of the cumulative deferred tax account balance which would appear in Amethyst's balance sheet at the end of each year.

No answers are published for the following two problems.

10.8 Wavendon Limited: Writing-down allowances

Wavendon Limited is preparing its accounts for the year ended 30 June 2003. In order to estimate its tax liability, the company is about to calculate its writing-down allowances, on the basis of the following data:

	£'000
Purchase of fixed assets in year:	
Plant and equipment	250
Industrial buildings	50
Office building (modification)	60
Tax writing-down value of fixed assets (at 30 June 2003):	
Plant and equipment	836
Industrial buildings (cost £1 000 000)	280
Disposal of fixed assets in the year:	
Plant and equipment: cost	20
writing-down value for tax	6
proceeds of sale	9
Depreciation charge in the accounts	225
Credit balance on deferred taxation account at 1 July 2003	300

10.8 Wavendon Limited *continued*

Required

1 Calculate the writing-down allowances for the year ended 30 June 2004.
2 Assuming full deferred taxation, calculate the charge or credit to the profit and loss account in respect of deferred tax in 2004. (The company pays tax @ 30 per cent.)

10.9 Brotherton's Foods Limited: Tax computation

Brotherton's Foods Limited was established in 1982. Its draft accounts for the year ended 30 June 2004 show a profit on ordinary activities before tax of £1 830 000.

Among the items charged in arriving at the profit were the following:

		£'000
(a) Write down of obsolescent stock		104
(b) Depreciation:	plant and equipment	200
	industrial buildings	20
	office premises	5
(c) Legal expenses in connection with debt collection		25
(d) Entertaining:	overseas customers	6
	staff	8
	other	4
(e) Provision for bad debts:	specific	50
	general	25

Tax writing down allowances for the year amount to £300 000.

On 25 October 2003, the company paid a final dividend of 6p per share (net) for the year ended 30 June 2003. It is planning on 23 October 2004 to pay a final dividend of 7p per share (net) for the year ended 30 June 2004. No interim dividend was paid in either year. 10 million shares have been outstanding throughout the two years.

Required

1 Calculate the corporation tax payable on the results of the year ended 30 June 2004.
2 Prepare in summarized form as much as you can of Brotherton's Foods Limited's profit and loss account for the year ended 30 June 2004.

10.7 Amethyst Limited

Solution

(a) Writing-down allowances

	£'000
Cost	1 280
Year 1 wda 25%	320
EOY 1 wdv	960
Year 2 wda 25%	240
EOY 2 wdv	720
Year 3 wda 25%	180
EOY 3 wdv	540
Year 4 wda (balance*)	540
EOY 4 wdv	nil

*Assuming the 'pool' system is not used. If it were, the allowance in Year 4 would be £135k, and the £405k would remain in the 'pool'. Any disposal proceeds would simply be deducted from the balance in the 'pool'.

(b) Corporation tax payable

	Year 1 £	Year 2 £	Year 3 £	Year 4 £	TOTAL £
Profit before depreciation	600	600	600	600	2 400
Tax writing-down allowances	320	240	180	540	1 280
Taxable profit	280	360	420	60	1 120
Corporation tax @ 30%	84	108	126	18	336

(c) Profit and loss account summary

	Year 1 £	Year 2 £	Year 3 £	Year 4 £	TOTAL £
Profit before depreciation	600	600	600	600	2 400
Depreciation	320	320	320	320	1 280
Profit before tax	280	280	280	280	1 120
Tax	84	84	84	84	336
Profit after tax	196	196	196	196	784
Actual tax liability	84	108	126	18	336
Deferred tax provision	–	(24)	(42)	66	0
'Tax expense'	84	84	84	84	336

(d) Deferred tax *asset* account 0   24   66   0

Rather a tricky question, as the straight line book depreciation is the same as tax writing-down allowances in Year 1 and *higher* in Years 2 and 3!

Section 11
Cash flow statements

WHY PROFIT AND CASH MAY DIFFER

So far we have been looking at profit and loss accounts and balance sheets prepared on the basis of accrual accounting. That means including revenues and expenditures when they arise, regardless of when the company receives or pays cash. In practice, however, company managers have to worry about cash as well as about profit or loss.

Both profit and cash are important; but they are not the same. Profit is a surplus of income over expenses, an increase in well-offness. Cash is a liquid asset, a means of payment.

In Section 1 we saw the links between the financial statements. The balance sheet gives a static picture of a company's financial position at a single point in time, while the profit and loss account and cash flow statement summarize flows during the year. We have seen that studying relationships between figures – financial ratios – can provide useful insights and raise important questions. In this section we discuss how a close study of cash flows can also be revealing.

Shown below are some of the main reasons why the increase or decrease in a firm's cash position may differ from its profit or loss during a period. Apart from the capital items, most of them result from differences of timing.

Creditors and debtors	**Capital items**
Purchases on credit	Borrowing
Payment of creditors	Repayment of borrowing
Sales on credit	Issuing shares for cash
Receipts from customers	Payment of dividends
Real assets	**Write-downs of assets**
Purchases of fixed assets	Depreciation of fixed assets
Purchases of stocks	Writing down cost of stock
Sales of fixed assets	Provision for bad debts

Hence the pattern of cash flows in a period may not reflect at all closely what the profit and loss account shows. For example, a company that is short of cash may borrow, take a long time to pay suppliers, or sell off or delay purchasing fixed assets. In general when liquidity is a problem, time-horizons of decision-makers tend to become shorter.

An important aspect of financial planning is trying to forecast future cash receipts and payments, in order to ensure that enough cash is on hand when needed to make payments. Failure to pay creditors on the due date may, in the extreme, lead to the winding-up of a business *even if* it is making a profit.

CASH FLOW STATEMENTS

FRS 1/IAS 7 requires medium and large companies (see page 8) to publish a cash flow statement as part of their annual accounts. Its aim is to show cash flows into and out of a company during the year. This is 'in order to assist users of the financial statements in their assessment of the reporting entity's liquidity, viability and financial adaptability'. (The requirement for a cash flow statement does *not* appear in the UK Companies Act.)

In preparing cash flow statements, most companies use the 'indirect method', which uses balance sheet differences to arrive at *funds flows* (representing movements in both cash and credit). Excluding the credit and accrual elements then translates these into *cash flows*. (The alternative 'direct method' of preparing cash flow statements in effect presents a classified summary of the cash book.)

As with the financial ratios we discussed in detail in sections 2 and 3, looking at cash flow figures over several years is often more useful than the results for a single year (or even two). This is partly because twelve months is a short period in the lives of most business enterprises, and partly because it becomes clearer whether particular cash flows are 'typical' or not.

A somewhat simplified version of Tesco plc's group cash flow statement for 2004 is set out opposite, following the FRS 1 format. There are separate headings for servicing of finance, taxation, equity dividends paid; and capital expenditure is split from acquisitions and disposals. A note is required reconciling 'operating profit' (from the profit and loss account) with the 'net cash inflow from operating activities' (at the top of the cash flow statement).

TESCO PLC: GROUP CASH FLOW STATEMENT

53 weeks ended 28 February 2004	2004	2003
	£m	£m
Net cash inflow from operating activities (a)	**2 942**	**2 375**
Dividends from joint ventures and associates	60	11
Servicing of finance	(296)	(218)
Interest received	41	37
Interest paid	(337)	(255)
Taxation: Corporation tax paid	(326)	(366)
Capital expenditure	(2 177)	(2 000)
Payments to acquire tangible fixed assets	(2 239)	(2 032)
Receipts from sale of tangible fixed assets	62	32
Acquisitions and disposals	(272)	(436)
Purchase of subsidiaries	(216)	(386)
Invested in joint ventures and associates	(56)	(50)
Equity dividends paid	(303)	(368)
Net cash outflow before financing	**(372)**	**(1 002)**
Financing	639	971
Ordinary shares issued for cash	868	73
Purchase of own shares	(51)	(52)
Net (decrease)/increase in loans	(178)	950
Increase/(decrease) in cash and liquid resources	**267**	**(31)**

Note (a): Reconciliation with operating profit

	2004	2003
Operating profit	**1 735**	**1 484**
Depreciation and amortization	752	602
Net decrease in working capital	455	289
Increase in goods held for resale	(92)	(129)
Decrease in development property	15	3
Decrease/(increase) in debtors	17	(28)
Increase in trade creditors	261	238
Increase in other creditors	254	205
Net cash inflow from operating activities	**2 942**	**2 375**

ALTERNATIVE FORMATS

There is some dispute about the most suitable format for a cash flow statement, and indeed about how much flexibility should be allowed. IAS 7 requires three main headings: operations, investment and financing; while FRS 1 requires seven separate headings. As shown on the right, we ourselves prefer a somewhat different format.

Many analysts are concerned with the longer-term ability of companies to generate cash, rather than just with the cash movements in a single period. Like them, we prefer to highlight separately the key movements which show operating performance, and management decisions about working capital, about fixed asset investment and about the financing of the business. We do this in a 'cash flow statement' which starts with operating profit and shows 'net funds from operations' before disclosing separately the changes in working capital.

The FRS 1 approach uses working capital movements to translate 'funds flows' (cash and credit) into 'cash flows'. But this reflects only one aspect of changes in working capital. The second aspect, which may be more important, is the conscious decision by management to invest more or less in working capital.

For example, reductions in total working capital for a company whose ratios formerly used to reflect industry norms may indicate short-term financial pressure. The company may in effect be using working capital to finance fixed asset investment. But the standard cash flow statement does not disclose the change in working capital as such (only in a separate note).

Further, 'fixed asset investment' might look low, even at a time of heavy investment, merely because purchase invoices relating to the year had not yet been paid. While the FRS 1 statement reflects *cash* movements, it may be of more interest to the analyst looking at longer-term trends to know what commitments have been incurred in a period.

In our preferred restated format, one can compare the movements in both working capital and fixed assets with net funds from operations to determine the extent to which a company has been able to finance its investment from internally generated operating funds. The lower part of the statement, as with the other formats, shows how the company has financed any deficit ('financing requirement') or invested any surplus.

The three alternative formats are compared on the right, first our preferred format, then the FRS 1 format with its seven separate headings, then the IAS 7 format emphasizing the three main headings: operations, investment and financing. The IAS 7 format allows alternative treatments for interest paid and received, tax and dividends, as follows:

- A may be included in Operations or Financing
- B may be included in Operations or Investment
- C is included in Operations unless specifically identified with Investment or Financing.

The table below compares in outline three different formats for cash flow statements. From left to right they are: our own preferred format; the FRS 1 format; and the IAS 7 format. As well as a number of differences, clearly there are also similarities between the various formats.

MCA preferred	FRS 1	IAS 7
Operating profit		
+ Depreciation		
Interest received		
Gross funds from operation	*Operating profit*	
Interest paid		
Tax paid	*+ Depreciation*	
Dividends paid		
	+/– stocks	
Net funds from operations	*debtors*	
	creditors	
Changes in working capital		
Net cash from operations	**Operating activities**	**Operating activities**
	Interest paid*	Interest paid A
	Interest etc. received*	Interest etc. received B
		Tax paid C
	Tax paid	Dividends paid A
Investment in fixed assets	**Capital expenditure & financial investment**	**Investing activities**
	Acquisitions & disposals	
	Equity dividends paid	
Financing	**Financing**	**Financing activities**
(Equity)	(Equity)	(Equity)
(Debt)	(Debt)	(Debt)
Change in:	*Change in:*	*Change in:*
Liquid resources	Cash less overdrafts	Cash and cash equivalents

* Returns on investment and servicing of finance

TESCO PLC: RESTATED GROUP CASH FLOW STATEMENT

53 weeks ended 28 February 2004	2004 £m	2003 £m
Operating profit	**1 735**	**1 484**
Dividends from joint ventures and associates	60	11
Interest received	41	37
	1 836	1 532
Non-cash item: Depreciation and amortization	752	602
Gross funds from operations	**2 588**	**2 134**
Financing costs and tax:	(966)	(989)
Interest paid	337	255
Tax paid	326	366
Dividends paid	303	368
Net funds from operations	**1 622**	**1 145**
Decreases in working capital:	455	289
Stocks	(77)	(126)
Debtors	17	(28)
Creditors	515	443
Net cash from operations	**2 077**	**1 434**
Sale of tangible fixed assets	62	32
Total cash available	2 139	1 466
Fixed asset investment	(2 511)	(2 468)
Purchase of tangible fixed assets	2 239	2 032
Purchase of subsidiaries	216	386
Purchase of interests in joint ventures	56	50
Financing requirement	**(372)**	**(1 002)**
External financing		
Ordinary share capital	868	73
Purchase of own shares	(51)	(52)
Net (decrease)/increase in loans	(178)	950
(Increase)/decrease in cash and liquid resources	(267)	31
	372	1 002

INTERPRETING TESCO'S CASH FLOWS

The statement on the left shows cash flows for 2003 and 2004. From these figures we can see a number of things:

- Operating profit rose 17 per cent, from £1 484m to £1 735m.
- Following heavy investment in fixed assets, depreciation rose by 25 per cent.
- Interest paid was up by one-third, but tax paid was down by 10 per cent.
- Net funds from operations were up by 40 per cent, from £1 145m to £1 622m.
- Working capital figures again reflect a significant decrease, due to creditors.
- Tangible fixed asset investment is (net) 10 per cent up at £2 177m.
- The financing requirement is well down on 2003's £1 002m.
- Whereas 2003's financing requirement was almost entirely met by borrowing, in 2004 there was a significant issue of equity shares.

The five years' figures below add some extra insight:

- In all five years working capital decreased (as one would expect with growing turnover, given the large excess of current liabilities over current assets).
- 2004 is the only year of the five in which net debt has not risen. (Between 1999 and 2003 the debt ratio rose from 32 per cent to 43 per cent.)

TESCO PLC: Summary of restated group cash flow statements 2000–2004

	2000 £m	2001 £m	2002 £m	2003 £m	2004 £m
Operating profit	**1 030**	**1 166**	**1 322**	**1 484**	**1 735**
Depreciation	435	476	534	602	752
Net financing costs and tax	(606)	(687)	(852)	(941)	(865)
Net funds from operations	**859**	**955**	**1 004**	**1 145**	**1 622**
Net decrease in working capital	48	295	182	289	455
Net cash from operations	**907**	**1 250**	**1 186**	**1 434**	**2 077**
Net spending on tangible fixed assets	(1 211)	(1 910)	(1 835)	(2 000)	(2 177)
Net acquisitions of subsidiaries etc.	1	(76)	(96)	(436)	(272)
Financing requirement	**(303)**	**(736)**	**(745)**	**(1 002)**	**(372)**
Financing: net equity	2	30	(3)	21	817
net debt	331	895	892	950	(178)
Increase/(decrease) in liquid resources	30	189	2 144	(31)	267

KEY ASPECTS OF CASH FLOW

The two versions of Tesco's cash flow statement contain the same basic information, but they summarize it differently. The restated format contains many lines of interest.

Operating profit

Operating profit includes credit sales and purchases in the period. It represents one of the best measures of a company's performance, on an accrual accounting basis, before financing or tax. The profit trend signals possible changes in the business environment and in management's ability to respond.

Net funds from operations

This line represents the 'lifeblood' of the enterprise after adjusting operating profit to allow for any 'non-cash' items used to calculate profits (the main one being depreciation), and after payments for financing (interest and dividends) and for tax. In theory a company can reduce or omit dividend payments, but in practice they are regular requirements and restrict the funds left for investment in the business. Tesco's figures show increasing positive amounts every year.

Change in working capital

The change in working capital shows whether the enterprise is absorbing funds or (as with Tesco) releasing them. Certain items would normally increase with growth in turnover. Allowing for any changes in the ratios relative to industry norms may help analysts to detect signs either of financial stress or of loose control over working capital.

Net cash from operations

The net cash from operations is available for fixed asset investment. It reflects the position after allowing for the change in working capital. The term 'free cash flow' is sometimes used to mean the internally generated cash flow that is available for either investment in expansion or distribution to shareholders, *after* allowing for 'replacement' investment. Where a company is growing, however, it may not be easy to tell how much of the expenditure on tangible fixed assets has been needed to sustain the ongoing business, and how much has expanded it.

Purchases of tangible fixed assets

Companies must invest in tangible fixed assets to maintain their productive capacity. In the absence of inflation (see Section 13) and technical change, a non-growth business would probably need to invest about as much as historical money cost depreciation. The trend in capital spending over the past five years may signal the required level, assuming that the same policies continue.

Acquisitions of subsidiaries

Another major use of funds may be to acquire other companies. Such items may be large, but hard to predict.

Financing requirement

This residual amount broadly indicates whether or not the company's ongoing operations are generating the cash needed for fixed asset investment (including growth). In Tesco's case that was clearly not so in any of the five years. In years when significant investment is taking place (as with Tesco), that is not necessarily a cause for concern.

But continuous financing requirements over a five-year period suggest that the existing rate of growth depends on regular injections of external finance. This may reflect strong growth which shareholders and/or lenders are prepared to finance, but it may suggest that past investments are producing an inadequate rate of return. In Tesco's case, however (as we saw in Section 2) return on capital employed has remained steady at around 10 or 11 per cent – on total assets less current liabilities which *doubled* in the four years between 2000 and 2004.

External financing

The final part of the statement shows how a surplus is being invested, or how a financing requirement is being met. For the latter the alternatives are: issuing more equity capital, net borrowing, or running down liquid resources.

Liquid resources

At least part of the cash held at year-end is 'operating' in nature and will be absorbed in operations in the next period. It is needed to run the business. There may, however, be surplus cash, perhaps as a temporary result of raising new equity capital or borrowing. Any such surplus cash is not really 'working capital'; it is 'negative financing'. It is rarely possible, however, to split cash between the two, so as a rule we *exclude* cash from working capital and show it all in the final part of the statement.

DERIVING A CASH FLOW STATEMENT

In the UK medium and large companies must publish cash flow statements, but not small companies (see page 8), nor *divisions* of larger companies. Since they can be useful for analysts, it is important to be able to derive cash flow statements from published balance sheets and profit and loss accounts, together with the notes to the accounts.

We saw a simple example in Section 1 (page 6), and we now work through a somewhat more complex case – Harris & Clark plc. We shall use the simplest system for preparing cash flow statements, the 'indirect' method. It starts with the differences between the opening and closing balance sheets, analyses in detail the retained profit for the period, and then makes certain adjustments (for depreciation of fixed assets, for accruals, debtors and creditors, and for taxation and dividends).

The profit and loss account for Harris & Clark plc for 2004 appears on this page (right), and the balance sheets showing the position as at the end of 2003 and 2004 on the next page (left). Our main task in the analysis is to separate out entries which represent flows of funds from those which are merely book entries (such as depreciation). We shall then convert the funds flows into cash flows by adjusting for changes in debtors and creditors. We thus remove the (change in) credit element from the funds flows.

The cash flow statement itself, in the standard UK format, appears on page 209 (right). We treat cash inflows (receipts or sources) as positive, and cash outflows (payments or uses) as negative.

To prepare the cash flow statement, the main steps are as follows:

1 Enter the profit and loss account figures in the left-hand column of the worksheet; and show each amount either as a 'funds flow' (that is, a flow of either cash or credit) or as a 'book entry'.
2 Enter the balance sheet differences (2004 figures less those for 2003) in the 'differences' column of the balance sheet worksheet (sources are positive, uses are negative (in parentheses)). Analyse each of them between funds flows and book entries (using details from the notes where necessary).
3 Transfer the 'book entries' from the profit and loss account into the 'book entries' column of the balance sheet worksheet.
4 Transfer the final line of the profit and loss account into the balance sheet worksheet (under 'Capital and reserves'). Here this comprises £62m funds inflow [£83m – £21m dividend paid] and (£48m) book entries.
5 Total all three balance sheet worksheet columns and make sure they balance (that is, add to zero).
6 Transfer the detailed amounts from the funds flow columns in *both* worksheets to the cash flow statement, adjusting the funds flows to cash flows in the process by means of the changes in working capital.

HARRIS & CLARK plc
Profit and loss account for the year ended 31 December 2004

	P&L account £m	Funds flows £m	Book entries £m
Turnover	510	510	
Depreciation	(28)		(28) (b)
Other operating expenses	(412)	(412)	
Operating profit	70		
Interest expense	(15)	(15)	
Profit before tax	55		
Tax	(20)		(20) (a)
Profit after tax	35	83	(48)

Notes

(a) The cash flow statement shows tax actually *paid* in the year, so we show it as a 'book entry' here, and adjust it later to allow for the change in the year-end liability.

(b) Depreciation is obviously a 'book entry', being merely an allocation of part of the cost of tangible fixed assets. Fixed asset details (from a note to the accounts) are:

	Cost £m	Depreciation £m
At 1 January 2004	375	160
Additions in year	60	
Charge for year		28
Disposals in year	(10)	(7)
At 31 December 2004	425	181

(c) £3m proceeds from fixed asset disposals in this case exactly equal the net book value (cost £10m less accumulated depreciation £7m); so there is no profit or loss on disposal.

(d) During the year the company issued 24 million ordinary £1 shares @ 125p each.

(e) During the year the company paid dividends of £21m. Hence the increase in retained profit was £14m (£35m – £21m).

HARRIS & CLARK plc
Balance sheet at 31 December 2004

	2004	2003	Difference	Funds flows	Book entries
	£m	£m	£m	£m	£m
Fixed assets					
Tangible: cost	425	375	(50)	(60) add.	10 disp.
depn	(181)	(160)	21		28 + (7)
net b.v.	244	215		3 sale (c)	(3) nbv (c)
Investments	40	30	(10)	(10)	
	284	245			
Current assets					
Stocks	100	80	(20)	(20)	
Debtors	81	75	(6)	(6)	
Cash	45	40	(5)	(5)	
	226	195			
Current liabilities					
Trade creditors	65	60	5	5	
Taxation (a)	20	14	6	(14)	20
	85	74			
TA-CL	425	366			
Long-term loans	(125)	(110)	15	15	
	300	256			
Capital and reserves					
Share capital	124	100	24 (d)	24	
Share premium	6	–	6 (d)	6	
Retained profit	170	156	14 (e)	62	(48)
	300	256	–	–	–

For notes, see under profit and loss account (on left).

HARRIS & CLARK plc
Cash flow statement, year ended 31 December 2004

	£m
Operating activities	
Operating profit	70
Depreciation	28
Change in working capital	(21)
Stocks	(20)
Debtors	(6)
Trade creditors	5
Net cash flow from operating activities	77
Interest paid	(15)
Taxation paid	(14)
Investing activities	(67)
Tangible fixed assets acquired	(60)
Proceeds from disposals	3 (c)
Investments	(10)
Dividends paid	(21) (e)
Net cash outflow before financing	(40)
Financing activities	45
Share capital issued	30
Loans borrowed	15
Increase in cash balance	5

Interpreting Harris & Clark plc's cash flows

With only a single year's figures, it is hard to get far with the interpretation of Harris & Clark's cash flow statement for the year 2004.

The 25 per cent increase in stocks looks large compared with less than 10 per cent for debtors and trade creditors. End of year stocks represent nearly a quarter of operating expenses (and the fraction would be even higher if related to cost of goods sold).

A relatively small part of the £67m net investment in fixed assets is coming from internally generated funds (£27m). [£77 – 15 – 14 – 21]

Most of the £40m financing requirement in 2004 was met by an issue of ordinary share capital; but this is unlikely to be a regular event. An analyst might be especially interested in the likely level of investment in stocks and tangible fixed assets in 2005, and how this is expected to be financed.

SECTION 11 SUMMARY

This section has looked at cash flow statements as an extra source of financial information. There are several reasons, mostly flowing from timing differences, why cash flows in a period may not directly reflect profits under accrual accounting rules. A trend in cash flows over a number of years is likely to be more useful than the figures for only a year or two.

Cash flow statements (as in IAS 7) basically contain three main headings: operations, investment and financing; though FRS 1 requires seven separate headings.

We showed two years' published cash flow statements for Tesco plc; and we also set out the figures in our own preferred format which shows the changes in working capital.

The key items in the restated cash flow statement include net funds from operations. The financial surplus (or requirement) for a period reveals the extent to which these covered the investment in working capital and in fixed assets. A succession of deficits (financing requirements) for a number of years might raise questions.

One can compile a cash flow statement (by the 'indirect' method) from the opening and closing balance sheets, the profit and loss account for the period, and the notes to the accounts. This involves analysing items to distinguish 'book entries' from flows of funds (of cash and credit). The standard layout shows sources of funds (receipts) as positive and uses of funds (payments) as negative.

The main adjustments, under the 'balance sheet differences' method, are to expand on the 'profit for the year', and to allow for various fixed asset items, such as depreciation and any profit or loss on disposals. One also needs to adjust tax, debtors, creditors, and accruals in order to determine the actual amounts paid in the year.

In the problems following the text of this section, Problem 11.1 comprises definitions. Problem 11.2 gives an opportunity to restate Tomkins plc's published cash flow statement into our preferred alternative format. Problem 11.3 provides another example of the indirect method (as worked through in the text). Problem 11.4 gives a detailed example using the columnar method of analysis, which may be more suitable for complex accounts.

PROBLEMS

11.1 Definitions

Please write down on this page your definitions of the terms shown. Then check your answers with those overleaf.

(a)　Financing activities

(b)　Liquid resources

(c)　Depreciation

(d)　Cash flow statement

(e)　Working capital (for cash flow statement purposes)

(f)　Investment activities

(g)　'Free cash flow'

(h)　Funds flows

(i)　Financing requirement

(j)　Operating activities

11.1 Definitions

(a) **Financing activities** describe how a business gets external money to finance its assets. There are two main external sources: net borrowing (gross new borrowing less repayments of existing debt); and new issues of equity shares, which includes new equity shares issued *for cash*, but not shares issued in payment for an acquisition of another company, or scrip dividends issued in lieu of cash dividends. In addition, of course, there may be internally generated cash from operations, sometimes simplified to 'retained earnings plus depreciation'.

(b) **Liquid resources** comprise cash and marketable securities. This is close to the IAS 7 description 'cash and cash equivalents' (the FRS 1 treatment is somewhat different). Bank overdrafts are not netted off, being part of borrowing. The cash flow statement 'explains' the change in liquid resources during the period.

(c) **Depreciation** is the regular writing-off of part of the cost of a tangible fixed asset (for intangibles it is called 'amortization'). It is often the largest single item of non-cash expense which therefore needs to be 'added back' to profit to get to 'internally generated cash flow'.

(d) A **cash flow statement** is one of the three main financial statements required by FRS 1/IAS 7 (but not by the UK Companies Act). It is backward-looking, though a similar format can be used for forward-looking estimates too. The precise format varies somewhat between FRS 1 and IAS 7, but in both the three main kinds of cash flow are: operations, investment and financing.

(e) **Working capital** (for cash flow statement purposes) comprises stocks [inventories], debtors [accounts receivable] and creditors [accounts payable]. It does not include cash or bank overdrafts, which are regarded respectively as liquid resources and borrowing, nor taxation which cash flow statements treat separately.

(f) **Investment activities** comprise investment in fixed assets and acquisitions of subsidiaries as well as investments in joint ventures and associates and in other financial investments. They also include proceeds from sales of such assets. The amounts involved can vary from year to year, so identifying reliable trends may not be easy.

(g) **'Free cash flow'** is sometimes taken to refer to cash available either for expansion investment or for additional distribution to shareholders. But it is very hard to quantify, since it is normally impossible to tell (at least from the outside) how much of investment in fixed assets is needed to 'maintain' the level of activity.

(h) **Funds flows** represent flows of cash *and credit*, from which the credit element needs to be removed to leave cash flows only.

(i) **Financing requirement** is normally the excess of spending on investment over cash generated from operations (though net 'investment activities' could generate cash and operations could absorb it). There are three basic ways to meet this (external) financing need: by issuing new equity shares for cash; by (net) borrowing; or by running down liquid resources.

(j) **Operating activities** represent operating profit (before interest and tax), plus depreciation, plus or minus the change in working capital. In the FRS 1/IAS 7 formats, the details are not shown as part of the cash flow statement, but as a separate note.

11.2 The BOC Group plc (A): Restating cash flow statement

The BOC Group plc's published cash flow statement for 2003 is shown opposite (somewhat simplified), together with information from Note 27 to the accounts.

You are asked to use a separate piece of paper to:

(a) restate the figures for 2003 and 2002 in our suggested format shown on pages 205 and 206.

(b) comment on the salient points.

A solution to this problem is shown overleaf.

Note (a) Net cash inflow from operating activities

	2003 £m	2002 £m
Operating profit	505	500
Depreciation and amortization	333	331
Net retirement benefits charge less contributions	6	50
Operating profit of joint ventures and associates	(98)	(75)
Change in stocks	(17)	14
Change in debtors	3	(38)
Change in creditors	11	57
Other	(43)	(80)
Net cash inflow from operating activities	**700**	**759**

THE BOC GROUP PLC
Group cash flow statement
Years ended 30 September

	2003 £m	2002 £m
Net cash inflow from operating activities (a)	700	759
Dividends from joint ventures and associates	35	34
Returns on investment and servicing of finance	(94)	(91)
Interest paid	(99)	(91)
Interest received	17	18
Dividends paid to minorities in subsidiaries	(12)	(14)
Tax paid	(91)	(96)
Capital expenditure and financial investment	(233)	(324)
Purchase of tangible fixed assets	(281)	(352)
Sales of tangible fixed assets	37	32
Net sales/(purchases) of other investments	11	(4)
Acquisitions and disposals	(119)	(215)
Acquisitions of businesses	(136)	(215)
Disposals of businesses	4	11
(Investments)/divestments in joint ventures and associates	13	(11)
Equity dividends paid	(192)	(187)
Net cash inflow/(outflow) before financing	6	(120)
Net sales of short-term investments	16	53
Financing	(125)	89
Issue of shares	4	25
(Decrease)/increase in debt	(129)	64
(Decrease)/increase in cash	(103)	22

11.2 The BOC Group plc (A)

Solution

Restated group cash flow statement years ended 30 September

	2003 £m	2002 £m
Operating profit	**505**	**500**
Less: Operating profit of joint ventures and associates	(98)	(75)
	407	425
Interest and dividends received	52	52
Depreciation and amortization	333	331
	792	808
Interest paid and dividends to minorities	(111)	(109)
Tax paid	(91)	(96)
Equity dividends paid	(192)	(187)
Other	(37)	(30)
	(431)	(422)
Net funds from operations	**361**	**386**
Changes in working capital	(3)	33
Decrease/(increase) in stocks	(17)	14
Decrease/(increase) in debtors	3	(38)
Increase in creditors	11	57
Net cash from operations	**358**	**419**
Sales of tangible fixed assets	37	32
Net sales of short-term investments etc.	40	38
Total cash available	435	489
Purchase of tangible fixed assets	(281)	(352)
Net acquisition of businesses	(132)	(204)
Net cash inflow/(outflow) before financing	**22**	**(67)**
Financing		
Issue of equity shares	4	25
(Decrease)/increase in debt	(129)	64
(Decrease)/increase in cash	**(103)**	**22**

Comments

1 There was little change in operating results between the two years.

2 Purchases of tangible fixed assets in 2003 were £52m (16%) *less* than depreciation, which suggests some reduction in the overall size of the business.

3 The small financing requirement in 2002 was met mainly by net borrowing of £64m which, however, was more than offset by the £129m net reduction in debt in 2003.

4 Certain minor headings in the published cash flow statement have been combined in the restated version. This is always a matter of judgement, but too much detail in a single statement can be hard for the reader to digest.

11.3 Chapman Piper Limited: Preparing a cash flow statement (balance sheet difference) using the FRS 1 format

The 2004 accounts for Chapman Piper Limited are set out here, the profit and loss account on this page, and the balance sheet on the next page.

You are asked to use the worksheets on the next two pages to complete the cash flow statement for 2004 shown on page 217 (right).

When you have finished check your answer with the solution set out on pages 218 and 219.

CHAPMAN PIPER LIMITED
Profit and loss account for year ended 31 December 2004

	2004 £'000		2003 £'000	
Turnover		13 000		11 000
Cost of sales		7 500		6 500
		5 500		4 500
Distribution costs	2 000		1 600	
Administrative expenses	900		800	
		2 900		2 400
Operating profit		2 600		2 100
Tax		800		700
Profit after tax		1 800		1 400

Notes

1   Trading profit has been determined after taking into account

	£'000
Depreciation	200
Loss on disposal of fittings	10

2   During the year the freehold shop was revalued and the increase in value of £1.2 million has been included in a revaluation reserve.

3   Movements in fittings in the year were

	Cost £'000	Depreciation £'000
Balance 31 December 2003	2 000	(200)
Additions	500	
Disposals	(200)	40
Depreciation for year		(200)
Balance 31 December 2004	2 300	(360)

4   Dividends of £1.0m were paid in 2004.

CHAPMAN PIPER LIMITED

Profit and loss account year ended 31 December 2004 (£'000)

	Profit and loss account	Funds flows	Book entries
Turnover			
Cost of sales			
Distribution costs			
Administrative expenses			
Trading profit			
Tax			
Profit after tax			

CHAPMAN PIPER LIMITED
Balance sheet at 31 December 2004

	2004 £'000		2003 £'000
Fixed assets			
Freehold shop at valuation		4 200	3 000
Fittings at cost	2 300		2 000
Less: Depreciation	360		200
		1 940	1 800
		6 140	4 800
Current assets			
Stock	1 710		1 300
Debtors	2 025		1 825
Cash	750		400
	4 485		3 525
Less: **Creditors due within one year**			
Tax	800		700
Trade creditors	700		500
	1 500		1 200
		2 985	2 325
Total assets less current liabilities		9 125	7 125
Share capital and reserves			
Called up share capital		5 000	5 000
Revaluation reserve		1 200	–
Retained profit		2 925	2 125
		9 125	7 125

CHAPMAN PIPER LIMITED

**Balance sheet at
31 December 2004**

(£'000)

	Balance sheet differences	Funds flows	Book entries
Assets			
Freehold shop			
Fittings			
Stocks			
Debtors			
Cash			
Shareholders' funds			
Share capital			
Revaluation reserve			
Retained profit			
Liabilities:			
Trade creditors			
Tax			

CHAPMAN PIPER LIMITED

Cash flow statement for the year ended 31 December 2004

£'000

Operating activities
Trading profit
Depreciation
Loss on disposal of fittings

Dividends paid

Taxation paid

Increase in working capital
Stocks
Debtors
Creditors

Investment in fixed assets
Fittings
Disposal of fittings

Surplus (deficit) before financing

Financing
Issue of shares

Increase (decrease) in cash

11.3 Chapman Piper Limited

Solution

CHAPMAN PIPER LIMITED

Profit and loss account year ended 31 December 2004 (£'000)	Profit and loss account	Funds flows	Book entries	
Turnover	13 000	13 000		
Cost of sales (balancing item)	(7 290)	(7 290)		
Distribution costs	(2 000)	(2 000)		
Administrative expenses	(900)	(900)		
Depreciation	(200)		(a)	(200)
Loss on disposal of FA	(10)		(b)	(10)
Operating profit	2 600	2 810		(210)
Tax	(800)		(c)	(800)
Profit after tax	1 800	2 810		(1 010)

CHAPMAN PIPER LIMITED

Balance sheet at 31 December 2004 (£'000)	Balance sheet differences	Funds flows	Book entries	
Assets				
Freehold shop	1 200		(d)	1 200
Fittings (net)	140		(a)	(200)
Additions		500		
Disposals		(160)		
Loss on disposal		10	(b)	(10)
Stocks	410	410		
Debtors	200	200		
Cash	350	350		
	2 300	1 310		990
Shareholders' funds				
Share capital	–	–		
Revaluation reserve	1 200		(d)	1 200
Retained profit	800	1 810		(1 010)
Liabilities				
Trade creditors	200	200		
Tax	100	(700)	(c)	800
	2 300	1 310		990

CHAPMAN PIPER LIMITED
Cash flow statement for the year ended 31 December 2004

	£'000
Operating activities	
Operating profit	2 600
Depreciation	200
Loss on disposal of fittings	10
	2 810
Dividends paid	(1 000)
Taxation paid	(700)
Net funds from operations	1 110
Increase in working capital	
Stocks	(410)
Debtors	(200)
Creditors	200
	700
Investment in fixed assets	
Fittings	(500)
Disposal of fittings	150
	(350)
Surplus (deficit) before financing	350
Financing activities	
Increase in cash	350

Comments
Again with only a single year's figures to comment on, there is not much to say.

- Net funds from operations comfortably cover net investment in working capital and in fixed assets.
- The financial surplus is simply reflected in an increase in the cash balance from £400 000 to £750 000.
- The year's profit after tax is £1 800 000, but retained profit in the balance sheet has increased by only £800 000 because the company paid dividends of £1 000 000 in 2004.

11.4 Harris & Clark plc: Preparing a cash flow statement (columnar analysis)

When we dealt with transaction analysis in Section 4, we found it useful to enter transactions in columnar analysis sheets. These allowed us to see easily how the entries were incorporated in the accounting headings. The same approach provides a useful framework for cash flow analysis: it is illustrated on the opposite page.

The columnar analysis shows clearly the link between the three financial statements; and sets out in a single statement the adjustments needed to the actual accounting figures to identify the operating and other flows. The columnar approach is also the best method for complex sets of accounts where adjustments affecting a number of items have to be viewed simultaneously.

The columnar worksheet includes columns for each balance sheet heading with additional columns for 'cash flows' and for 'profit of the year'. The opening and closing balances have been entered from the Harris & Clark balance sheets on page 209. The worksheet also includes the items shown in the profit and loss account and notes.

In the worksheet the double-entry principles underlying the balance sheet figures are continued. The two sides of the worksheets should continue to balance. Thus, it is possible to have a positive entry on both sides, a negative entry on both sides, or positive and negative entries on the same side.

The detailed steps needed to complete the worksheet are set out below and you are asked to follow each step in turn.

1 Enter operating profit in the 'profit of the year' column and in 'funds from operations'.
2 The other entries which appear in the profit of the year column are:

- *Interest expense* – on the other side this is a cash flow.
- *Taxation* – this is the tax provision based on the profits of the year. The other side appears in tax payable. The cash outflow for tax in the year is the opening balance plus the provision, less the closing balance.
- *Dividends* – this is the appropriation of profits for the year. The other side is entered in the dividends payable column. The dividend payment in the year is then calculated by determining the difference between the total of the opening balance plus the appropriation, and the closing balance.
- *Retained profit* – the retained profit is deducted and entered in the 'reserve' column (transferred to reserve).

3 Using the information disclosed in the tangible fixed asset note (b):

- additions represent an outflow of funds. They are added in the tangible fixed asset column and deducted in the cash flow column.
- the depreciation provision is a 'book entry'. It is deducted in the tangible fixed asset column and added in the funds from operations column. It was deducted in arriving at the trading profit; and as a 'non-cash charge' is now added back to give 'funds from operations'.
- the cost of disposals of 10 are deducted from tangible fixed assets. The other side is part of a flow and appears in the 'Sale of FA' column.
- depreciation on disposals is entered as a positive figure in the tangible fixed asset column (it eliminates some depreciation) and as a negative figure in the 'Sale of FA' column. The net book value of the disposal was $10 - 7 = 3$.

4 Using the information shown in Note (d) relating to share capital:

- share capital increases by 24 as does the cash flow column.
- share premium increases by 6 and so does the cash flow column.

5 We now have taken into account the information contained in the notes. Since there is no further information, the next step is to transfer the balance on the 'Sale of FA' column to the cash flow column and the balance on the 'Funds from operations' column to the cash flow column.
6 The next step is to total the columns, calculate the differences between the column totals and the closing balance sheet figures and to transfer the differences to the cash flow column. It is assumed that since they have not been identified as book entries they must be cash flows.
7 Finally, transfer the figures to the cash flow statement (page 209).

The answer to the following problem is shown at the end of the book.

11.5 Tesco plc: IAS format

Refer to Tesco plc's 2004 cash flow statement (on page 204), and restate it (with comparative figures) in the IAS format (noted on page 205).

No answer is published for the following problem.

11.6 Hamilton Pumps Limited (C): Preparing a cash flow statement

Refer again to Problem 2.6 Hamilton Pumps Limited (A) (on page 40). From the balance sheets at 31 December 2003 and 2004, and the profit and loss account for the year ended 31 December 2004, prepare a cash flow statement in a suitable format.

Harris & Clark plc – Cash flow statement: Year ended 31 December 2004. Worksheet

Assets   **Liabilities**

Tangible FA (net)	FA Invest-ments	Stocks	Trade debtors	Cash	Sale of FA	Funds from operations	Cash flows	£'000	Share capital and reserves	Profit of year	Loans	Trade creditors	Tax payable
215	30	80	75	40				**Opening balances** (=440) Operating profit P&L Interest expense P&L Tax P&L Retained profit P&L FA – Additions Note b Depreciation Note b Disposal (cost) Note b Disposal (acc. depr) Note b FA – Disp proceeds Note c Share capital Note d Share premium Note d **Funds from operations**	256		110	60	14
								FA investments Stocks Trade debtors Cash Loans Trade creditors Tax paid Dividends paid					
244	40	100	81	45			–	**Closing balances** (= 510)	300		125	65	20

Please check your answer against the solution overleaf, and then against the full cash flow statement on page 209.

11.4 Harris & Clark plc – Cash flow statement: Year ended 31 December 2004

Solution

Assets   **Liabilities**

Tangible FA (net)	FA Invest-ments	Stocks	Trade debtors	Cash	Sale of FA	Funds from operations	Cash flows	£'000	Share capital and reserves	Profit of year	Loans	Trade creditors	Tax payable
215	30	80	75	40				**Opening balances** (=440)	256		110	60	14
						70		Operating profit P&L		70			
							(15)	Interest expense P&L		(15)			
								Tax P&L		(20)			20
								Profit P&L	35	(35)			
60							(60)	FA – Additions Note b					
(28)						28		Depreciation Note b					
(10)					10			Disposal (cost) Note b					
7					(7)			Disposal (acc. depr) Note b					
					(3)		3	FA – Disp proceeds Note c					
							{20	Share capital Note d	20				
							{10	Share premium Note d	10				
						(98)	98	**Funds from operations**					
244	30	80	75	40	–	–	56	(= 525)	321	–	110	60	34
	10						(10)	FA investments					
		20					(20)	Stocks					
			6				(6)	Trade debtors					
				5			(5)	Cash					
							15	Loans			15		
							5	Trade creditors				5	
							(14)	Tax paid					(14)
							(21)	Dividends paid	(21)				
244	40	100	81	45			–	**Closing balances** (= 510)	300		125	65	20

Section 12
International accounting

CONTEXT

International trade and multinational businesses expanded vastly during the second half of the twentieth century. World exports grew in real terms by about 6 per cent a year, more than twice as fast as real national product per head. As a result many people need to understand how other countries report business performance and financial position.

There are still serious obstacles to understanding accounts across national borders: different languages and cultures; different legal systems and tax rules; different currencies, and different business and accounting practices.

There are also moves leading towards international harmonization of accounting. The International Accounting Standards Board [IASB] has published thirty-six standards (see page 275) which, from 2005, the European Union is requiring all listed groups in its 25 member-states to follow.

The most critical countries for international accounting are the United States and the United Kingdom, whose stock markets have long had large equity capitalizations. Also important are France, Germany, the Netherlands and Switzerland. As the table below shows, equity market capitalizations of the so-called 'Anglo-Saxon' countries represent about 68 per cent of the world total.

Stock market valuations of equities	% of total	
USA	51	
UK	10	
Other ex-British colonies	7	
France	4	
Germany	3	
Netherlands	2	
Other European Union countries	7	
Switzerland	3	19
Japan	9	
Rest of world	4	13
	100	
31 December 2004	$24 trillion	

In this section we concentrate mainly on contrasts between UK and US accounting. We shall look first at different balance sheet formats, then at certain key differences in accounting practice and in terminology. We shall also consider contrasts between UK and international accounting standards. We then look briefly at multinational companies and their reporting of regional results. Finally we review the translation of foreign currencies into the reporting currency for accounting purposes.

UK/US BALANCE SHEET FORMATS

UK law enacts EU directives aiming to standardize the formats of company accounts throughout Western Europe. Schedule 4 to the Companies Act 1985 (as amended by the Companies Act 1989) contains the provisions relating to the form and content of accounts (see Appendix 5 on pages 277 to 281). Section A sets out general rules relating to disclosure; and Section B contains the two permitted balance sheet formats and the four profit and loss account formats.

In this book we began by using the 'net asset' format. First, this format lists fixed assets and working capital (= net assets), and then shows the main sources of long-term funds, namely long-term borrowing and shareholders' funds (= capital employed). This is a useful format while learning about accounts; but in practice, most UK companies deduct 'creditors: due after one year' from 'total assets less current liabilities'. This gives a figure which balances with 'capital and reserves' (including any minority interests). An example of this layout is shown opposite (top) for General Trading Limited (see also page 6).

Instead of the British 'vertical' layout, American balance sheets sometimes use the 'horizontal' layout, which shows assets on the left and liabilities and equity on the right. An example is set out opposite (below) for General Trading Inc. This also shows that the American balance sheet has a different order: it shows the most liquid assets at the top, and the least liquid assets at the bottom. The liabilities and equity side follows a similar pattern.

In the American version of General Trading's 2005 balance sheet we have used US terminology. The only items with exactly the same names are 'cash' and 'current assets'!

The American balance sheet may look strange at first sight, but in practice it is not too difficult to cope with these differences in format and terminology. An example of an actual American horizontal balance sheet is shown in Problem 12.2 H.J. Heinz Company (page 233). A number of large American companies now use a vertical balance sheet format, though with the items in a different order from UK balance sheets.

British format (vertical)

GENERAL TRADING LIMITED

Balance sheet at 31 March 2005	£'000
Tangible fixed assets	800
Current assets	900
Less: **Creditors due within one year** (current liabilities)	(300)
Net current assets (working capital)	600
Total assets less current liabilities	1 400
Less: **Creditors due after one year**	(180)
	1 220
Capital and reserves	
Called up share capital	1 000
Profit and loss account	220
	1 220

American format (horizontal)

GENERAL TRADING INC.
Statement of financial position as of March 31 2005

Current assets	$'000		Current liabilities	$'000	
Cash	150		Income taxes	30	
Accounts receivable	350		Accounts payable	270	
Inventories	400				300
		900			
			Long-term debt		180
Property			**Stockholders' equity**		
Real estate	300		Common stock	1 000	
Plant & equipment	500		Retained earnings	220	
		800			1 220
		1 700			1 700

DIFFERENCES IN UK/US ACCOUNTING PRACTICES

We have already mentioned in earlier sections the main differences in accounting practice between the UK and the US, which we briefly review here. It is worth emphasizing that the overall aims of accounting in the two countries, and the detailed accounting rules, are mostly very similar.

US accounting standards usually require all listed companies to follow the same approach, but in some areas UK standards allow alternatives. There are many more US standards than UK ones because the US FASB issues new standards with a new number, while UK (and IAS) practice is to amend earlier standards under the original number.

All the differences below (set out in order of section reference) can affect reported profit as well as the balance sheet.

- US companies have to expense all research and development expenditure (other than on certain fixed assets). UK companies may capitalize development spending which meets certain conditions (see Section 5), but in fact most UK companies expense all research and development expenditure (other than on fixed assets).
- Many US companies use the LIFO (Last In First Out) method of valuing stock (see Section 6), which is not used in the UK and now forbidden under IAS. The effect is to reduce US companies' profits (and assets) – and tax – in times of rising prices.
- US companies adhere firmly to historical money cost, while UK companies *may* revalue land, buildings and plant and equipment upwards (see Section 7). This affects return on investment and gearing, though the impact on profit is usually small. UK companies *may* capitalize borrowing costs related to the construction of fixed assets, whereas this is compulsory in the US for 'qualifying assets'.
- US companies capitalize purchased goodwill arising on acquisitions (see Section 9), but do not amortize it against profit. Instead they have an annual 'impairment review'. UK companies normally do amortize goodwill, though they undertake impairment reviews for goodwill assumed to have an 'indefinite' life. (The former UK practice of writing off goodwill directly against reserves is no longer allowed; but very few UK companies have reinstated goodwill once it has been written off against reserves. Hence a significant difference in UK accounts remains.) Merger accounting is no longer allowed in the US, as it still is in the UK.

UK/US TERMINOLOGY

The following accounting terms are different in the UK and the US. Items marked with an asterisk (*) may be used in both countries.

UK	US
BALANCE SHEET*	**STATEMENT OF FINANCIAL POSITION**
Fixed assets	
Tangible: land and buildings*	Property (real estate)
plant and machinery	plant and equipment*
Current assets	
Stocks	Inventories*
Debtors	Accounts receivable*
Creditors: due within one year	**Current liabilities***
Bank loans and overdrafts	Notes payable
Creditors	Accounts payable*
Corporation tax	Income taxes
Net current assets	n/a
Creditors: due after one year	**Long-term debt***
Capital and reserves	**Shareholders' equity**
Called up share capital –	Capital stock –
ordinary	common
preference (non-equity)	preferred
Share premium	Paid-up surplus
Revaluation reserve	n/a
Profit and loss account	Retained earnings*
PROFIT AND LOSS ACCOUNT	**INCOME STATEMENT**
Turnover	Net sales
Profit after tax	Net income
Company	Corporation
Gearing	Leverage
Merger	Pooling of interests
Acquisition	Purchase
Bonus issue, scrip issue	Stock dividend

See also the list of synonyms in Appendix 1 (page 273).

UK VERSUS INTERNATIONAL ACCOUNTING

At the start of this section we mentioned six obstacles to understanding accounts across national borders. In comparing UK and US accounts, only one, currency, is a major problem. Language, culture, legal systems, tax rules and accounting practices are all similar (though certainly not identical). And, as we have just seen, there are a number of major differences in accounting practice in specific areas

When we come to compare UK accounting with other countries, however, the obstacles multiply. Apart from former British colonies, probably the Netherlands is closest to the UK/US approach. It has a mature capital market (the Amsterdam stock exchange was founded as long ago as 1602), with three large multinational companies in Philips, Royal Dutch Shell and Unilever. In all three countries general business acceptance of accounting rules has been important (at least until recently). But differences in language and in legal systems still represent serious hurdles.

For France, Germany (and Switzerland) and Japan, problems of comparing with UK/US accounting are even greater, because the basic philosophy has been different. And government influence on accounting has been far more evident, though this is now changing. For example, for many years it was normal for the tax rules to determine what accounts charged for depreciation of fixed assets. (Hence there would often be no need for deferred tax (see Section 10).) More important, the charge in the accounts might not represent a sensible commercial estimate.

Large family shareholdings in France and Germany may have reduced pressures for accounts to be transparent. Since capital markets and outside shareholders have had less influence, accounting has tended to be conservative. The emphasis has been on financial soundness in balance sheets, with hidden (secret) reserves quite usual. In contrast, in the UK and the US, the need to report to more 'mobile' and more numerous public owners has led accounts to focus more on reported annual earnings (which transfers to or from secret reserves could easily distort.)

The EU now holds that the aim of accounts is to present 'a true and fair view' of a company's performance and financial position. In this respect it has accepted the long-standing UK approach. But not all member-states will understand exactly the same thing by the phrase (any more than all British accountants do).

Listed groups in all EU member-states, including the UK, will have to comply with international accounting standards (IAS) as from 2005. Because the Anglo-American approach has been prominent ever since the International Accounting Standards Committee was first formed in 1973, this may be less of a problem for the UK than for most other EU member-states. Before long, UK standards may change to conform precisely to IAS. But for the time being there remain some important differences.

Some of the main differences between UK and international accounting standards as at 31 March 2004 are briefly noted below. Sometimes (*) a choice is allowed.

- IFRS 3 requires all business combinations to be accounted for by the purchase method and prohibits merger (pooling of interest) accounting.
  FRS 6 requires merger accounting if certain criteria are met (see Section 9).

- IFRS 3 prohibits amortization of goodwill, and requires regular impairment tests.
  FRS 10 requires amortization of all goodwill not estimated to have an 'indefinite life', normally over not more than 20 years (see Section 9).

- IAS 38 requires certain development costs to be capitalized as an intangible asset.
  * *SSAP 9 permits capitalizing development costs if they meet similar criteria (see Section 6).*

- * IAS 38 allows a choice between showing intangible assets at cost or at regular revaluation, less any depreciation or impairment losses.
  FRS 10 does not allow intangible assets to be revalued (see Section 7).

- * IAS 31 allows a choice between reporting an interest in a joint venture using either proportionate consolidation or the equity method.
  FRS 9 does not permit proportionate consolidation (see Section 9).

- IAS 19 requires actuarial gains and losses on employee defined benefit schemes to be recognized in the profit and loss account if they do not exceed 10 per cent of the greater of the scheme's gross assets or gross liabilities [the 10 per cent 'corridor'].
  * Recognition of actuarial gains and losses exceeding the 10 per cent 'corridor' *may* be spread forward over the average remaining working lives of the employees in the scheme, or according to a more accelerated schedule.
  FRS 17 requires immediate recognition in the statement of total recognized gains and losses of all actuarial gains and losses (see Section 5).

- IAS 12 prohibits discounting deferred tax assets and liabilities.
  * *FRS 19 permits discounting deferred tax assets and liabilities (see Section 10).*

MULTINATIONALS

Precise definition of a 'multinational' company is not easy. For a UK group we suggest at least 50 per cent of sales, profits and assets should be outside the UK. Moreover one might argue that not more than 50 per cent of sales, profits or assets should come from any single country.

It is hardly surprising that companies based in smaller countries find it easier to meet these requirements than companies in the United States or Japan. Thus Nestle, for example, based in Switzerland, is clearly a multinational, whereas large US companies such as General Motors, even with very extensive overseas operations, may still have more than half of their sales and profits arising 'at home' in the US. Hence international accounting may be a more important topic for UK companies, as a rule, than for American or Japanese (or, in future perhaps, 'Euroland').

To illustrate what UK multinationals look like, we list here five large businesses. We show the percentage split of sales, profits and assets (as required by SSAP 25), and of employees (which many companies also choose to report).

Each of the companies define the regions of the world in a different way. While this makes it harder to compare the companies directly, no doubt each group chooses a split which suits its own business.

All five groups refer to 'Europe', though Rio Tinto, oddly, combines it with 'other countries'. Two groups refer to 'USA', two to 'North America' (presumably USA and Canada), and British American Tobacco refers to America-Pacific. Two groups refer to 'Latin America', Rio Tinto (more 'British'?) to 'South America'. One group refers to 'Africa', one to 'Africa and Middle East' and one to 'Africa, Middle East and Turkey'. Two groups refer to 'Asia-Pacific' or 'Asia and Pacific'. GlaxoSmithKline has only three groups: USA, Europe and 'Rest of the World', Shell has four groups: Europe, USA, 'Other Eastern Hemisphere' and 'Other Western Hemisphere'. Finally, Rio Tinto has two 'unusual' regions: 'Australia and New Zealand' (which represents over 50 per cent of profits and assets) and 'Indonesia'.

Few UK companies appear to translate their annual report and accounts into foreign languages, though American investors would not need this. Many do, however, provide detailed notes of major differences between UK and US accounting practices. Indeed GlaxoSmithKline's note on this topic takes up no less than *eleven pages* in its latest annual report!

UK MULTINATIONALS: REGIONAL ANALYSIS

	Sales %	Profits %	Assets %	Employees %
BRITISH AMERICAN TOBACCO				
America-Pacific	32	39	19	15
Asia-Pacific	14	20	17	18
Latin America	11	23	6	22
Europe	36	3	47	30
Africa and Middle East	7	15	11	15
Employees: excluding Associates				
GLAXOSMITHKLINE				
USA	48	31	21	24
Europe	33	48	64	44
Rest of the World	19	21	15	18
RIO TINTO				
North America	26	19	31	27
Australia and New Zealand	23	54	56	29
South America	18	11	4	7
Africa	22	3	4	17
Indonesia	7	16	3	10
Europe and other countries	4	(3)	2	10
ROYAL DUTCH SHELL			(fixed)	n/a
Europe	36	41	33	
Other Eastern Hemisphere	19	27	29	
USA	37	29	27	
Other Western Hemisphere	8	3	11	
UNILEVER				
Europe	43	47	46	24
North America	23	20	31	8
Africa, Middle East and Turkey	8	8	5	22
Asia and Pacific	16	19	5	33
Latin America	10	6	13	13

FOREIGN CURRENCY TRANSLATION

In recent years various groups have acquired businesses abroad or built up foreign interests from retained profits. Many multinational companies have thus emerged, each controlling a number of different foreign offshoots. Accounting for such groups poses special problems when foreign exchange rates fluctuate. There are two ways to translate the accounts of foreign operations into the holding company's domestic currency: the 'closing rate' method or the 'temporal' method.

SSAP 20/IAS 21 regards a holding company's investment as being in a foreign operation's whole business. So it uses the same rate of exchange (the closing rate) for all assets and liabilities (in effect, for the 'net investment' in the equity). SSAP 20 says: 'consolidated statements should reflect the financial results and relationships as measured in the foreign currency financial statements prior to translation.'

Groups should normally use the closing rate method to translate all assets and liabilities of foreign operations into the reporting currency. IAS 21 says they should translate foreign profits or losses at an average rate for the period (SSAP 20 also permits use of the closing rate), and record exchange differences as a movement on reserves. Retranslating opening equity (= net assets) at the year-end closing rate will cause an exchange difference which also goes direct to reserves.

The temporal method regards transactions as part of a single worldwide system (the rationale for group accounts in the first place), and uses historical exchange rates for non-monetary assets. Group accounts should use it only where the foreign entity's trade is closely linked with the holding company, or in countries with very high inflation. The temporal method resembles the constant purchasing power (CPP) method of inflation accounting (see Section 13).

The charts opposite show significant movements in exchange rates between 1999 and 2004 for the pound, the US dollar and the euro. The euro lost more than 25 per cent of its value against the US dollar in 1999–2000 (which few experts predicted), but regained it all and more in 2002–2003. Such big changes make it difficult for multinational companies to make sensible long-term business decisions (for example, about where to locate factories). They also make it much harder to understand accounts.

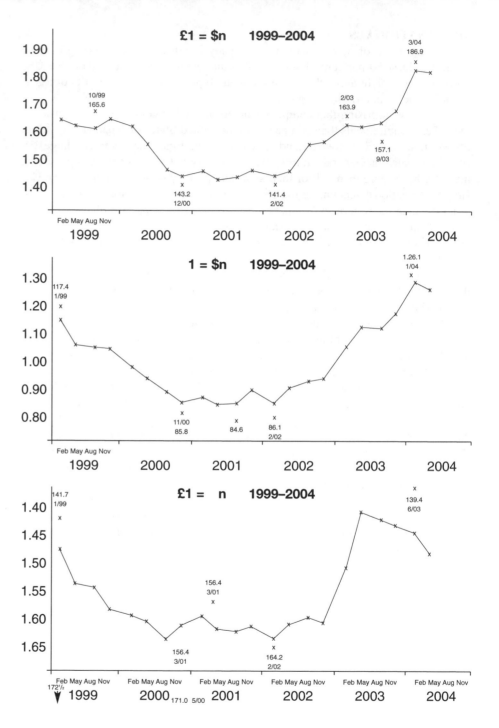

228

Example

The accounts on the right show the balance sheet at 31 December 2004, and the profit and loss account for the year ended on that date, for Overseas Trading Limited. When the company started trading at the end of 2003 its balance sheet showed (in $'000): plant and equipment $900, net current assets $600, less loan $300 = called up share capital $1 200.

The company trades in stock which turns over very quickly, and is therefore treated in the example in the same way as liquid assets. During the year there was no change in the fixed assets, or in the loan. At the start of the year the exchange rate was $3 = £1, but this had become $2 = £1 by the end of the year. The year's average rate of $2.5 = £1 has been used to translate profits.

The accounts opposite have been prepared on two bases, using the closing rate method and the temporal method respectively. According to the closing rate method, the profit for the year – $600 – amounted to £240; and return on equity was 27 per cent (it was 33 per cent in dollar terms). Under the temporal method, profit for the year was £367; and return on equity was 48 per cent.

The closing rate method credits the gain on exchange (£260) to reserves; while the temporal method credits the gain on exchange (£120) to profit:

Closing rate method

Profit for year $600: at average rate ($2.5)	= £240	
at closing rate ($2.0)	= £300	
		£60
Opening net assets $1 200: at opening rate ($3.0)	= £400	
at closing rate ($2.0)	= £600	
		£200
Total gains on exchange		£260

Temporal method

Opening net monetary assets $300: at opening rate ($3.0)	= £100	
at closing rate ($2.0)	= £150	
		£50
Cash generated in year $700*: at average rate ($2.5)	= £280	
at closing rate ($2.0)	= £350	
		£70
Gain on exchange		£120

*$700 = $600 profit after tax plus $100 depreciation.

OVERSEAS TRADING LIMITED

Balance sheet at 31 December 2004

	Foreign currency $'000		Closing rate method £'000		Temporal method £'000
Plant and equipment	900	2.0	450	3.0	300
Less: Depreciation	100	2.0	50	3.0	33
	800		400		267
Net current assets	1 300	2.0	650	2.0	650
Less: Loan	(300)	2.0	(150)	2.0	(150)
	1 800		900		767
Called up share capital	1 200	3.0**	400	3.0	400
Reserve: Gain on exchange	—	*	260		—
Profit and loss account	600	2.5	240	*	367
	1 800		900		767

Profit and loss account
Year ended 31 December 2004

Turnover	1 500	2.5	600	2.5	600
Cost of sales	(470)	2.5	(188)	2.5	(188)
Depreciation	(100)	2.5	(40)	3.0	(33)
Gain on exchange	—		—	*	120
	930		372		499
Interest	(30)	2.5	(12)	2.5	(12)
Profit before tax	900		360		487
Tax	(300)	2.5	(120)	2.5	(120)
Profit after tax	600	2.5	240		367

---

*no single exchange rate applies

**historical rate used for original investment

SECTION 12 SUMMARY

In this section we noted the rapid growth of world trade in the last fifty years and the spread of multinational enterprise. This has led to an increasing need for accounting across national borders.

In addition to all the problems of comparing accounts even within one country, there are several special obstacles to international comparisons. These are: different languages and cultures, legal systems and tax rules, currencies and accounting practices. The International Accounting Standards Board (IASB) has for many years been working to try to harmonize global accounting.

Even though the philosophies and practices of UK and US accounting are similar as a rule, we noted a number of differences – in balance sheet formats, in terminology and (most importantly) in certain accounting practices. These were in respect of: research and development costs, valuing stock, revaluing fixed assets, merger accounting and treatment of goodwill.

We also briefly compared UK accounting with that of some other countries. The UK and the US, where the stock market has long had a big influence, tend to emphasize annual earnings. In other countries in Europe, where family shareholders and banks are often long-term investors, balance sheet soundness has been more important. We noted that from 2005 listed groups in EU member-states will have to follow international accounting standards, and we listed some of the key remaining differences with UK accounting.

Next we noted the requirements for geographical segmental reporting of sales, profits and assets by multinationals, and we saw how companies based in smaller countries are likely to have larger proportions of sales, profits and assets located 'abroad'.

Finally we looked at the difficult topic of foreign currency translation. We noted the two main methods (the closing rate method – which is usual – and the temporal method), and showed in outline how each method works. (If you want to see how much difference foreign currencies can make, without getting too bogged down in accounting technicalities, Problem 12.9 may be of interest.)

Large currency fluctuations since about 1970 have caused serious problems for the managements of multinational companies in measuring and reporting the financial results of their world-wide operations. It is by no means clear that the next thirty or forty years will be less turbulent in this respect.

PROBLEMS

12.1 Definitions
Write down below your definition of the terms shown. Then compare your answers with the definitions overleaf.

(a)   Translating a foreign currency

(b)   The 'closing rate' method

(c)   Net monetary assets

(d)   A multinational company

(e)   Converting a foreign currency

(f)   Non-monetary assets

(g)   The horizontal format

(h)   The 'temporal' method

(i)   The 'average rate' method

(j)   Hidden reserves

12.1 Definitions

(a) **Translating a foreign currency** means expressing (or re-stating) one currency in terms of another. (In contrast, 'conversion' means literally *exchanging* one currency for another.) Translation is thus an accounting concept rather than a financial one. IAS 21 allows companies to present accounts in *any* currency.

(b) **The 'closing rate' method** is a method of translating foreign currency amounts into terms of the holding company's domestic currency for the purpose of group accounts. UK companies normally use it for balance sheets and sometimes do so for profit and loss accounts.

(c) **Net monetary assets** represents the excess of monetary assets over monetary liabilities. A simple way to measure the amount is to deduct long-term liabilities from net current assets (that is, from net working capital). This involves treating stock as if it were a 'monetary' asset, which while untrue is often convenient and makes little difference to the result.

(d) **A multinational company** operates in many countries. A 'genuine' multinational should have (a) more than half its sales, profits and assets outside its home country and (b) not more than half its sales, profits or assets deriving from any one foreign country. On this basis, few US or Japanese companies would qualify, but several Dutch, Swiss and UK companies would.

(e) **Converting a foreign currency** means literally exchanging a foreign currency (into the domestic currency), for example, changing $180 into £100. (For the contrast with 'translation', see (a) above.)

(f) **Non-monetary assets** are 'real' assets, such as tangible fixed assets, not consisting of money or amounts payable in money (such as debtors). The distinction is important both for the temporal method of foreign currency translation (see (h) below) and for constant purchasing power (CPP) accounting (see Section 13), which the temporal method resembles.

(g) **The horizontal format** is a balance sheet layout that some US companies still use, rather than the vertical format that the Companies Act requires in the UK (following the EU's Fourth Directive).

(h) **The 'temporal' method** is a method of translating subsidiaries' foreign currency accounts into terms of the holding company's domestic currency for the purposes of group accounts. For non-monetary assets it uses the exchange rate at the date of purchase. It is suitable in high-inflation countries.

(i) **The 'average rate' method** is a method of translating foreign currencies in the profit and loss account. As the name implies, it uses an 'average' rate of exchange for the accounting period, rather than the closing rate. IAS 21 requires it, and most UK companies use it.

(j) **Hidden reserves** ('secret' reserves) are amounts which company accounts do not disclose, because they either understate assets or overstate liabilities. It matters if the true financial position is 'better' than that shown, because it enables managers to mis-state current profits (by drawing secretly on such reserves in times of trouble).

12.2 H.J. Heinz Company: Restating a US balance sheet

Restate this US company's group balance sheet as at 28 April 2004 in the normal vertical UK format, using UK terminology. You may prefer to group certain items which UK companies would show in detail in the Notes. When you have completed your restated balance sheet, check it against our solution overleaf.

H.J. Heinz Company: Consolidated Balance Sheet at 28 April 2004

Assets (dollars in thousands)

Current assets

Cash and cash equivalents	1 180 039
Receivables (net of allowances: $21 313)	1 093 155
Inventories:	
Finished goods and work-in-process	890 813
Packaging material and ingredients	266 119
Total inventories	1 156 932
Prepaid expenses	165 177
Other current assets	15 493
Total current assets	3 610 796

Property, plant and equipment:

Land	65 836
Buildings and leasehold improvements	796 966
Equipment, furniture and other	2 864 422
	3 727 224
Less accumulated depreciation	1 669 938
Total property, plant and equipment, net	2 057 286

Other non-current assets:

Goodwill	1 959 914
Trademarks, net	643 901
Other intangibles, net	149 920
Other non-current assets	1 455 372
Total other non-current assets	4 209 107
Total assets	9 877 189

Liabilities and Shareholders' Equity (dollars in thousands)

Current Liabilities:

Short-term debt	11 434
Portion of long-term debt due within one year	425 016
Accounts payable	1 063 113
Salaries and wages	50 101
Accrued marketing	230 495
Other accrued liabilities	361 596
Income taxes	327 313
Total current liabilities	2 469 068

Long-term debt and other liabilities:

Long-term debt	4 537 980
Deferred income taxes	313 343
Non-pension postretirement benefits	192 599
Minority interest	104 645
Other	365 365
Total long-term debt and other liabilities	5 513 932

Shareholders' equity:

Capital stock:

Third cumulative preferred, $1.70 first series, $10 par value	94
Common stock, 431 096 485 shares issued, $.25 par value	107 774
	107 868
Additional capital	403 043
Retained earnings	4 856 918
	5 367 829
Less:	
Treasury shares, at cost (79 139 249 shares)	2 927 839
Unearned compensation	32 275
Accumulated other comprehensive loss	513 526
Total shareholders' equity	1 894 189
Total liabilities and shareholders' equity	9 877 189

12.2   H. J. Heinz Company
Solution

H. J. HEINZ COMPANY
Consolidated Balance Sheet at 28 April 2004

		$ million
Fixed assets		
Tangible fixed assets	Note 1	2 057
Intangibles	Note 2	2 754
Other non-current assets		1 455
		6 266
Current assets		
Stocks	Note 3	1 157
Debtors	Note 4	1 274
Cash etc.		1 180
		3 611
Less: **Creditors due within one year**		
Short-term borrowings	Note 5	(437)
Other creditors	Note 6	(2 032)
		(2 469)
Net working capital		1 142
Total assets less current liabilities		7 408
Creditors due after one year		
Long-term borrowings		(4 538)
Provisions for liabilities and charges	Note 7	(871)
Minority interest		(105)
		1 894
Capital and reserves		
Called up share capital		108
Share premium account		403
Retained profits		4 857
Other reserves		(546)
		4 822
Less: Treasury shares at cost (67.7m shares)		(2 928)
		1 894

Note 1. Tangible fixed assets	$ million
Land and buildings, at cost	863
Equipment and furniture, etc., at cost	2 864
	3 727
Less: accumulated depreciation	1 670
Net book value	2 057

Note 2. Intangibles	
Goodwill	1 960
Other intangibles net	794
	2 754

Note 3. Stocks	
Packaging material and ingredients	266
Finished goods and work-in-progress	891
	1 157

Note 4. Debtors	
Trade debtors (net of provisions 21)	1 093
Prepayments, etc.	181
	1 274

Note 5. Short-term borrowings	
Short-term borrowings	12
Long-term borrowings, due within one year	425
	437

Note 6. Other creditors (current)	
Trade creditors	1 063
Accrued liabilities	642
Taxation	327
	2 032

Note 7. Provisions for liabilities and charges	
Deferred taxation	313
Non-pension post-retirement benefits	193
Other	365
	871

12.3 A common language?

Can you identify the UK equivalents for each of the following US accounting terms? Answers are shown overleaf.

(a) Net sales
(b) Common stock
(c) Inventories
(d) Income statement
(e) Inc.
(f) Current liabilities
(g) Long-term debt
(h) Accounts payable

12.4 Vice versa

Can you identify the US equivalents for each of the following UK accounting terms? Answers are shown overleaf.

(a) Gearing
(b) Capital and reserves
(c) Balance sheet
(d) Merger
(e) Tangible fixed assets
(f) Share premium
(g) Profit after tax
(h) Debtors

12.5 Diageo plc (B): Restating a UK balance sheet

You will find the 2003 group balance sheet of Diageo plc set out on page 173. Please attempt, on a separate sheet of paper, to restate this UK group's balance sheet into the horizontal US format, using US terminology.

When you have completed your attempt (ensure the balance sheet balances!), check with our proposed solution overleaf. (Hint: You may need to re-arrange some of the items.)

12.6 The BOC Group plc (B): UK/US accounting differences

The BOC Group plc has extensive business in the United States. The company reports to its shareholders how various items have been treated in its (UK) accounts, and how they would appear under US GAAP (Generally Accepted Accounting Principles).

Write down, in two or three sentences each, what you would expect BOC to say about each of the following three items. When you have done so, check overleaf against what the company actually did say on each item in its 2003 Annual Report.

(a) Goodwill

(b) Pensions

(c) Revaluation of fixed assets

12.3 A common language?

Solution

(a) Turnover
(b) Ordinary shares
(c) Stocks
(d) Profit and loss account
(e) Ltd. ['limited'] or plc ['public limited company']
(f) Creditors due within one year
(g) Creditors due after one year
(h) Trade creditors

12.4 Vice versa

Solution

(a) Leverage
(b) Shareholders' equity
(c) Statement of financial position
(d) Pooling of interests
(e) Property plant and equipment [PPE]
(f) Paid-in surplus
(g) Net income
(h) Accounts receivable

12.6 The BOC Group plc (B)

Solution

(a) Goodwill

FRS 10 requires goodwill on acquisitions to be capitalized and amortized over a period not exceeding 20 years.

Under US GAAP goodwill continues to be capitalized although amortization is no longer charged to the income statement. Instead an annual impairment test is carried out, with any identified impairment loss recorded in the income statement.

(b) Pensions

FRS 17 requires that past service costs are recognized in full in the period in which they become vested. SFAS87 (US) requires past service costs to be amortized over the remaining service lives of the employees to whom the amendments relate.

UK GAAP recognizes the actuarial gains and losses (arising during the accounting period) in full in the year in which they arise in the statement of total recognized gains and losses. Under US GAAP, the actuarial gains and losses which exceed ten per cent of the value of assets or liabilities at the start of the accounting period are amortized over the remaining service lives of scheme members.

236

(c) Revaluation of fixed assets

With the Group's adoption of FRS 15 in 2000, the Group no longer revalues fixed assets (though the net book value of land and buildings still includes £38m from earlier revaluations).

Under US GAAP revaluations of fixed assets are not permitted.

12.5 Diageo plc (B): Group balance sheet restated in US horizontal format

Solution

DIAGEO plc
Consolidated statement of financial position as at June 30 2003

	£m		£m
Current assets		**Current liabilities**	
Cash and liquid resources	1 191	Short-term debt	3 563
Receivables	2 173	Other creditors	3 283
Inventories	2 193		6 846
	5 554		
		Long-term liabilities	
Property plant and equipment		Long-term debt	2 981
Land and buildings	904	Provisions	869
Plant, machinery, etc.	2 047	Other creditors	18
	2 951		3 868
less: accumulated depreciation	(977)		
	1 974	**Shareholders' equity**	
		3.1m ordinary shares	897
Other non-current assets		Paid-in surplus	1 327
Investments	3 222	Revaluation reserve	120
Goodwill, brands and other	5 931	Retained earnings	1 207
Long-term receivables	897	Other	3 046
	10 050		6 597
		less: Treasury shares	(259)
			6 338
		Minority interests: equity	186
		: non-equity	343
			529
Total assets	17 581	Total liabilities and equity	17 581

Note: All the asset items except cash and inventories have been changed, either as to presentation or as to amount.

Answers to the following three problems are given at the end of the book.

12.7 Parkside Limited (A): The closing rate method

Parkside Limited, a UK company, established a wholly-owned Ruritanian subsidiary, Blue Moon, in 2003 when the exchange rate was £1 = R$4.00. Parkside uses the closing rate method for incorporating Blue Moon's accounts in the group accounts for the year ended 31 December 2005. At 31 December 2004, the exchange rate was £1 = R$3.00. The average rate for the year 2005 was £1 = R$2.50; and the closing rate at 31 December 2005 was £1 = R$2.00.

The summarized profit and loss account and balance sheet for Blue Moon for 2005 are shown below in terms of Ruritanian dollars. You are asked:

(a) to show how Blue Moon's Ruritanian dollar accounts should be translated into pounds for inclusion in the Parkside group accounts. In particular, calculate 'exchange differences' for the year 2005, and show where this item would appear in the group accounts;

(b) how would the amounts to include in the 2005 Parkside group accounts be different using the average rate for the year instead of the closing rate to translate the profit and loss account?

Blue Moon: Profit and loss account, year ended 31 December 2005

	R$'000
Sales	7 000
Depreciation (1/6 x 1 800)	300
Other expenses	6 560
Profit	140

Blue Moon: Balance sheet as at 31 December

	2005	2004
	R$'000	R$'000
Fixed assets	1 200	1 500
Working capital	560	360
	1 760	1 860
(Long-term debt)	(720)	(960)
	1 040	900
Capital and reserves:		
Called up share capital	200	200
Retained profits	840	700
	1 040	900

12.8 Parkside Limited (B): The temporal method

Refer to the information in 12.7 Parkside Limited (A).

Fixed assets, all acquired in 2003 for R$1 800, when the exchange rate was £1 = R$4.00, are being written off on the straight line method over six years (zero residual value). You are asked to show how Blue Moon's Ruritanian dollar accounts should be translated into pounds for inclusion in the Parkside group accounts for 2005 if the temporal method were used. Assume that the average rate for the year (£1 = R$2.50) is used for the profit and loss account.

12.9 Global Investor

An investor with £3 million to invest in listed equities at 1 January 2002 decided to split his funds equally between American, British and European stocks, in each case investing in 'index' funds which exactly matched the Standard & Poor's 500, the FTSE 100, and the Eurostoxx respectively. After one year he calculated the value of each of his three different holdings, and decided to transfer £50 000 from British into European stocks in order to roughly equalize the holdings again.

The level of the indexes at 1 January 2002, 2003 and 2004 were as follows:

	S&P 500	FTSE 100	Eurostoxx
1 January 2002	1 150	5 200	315
1 January 2003	900	4 000	200
1 January 2004	1 050	4 500	240

The exchange rates between the currencies on those three dates were:

	£1 = $n	1 = $n	£1 = n
1 January 2002	$1.44	$0.90	1.60
1 January 2003	$1.575	$1.05	1.50
1 January 2004	$1.80	$1.20	1.50

You are asked:

(a) If the investor again wants (roughly) to equalize his holdings in terms of £ on 1 January 2004, how much should he transfer from and to which index funds?

(b) For each of the two years, how much profit or loss overall has the investor made:
  (i)   in terms of £?
  (ii) in terms of $?
  (iii) in terms of ?

(c) How can you reconcile your answers in (b)?

No answers are shown to the following problems.

12.10 Grand Imperial plc (A): Closing rate method

Grand Imperial plc, a UK Company, established a wholly-owned Bolonian subsidiary, Ananam, in 1997, when the exchange rate was £1 = 12 Bolonian pesos (Bp).

Recent exchange rates have been as follows:

£1 = Bp	2002	2003	2004
Average rate for the year	6.00	4.50	3.50
Closing rate	5.00	4.00	3.00

Ananam's summarized accounts for 2003 and 2004 in terms of Bolonian pesos, are shown opposite. Grand Imperial uses the average rate for the year to translate profits and losses.

You are asked to show, on a separate sheet of paper, what amounts for Ananam would be included in Grand Imperial plc's group accounts for 2003 and 2004; and to explain how exchange differences for each year have been calculated.

12.11 Grand Imperial plc (B): Temporal method

You are asked to show what amounts for Ananam would be included in Grand Imperial plc's group accounts for 2003 and 2004 assuming the temporal method is used.

Details of purchases of plant and equipment have been as follows:

Date	Exchange rate £1 =	Cost Bp'000
1997	12 Bp	3 600
1998	10	3 000
1999	9	1 800
2000	8	800
2001	7.50	1 500
2002	6	1 200
		11 900
2003	4.50	1 350
		13 250
2004	3.50	1 400
		14 650

The freehold land was acquired for 4.8 million Bp in 1997.

Ananam: Profit and loss account for year	2003 Bp'000	2004 Bp'000
Sales	26 480	30 240
Depreciation	1 325	1 465
Other operating expenses	23 265	27 045
Profit before interest and tax	1 890	1 730
Interest	630	770
Profit before tax	1 260	960
Tax	495	385
Profit after tax	765	575

No dividends were paid in respect of either year.

Ananam: Balance sheet at 31 December	2002 Bp'000	2003 Bp'000	2004 Bp'000
Fixed assets			
Freehold land	4 800	4 800	4 800
Plant and equipment: Cost	11 900	13 250	14 650
(Accum. depn.)	(5 040)	(6 365)	(7 830)
Net	6 860	6 885	6 820
	11 660	11 685	11 620
Working capital	6 420	8 160	9 800
(Long-term debt)	(4 000)	(5 000)	(6 000)
	14 080	14 845	15 420
Capital and reserves			
Share capital	6 000	6 000	6 000
Retained profits	8 080	8 845	9 420
	14 080	14 845	15 420

Section 13
Inflation accounting

BACKGROUND

From 1970 to 1990, inflation rates in most countries were high and fluctuating. In these twenty years, with inflation exceeding 10 per cent a year, the pound lost nearly 85 per cent of its purchasing power, an unprecedented rate of inflation over such a long peacetime period. This led to an intensive review of the usefulness of historical money cost (HMC) accounting in times of rapid inflation.

After years of discussion, in January 1973 the UK Accounting Standards Committee proposed a system of 'current purchasing power' (CPP) accounting. A more accurate and less confusing name with the same acronym, which we prefer, is Constant Purchasing Power accounting. (In the United States CPP is known as either 'general price level accounting' (GPLA) or 'constant dollar' accounting.)

Because of the widespread impact of changing the system of accounting, the British government set up the Sandilands Committee to look into the question. Its 1975 report rejected CPP accounting, and proposed instead 'current cost accounting' (CCA).

After much public debate and two CCA Exposure Drafts, the Accounting Standards Committee – following government instructions – finally published a current cost accounting standard in 1980. It required larger UK companies, in addition to HMC accounts, to publish at least supplementary CCA accounts. In the United States a similar process of discussion and political intervention meant that large US companies, in addition to HMC accounts, had to publish summary CCA *and* CPP figures.

The CPP accounting standard [SSAP 7] was withdrawn when the government committee proposed CCA and the CCA standard itself [SSAP 16] was dropped in 1985, when it became clear that CCA had failed to establish itself.

From 1990 to 2004 UK inflation averaged less than 3 per cent a year. This low rate, mirrored in most other currencies, helps explain why interest in 'inflation accounting' has faded in the past fifteen years. But we continue to include this section because inflation might return.

IAS 29 requires the use of constant purchasing power accounting in 'hyperinflationary' economies. That means where the cumulative inflation rate approaches 100 per cent over three years, which is an *annual* rate of 25 per cent or more.

In this section we consider how to measure 'inflation' and the ways in which it can seriously distort historical money cost accounts. In reviewing the basic principles of the two main methods of 'inflation accounting', we look first at constant purchasing power (CPP) accounting and then at current cost accounting (CCA).

PROBLEMS WITH HISTORICAL MONEY COST ACCOUNTS

High rates of inflation cause historical money cost (HMC) accounts to mislead readers because:

- they show fixed assets at purchase costs of many years earlier;
- they understate expenses, especially depreciation of fixed assets;
- they overstate profit, which, if paid out in dividends, impairs real capital;
- return on investment ratios relate overstated profit to understated investment;
- trends over time may reflect growth in money terms not 'real' growth rates.

When inflation exceeds (say) 5 per cent a year over a period of years, historical money cost accounts may greatly understate the real cost of long-life assets on the balance sheet and hence understate depreciation (see page 243), and greatly overstate profit.

Many large UK companies have revalued upwards some of their interests in land and buildings (see Section 7). But infrequent revaluations scarcely affecting *depreciable* fixed assets have done little to overcome performance measurement problems due to inflation.

Errors inside companies

In times of inflation, historical money cost figures may easily mislead decision-makers. In particular, managers may:

- overlook the need to improve low (or negative) real profit levels;
- fix prices too low, if HMC accounts understate costs and overstate profits;
- allocate resources wrongly, on the basis of misleading HMC segment results;
- pay excessive dividends, if HMC accounts overstate profit.

Errors outside companies

Many different kinds of 'outsiders' use company accounts. In particular, decisions by the following groups using historical money cost data in times of inflation may have damaging results:

- Lenders and equity investors – in allocating resources between different companies
- Employees – in wage bargaining
- Governments – in relation to taxes on profits, purchasing, regulation and price controls

Thus using historical money cost accounts in times of inflation may have serious and widespread consequences. A better system of accounting would properly allow for the impact of inflation on accounts. Over the years two different systems have emerged: constant purchasing power (CPP) accounting and current cost accounting (CCA). The table opposite contrasts their different approaches.

TWO CONTRASTING METHODS OF 'INFLATION ACCOUNTING'

The two main methods of 'inflation accounting' take different views of 'capital': hence use different ways to measure 'profit'.

Constant purchasing power (CPP) accounting seeks to maintain the *purchasing power of shareholders' equity*; and uses changes in the Retail Prices Index (RPI) as the basis for adjusting historical money cost (HMC) accounts. In effect CPP proposes to *change the unit of measurement* in accounting from money to a 'unit of constant purchasing power'. But CPP is still a form of historical cost accounting.

Current cost accounting (CCA), on the other hand, aims to maintain the *productive capacity of a company's assets:* and reflects the specific price changes applying to a going concern. CCA continues to use money as the unit of measurement, but proposes to *switch from past costs to current values*.

CPP allows for 'general inflation' but not for 'relative price changes'. If a product's money price increases by 12 per cent in a period in which the RPI increases by 7 per cent, CPP attributes 7 percentage points of the price rise to 'general inflation' (which CPP allows for), and 5 percentage points to 'relative price changes' (which CPP ignores).

But CCA regards the price changes which are relevant to a textile company (say) as those relating to a sample of textile products, and not a 'household shopping basket'. This 'entity' viewpoint implies a difference between CCA and HMC accounting even when 'prices in general' are stable (according to the RPI). For, in a dynamic economy, the money prices of specific goods and services will fluctuate, whether there is 'general inflation' or not.

The table below summarizes the contrast between CPP and CCA. Because CPP tries to allow for general inflation and CCA for specific price changes (up or down), they are not strictly alternatives *to each other*. Hence there is no logical inconsistency in *combining* CPP with CCA in the bottom right quadrant.

		DEFINITION OF 'COST'	
		Past cost	Current value
UNIT OF ACCOUNT	Monetary unit	Historical money cost (HMC)	Current cost accounting (CCA)
UNIT OF ACCOUNT	Unit of constant purchasing power	Constant purchasing power (CPP)	Combination of CPP and CCA

MEASURING THE RATE OF INFLATION

Inflation, in simple terms, is 'too much money chasing too few goods'. If the money supply increases faster than the supply of goods and services, then (subject to certain qualifications) prices expressed in money terms tend to rise over time, and there is 'inflation'.

For many people in the United Kingdom, the 'rate of inflation' means the rate of increase in the monthly Retail Prices Index (RPI). This index measures changes over time in the money cost of a representative sample of goods – an average family's 'household shopping basket'. The rate of inflation which the RPI signals is only approximate. The buying pattern of many families may not correspond exactly to that of the 'average' family; and patterns of spending, and the technical qualities of goods, change over time, which can be hard to allow for precisely. Appendix 4 (on page 276) gives details of the RPI in recent years.

Over the thirty-five year period from 1970 to 2004, the average level of retail prices in the UK multiplied about ten times. (The second edition of this book, in 1974, cost £3.95.) In the last fifty years money prices have increased more than in the whole of the rest of sterling's thousand-year history. No wonder that accountants and others have spent so much effort trying to solve the accounting problems posed by inflation.

Currency debasement

So far we have been talking about money prices rising, with the RPI reflecting the 'average' rate of increase. But another approach is to measure the *fall* in the 'purchasing power' of the pound. This is what the constant purchasing power approach does. From this point of view, 'inflation' of money prices represents 'debasement' of the currency unit. The percentages are not the same: when the RPI doubles (increases by 100 per cent), the purchasing power of the pound halves (falls by 50 per cent).

In the nineteenth century, when modern accounting principles and methods were starting to emerge in the UK, the purchasing power of the pound was stable. In those days, money accounting was the same as constant purchasing power accounting. That is why the sharply falling value of the pound in the second half of the twentieth century proved such a shock.

The pound's purchasing power halved between 1945 and 1965; it halved again between 1965 and 1975; and it halved *again* between 1975 and 1980. In the last twenty-five years the pound has lost a further 65 per cent of its 1980 purchasing power. In all, between 1945 and 2004 the pound lost more than 95 per cent of its purchasing power. This has had a devastating effect on historical money cost accounts.

HISTORICAL MONEY COST ACCOUNTING

Accountants have used historical money cost (HMC) accounting for many years to measure companies' financial performance and position. As we have seen in earlier sections, there are problems in measuring and recording certain kinds of assets, and in matching costs against revenues to determine profit or loss. Even so, on the whole, HMC accounting has been an adequate system for practical purposes, in the absence of prolonged rapid inflation.

The concept of 'capital' in HMC accounts is 'the money amount of the shareholders' equity interest'. When there is no general inflation (when the 'purchasing power of money' is stable), then 'money capital' is the same thing as 'purchasing power capital'. As we saw in Section 5 (page 93), the increase in shareholders' funds between one balance sheet date and the next – after allowing for capital changes, such as new issues of shares and for dividends – represents the profit or loss for the period. But in times of inflation that approach can give a false impression.

Example

In the example below, Paint Making Limited started trading at the beginning of 2004. Straight line depreciation on equipment was based on an eight-year life. Profit for 2004 was £30 000, of which £24 000 was paid out in dividends. Thus the company could legally have paid out an extra £6 000 in dividends. That would have left the shareholders' funds at £200 000, exactly the same money amount as at the beginning of 2004.

PAINT MAKING LIMITED

HMC balance sheet at 31 December 2004	£'000	HMC profit and loss account Year ended 31 December 2004		£'000
Fixed assets				
Land and buildings at cost	40	Turnover		480
Equipment: Cost	120	Cost of goods sold	360	
Depreciation	15	Depreciation	15	
	105	Admin. expenses	60	
Net current assets	61			
	206			435
		Profit before tax		45
Capital and reserves		Tax		15
Called up share capital	200	Profit after tax		30
Profit and loss account	6	Dividends		24
	206	Retained profit		6

CONSTANT PURCHASING POWER (CPP) ACCOUNTING

In the early 1970s the UK accounting profession supported the constant purchasing power (CPP) method of inflation accounting; and in 1974 issued SSAP 7 as the accounting standard on 'Accounting for changes in the purchasing power of money'. The title made it clear that the 'problem' which inflation causes is changes in the accounting unit of measurement (money).

CPP aims to adjust HMC accounts solely for changes in the *general* purchasing power of money. It is, in fact, strictly still a form of 'historical cost' accounting; but it uses as the unit of account not the monetary unit but a 'unit of constant purchasing power'. According to this approach, if there were no general inflation, CPP would be identical with HMC. There would be no need for 'inflation accounting', since there would be no (general) inflation. In measuring profit or loss, CPP aims to *maintain the purchasing power of the shareholders' equity*. It looks at accounts from the shareholders' viewpoint.

CPP accounting requires accounts to express all financial amounts in units of the same 'purchasing power' – normally (but not necessarily) that of the monetary unit at the closing balance sheet date. CPP argues that HMC accounts add together amounts stated in *different* units of measurement (even though in the UK money amounts of different years are all called 'pounds'). So CPP indexes all money amounts in HMC accounts by reference to the change in the RPI between the date when each item occurred and the base date (normally the closing balance sheet date).

CPP regards money of different dates as being, in effect, 'foreign currencies'; it uses an index system to translate money amounts into terms of the *same* 'currency', much as the 'temporal system' does (see Section 12). CPP 'dates' purchasing power amounts by means of a subscript before the £ symbol; thus, $_{05}£150$. CPP calculates profit or loss for a period by measuring the change in the *purchasing power* of the shareholders' equity interest (after excluding new capital issues, dividends paid, and so on). The basic question which CPP raises is whether in times of rapid inflation it is more *useful* to account in terms of money or in terms of (constant) purchasing power.

IAS 21 allows companies to use any currency they choose to present accounts; so there seems to be nothing to stop companies (for example) using 'constant 2005 pounds' as part of a CPP approach.

Paint Making Limited – Example

CPP accounts for Paint Making Limited for the year 2004 are set out opposite. They allow for inflation of 15 per cent in 2004. (We take a high rate of inflation to help illustrate the process of adjustment to HMC accounts.) The RPI is assumed to stand at 100.0 in December 2003 and at 115.0 in December 2004, with the rate of inflation steady throughout the year.

PAINT MAKING LIMITED

CPP balance sheet
at 31 December 2004

$_{04}£'000$

Fixed assets

Land and buildings at cost	(40 x 1.15)	46
Equipment: Cost	(120 x 1.15)	138
Depreciation		17
		121
Net current assets		61
		228

Capital and reserves

Called up share capital	(200 x 1.15)	230
Profit and loss account	(see details)	(2)
		228

CPP profit and loss account
Year ended 31 December 2004

$_{04}£'000$

Turnover	(480 x 1.07)		513
Cost of goods sold	(360 x 1.07)	385	
Depreciation		17	
Administration expenses	(60 x 1.07)	64	
			466
			47
Loss on monetary assets	(see details)		7
Profit before tax			40
Tax	(15 x 1.07)		16
Profit after tax			24
Dividends	(24 x 1.07)		26
Retained profit for the year			(2)

Balance sheet

The figures need explaining. The money cost of fixed assets purchased at the start of 2004 must be multiplied by 1.15 to express their cost in end-2004 pounds. Thus the CPP accounts show land and buildings at £46 000 (£40 000 x 115/100) and restate plant and equipment figures in a similar way. This is not to 'revalue' fixed assets, certainly not at 'current values'; but to *restate their original cost* in terms of up-to-date purchasing power. It is a process of 'translation'. Thus constant purchasing power accounting is really a form of historical cost accounting; but it indexes original money costs to allow for subsequent general inflation. CPP restates share capital in the same way as the cost of fixed assets.

The HMC balance sheet already expresses closing net current assets in end-of-year pounds, so CPP accounts do not need to restate the amount.

Profit and loss account

The profit and loss account items (apart from depreciation) require adjustment too, but of a different magnitude. We assume that the figures in the HMC profit and loss account represent 'average-of-the-year' pounds; and we further assume that inflation occurred at a steady rate all through the year. Hence we multiply the 2004 profit and loss account items by 1.07 (that is, 115.0/107.5) to translate from mid-2004 pounds to end-2004 pounds.

Depreciation is different. Here we simply take one-eighth of the adjusted (CPP) cost figure. This results in a CPP charge of £17 000 in end-2004 pounds, instead of the £15 000 charged in the HMC accounts.

The difference between HMC and CPP depreciation could be much larger with older fixed assets, or with a higher rate of inflation. For example, with average inflation of 10 per cent a year and a fifteen-year asset life, the average understatement over the asset's whole life is 97 per cent, as the table below shows.

HMC depreciation understatement

$\dfrac{\text{CPP-HMC}}{\text{HMC}}$ as a %	Inflation rate per year		
	5%	10%	15%
Life in years			
10	30	63	99
15	45	97	157
20	60	135	220

We assume the HMC tax charge of 15 is not affected by the CPP adjustments; here it is simply multiplied by 1.07 like most other profit and loss items

Loss on monetary assets

In CPP accounts there is an *extra* profit and loss account item which does not appear at all in HMC accounts. This is the item: 'loss on monetary assets' (or 'gain on monetary liabilities'). It arises in CPP accounts because the measuring unit is a unit of constant purchasing power. (It does not arise in HMC accounts, of course, where the measuring unit *is* money.)

In Paint Making's case, we shall assume that all net current assets are 'monetary' in nature. (Treating stocks in this way normally makes little difference in practice.) We then calculate the amount of the (purchasing power) loss on monetary assets as follows:

		$_{04}$£'000
Opening working capital*	(40 x 1.15)	46*
Closing working capital		61
Average working capital		53$\frac{1}{2}$*
Loss of purchasing power in year:		
Percentage**		13%**
In CPP terms* (53$\frac{1}{2}$ x 0.13)		7

* in end-of-period pounds

** increase in RPI was 15.0 per cent, hence loss of purchasing power in year was $100 - (100/115) = 13.0\%$

Conclusion

We see that on a CPP basis, in 2004 Paint Making Limited distributed some of its dividends out of (purchasing power) 'capital' – in contrast to what the HMC accounts showed. We can also see that while HMC return on end-of-year equity in 2004 was 14.6 per cent (30/206), the CPP figure was only 10.5 per cent (24/228).

In this example we are using only the figures for 2004. If we had figures for earlier years, we would have made a further adjustment to restate the earlier years' figures in terms of end-2004 purchasing power. (Problem 13.2 at the end of this section deals with such adjustments.)

CURRENT COST ACCOUNTING (CCA)

SSAP 16, the accounting standard on current cost accounting (CCA), was issued in 1980 (and withdrawn in 1985). It required annual financial statements for all but small companies to include current cost accounts as well as historical money cost (HMC) figures. Companies could publish either CCA or HMC accounts as the 'main' accounts, with extra information either in the notes or in the form of supplementary accounts.

CCA regards as the main problem changes in the prices of fixed assets and stocks. Hence CCA adjustments to HMC accounts aim to show such 'real' assets at their estimated *current* costs (not their actual historical costs), both in the balance sheet and in the profit and loss account.

CCA extends to all real assets on a regular and systematic basis the *ad hoc* revaluations that some HMC accounts apply to some fixed assets from time to time (see Section 7). Changes in asset 'costs' appear in a revaluation reserve in the CCA balance sheet (as part of shareholders' funds).

CCA, in contrast to CPP, is not a system of accounting for general inflation. The case for using current costs rather than historical costs is (in theory) just as strong when there is no general inflation. CCA takes the view that companies are concerned, not so much with 'general' inflation, but with the specific price changes of the goods they themselves buy and sell. In effect, CCA takes an 'entity' view. Therefore CCA includes current costs (rather than historical costs) of the specific assets a business uses. This aims to ensure the business *maintains its operating capability*, as represented by its fixed assets, stocks, and monetary working capital.

'Current cost operating profit' (before interest and tax) matches current costs against sales turnover to determine the current cost profit or loss from operations. It makes three adjustments to HMC operating profits:

1   A *depreciation adjustment*, being the difference between depreciation based on current costs of fixed assets, and that based on historical money costs.
2   A *cost of sales adjustment* (COSA), being the difference between the current costs of stocks consumed in the period and their historical money costs.
3   A *monetary working capital adjustment* (MWCA), being the amount needed to maintain the real volume of 'monetary working capital' (which is roughly working capital less stocks).

Balance sheet valuations

SSAP 16 required CCA balance sheets to show assets at their 'value to the business', defined as 'the lower of net current replacement cost and recoverable amount'. Recoverable amount is the higher of an asset's net realizable value (on disposal) and, where applicable, the amount recoverable from its further use. The diagram below illustrates.

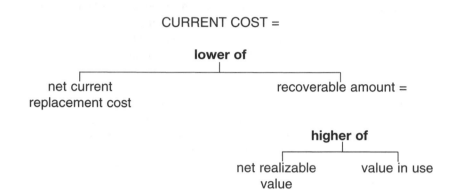

CURRENT COST =

lower of

net current replacement cost   recoverable amount =

higher of

net realizable value   value in use

Because the CCA balance sheet includes only those same assets which appear in an HMC balance sheet (though some at different values), it does *not* attempt to disclose the 'total value' of the business. Thus our comments in Section 1 (page 3) about the misleading nature of the American expression 'net worth' *apply with equal force to CCA balance sheets*.

For plant and machinery, CCA accounts use the current replacement cost net of depreciation. Companies must obtain current costs for each distinct kind of asset, such as production machinery, vehicles, office equipment, and so on. They normally do so by applying to the historical money cost the change in a relevant asset index since the date of acquisition. In rare cases companies might use 'economic value', that is, the net present value of the expected remaining cash flows from using an asset.

The current cost of stock will normally be obtained by adjusting historical money costs by the use of suitable specific price indices (or possibly from current price lists). If the difference between HMC and CCA stocks at the balance sheet date is small, CCA balance sheets may use the same figure as for HMC. But the current cost profit and loss account will still need to make a cost of sales adjustment (COSA). Thus CCA aims to get the profit and loss account advantages of the LIFO method of valuing stock without its balance sheet disadvantages.

Paint Making Limited – Example

We assumed that the RPI in Paint Making Limited's case stood at 100.0 in December 2003 and at 115.0 in December 2004. These were the 'general index' numbers we used in preparing CPP accounts. For CCA accounts, however, we need different *specific* price indices for each of the main types of asset. Let us assume that professional valuers valued Paint Making's land and buildings at £50 000 at December 2004, and that the relevant specific price indices changed as follows:

	end 2003	end 2004
Equipment	100.0	110.0
Monetary working capital	100.0	120.0

Balance sheet

The CCA balance sheet adjusts the equipment's historical cost by reference to the change in its specific price index (£120 000 x 110/100 = £132 000); and the one-eighth straight line depreciation is then calculated on the gross *current* cost.

The HMC balance sheet already shows the net current assets at 'current cost' levels, so no adjustment is needed; but we use the change in the monetary working capital index to calculate the necessary profit and loss account charge.

PAINT MAKING LIMITED

CCA balance sheet at 31 December 2004

	£'000
Fixed assets	
Land and buildings, valuation	50
Equipment: Current cost	132
Depreciation	16
	116
Net current assets	61
	227
Capital and reserves	
Called up share capital	200
CC revaluation reserve	31
Profit and loss account	(4)
	227

CCA profit and loss account Year ended 31 December 2004

		£'000
Turnover		480
Cost of goods sold	360	
Depreciation	15	
Admin. expenses	60	
		435
HMC profit before tax		45
Current cost adjustments:		
Depreciation adjustment	1	
MWCA (inc. COSA)	9	
		10
Current cost profit before tax		35
Tax		15
Current cost profit after tax		20
Dividends		24
Current cost balance retained		(4)

Profit and loss account: current cost adjustments

The current cost profit and loss account for Paint Making Limited shows three 'current cost adjustments' to the HMC trading profit before tax:

1   The depreciation adjustment in 2004 is simply the excess of CCA depreciation (£16 000) over HMC depreciation (£15 000).
2   The monetary working capital adjustment (MWCA) here covers the whole of the net current assets (that is, *including stocks*). To calculate the MWCA the 'averaging' method uses opening (100), closing (120), and average (assumed 110) index numbers for 2004, as shown below:

	£'000	Average prices £'000
Closing net current assets	61 x 110/120 =	56
Opening net current assets	40 x 110/100 =	44
Increase in year 2004	21	(12)
of which *volume* change =	12	
leaving as due to *price*	9 (MWCA)	

That part of the change in net current assets due to *price* changes, rather than to volume changes, is the monetary working capital adjustment (MWCA); it appears in the profit and loss account as a current cost adjustment to the HMC operating profit; and increases the current cost revaluation reserve in the balance sheet.

3   In Paint Making Limited's case the cost of sales adjustment (COSA) is included in the MWCA. Often the price index for stocks also applies to monetary working capital and the two adjustments can be combined; but where different indices are appropriate, then two separate calculations must be made.

Conclusion

The current cost operating profit in 2004 now becomes £35 000 and the profit after tax £20 000. As a result, in the current cost accounts it appears that dividends paid in 2004 have exceeded available current cost profits after tax by £4 000; and this deficit reduces capital and reserves in the balance sheet.

The current cost revaluation reserve of £31 000 consists of the increase in valuation of land and buildings (+ 10) and of gross equipment (+ 12), together with the MWCA (+ 9).

The CCA return on end-of-year equity is 8.8 per cent in 2004 (20/227). Like the CPP figure, this percentage is lower than that derived from the HMC accounts.

Gearing adjustment

In the Paint Making example, we have so far considered the three current cost adjustments to HMC operating profit:

1 Depreciation adjustment.
2 Cost of sales adjustment (COSA).
3 Monetary working capital adjustment (MWCA).

In addition, when a proportion of the net operating assets is financed by net borrowing, SSAP 16 required a further adjustment – the 'gearing adjustment'. This would normally *reduce* the effect of the three current cost operating adjustments. The gearing adjustment reflects the extent to which current cost operating adjustments do not have to be financed from equity funds because of the existence of debt capital.

SSAP 16 required two steps to calculate the gearing adjustment:

(a) Express 'net borrowing' (that is, borrowing less cash) as a proportion of net operating assets (in current cost terms).
(b) Multiply the total of the three current cost operating adjustments by the 'borrowing proportion' so determined.

When SSAP 16 was being introduced there was much debate about the gearing adjustment, and how to calculate it. Paint Making's accounts contain no debt, so require no gearing adjustment.

13.3 Paint Making Limited (B):
Solution (continued from page 250)

(b) (i) **MWCA**	£'000		£'000
Closing net current assets	84 × 127½/135 =		79
Opening net current assets	61 × 127½/120 =		65
Increase in year 2005	23		14
of which *volume* change	14		
leaving as due to *price*:	9		

(ii) **Current cost revaluation reserve**	£'000
At 31 December 2004	31
Plus: Land and buildings	10
Equipment	10
Monetary working capital	9
	60
Less: Backlog depreciation (36-16-18)	2
At 31 December 2005	58

SECTION 13 SUMMARY

In this section we have tried to cover the problem of 'inflation accounting' as simply as possible. We noted fluctuating rates of UK inflation averaging 10 per cent a year between 1970 and 1990, and less than 3 per cent a year since 1990. We noted how in times of inflation historical money cost (HMC) accounts overstate profits and understate assets.

CPP

Constant purchasing power (CPP) accounting regards the accounting problem of inflation as being the fall in the value ('purchasing power') of the monetary unit. It seeks to maintain the *purchasing power* of shareholders' equity but still in a historical cost context. Hence CPP adjusts all items in HMC accounts according to the date on which they arose, by applying a single index of 'general inflation' (the RPI).

The main CPP adjustments within a period are:

1 to fixed assets and depreciation;
2 in respect of gains (or losses) on net monetary liabilities (or assets). (Stocks are usually regarded as 'monetary' for this purpose.)

There is also an important CPP adjustment to prior years' results in order to restate all figures in accounts and in summary statistics into terms of the same ('constant') purchasing power. This permits sensible comparisons of trends over periods of five to ten years.

CCA

Current cost accounting (CCA) regards changes in prices of fixed assets and stocks as the main problem of inflation. It seeks to maintain the operating capacity of the business. We noted the different CCA adjustments to HMC accounts:

1 Revalue fixed assets and stocks.
2 Calculate the three CCA operating adjustments:
    (a) depreciation adjustment
    (b) cost of sales adjustment (COSA)
    (c) monetary working capital adjustment (MWCA).
    (Note: (b) and (c) may be combined.)
3 Calculate the gearing adjustment.

The current cost (revaluation) reserve consists of unrealized gains as well as realized gains which have passed through the CCA profit and loss account. The three current cost adjustments are applied to the HMC operating profit before interest and tax, to arrive at current cost operating profit.

The gearing adjustment reduces the CCA operating adjustments by the extent of the gearing proportion. This is intended to avoid double counting in respect of price changes effectively financed by debt capital.

PROBLEMS

13.1 Definitions

Please write out below your understanding of what the following terms mean. If you need to, use extra paper. When you have completed writing out your answers, compare them carefully with those shown overleaf.

(a) General inflation

(f) The CCA depreciation adjustment

(b) A unit of constant purchasing power

(g) The CCA cost of sales adjustment (COSA)

(c) Loss on monetary assets

(h) The CCA monetary working capital adjustment (MWCA)

(d) Operating capability

(i) Current cost 'value to the business'

(e) Current cost operating profit

(j) The CCA gearing adjustment

13.1 Definitions

(a) **General inflation** is measured in the UK by increases in the monthly Retail Prices Index (RPI), which records changes in the money cost over time of a representative sample of retail goods – loosely an average family's 'household shopping basket'. (The Gross Domestic Product (GDP) deflator is an alternative measure.) The reciprocal of general inflation is 'currency debasement', a fall in the purchasing power of money.

(b) **A unit of constant purchasing power** is what CPP accounting uses as the unit of account (instead of money, as in HMC accounting). It stems from an index measuring general inflation, such as the RPI. As a matter of practical convenience, CPP accounts normally use 'end-of-most-recent-period' purchasing power units, but in principle one could use CPP units of *any* date. Use of CPP units is helpful, in times of inflation, in comparing financial amounts over time in 'real' terms.

(c) **Loss on monetary assets** is the loss of purchasing power in respect of average net monetary assets during a period. These would normally include stock (as a simplifying assumption) and would comprise: working capital less long-term borrowing. In times of inflation there will be a *gain* of purchasing power in respect of any net monetary *liabilities*.

(d) **Operating capability** is the volume of a given quality of goods and services which a business can produce with its existing resources. In accounting terms it means net operating assets (fixed assets, stocks and monetary working capital) at current cost. This concept of 'capital' underpins current cost accounting (CCA). It contrasts with:

● historical money cost (HMC) accounting, which aims to maintain the *money amount* of shareholders' funds (share capital and reserves); and
● constant purchasing power (CPP) accounting, which aims to maintain the *purchasing power* of shareholders' funds.

(e) **Current cost operating profit** is the surplus arising from business after allowing for the impact of price changes on the funds needed to maintain its capacity. There are three main adjustments to historical money cost profit:

● the depreciation adjustment;
● the cost of sales adjustment (COSA); and
● the monetary working capital adjustment (MWCA).

(f) **The CCA depreciation adjustment** allows for the impact of price changes in charging for depreciation of fixed assets. It is the difference between current cost and historical money cost depreciation for a period.

(g) **The CCA cost of sales adjustment (COSA)** allows for the impact of price changes in charging for stock consumed. It is the difference between the current cost and the historical money cost of stock charged during the period. One can calculate COSA either item by item or by the 'averaging method', using an index of relevant price changes.

(h) **The CCA monetary working capital adjustment (MWCA)** represents the change in the amount of finance needed for MWC as a result of changes in the input prices of goods and services. Where stock is mostly financed by net creditors, the credit for MWCA will largely offset the debit for COSA. The averaging method is used to calculate MWCA, which may be combined with COSA.

(i) **Current cost 'value to the business'** is normally net current replacement cost, unless there is a permanent reduction to less than that amount. If so, then 'value to the business' is the *higher* of:

● the asset's net realizable value; and
● the amount recoverable from its further use.

(j) **The CCA gearing adjustment** reduces the current cost operating adjustments to the extent that net assets are financed by net borrowing and thus do not require equity funds. It reduces those adjustments by the proportion of net borrowing to net borrowing plus equity. ('Net borrowing' is the excess of all money liabilities, except those in MWC, over the aggregate of all current assets not subject to a COSA or in MWC.) The gearing adjustment does not depend on the company's intention to maintain the same gearing in future.

13.2 Paint Making Limited (A): CPP accounts for 2005

Refer back to the Paint Making Limited example on pages 241 to 243. Assume the rate of RPI inflation in 2005 was 10 per cent. Thus the RPI, which stood at 100.00 in December 2003 and at 115.0 in December 2004, stood at 126.5 in December 2005. As before assume the rate of inflation was steady throughout the year (so that the mid-2005 RPI may be taken as 120.6). No further fixed assets have been acquired.

Required

(a) Prepare CPP accounts for 2005.
(b) To provide comparative figures for the above, *restate* the 2004 CPP figures (shown in end-2004 pounds on page 242) in terms of end-2005 pounds.

The 2005 HMC accounts for Paint Making Limited are shown opposite.

13.3 Paint Making Limited (B): CCA accounts for 2005

Refer back to the Paint Making Limited example on pages 241 and 245.
Assume the relevant specific price index levels were as follows:

	end 2003	*end 2004*	*end 2005*
Plant and equipment	100.0	110.0	118.0
Monetary working capital	100.0	120.0	135.0

The value of land and buildings has risen to £60 000 by December 2005.

Required

(a) Prepare CCA accounts for 2005.
(b) Explain your calculation of:
  (i) MWCA
  (ii) Current cost revaluation reserve at December 2005.

The 2005 HMC accounts for Paint Making Limited are shown opposite.

PAINT MAKING LIMITED

HMC balance sheet
at 31 December 2005

	£'000
Fixed assets	
Land and buildings at cost	40
Equipment: Cost	120
Depreciation	30
Net	90
Net current assets	84
	214
Capital and reserves	
Called up share capital	200
Profit and loss account	14
	214

HMC profit and loss account
Year ended 31 December 2005

		£'000
Turnover		600
Cost of goods sold	450	
Depreciation	15	
Administration expenses	75	
		540
Profit before tax		60
Tax		20
Profit after tax		40
Dividends		32
Retained profit for the year		8

13.2 Paint Making Limited (A): CPP

Solution

PAINT MAKING LIMITED		(a)	(b)	
		2005	**2004**	**2004**
CPP balance sheet at 31 December		$_{05}$£'000	$_{05}$£'000	$_{04}$£'000
Fixed assets				
Land and buildings at cost	(40 x 1.265)	51	51	46
Equipment: Cost	(120 x 1.265)	152	152	138
Depreciation		38	19	17
Net		114	133	121
Net current assets		84	67	61
		249	251	228
Capital and reserves				
Called up share capital	(200 x 1.265)	253	253	230
Profit and loss account	(see details)	(4)	(2)	(2)
		249	251	228

CPP profit and loss account Year ended 31 December		$_{05}$£'000	$_{05}$£'000	$_{04}$£'000
Turnover	(600 x 1.05)	630	564	513
Cost of goods sold	(450 x 1.05)	472	423	385
Depreciation		19	19	17
Administration expenses	(75 x 1.05)	79	70	64
		570	512	466
		60	52	47
Loss on monetary assets		7*	8	7
Profit before tax		53	44	40
Tax	(20 x 1.05)	21	18	16
Profit after tax		32	26	24
Dividends	(32 x 1.05)	34	28	26
Retained profit for the year		(2)	(2)	(2)

*Average working capital 75.5 x $^{1}/_{11}$.

13.3 Paint Making Limited (B): CCA

Solution

PAINT MAKING LIMITED		
CCA balance sheet at 31 December	**2005** £'000	**2004** £'000
Fixed assets		
Land and buildings	60	50
Equipment: Current cost	142	132
Depreciation	36	16
	106	116
Net current assets	84	61
	250	227
Capital and reserves		
Called up share capital	200	200
Revaluation reserve	58	31
Profit and loss account	(8)	(4)
	250	227

CPP profit and loss account Year ended 31 December	£'000	£'000
Turnover	600	480
Cost of goods sold	450	360
Depreciation	15	15
Administration expenses	75	60
	540	435
HMC profit before tax	60	45
Current cost adjustments:		
Depreciation adjustment	3	1
Monetary working capital adjustment	9	9
Current cost profit before tax	48	35
Tax	20	15
Current cost profit after tax	28	20
Dividends	32	24
Retained profit for the year	(4)	(4)

Solution continued at foot of page 246 (left).

Section 14

Interpreting company accounts

INTRODUCTION

We have now completed Sections 2 to 13, which we introduced in Section 2 (page 29) with the comment: 'It is important for people who use accounting figures to understand what those figures really mean. They should know how companies record transactions and summarize them in accounts; and they should recognize the various possible ways to value assets and to measure profit or loss.'

Now we know in more detail what is involved, it is clear that external analysts must be cautious in examining accounts. This applies whether they are shareholders (actual or potential), employees, creditors, customers, professional financial analysts or government officials. Indeed, analysis often raises questions rather than providing conclusions.

Users must be aware of the normal margins of error which are inevitable in compiling accounts for large and complex enterprises. They must also recognize the extent to which subjective judgements affect critical areas of valuing assets (or providing for deductions from cost) and hence of measuring profit or loss. Indeed recent moves to include more assets in accounts at 'fair values', rather than at cost, will increase the margins or error as well as adding to volatility from year to year.

We have looked at accounting statements from various angles: basic concepts and structure; financial ratios; recording transactions; measuring profit or loss; stocks and fixed assets; capital structure; groups; taxation; cash flows; international accounting and inflation accounting.

In this final section we shall consider:

1. accounting matters requiring special attention;
2. financial analysis and economic reality;
3. disclosure and accounting conventions;
4. comparisons over time and between companies.

We shall then examine Tesco plc's 2004 accounts in detail, drawing on the knowledge we have been gaining about company accounts throughout the book. We shall review the four main steps in analysing accounts.

1. Overview*
2. Ratio analysis
3. Business segments
4. Cash flows*

*These have already been dealt with in Section 2 and Section 11 respectively.

Finally we shall interpret the results.

ACCOUNTING MATTERS REQUIRING SPECIAL ATTENTION

We summarize here some items in accounts where the analyst may need to exercise special care, under four headings: capital employed; fixed assets; working capital; profit and loss account. Many balance sheet items will also affect the profit and loss account.

Analysts may sometimes need to adjust published figures to make comparisons over time or between companies more valid. This may be where alternative accounting treatments are possible or where historical money costs fail to reflect the impact of inflation. It may require special effort to obtain five- or ten-year statistics for certain profit and loss account and balance sheet items. Where adequate detail is missing, great care will be essential before drawing conclusions.

Capital employed

Has called up ordinary share capital increased during the period?
> If so, why? Rights issue? Bonus (scrip) issue? Acquisition?
> Have any dividends been 'paid' in shares, rather than in cash?

Do 'per share' figures use properly weighted number of shares?
> Are prior years' figures comparable?

Which items have caused significant movements on reserves?
> Do any of them really belong in the profit and loss account?

Are there any minority interests?
> Have there been any significant changes during the year?

Is there any preference (non-equity) capital?

Is any long-term debt convertible into ordinary shares?
> On what terms?
> Have per share figures been calculated on a 'fully diluted' basis?

Is any long-term debt repayable in the fairly near future?
> If so, will it probably need to be refinanced with more debt?

Are there significant borrowings in foreign currencies?
> Do they seem to be matched by foreign assets?
> How are exchange gains and losses treated?

Has all lease financing been correctly identified?
> Are any 'operating' leases really 'finance' leases?

Should short-term borrowing be included in capital employed?

Should any cash balances be offset against short-term borrowing?

Is the treatment of pensions appropriate?

What deferred taxation policy is being followed?

Fixed assets

Have there been any substantial acquisitions or disposals in the period?

How have acquisitions been accounted for?
> By acquisition accounting with fair values attached to assets?
> By merger accounting with historical book values?

What accounting policy is being used for purchased goodwill?
> Amortization? (Over what period?)
> Or regular impairment testing?

Has goodwill in the past been written off against reserves?
> How much? Is adjustment needed?

Where tangible fixed assets are shown at 'historical cost':
> How old are they? What is their estimated current value?
> How would revaluation affect the depreciation charge?
> Has any debt interest been capitalized?

Where tangible fixed assets are shown at 'valuation':
> When was the valuation made, and on what basis?
> How have values changed since that date?
> Might the assets be more valuable if used for some other purpose?

What methods of depreciation are used?
> What asset lives are used?
> Has adequate provision been made for technological obsolescence?

Are any assets leased? What is their value?
> How much are the annual rentals? How long is the commitment?

Has the status of any investments changed during the period?
> Subsidiaries? Associates? Joint ventures? Trade investments?
> Non-consolidated subsidiaries?

What is the difference between cost and market value of listed investments?
> Is market value used if lower than cost?

Working capital

On what basis has stock and work-in-progress been valued?
    What provision has been made for slow-moving stock and losses?

How are contracts in progress valued?
    How much profit has been taken so far?
    Are provisions for contingencies adequate?

Are sufficient details of debtors given?
    What amount is owed in foreign currencies?
    How much has been provided for bad debts?
    Can the total be split between domestic and foreign debtors?
    Are there any long-term debtors?

How much 'revenue' expenditure is being carried forward to future periods?
    What does it represent? Development? Advertising?
    Is the amount deferred increasing from period to period?

Is any tax recoverable shown as an asset?
    How certain of recovery is it?

Is cash distinguished from interest-bearing short-term investments?
    How does the total of liquid resources compare with short-term borrowing?
    Do net liquid resources look either excessive or inadequate?

Have any bank overdrafts been outstanding for more than twelve months?
    If so, should they be regarded as medium-term liabilities?

Are any 'provisions' included in current liabilities?
    What is their nature? Are the amounts adequate?

Are trade creditors affected by fixed asset purchases?

Profit and loss account

How are sales and trading profit split among the main activities?
    To what extent are changes due to price changes?
    To what extent to volume changes?
    Does inter-company transfer pricing policy distort the analysis?
    What is the impact of foreign exchange differences?
    How much interest payable, if any, has been capitalized?

Which method is used to translate overseas profits?
    The average exchange rate for the year?
    The closing rate?
    Has the reporting currency's exchange rate changed much in the year?

Has the apparent proportion of profit taken in tax changed?
    What deferred taxation policy is being followed?

Has the share of profit (or loss) of minority interests in subsidiaries changed? If so, is it clear why?

Were any mergers, acquisitions or disposals made in the year?
    For what fraction of the year were sales and profits included?

Are profits and losses on sales of fixed assets:
    Treated as adjustments of depreciation charges?
    Disclosed separately in the profit and loss account?

What has been included in exceptional items?
    Should any of these items be regarded as 'ordinary' activities?
    Do any items tend to recur year after year?

Is it clear which items are shown in the Statement of Total Recognized Gains and Losses without going through the profit and loss account?
    Is such treatment appropriate in each case?

FINANCIAL ANALYSIS AND ECONOMIC REALITY

Financial analysis is a means of finding out about a company's performance over time in the markets in which it operates. We also want to know about its financial status (level of debt and short-term liquidity). The diagram opposite shows a framework which we can use for these purposes. We can relate some items to others (for example profit to sales and profit to investment). But to understand the economic realities of the business in its market environment, we need to identify *changes* taking place through time.

To achieve success a company must perform well in three competitive markets – financial markets, product/customer markets and markets for labour and other supplies. Some financial measures show directly a company's degree of success in the financial and product/customer markets. While there is increasing pressure for companies to report on staff recruitment and training, accounts do not directly reflect success in the labour markets. In the longer term, though, poor performance in relation to employees is likely to result in low or negative profit.

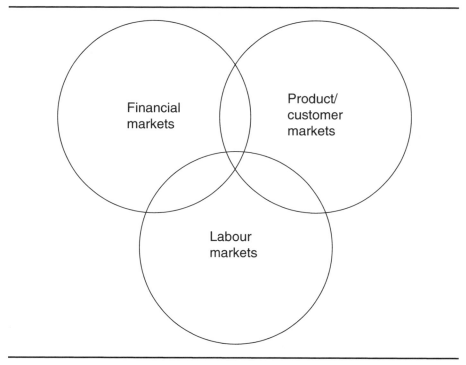

The diagram opposite represents the financial and accounting links between these markets. On the left-hand side, success in financial markets is reflected in the company's share price. On the right-hand side, success in product/customer markets can be measured in terms of sales and profit growth, and in the utilization of assets.

Here detailed accounting numbers directly indicate levels of performance; and changes in them over time reflect both internal changes within the company and external changes in the business environment.

Between share price, which looks forward, and accounting return on equity, which looks backward, the link is only tenuous, certainly in the short term. The bigger the changes affecting a company, the less will past results be a good guide to likely future achievement. General conditions in the financial markets affect share prices: they also reflect the market's view of uncertainty – both the risks inherent in the business, and those related to the methods of financing. Volatility of past earnings and comparisons with other companies in the same industry may help show whether returns have been adequate in relation to risk.

The remaining boxes in the diagram represent a comprehensive accounting model with parts directly linked to each other. It is thus possible to identify, for example, whether a falling return on equity is caused by increasing charges for interest or for tax. Similarly, changes in return on net assets may be due to changes in margins or asset utilization. These in turn may be caused by changes in volume, prices, costs, and the level of use of fixed assets and working capital.

Financial analysis directs attention to where change is taking place. Rarely will the accounting numbers *explain* the reasons for a change; but analysts with clearly defined questions are more likely to obtain relevant answers.

Seeing declining overall margins they may discover that the problem lies in two out of several product lines; but they then need to find out from management *why* profit is declining – is it increased costs or lower prices, and what is causing them? We saw in Section 2 how to extend the accounting model in detail by using the pyramid of ratios. This enables analysts to break down profit/sales and sales/net assets into their constituent parts.

The framework of the pyramid can apply in two directions – either breaking down aggregate figures into more detail, or building them up from below. Similarly, financial analysis using the framework opposite moves from left to right within the diagram: changes in return on equity are 'explained' by changes in one or more elements to its right. In planning, management can use the same model, moving from right to left: to discover, for example, what happens to return on equity if sales volume increases by 20 per cent, or if asset utilization increases by 10 per cent.

Such a framework, although crude, can help to diagnose what affects success or failure, and to assess the impact of management decisions on financial performance. But this accrual accounting framework does not show cash flows, and even profit-making companies can still experience cash problems. Solvency and liquidity ratios will reflect these; but it is wise to use such ratios in conjunction with detailed cash flow statements covering a number of years.

FRAMEWORK FOR LINKING FINANCIAL AND BUSINESS OBJECTIVES

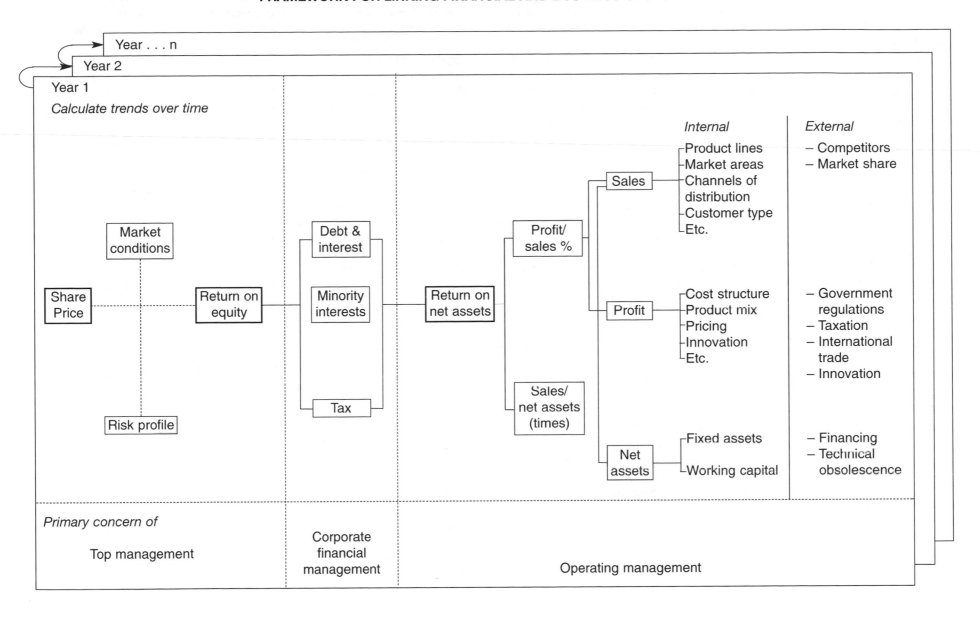

DISCLOSURE AND ACCOUNTING CONVENTIONS

Except where the results of completed transactions are being measured, accounting profit or loss for going concerns is not a matter of certainty, but involves subjective judgement. The larger the number of incomplete transactions, the longer their timespan, and the greater their size, the wider will be the range of possible figures for profit or loss.

The requirement for accounting treatment to be 'consistent' from year to year aims to minimize distortions due to changes in opinion. In a changing business environment, however, accounting treatment may properly adapt from time to time (subject to adequate disclosure).

Accounting conventions owe much to their historical roots, and conservatism ('prudence') is a basic feature. This often leads to a tendency to understate the position. Intangible assets such as goodwill or trademarks may be extremely valuable, as may the results of research or of brand development. Yet because they are not tangible, and often cannot be realized separately, balance sheets may omit such items completely, unless they have been explicitly purchased outside for a definite cost.

Company chairmen often say that their company's most important asset is its employees. But balance sheets do not normally show this 'asset', nor is any capital sum usually payable directly on 'acquiring' employees. (Football clubs are a well-known exception.) Hence in the accounts of firms providing services rather than selling goods, 'return on capital' ratios may seem very high.

In periods of inflation, the accounting convention of using historical money cost fails to reflect the real position. As we saw in Section 13, inflation affects the level of profit or loss as well as many of the balance sheet figures. Companies need to retain sufficient reported money 'profits' in the business, otherwise there is a serious danger of distributing real capital in the mistaken belief that it is 'profit'.

We noted on page 8 that there are modern pressures for increasing disclosure, both to comply with the Companies Act and to follow accounting standards. Clearly accounting regulation has costs as well as benefits. When we were working on the first edition of this book, ICI's 1968 accounts contained five page of notes. Diageo's 2003 accounts contain fifty pages of notes, plus sixteen more pages of similar material.

COMPARISONS OVER TIME AND BETWEEN COMPANIES

The trend in a company's results over a number of years is likely to provide a more useful means of appraising its performance and financial position than the results for a single year. Consistency is important, and the analyst using published figures may require adjustments in order to disclose a realistic trend. Certainly the effects of inflation are likely to be important in looking at trends over longer periods of time. Given the increasing volatility of accounts, for certain purposes (such as computing earnings per share) it may make sense to use three-year averages rather than annual figures.

Comparing the published results of different companies is much less trustworthy than comparisons over time for a single company. That may be a pity but it is a fact. Companies, even in the same 'industry', may engage in different activities. They may be of unequal size, or they may have started at different points in time. Thus in the stores sector, one company may be a supermarket chain, another a department store, and a third a small specialist grocer. All are in the 'retail trade'; but what does comparing their results show? International comparisons are even more hazardous.

At a more technical accounting level, companies may not have adopted the same approach in preparing their accounts. We have seen earlier the differences in profits and assets which can stem from alternative approaches to expenditure allocation, valuing stock, valuing and depreciation of fixed assets, deferred taxation, and so on. Later in this section we shall explicitly adjust financial ratios to allow for the alternative possible treatments of goodwill in accounts.

Financial information about leading companies appears daily in the financial press. Various investment services, and publications such as *The Times 1000*, provide longer-term data about the financial results of a whole range of companies. They use data from published accounts over the previous five or ten years, often adjusted to try to make them more comparable with other companies' figures. Adjustments may include standardizing the tax charge and excluding 'non-recurring' exceptional profits or losses.

Detailed comparisons between the results of different companies within an industry are also made, for example by trade federations. The compilers of such statistics are well aware of the problems inherent in published accounts. They make extensive amendments to published data by using extra information provided in confidence. Such adjustments are essential to obtain meaningful detailed comparisons, as we saw in Section 2 with the example of Brown and Green (pages 32 and 33). Analysts without access to the required level of detail must be sure to move with considerable caution.

Finally we would emphasize again what we said on page 7: anyone studying a company's performance should pay careful attention not only to the accounts (and notes), but also to the chairman's statement and the Operating and Financial Review.

ANALYSIS OF TESCO'S 2004 ACCOUNTS

Substantial extracts from the 2004 accounts of Tesco plc are set out on the next several pages (pages 258 to 264). Please study them carefully in order to prepare a financial analysis. The steps needed are as follows:

- Study the overview analysis (this page, top, from Section 2, page 20).
- Study the five-year cash flow summary (this page, foot, from Section 11, page 206).
- Study a segment analysis (prepared from Tesco's Note 2, not reproduced).
- Analyse the financial ratios for 2003 and 2004. Worksheets are on pages 265 and 267, and our worked solutions appear on pages 266 and 268.
- Prepare amended financial ratios for 2003 and 2004 after adding back (capitalizing) goodwill written off against reserves and providing for amortization. The worksheet is on page 269 with an explanation. Our worked solutions appear on page 270.
- Prepare an interpretation of the figures shown in the accounts (including the notes), together with the overview and cash flow summary (this page), the segment analysis (page 259), and the summary of ratios (page 271).

You may wish to use the analysis forms in Appendix 7 (pages 283 to 290), though worksheets are provided for the financial ratio analysis (on pages 265, 267 and 269).

The overview analysis opposite (top) was taken from Section 2 (page 20). You may wish to remind yourself of our introductory comments there.

The cash flow summary opposite (foot) was taken from Section 11 (page 206). You may wish to refer back to our comments there.

In Tesco's annual report, the Notes to the Accounts comprise 26 pages, so we have omitted some notes altogether and abbreviated others.

TESCO PLC: OVERVIEW 2000–2004

52 weeks ended February

	2000	2001	2002	2003	2004*
Key figures					
Turnover (£ billion)	18.6	20.8	23.4	26.0	30.8
Operating profit (£ million)	1 030	1 166	1 322	1 484	1 735
Total assets less CL (£ billion)	6.4	7.3	8.7	11.1	12.9
Earnings per share (pence)	[9.48]	10.63	12.05	13.54	15.05
'Average' share price (pence)	173	217	258	207	210
Annual rate of change (%)					
Turnover	9.6	11.7	12.5	11.1	18.5
Operating profit	8.1	12.6	13.5	13.3	21.4
Total assets less CL	13.5	15.1	19.1	27.2	16.3
Earnings per share	10.2	12.1	13.4	12.4	11.2
Average share price	0	25	19	(20)	1
Retail Prices Index (Average)	1.1	3.0	2.1	1.4	3.0

* 53 weeks

TESCO PLC: GROUP CASH FLOW SUMMARY 2000–04

52 weeks ended February

	2000 £m	2001 £m	2002 £m	2003 £m	2004* £m
Operating profit	1 030	1 166	1 322	1 484	1 735
Depreciation	435	476	534	602	752
Net financing costs and tax	(606)	(687)	(852)	(941)	(865)
Net funds from operations	859	955	1 004	1 145	1 622
Net decrease in working capital	48	295	182	289	455
Net cash from operations	907	1 250	1 186	1 434	2 077
Net spending on tangible fixed assets	(1 211)	(1 910)	(1 835)	(2 000)	(2 177)
Net acquisitions of subsidiaries, etc.	1	(76)	(96)	(436)	(272)
Financing requirement	(303)	(736)	(745)	(1 002)	(372)
Financing: net equity	2	30	(3)	21	817
net debt	331	895	892	950	(178)
Increase/(decrease) in liquid resources	30	189	144	(31)	267

* 53 weeks

ACCOUNTING POLICIES

Basis of preparation of financial statements

These financial statements have been prepared under the historical cost convention, in accordance with applicable accounting standards and the Companies Act 1985.

As in the prior year, the Group has continued to account for pensions and other post-employment benefits in accordance with SSAP 24 but has complied with the transitional disclosure requirements of FRS 17. These transitional disclosures are presented in note 27.

Basis of consolidation

The Group financial statements consist of the financial statements of the parent company, its subsidiary undertakings and the Group's share of interests in joint ventures and associates. The accounts of the parent company's subsidiary undertakings are prepared to dates around 28 February 2004 apart from Global T.H., Tesco Polska Sp. z o.o., Tesco Stores ČR a.s., Tesco Stores SR a.s., Tesco Kipa A.Ş., Samsung Tesco Co. Limited, Tesco Malaysia Sdn Bhd, Tesco Taiwan Co. Limited, Ek-Chai Distribution System Co. Ltd and C Two-Network Co. Ltd which prepared accounts to 31 December 2003. In the opinion of the Directors, it is necessary for the above named subsidiaries to prepare accounts to a date earlier than the rest of the Group to enable the timely publication of the Group financial statements.

The Group's interests in joint ventures are accounted for using the gross equity method. The Group's interests in associates are accounts for using the equity method.

Turnover

Turnover consists of sales through retail outlets and sales of development properties, excluding value added tax. The policy was revised this year in accordance with FRS 5 Application Note G 'Revenue Recognition' (issued November 2003). Turnover is now reported net of vouchers and on a commission-only basis for mobile phone airtime sales. Turnover is stated net of returns.

Stocks

Stocks comprise goods held for resale and properties held for, or in the course of, development and are valued at the lower of cost and net realisable value. Stocks in stores are calculated at retail prices and reduced by appropriate margins to take into account factors such as obsolescence, seasonality and damage.

Money market deposits

Money market deposits are stated at cost. All income from these investments is included in the profit and loss account as interest receivable and similar income.

Fixed assets and depreciation

Fixed assets are carried at cost and include amounts in respect of interest paid on funds specifically related to the financing of assets in the course of construction. Interest is capitalised on a gross basis.

Depreciation is provided on a straight-line basis over the anticipated useful economic lives of the assets.

The following rates applied for the Group and are consistent with the prior year:

- Land premia paid in excess of the alternative use value – at 2.5% of cost.
- Freehold and leasehold buildings with greater than 40 years unexpired – 2.5% of cost.
- Leasehold properties with less than 40 years unexpired are amortised by equal annual instalments over the unexpired period of the lease.
- Plant, equipment, fixtures and fittings and motor vehicles – at rates varying from 10% to 33%.

Goodwill

Goodwill arising on acquisitions is capitalised and amortised on a straight-line basis over its useful economic life, up to a maximum of 20 years.

Impairment of fixed assets and goodwill

Fixed assets and goodwill are subject to review for impairment in accordance with FRS 11, 'Impairment of Fixed Assets and Goodwill'. Any impairment is recognised in the profit and loss account in the year in which it occurs.

Leasing

Plant, equipment and fixtures and fittings which are the subject of finance leases are dealt with in the financial statements as tangible fixed assets and equivalent liabilities at what would otherwise have been the cost of outright purchase.

Rentals are apportioned between reductions of the respective liabilities and finance charges, the latter being calculated by reference to the rates of interest implicit in the leases. The finance charges are dealt with under interest payable in the profit and loss account.

Leased assets are depreciated in accordance with the depreciation accounting policy over the anticipated working lives of the assets which generally correspond to the primary rental periods. The cost of operating leases in respect of land and buildings and other assets is expensed as incurred.

Taxation

The amount included in the profit and loss account is based on pre-tax reported income and is calculated at current local tax rates, taking into account timing differences and the likelihood of realisation of deferred tax assets and liabilities.

Deferred taxation

Deferred tax is recognised in respect of all timing differences that have originated but not reversed by the balance sheet date and which could give rise to an obligation to pay more or less taxation in the future. Deferred tax assets are recognised to the extent that they are regarded as recoverable. They are regarded as recoverable to the extent that on the basis of all available evidence, it is regarded as more likely than not that there will be suitable taxable profits from which the future reversal of the underlying timing differences can be deducted. Deferred tax is measured on a non-discounted basis at the tax rates that are expected to apply in the periods in which timing differences reverse, based on tax rates and laws substantively enacted at the balance sheet date.

Pensions

The expected cost of pensions in respect of the Group's defined benefit pension schemes is charged to the profit and loss account over the working lifetimes of employees in the schemes. Actuarial surpluses and deficits are spread over the expected remaining working lifetimes of employees. Note 27 in the financial statements provides further detail in respect of pension costs and commitments.

Post-retirement benefits other than pensions

The cost of providing other post-retirement benefits, which comprise private healthcare, is charged to the profit and loss account so as to spread the cost over the service lives of relevant employees in accordance with the advice of qualified actuaries. Actuarial surpluses and deficits are spread over the expected remaining working lifetimes of relevant employees.

Foreign currencies

Assets and liabilities in foreign currencies are translated into sterling at the financial year end exchange rates. Profits and losses of overseas subsidiaries are translated into sterling at average rates of exchange. Gains and losses arising on the translation of the net assets of overseas subsidiaries, less exchange differences arising on matched foreign currency borrowings, are taken to reserves and disclosed in the statement of total recognised gains and losses. Gains and losses on instruments used for hedging are recognised in the profit and loss account when the exposure that is being hedged is itself recognised.

Financial instruments

Derivative instruments utilised by the Group are interest rate swaps, floors and caps, forward start interest rate swaps, cross currency, swaps, forward rate agreements and forward exchange contracts and options. Termination payments made or received in respect of derivatives are spread over the life of the underlying exposure in cases where the underlying exposure continues to exist. Where the underlying exposure ceases to exist, any termination payments are taken to the profit and loss account.

Interest differentials on derivative instruments are recognised by adjusting net interest payable. Premia or discounts on derivative instruments are amortised over the shorter of the life of the instrument or the underlying exposure.

Currency swap agreements are valued at closing rates of exchange. Forward exchange contracts are valued at discounted closing forward rates of exchange. Resulting gains or losses are offset against foreign exchange gains or losses on the related borrowings or, where the instrument is used to hedge a committed future transaction, are deferred until the transaction occurs or is extinguished.

GROUP PROFIT AND LOSS ACCOUNT
53 weeks ended 28 February 2004

	Note	2004	2003 restated
		£m	£m
Sales at net selling prices		33 557	28 280
Turnover including share of joint ventures		31 050	26 197
Less: share of joint ventures' turnover		(236)	(193)
Group turnover excluding VAT		30 814*	26 004
Operating expenses**:			
Normal operating expenses		(28 925)*	(24 444)
Employee profit-sharing		(57)	(51)
Integration costs		(45)	(4)
Goodwill amortization		(52)*	(21)
Operating profit		1 735*	1 484
Share of profit of joint ventures and associates		97	70
Net loss on disposal of fixed assets		(9)	(13)
Profit before interest and tax		1 823	1 541
Net interest payable		(223)	(180)
Profit before tax		1 600	1 361
Tax on profit		(498)	(415)
Profit after tax		1 102	946
Minority interests		(2)	–
Profit for the financial year		1 100	946
Dividends		(516)	(443)
Retained profit for the financial year		584	503
Earnings per share		15.05	13.54
Dividend per share		6.84	6.20

*Including acquisitions:
turnover £131m; op. exs £121m; goodwill amortization £4m; operating profit £6m.

** of which administration expenses £577m (£488m).

SEGMENT ANALYSIS

In Tesco's case, segment analysis is limited. The following details (simplified) are taken from Note 1 (not reproduced). Apart from a very small amount of property development activity, the only 'class' of business is retailing (not now by any means only food retailing). But from a geographical point of view, overseas business has been growing rapidly and now represents nearly 20 per cent both of turnover and of profits. (In 2004 Europe represented about 55% of overseas turnover and about two-thirds of profit.) Notice how overseas profit margins have been increasing, especially in the last two years.

In other businesses segment analysis may be really helpful in analysing the aggregates in group accounts between sales, profits and assets.

	2000	2001	2002	2003	2004
Turnover (£b)					
UK	16.8	18.2	19.8	21.3	24.8
Overseas	1.8	2.6	3.6	4.7	6.0
Total	18.6	20.8	23.4	26.0	30.8
Sales growth (%)					
UK	6	8	9	8	16
Overseas	37	43	38	31	29
Total	9	12	13	11	19
Assets (£b)					
UK	5.7	6.3	7.1	8.4	9.0
Overseas	1.1	1.5	2.0	2.9	3.1
Total	6.8	7.8	9.1	11.3	12.1
Operating profit (£m)					
UK	993	1 100	1 213	1 297	1 526
Overseas	50	74	119	212	306
Total (inc. joint ventures)	1 043	1 174	1 332	1 509	1 832
Profit/Sales (%)					
UK	5.9	6.0	6.1	6.1	6.2
Overseas	2.8	2.9	3.3	4.5	5.1
Total	5.6	5.6	5.7	5.8	5.9
Profit/Assets (%)					
UK	17.5	16.4	17.0	15.4	17.0
Overseas	4.4	5.0	6.0	7.4	9.9
Total	15.2	14.3	14.6	13.4	15.2

BALANCE SHEETS
28 February 2004

	Group		Company	
	2004	2003	2004	2003
	£m	£m	£m	£m
Fixed assets				
Intangible assets	965	890	–	–
Tangible assets	14 094	12 828	–	–
Investments	34	59	9 077	7 820
Net investments in joint ventures	309	266	143	158
Investments in associates	21	18	–	–
	15 423	14 061	9 220	7 978
Current assets				
Stocks	1 199	1 140	–	–
Debtors	840	662	1 624	1 012
Investments	430	239	99	–
Cash at bank and in hand	670	399	–	–
	3 139	2 440	1 723	1 012
Creditors falling due within one year	(5 618)	(5 372)	(2 456)	(1 961)
Net current liabilities	(2 479)	(2 932)	(733)	(949)
Total assets less current liabilities	12 944	11 129	8 487	7 029
Creditors falling due after one year	(4 368)	(4 049)	(3 950)	(3 772)
Provisions for liabilities and charges	(586)	(521)	–	–
Net assets	7 990	6 559	4 537	3 257
Capital and reserves				
Called up share capital	384	362	384	362
Share premium account	3 470	2 465	3 470	2 465
Other reserves	40	40	–	–
Profit and loss account	4 051	3 649	683	430
	7 945	6 516	4 537	3 257
Minority interests	45	43	–	–
Capital employed	7 990	6 559	4 537	3 257

AUDITORS OPINION

In our opinion, the financial statements give a true and fair view of the state of affairs of the company and the Group at 28 February 2004 and of the profit and cash flows of the Group for the year then ended; (and) have been properly prepared in accordance with the Companies Act 1985; ...

PricewaterhouseCoopers LLP, London, 19 April 2004.

Reconciliation of movements in shareholders' funds

53 weeks ended 28 February 2004

	Group		Company	
	2004	2003	2004	2003
	£m	£m	£m	£m
Profit for the financial year	1 100	946	771	618
Dividends	(516)	(443)	(516)	(443)
	584	503	255	175
(Loss)/gain on foreign currency net investments	(157)	22	(2)	–
New share capital subscribed less expenses	844	421	869	433
Pay ment of dividends by shares in lieu of cash	158	40	158	40
Net addition to shareholders' funds	1 429	986	1 280	648
Opening shareholders' funds	6 516	5 530	3 257	2 609
Closing shareholders' funds	7 945	6 516	4 537	3 257

Selected Notes

NOTE 5   Profit on ordinary activities before taxation

	2004	2003
	£m	£m
Profit on ordinary activities is stated after charging the following:		
Depreciation of tangible fixed assets:		
– owned assets	631	542
– under finance leases	69	39
Goodwill amortisation	54	23
Operating lease costs (a)	221	172
Employment costs (note 6)	3 234	2 653

(a) Operating lease costs include £55m for hire of plant and machinery (2003 – £39m).

NOTE 6   Employment costs

	2004	2003
	£m	£m
Employment costs during the year		
Wages and salaries	2 891	2 385
Social security costs	183	146
Other pension costs (note 27)	160	122
	3 234	2 653

Number of persons employed

The average number of employees during the year was: UK 230 680 (2003 – 203 766). Rest of Europe 49 362 (2003 – 42 280), Asia 30 369 (2003 – 24 754) and the average number of full-time equivalents was: UK 152 408 (2003 – 133 051), Rest of Europe 42 399 (2003 – 35 372) and Asia 28 528 (2003 – 19 759).

NOTE 7 *Directors' emoluments and interests*

1 Directors' emoluments

	Fixed emoluments		Performance-related emoluments			Total 2004	Total 2003
	Salary £000	Benefits £000	Profit-sharing £000	Short-term £000	Long-term £000	£000	£000
Mr J A Gardiner	396	35	–	–	–	431	427
Sir Terry Leahy	955	36	3	1 091	892	2 977	2 838
Mr D E Reid (c)	691	89	3	821	1 120	2 724	2 610
Mr R S Ager (b)	463	37	3	679	452	1 634	1 425
Mr C L Allen	47	–	–	–	–	47	41
Mr R F Chase	49	–	–	–	–	49	28
Mr P A Clarke	531	65	3	619	439	1 657	1 431
Mr E M Davies (a)	28	–	–	–	–	28	–
Dr H Einsmann	44	–	–	–	–	44	36
Mr J Gildersleeve (b)	614	96	3	851	597	2 161	1 928
Mr A T Higginson	538	37	3	619	462	1 659	1 513
Mr K J Hydon (a)	1	–	–	–	–	1	–
Mr T J R Mason	538	12	3	619	509	1 681	1 561
Mrs V Morali	44	–	–	–	–	44	36
Mr G F Pimlott	72	–	–	–	–	72	59
Mr D T Potts	531	34	3	619	474	1 661	1 442
	5 542	441	24	5 918	4 945	16 870	15 375

(a) Appointed during the year.
(b) Retired from the Tesco Group in March 2004. Mr R S Ager and Mr J Gildersleeve were awarded bonuses of £150 000 each, which have been sacrificed in return for pension augmentation.
(c) Mr D E Reid has sacrificed an amount of £430 000 from his long-term bonus relating to overseas business growth in return for pension augmentation. Mr D E Reid resigned as an Executive Director in December 2003 and was appointed Non-executive Chairman in April 2004.

7 Disclosable interests of the Directors, including family interests

	28 Feb 2004		22 Feb 2003	
	Ordinary shares	Options to acquire ordinary shares	Ordinary shares	Options to acquire ordinary shares
Mr J A Gardiner	669 111	–	627 805	–
Sir Terry Leahy	4 915 893	3 762 101	3 754 973	3 344 457
Mr D E Reid	189 682	2 952 071	2 450 973	3 080 683
Mr R S Ager	1 971 071	2 282 478	1 448 706	1 830 799
Mr R F Chase	50 000	–	–	–
Mr P A Clarke	983 778	2 031 112	631 795	1 529 709
Mr E M Davies	2 400	–	–	–
Dr H Einsmann	92 150	–	–	–
Mr J Gildersleeve	1 829 760	3 131 132	1 272 629	2 648 609
Mr A T Higginson	1 160 023	2 172 136	679 897	1 646 967
Mr K J Hydon	30 093	–	–	–
Mr T J R Mason	1 519 084	2 261 653	1 087 172	1 961 091
Mr G F Pimlott	33 418	–	32 529	–
Mr D T Potts	1 250 063	2 024 400	774 912	1 521 509

Options to acquire ordinary shares shown above comprise options under the executive share option schemes (1984), (1994), (1996) and the savings-related share option scheme (1981) (note 26).

NOTE 9 *Taxation*

(a) Analysis of charge in year

Current tax	£ million
UK corporation tax @ 30.0%	433
Prior year items	(64)
Overseas taxation	33
Share of joint ventures and associates	27
	429*

Deferred tax	
Origination and reversal of timing differences	29
Prior year items	41
Share of joint ventures and associates	(1)
	69

Tax on profit on ordinary activities	**498**

*2003 – £353m

(b) Factors affecting the tax charge for the year 2004

	%
Standard rate of corporation tax	**30.0**
Effects of:	
Expenses not deductible for tax purposes*	4.1
Capital allowances in excess of book depreciation	(3.9)
Differences in overseas taxation rates	(0.9)
Timing of tax relief of share-based payments	1.4
Prior year items	(4.0)
Other items	0.1
Effective rate of corporation tax for the year**	**26.8**

Notes:
* Primarily goodwill amortization and non-qualifying depreciation
** £429m ÷ £1 600m

NOTE 8   Net interest payable

	2004		2003	
	£m	£m	£m	£m
Interest receivable and similar income on money market investments and deposits		49		65
Less interest payable on:				
Short-term bank loans and overdrafts repayable within five year	(85)		(104)	
Finance charges payable on finance leases	(19)		(5)	
4% unsecured deep discount loan stock 2006 (a)	(11)		(10)	
4% RPI bonds 2016 (b)	(18)		(12)	
3.322% LPI bonds 2025 (c)	(15)		(10)	
8¾% bonds 2003	–		(17)	
6% bonds 2006	(9)		(9)	
7½% bonds 2007	(25)		(24)	
6% bonds 2008	(15)		(15)	
5⅛% bonds 2009	(18)		(18)	
6⅝% bonds 2010	(10)		(10)	
6% bonds 2029	(12)		(12)	
5¼% Euro bonds 2008	(18)		(13)	
4¾% Euro bonds 2010	(26)		(4)	
5½% bonds 2033	(11)		(2)	
5½% bonds 2019	(20)		(4)	
Other bonds	(8)		(20)	
Interest capitalised	62		62	
Share of interest of joint ventures and associates	(14)		(18)	
		(272)		(245)
		(223)		(180)

(a)   Interest payable on the 4% unsecured deep discount loan stock 2006 includes £6m (2003 – £5m) of discount amortisation.

(b)   Interest payable on the RPI bond 2016 includes £8m (2003 – £2m) of RPI related amortisation.

(c)   Interest payable on the LPI bond 2025 includes £6m (2003 – £1m) of RPI related amortisation.

NOTE 10   Dividends

	2004 Pence/share	2003 Pence/share	2004 £m	2003 £m
Declared interim	2.07	1.87	151	131
Proposed final	4.77	4.33	365	312
	6.84	6.20	516	443

NOTE 14   Fixed asset investments

	Group						Company
	Joint ventures (b)	Associates (c)	Own shares (d)	Other investments	Shares in Group undertakings (a)	Loans to Group undertakings	Joint ventures (b)
	£m	£m	£m	£m	£m	£m	£m
At 22 February 2003	266	18	53	6	4 505	3 315	158
Additions	11	8	46	–	1 019	238	6
Share of profit/(loss) of joint ventures and associates	63	(4)	–	–	–	–	–
Goodwill amortisation	(1)	(1)	–	–	–	–	–
Income received from joint ventures and associates	(24)	–	–	–	–	–	–
Disposals	(6)	–	(71)	–	–	–	(21)
At 28 February 2004	309	21	28	6	5 524	3 553	143

NOTE 13   Tangible fixed assets

	Land and buildings £m	Plant, equipment fixtures and fittings and motor vehicles £m	Total £m
Cost			
At 22 February 2003	12 493	4 132	16 625
Currency translation	(277)	(65)	(342)
Additions at cost (a)	1 556	729	2 285
	13 772	4 796	18 568
Acquisitions	60	3	63
Disposals	(114)	(320)	(434)
At 28 February 2004	13 718	4 479	18 197
Depreciation			
At 22 February 2003	1 538	2 259	3 797
Currency translation	(10)	(21)	(31)
Change for period	251	449	700
	1 779	2 687	4 466
Disposals	(70)	(293)	(363)
At 28 February 2004	1 709	2 394	4 103
Net book value (b) (c)			
At 28 February 2004	12 009	2 085	14 094
At 22 February 2003	10 955	1 873	12 828
Capital work in progress included above (d)			
At 28 February 2004	353	100	453
At 22 February 2003	553	128	681

(a)   Includes £62m in respect of interest capitalised principally relating to land and building assets. The capitalisation rate used to determine the amount of finance costs capitalised during the period was 6.0%.

(b)   Net book value includes capitalised interest at 28 February 2004 of £518m (2003 – £463m).

Plant, equipment, fixtures and fittings and motor vehicles subject to finance leases included in net book value are:

	Cost £m	Depreciation £m	Net book value £m
At 22 February 2003	740	469	271
Movement in the period	102	103	(1)
At 28 February 2004	842	572	270

(c)   The net book value of land and buildings companies:

	2004 £m	2003 £m
Freehold	11 023	9 992
Long leasehold – 50 years or more	501	493
Short leasehold – less than 50 years	485	470
At 28 February 2004	12 009	10 955

(d)   Capital work in progress does not include land.

NOTE 16 Debtors

	Group		Company	
	2004 £m	2003 £m	2004 £m	2003 £m
Amounts owed by Group undertakings	–	–	1 260	776
Prepayments and accrued income	49	48	–	5
Other debtors	671	507	258	128
Amounts owed by undertakings in which Group companies have a participating interest	120	107	106	103
	840	662	1 624	1 012

Of the amounts owed by undertakings in which Group companies have a participating interest, £109m (2003 – £107m) is due after more than one year. Included in other debtors are amounts of £38m (2003 – £17m) due after more than one year.

NOTE 18 Creditors falling due within one year

	Group		Company	
	2004 £m	2003 £m	2004 £m	2003 £m
Bank loans and overdrafts (a) (b)	775	1 286	552	1 162
Trade creditors	2 434	2 196	–	–
Amounts owed to Group undertakings	–	–	1 189	351
Corporation tax	308	230	6	5
Other taxation and social security	190	170	3	–
Other creditors	1 142	851	323	20
Loans from joint ventures	10	2	–	–
Accruals and deferred income (c)	320	263	13	105
Finance leases (note 23) (d)	69	55	–	–
Dividends	370	319	370	318
	5 618	5 372	2 456	1 961

NOTE 19 Creditors falling due after more than one year

	Group		Company	
	2004 £m	2003 £m	2004 £m	2003 £m
4% unsecured deep discount loan stock 2006 (a)	110	104	110	104
Finance leases (note 23)	166	171	–	–
6% bonds 2006 (b)	150	150	150	150
0.7% 50bn Yen bonds 2006 (l)	285	285	285	285
7¹/₂% bonds 2007 (c)	325	325	325	325
6% bonds 2008 (d)	250	250	250	250
5¹/₄% 500m Euro bonds 2008 (l)	345	308	345	308
5¹/₈% bonds 2009 (e)	350	350	350	350
6⁵/₈% bonds 2010 (f)	150	150	150	150
4³/₄% 750m Euro bonds 2010 (l)	528	477	528	477
4% RPI bonds 2016 (g)	220	212	220	212
5¹/₂% bonds 2019 (h)	350	350	350	350
3.322% LPI bonds 2025 (i)	221	215	221	215
6% bonds 2029 (j)	200	200	200	200
5¹/₂% bonds 2033 (k)	200	200	200	200
Other bonds (l)	266	197	266	196
Other loans (m)	230	90	–	–
	4 346	4 034	3 950	3 772
Other creditors	22	15	–	–
	4 368	4 049	3 950	3 772

NOTE 24 Called up share capital

	Ordinary shares of 5p each	
	Number	£m
Authorised at 22 February 2003	9 632 000 000	482
Authorised during the year	–	–
Authorised at 28 February 2004	9 632 000 000	482
Allotted, called up and fully paid:		
At 22 February 2003	7 237 609 183	362
Share placing	315 000 000	16
Scrip dividend election	80 201 756	4
Share options	47 347 116	2
At 28 February 2004	7 680 158 055	384

During the financial year, 315 million shares were issued as an equity share placing, for net proceeds of £773m. In addition, 127.5 million shares were issued during the year for an aggregate consideration of £254m, which comprised £158m for scrip dividend and £96m for share options.

Between 28 February 2004 and 19 April 2004, options on 19 107 ordinary shares and 2 213 652 ordinary shares have been exercised under the terms of the savings-related share option scheme (1981) and the executive share option schemes (1984, 1994 and 1996) respectively.

As at 28 February 2004, the Directors were authorised to purchase up to a maximum in aggregate of 723 million ordinary shares.

NOTE 25 Reserves

	Group		Company	
	2004 £m	2003 £m	2004 £m	2003 £m
Share premium account				
At start of period	2 465	2 004	2 465	2 004
Premium on issue of shares less costs	851	422	851	422
Scrip dividend election	154	39	154	39
At end of period	3 470	2 465	3 470	2 465
Other reserves				
At 28 February 2004 and 22 February 2003	40	40	–	–
Profit and loss account				
At start of period	3 649	3 136	430	255
(Loss)/gain on foreign currency net investments	(157)	22	(2)	–
Issue of shares	(25)	(12)	–	–
Retained profit for the financial year	584	503	255	175
At end of period	4 051	3 649	683	430

Other reserves comprise a merger reserve arising on the acquisition of Hilliards plc in 1987.

In accordance with section 230 of the Companies Act 1985 a profit and loss account for Tesco PLC, whose result for the year is shown above, has not been presented in these financial statements.

The cumulative goodwill written-off against the reserves of the Group as at 28 February 2004 amounted to £718m (2003 – £718m). During the year, the qualifying employee share ownership trust (QUEST) subscribed for 30 million, 0.4% of called-up share capital at 28 February 2004 (2003 – 41 million, 0.6%), shares from the company. The amount of £25m (2003 – £12m) shown above represents contributions to the QUEST from subsidiary undertakings.

The net assets and results of acquired businesses are included in the consolidated accounts from their respective dates of acquisition.The following tables set out the effect of the material acquisitions by the Group in the year to 28 February 2004 on the consolidated balance sheet. Acquisition accounting has been applied in all cases. The fair values currently established for all acquisitions made in the year to 28 February 2004 are provisional. Fair values will be reviewed based on additional information up to 26 February 2005. The Directors do not believe that any net adjustments resulting from such a review would have a material effect on the Group. The goodwill arising on these acquisitions has been capitalised and is being amortised over 20 years.

C Two-Network
C Two-Network was acquired on 17 July 2003 and included in the consolidated balance sheet at 28 February 2004. The purchase consideration was £176m. The net assets of C Two-Network on acquisition and the provisional fair values were as follows:

	Book values of acquired business £m	Adjustments to align accounting policies £m	Revaluations £m	Fair values at date of acquisition £m
Fixed assets	13	2	(3)	12
Stock	8	–	–	8
Debtors	24	–	–	24
Cash	31	–	–	31
Creditors	(30)	(2)	–	(32)
Net assets acquired	46	–	(3)	43

Consideration
Cash	176

Goodwill	133

Kipa
Kipa was acquired on 11 November 2003 and included in the consolidated balance sheet at 28 February 2004. The purchase consideration was £96m. The net assets of Kipa on acquisition and the provisional fair values were as follows:

	Book values of acquired business £m	Adjustments to align accounting policies £m	Revaluations £m	Fair values at date of acquisition £m
Fixed assets	40	3	7	50
Stock	6	–	–	6
Debtors	1	4	–	5
Cash	24	(2)	–	22
Creditors	(19)	(7)	–	(26)
Provisions for liabilities and charges	(1)	1	–	–
	51	(1)	7	57
Minority interest				(5)
Net assets acquired				52

Consideration
Cash	93
Other	3

Goodwill	44

TESCO: PERFORMANCE RATIO ANALYSIS

	2004*	2003
Profitability		
Return on equity %		
Tax ratio %		
Return on net assets %		
Profit margin %		
Asset turnover		
Net asset turnover		
Tangible fixed asset turnover		
Stock days		

*53 weeks

When you have calculated all the ratios for both years, compare your answers with those shown overleaf.

TESCO: PERFORMANCE RATIO ANALYSIS

	2004*	2003

Profitability

Return on equity %
$$\frac{1\ 100}{7\ 945} = 13.9\% \qquad\qquad \frac{946}{6\ 516} = 14.5\%$$

Tax ratio %
$$\frac{429}{1\ 600} = 26.8\% \qquad\qquad \frac{353}{1\ 361} = 25.9\%$$

Return on net assets %
$$\frac{1\ 600 + 272}{12\ 944 + 844} = 13.6\% \qquad\qquad \frac{1\ 361 + 245}{11\ 129 + 1\ 341} = 12.9\%$$

Profit margin %
$$\frac{1\ 872}{31\ 050} = 6.0\% \qquad\qquad \frac{1\ 606}{26\ 197} = 6.1\%$$

Asset turnover

Net asset turnover
$$\frac{31\ 050}{13\ 788} = 2.25 \qquad\qquad \frac{26\ 197}{12\ 470} = 2.10$$

Tangible fixed asset turnover
$$\frac{31\ 050 - 236}{14\ 094 - 453} = 2.26 \qquad\qquad \frac{26\ 197 - 193}{12\ 828 - 681} = 2.14$$

Stock days
$$\frac{1\ 199 \times 371}{28\ 925} = 15.4 \qquad\qquad \frac{1\ 140 \times 364}{24\ 444} = 17.0$$

*53 weeks

Notes

(1) For the tax ratio we exclude deferred tax (Note 9).
(2) To calculate PBIT we add interest payable (net of amount capitalized) (Note 8) to profit before tax.
(3) We add short-term borrowings (Note 18) to total assets less current liabilities.
(4) We recognize Tesco's accounts are for 52 (or 53) weeks; not 365 (or 366) days.
(5) Tesco sells for cash; so there are no trade debtors.

	2004*	**2003**

Financial status ratios

Debt ratio %

Interest cover*
adding back capitalized interest

Current ratio

Acid test

Stock market ratios (Year-end share price: 258 (2004) and 162 (2003))
Weighted average number of shares: 7307m (2004) and 6989m (2003)

Earnings per share (pence)

Price/earnings ratio

Dividend yield %

Dividend cover

*53 weeks

When you have calculated all the ratios for both years, compare your answers with those shown overleaf.

TESCO: FINANCIAL RATIO ANALYSIS *(continued)*

	2004	**2003**

Financial status ratios

Debt ratio %

$$\frac{4\ 346 + 844}{12\ 944 + 844} = 37.6\%$$ $$\frac{4\ 034 + 1\ 341}{11\ 129 + 1\ 341} = 43.1\%$$

Interest cover*
adding back capitalized interest

$$\frac{1\ 600 + 334}{334} = 5.8$$ $$\frac{1\ 361 + 307}{307} = 5.4$$

Current ratio

$$\frac{3\ 139}{5\ 618} = 0.56$$ $$\frac{2\ 440}{5\ 372} = 0.45$$

Acid test

$$\frac{1\ 940}{5\ 618} = 0.35$$ $$\frac{1\ 300}{5\ 372} = 0.24$$

Stock market ratios (Year-end share price: 258 (2004) and 162 (2003))

Earnings per share (pence)

$$\frac{1\ 100}{7\ 307} = 15.05$$ $$\frac{946}{6\ 989} = 13.54$$

Price/earnings ratio

$$\frac{258}{15.05} = 17.1$$ $$\frac{162}{13.54} = 12.0$$

Dividend yield %

$$\frac{6.84}{258} = 2.7\%$$ $$\frac{6.20}{162} = 3.8\%$$

Dividend cover

$$\frac{15.05}{6.84} = 2.20$$ $$\frac{13.54}{6.20} = 2.18$$

*53 weeks

Notes
(1) We include short-term borrowings.
(2) We add back capitalized interest.
(3) For retailers the acid test ratio is normally unduly pessimistic, since most retailers' stocks are more 'liquid' than many other companies' debtors.

TESCO: FINANCIAL RATIOS ADJUSTED FOR GOODWILL WRITTEN OFF

The performance and financial status and stock market ratios we calculated earlier (on pages 266 and 268) were based on figures published by Tesco. As we noted above (page 256), adjustments sometimes need to be made to financial ratios in order to help improve comparisons between years or between companies.

One such major adjustment is capitalizing any purchased goodwill which has been written off against reserves. (This practice was permitted in the UK prior to FRS 15 in 1997.) In addition, it makes sense to provide for annual amortization against profit of such goodwill. Probably using the maximum normal life of twenty years is advisable unless there is reason to use some different life for goodwill. Such an adjustment restores total shareholders' funds and increases total assets, and can significantly affect return on equity and return on net assets and other ratios.

Tesco's 2004 accounts disclose (foot of Note 25) that cumulative goodwill written off against reserves amounted to £718 million at the end of 2004 (and the same amount, £718 million, at the end of 2003 too). We suggest you use the twenty-year life mentioned above in making necessary adjustments for amortization against profit, as well as capitalizing the goodwill itself, in adjusting the following ratios. Then please compare your answers with those shown overleaf.

	2004	**2003**
Return on equity %		
Return on net assets %		
Profit margin %		
Net asset turnover		
Debt ratio		

TESCO: FINANCIAL RATIOS ADJUSTED FOR GOODWILL WRITTEN OFF

The performance and financial status and stock market ratios we calculated earlier (on pages 266 and 268) were based on figures published by Tesco. As we noted above (page 256), adjustments sometimes need to be made to financial ratios in order to help improve comparisons between years or between companies.

One such major adjustment is capitalizing any purchased goodwill which has been written off against reserves. (This practice was permitted in the UK prior to FRS 15 in 1997.) In addition, it makes sense to provide for annual amortization against profit of such goodwill. Probably using the maximum normal life of twenty years is advisable unless there is reason to use some different life for goodwill. Such an adjustment restores total shareholders' funds and increases total assets, and can significantly affect return on equity and return on net assets and other ratios.

Tesco's 2004 accounts disclose (foot of Note 25) that cumulative goodwill written off against reserves amounted to £718 million at the end of 2004 (and the same amount, £718 million, at the end of 2003 too). We suggest you use the twenty-year life mentioned above in making necessary adjustments for amortization against profit, as well as capitalizing the goodwill itself, in adjusting the following ratios. Then please compare your answers with those shown overleaf.

	2004	**2003**
Return on equity %	$\dfrac{1\ 100 - 36}{7\ 945 + 718} = 12.3\%$	$\dfrac{946 - 36}{6\ 516 + 718} = 12.6\%$
Return on net assets %	$\dfrac{1\ 872 - 36}{13\ 788 + 718} = 12.7\%$	$\dfrac{1\ 606 - 36}{12\ 470 + 718} = 11.9\%$
Profit margin %	$\dfrac{1\ 872 - 36}{31\ 050} = 5.9\%$	$\dfrac{1\ 606 - 36}{26\ 197} = 6.0\%$
Net asset turnover	$\dfrac{31\ 050}{13\ 788 + 718} = 2.14$	$\dfrac{26\ 197}{12\ 470 + 718} = 1.99$
Debt ratio	$\dfrac{5\ 190}{13\ 788 + 718} = 35.8\%$	$\dfrac{5\ 375}{12\ 470 + 718} = 40.8\%$

TESCO PLC
Summary of key ratios, year ended 28 February

	2000	2001	2002	2003	2004
Profitability ratios					
*Return on equity %	11.6	12.0	12.7	12.6	12.3
Tax ratio %	27.6	26.9	28.0	25.9	26.8
*Return on net assets %	15.1	14.2	13.9	11.9	12.7
*Profit margin %	5.8	5.9	6.0	6.0	5.9
Asset turnover ratios					
*Net asset turnover (times)	2.60	2.41	2.33	1.99	2.14
Stock days	12.3	14.1	13.9	17.0	15.4
Financial status ratios					
Debt ratio %	32.3	38.1	41.3	43.1	37.6
Interest cover (times)	5.8	5.4	5.3	5.4	5.8
Current ratio	0.38	0.39	0.43	0.45	0.56
Stock market ratios					
Earnings per share (pence)**	[9.48]	10.63	12.05	13.54	15.05
Price/earnings ratio	18.0	24.7	20.9	12.0	17.1

* using figures adjusted for goodwill written off against reserves
** 2000 estimated, on new deferred tax basis

Data from Tesco's own statistics

	2000	2001	2002	2003	2004
Number of stores: UK	659	692	729	1 982*	1 878
Overseas	186	205	250	309	440
Sales area: m sq. ft.: UK	16.9	18.0	18.8	21.8	23.3
Overseas	7.1	10.4	13.7	18.1	22.1
Weekly sales per sq. ft.: UK	21.27	21.75	22.43	22.86	22.48
FT equiv '000 employees: UK	108	114	121	133	152
Overseas	27	38	51	55	71
Wages/UK employee: £'000	15.6	16.1	16.8	17.0	17.6

* including T&S stores from 2003

INTERPRETATION: TESCO PLC

53 weeks ended 28 February 2004

1 Tesco's turnover in 2004 increased by 15 per cent in real terms, compared with an average of just under 10 per cent a year in the previous four years. This is a very rapid rate of growth for such a large company: a total increase of 80 per cent in money terms in five years.

2 Overseas sales have risen from 10 per cent of the group total to 20 per cent over the five years and overseas profit margins have been rising steadily.

3 Return on net assets has fallen from over 15 per cent in 2000 to less than 13 per cent in 2004 (after adding back and amortizing goodwill previously written off against reserves). Return on equity has been steady at about 12 per cent a year, due to an increase in financial gearing.

4 Borrowing increased from 32 per cent of capital employed in 2000 to over 43 per cent in 2003. The gearing ratio fell back to 38 per cent in 2004 due to a share placing of just under £800 million and a small net repayment of debt.

5 In the previous three years, the total financing requirement of £2.5 billion was met almost entirely by borrowing. But the increase in trade and other creditors over the three years of some £1.3 billion significantly held down the amount needing to be financed by interest-bearing debt. Interest cover has remained consistently above 5 times.

6 Spending on tangible fixed assets has averaged £2.0 billion a year in the last four years.

7 Operating margin has been steady at 6.0 per cent or just under. At Tesco's volumes, one percentage point of profit margin represents about £300 million a year of before-tax profit . (This means about 3 pence, or 20 per cent, of earnings per share.)

8 The current ratio of 0.56 may not look high at first sight, but in fact is perfectly adequate for such a cash-generative business. Total current liabilities, excluding short-term borrowing, amount to less than two months' sales.

9 Current assets, on the other hand, are very low. Trading stocks represent on average only 15 days worth of (cost of) sales.

SECTION 14 SUMMARY

This final section has summarized a number of accounting matters requiring special attention when looking at accounts, under four headings: capital employed, fixed assets, working capital and profit and loss.

Then followed a framework for relating financial analysis to economic reality in the context of a number of specific competitive market environments over time.

We considered again aspects of disclosure and accounting conventions, and incomplete transactions, consistency and prudence.

Trends over a number of years are likely to be more useful to the analyst than numbers and ratios for a single year and we discussed some of the problems in trying to compare the financial results of different companies, especially between different countries.

The remainder of the section contained a detailed analysis of the 2004 accounts of Tesco plc. We reproduced many pages of Notes to the Accounts, though we abbreviated some and omitted others. Repeated from earlier in the book were the five-year Overview summary (Section 2) and the Cash Flow summary (Section 11).

A segment analysis in Tesco's case contained relatively little detail. Multinational companies might have more extensive splits between geographical areas (see page 227), as well as between business sectors. Perhaps soon Tesco will report separately its food and non-food business?

Then followed a detailed ratio analysis of performance ratios and financial status and stock market ratios, along the lines set out in Sections 2 and 3. We asked you only to calculate two years' ratios, but the summary of key ratios included figures for *five* years.

The adjustments of the ratios for goodwill previously written off against reserves showed the importance of amending ratios for accounting matters which require special attention. A similar adjustment is likely to be needed for some years yet for those UK companies which have written off against reserves significant amounts of goodwill.

Finally we interpreted the results of our analysis.

It should now be clear that careful analysis of a set of accounts can yield a great deal of information about a company's affairs, its performance and financial position. But to get a proper feel for the meaning of company accounts, one needs to understand their structure and the sort of judgements that those preparing accounts may have to make. One also needs the patience and determination to pursue the analysis as far as possible, over a number of years, while recognizing that often the result is unanswered questions rather than definite conclusions.

PROBLEMS

We regret that company annual reports, their accounts and notes, have now grown so voluminous that it is no longer reasonably practicable to reproduce them as problem material in this book without either taking up far too many pages, or using a very small font size, or omitting so much material that a misleading impression may be given.

Accordingly we suggest that readers who do wish to practise their skills in interpreting the meaning of company accounts arrange to get hold of a copy of the Annual Report and Accounts of one or more listed companies, whether British or foreign. These can normally be downloaded from the internet, or most companies will freely provide a hard copy.

Please feel free, if you wish, to photocopy and use the pro forma analysis forms set out in Appendix 7 from pages 283 to 290.

Appendix 1

Synonyms

* American expression
(*) originally American expression, now also found elsewhere

Accounts	= Financial statements (*)
Accounts payable (*)	= Creditors
Accounts receivable (*)	= Debtors
Acid test ratio	= Quick ratio
Amortization	= Depreciation [of intangibles]
Associated companies	= Related companies
Balance sheet	= Statement of financial position*
Bonus shares	= Scrip issues
Borrowing	= Debt
Capital allowances [tax]	= Writing down allowances [tax]
Capital and reserves	= Shareholders' funds; owners' equity*
Cash etc.	= Liquid resources
Common stock*	= Ordinary shares
Consolidated accounts	= Group accounts
Constant dollar accounting*	= Constant purchasing power accounting
Creditors	= Accounts payable (*)
Creditors due beyond one year	= Long-term liabilities
Creditors due within one year	= Current liabilities
Current liabilities	= Creditors due within one year
Debt	= Borrowing
Debtors	= Accounts receivable (*)
Deferred income	= Payments received in advance
Depreciation [of intangibles]	= Amortization
Earnings	= Profits; net income*
Financial statements (*)	= Accounts
Fixed assets	= Long-term assets
Gearing	= Leverage*
Group accounts	= Consolidated accounts
Holding company	= Parent company
Income statement*	= Profit and loss account
Inventories (*)	= Stocks
Leverage*	= Gearing
Liquid resources	= Cash etc.
Liquidation	= Winding-up
Long-term assets	= Fixed assets
Long-term liabilities	= Creditors due beyond one year
Merger	= Pooling of interests*; uniting of interests
Net current assets	= (Net) working capital
Net income*	= Profits; earnings
(Net) working capital	= Net current assets
Nominal value	= Par value
Operating profit	= Profit before interest and tax
Ordinary shares	= Common stock*
Owners (*)	= Shareholders
Owners' equity	= Shareholders' funds; capital and reserves
Paid-in surplus*	= Share premium
Par value	= Nominal value
Parent company	= Holding company
Payments received in advance	= Deferred income
Pooling of interests*	= Merger
Profit	= Earnings; net income*
Profit and loss account	= Income statement*
Profit before interest and tax	= Operating profit
Quick ratio	= Acid test ratio
Related companies	= Associated companies
Retained earnings	= Retained profit
Sales revenue	= Turnover
Scrip issues	= Bonus shares
Share premium	= Paid-in surplus*
Shareholders	= Owners (*)
Shareholders' funds	= Capital and reserves; owners' equity*
Shares	= Stock*
Statement of financial position*	= Balance sheet
Stocks	= Inventories (*)
Turnover	= Sales revenue
Uniting of interests	= Merger
Winding-up	= Liquidation
Writing-down allowances [tax]	= Capital allowances [tax]

Appendix 2

Acronyms and abbreviations

ASB	Accounting Standards Board (1990–)
ASC	Accounting Standards Committee (1970–90)
BS	Balance Sheet
BV	Book Value
CA	Current Assets
CCA	Current Cost Accounting
COGS	Cost Of Goods Sold
COSA	Cost of Sales Adjustment
CPP	Constant Purchasing Power
DPR	Dividend Payout Ratio
DPS	Dividend Per Share
DY	Dividend Yield
EBIT	Earnings Before Interest and Tax
EBITDA	Earnings Before Interest, Tax, Depreciation and Amortization
ED	Exposure Draft
EPS	Earnings Per Share
EY	Earnings Yield
FA	Fixed Assets
FASB	Financial Accounting Standards Board (USA)
FG	Finished Goods
FIFO	First In First Out
FRED	Financial Reporting Exposure Draft
FRS	Financial Reporting Standard (ASB)
GAAP	Generally Accepted Accounting Principles (USA)
GPLA	General Price Level Adjustments (USA)
HMC	Historical Money Cost
IAS	International Accounting Standard
IASB	International Accounting Standards Board
IASC	International Accounting Standards Committee
ICAEW	Institute of Chartered Accountants in England and Wales
IFRS	International Financial Reporting Standard
IOSCO	International Organization of Securities Commissions
LIFO	Last In First Out
Ltd	Limited
MI	Minority Interest
MV	Market Value
MWCA	Monetary Working Capital Adjustment

NBV	Net Book Value
NRV	Net Realizable Value
P & L	Profit and Loss
PAP	Pre-Acquisition Profit
PAT	Profit After Tax
PBIT	Profit Before Interest Payable and Tax
PBT	Profit Before Tax
P/E	Price/Earnings (ratio)
plc	Public Limited Company
RC	Replacement Cost
RE	Retained Earnings
RM	Raw Materials (stock)
RI	Residual Income
ROCE	Return on Capital Employed
ROFE	Return on Funds Employed
ROI	Return On Investment
RONA	Return on Net Assets
RPI	Retail Prices Index
SL	Straight Line (depreciation)
SSAP	Statement of Standard Accounting Practice (ASC)
SYD	Sum of the Years' Digits (depreciation)
TB	Trial Balance
VAT	Value Added Tax
WC	Working Capital
WIP	Work-In-Progress

Appendix 3
UK Accounting standards
as at 1 January 2005

Topic

SSAP

4	Government Grants
5	Value Added Tax
9	Stocks and Work in Progress
13	Research and Development
19	Investment Properties
20	Foreign Currency Translation
21	Leases and Hire Purchase Contracts
25	Segmental Reporting

FRS

1	Cash Flow Statements
2	Subsidiary Undertakings
3	Reporting Financial Performance
4	Capital Instruments
5	Reporting the Substance of Transactions
6	Acquisitions and Mergers
7	Fair Values in Acquisition Accounting
8	Related Party Disclosures
9	Associates and Joint Ventures
10	Goodwill and Intangible Assets
11	Impairment of Fixed Assets
12	Provisions and Contingencies
13	Derivatives: Disclosures
15	Tangible Fixed Assets
16	Current Tax
17	Retirement Benefits
18	Accounting Policies
19	Deferred Tax
20	Share-based Payment
21	Events After the Balance Sheet Date
22	Earnings Per Share
23	Changes in Foreign Exchange Rates
24	Hyperinflationary Economies
25	Financial Instruments: Disclosure
26	Financial Instruments: Measurement
27	Life Assurance
	Smaller Entities [FRSSE]

International accounting standards
as at 1 January 2005

Topic

IAS

1	Presentation of Financial Statements
2	Inventories
7	Cash Flow Statements
8	Accounting Policies, etc.
10	Events After the Balance Sheet Date
11	Construction Contracts
12	Income Taxes
14	Segment Reporting
16	Property, Plant and Equipment
17	Leases
18	Revenue
19	Employee Benefits
20	Government Grants
21	Changes in Foreign Exchange Rates
23	Borrowing Costs
24	Related Party Disclosures
26	Reporting by Retirement Benefit Plans
27	Consolidated and Separate Financial Statements
28	Investments in Associates
29	Hyperinflationary Economies
30	Disclosures in the Financial Statements of Banks etc.
31	Interests in Joint Ventures
32	Financial Instruments: Disclosures and Presentation
33	Earnings per Share
34	Interim Financial Reporting
36	Impairment of Assets
37	Provisions and Contingencies
38	Intangible Assets
39	Financial Instruments: Recognition and Measurement
40	Investment Property
41	Agriculture

IFRS

1	First-time Adoption of IFRS
2	Share-based Payment
3	Business Combinations
4	Insurance Contracts
5	Non-current Assets Held for Sale, etc.

Appendix 4
UK Retail Prices Index

A Post-war series

June	1947	100.0	to January 1956	153.4
January	1956	100.0	to January 1962	117.5
January	1962	100.0	to January 1974	191.8
January	1974	100.0	to January 1987	395.5
January	1987	100.0		

B Annual averages (January 1987 = 100.0)

1960	12.5	1970	18.5	1980	66.9	1990	126.1	2000	170.3
1961	12.9	1971	20.3	1981	74.8	1991	133.5	2001	173.4
1962	13.4	1972	21.7	1982	81.2	1992	138.5	2002	176.2
1963	13.7	1973	23.7	1983	85.0	1993	140.7	2003	181.3
1964	14.2	1974	27.5	1984	89.2	1994	144.1	2004	186.7
1965	14.8	1975	34.2	1985	94.6	1995	149.1		
1966	15.4	1976	39.8	1986	97.8	1996	152.7		
1967	15.8	1977	46.2	1987	101.9	1997	157.5		
1968	16.5	1978	49.9	1988	106.9	1998	162.9		
1969	17.4	1979	56.7	1989	115.1	1999	165.4		

C Annual rates of increase (calendar year)

1960	2%	1970	8%	1980	15%	1990	9%	2000	3%
1961	4%	1971	9%	1981	12%	1991	4%	2001	1%
1962	3%	1972	8%	1982	5%	1992	3%	2002	3%
1963	2%	1973	11%	1983	5%	1993	2%	2003	3%
1964	5%	1974	19%	1984	5%	1994	3%	2004	3%
1965	4%	1975	25%	1985	6%	1995	3%		
1966	4%	1976	15%	1986	4%	1996	3%		
1967	2%	1977	12%	1987	4%	1997	4%		
1968	6%	1978	8%	1988	7%	1998	3%		
1969	5%	1979	17%	1989	8%	1999	2%		

Appendix 5

Companies Act 1985, Schedule 4: Form and content of company accounts (as amended by Schedules 1 and 2 to the Companies Act 1989)

PART I: GENERAL RULES AND FORMATS (abbreviated)

Section A: General rules

1 (1) Subject to the following provisions: (a) every balance sheet of a company shall show the items listed in either of the balance sheet formats; and (b) every profit and loss account of a company shall show the items listed in any one of the profit and loss account formats; in either case in the order and under the headings and subheadings given.

   (2) Any headings or subheadings need not be distinguished by a letter or number.

2 (1) The directors of a company shall keep to the same format for the balance sheet and profit and loss account unless there are special reasons for a change.

   (2) Disclose particulars of any change in format, with reasons for the change.

3 (1) Any item may be shown in greater detail than required.

   (2) The following shall not be treated as assets in any balance sheet: (a) preliminary expenses; (b) expenses of any issue of shares or debentures; and (c) costs of research.

   (3) The directors of a company may adapt the arrangement for items with an Arabic number, where the special nature of the company's business requires it.

   (4) Items with Arabic numbers in any of the formats may be combined if either: (a) their individual amounts are not material; or (b) the combination helps understanding (in which case show the individual amounts in a note).

   (5) Do not include a heading or subheading if there is no amount for that item in respect of the financial year or the preceding year.

   (6) Every profit and loss of a company shall show the amount of a company's profit or loss on ordinary activities before taxation.

   (7) Every profit and loss account shall show separately: (a) any amount set aside to, or withdrawn from, reserves; and (b) aggregate dividends paid and proposed.

4 (1) For every item in a company's balance sheet or profit and loss account, show the corresponding amount for the preceding financial year.

   (2) Where that corresponding amount is not comparable, adjust it and disclose particulars of the adjustment and the reasons for it.

5 Amounts in respect of items representing assets or income may not be set off against amounts in respect of items representing liabilities or expenditure, or vice versa.

Section B: Required formats for accounts

Notes on balance sheet formats

1 *Called up share capital not paid* (A or C.II.5)
This item may be shown in either of the two positions.

2 *Concessions, patents, licences, trade marks, etc.* (B.I.2)
Include amounts only if the assets were either: (a) acquired for valuable consideration; or (b) created by the company itself.

3 *Goodwill* (B.I.3)
Include only to the extent that goodwill was acquired for valuable consideration.

4 *Own shares* (B.III.7 and C.III.2)
Show separately the nominal value of the shares held.

5 *Debtors* (C.II.1 to 6)
Show separately the amount falling due after one year.

6 *Prepayments and accrued income* (C.II.6 or D)
This item may be shown in either of the two positions.

7 *Debenture loans* (Format 1: E.1 and H.1; Format 2: C.1)
Show separately the amount of any convertible loans.

8 *Payments received on account* (Format 1: E.3 and H.3; Format 2: C.3)
Show in so far as they are not shown as deductions from stocks.

9 *Other creditors including taxation* (Format 1: E.8 and H.8; Format 2: C.8)
Show separately the amount for creditors in respect of taxation and social security.

10 *Accruals and deferred income* (Format 1: E.9 and H.9 or J; Format 2: C.9 or D)
In Format 1, position J is an alternative; in Format 2, position D.

11 *Net current assets (liabilities)* (Format 1, F)
Include any amounts shown under 'prepayments and accrued income'.

12 *Called up share capital* (Format 1, K.I; Format 2, A.I)
Show separately the amount of allotted and called up share capital.

13 *Creditors* (Format 2, C.1 to 9)
Show separately amounts falling due within one year and after one year.

Balance sheet formats

Format 1

A Called up share capital not paid *(1)*

B Fixed assets
  I Intangible assets
    1 Development costs
    2 Concessions, patents, licences, trade marks and similar rights and assets *(2)*
    3 Goodwill *(3)*
    4 Payments on account
  II Tangible assets
    1 Land and buildings
    2 Plant and machinery
    3 Fixtures, fittings, tools and equipment
    4 Payments on account and assets in course of construction
  III Investments
    1 Shares in group undertakings
    2 Loans to group undertakings
    3 Interests in associated undertakings
      Other participating interests
    4 Loans to undertakings in which the company has a participating interest
    5 Other investments other than loans
    6 Other loans
    7 Own shares *(4)*

C Current assets
  I Stocks
    1 Raw materials and consumables
    2 Work-in-progress
    3 Finished goods and goods for resale
    4 Payments on account
  II Debtors *(5)*
    1 Trade debtors
    2 Amounts owed by group undertakings
    3 Amounts owed by undertakings in which the company has a participating interest
    4 Other debtors
    5 Called up share capital not paid *(1)*
    6 Prepayments and accrued income *(6)*
  III Investments
    1 Shares in group undertakings
    2 Own shares *(4)*
    3 Other investments
  IV Cash at bank and in hand

D Prepayments and accrued income *(6)*

E Creditors: amounts falling due within one year
  1 Debenture loans *(7)*
  2 Bank loans and overdrafts
  3 Payments received on account *(8)*
  4 Trade creditors
  5 Bills of exchange payable
  6 Amounts owed to group undertakings
  7 Amounts owed to undertakings in which the company has a participating interest
  8 Other creditors including taxation and social security *(9)*
  9 Accruals and deferred income *(10)*

F Net current assets (liabilities) *(11)*

G Total assets less current liabilities

H Creditors: amounts falling due after more than one year
  1 Debenture loans *(7)*
  2 Bank loans and overdrafts
  3 Payments received on account *(8)*
  4 Trade creditors
  5 Bills of exchange payable
  6 Amounts owed to group undertakings
  7 Amounts owed to undertakings in which the company has a participating interest
  8 Other creditors including taxation and social security *(9)*
  9 Accruals and deferred income *(10)*

I Provisions for liabilities and charges
  1 Pensions and similar obligations
  2 Taxation, including deferred taxation
  3 Other provisions

J Accruals and deferred income *(10)*

K Capital and reserves
  I Called up share capital *(12)*
  II Share premium account
  III Revaluation reserve
  IV Other reserves
    1 Capital redemption reserve
    2 Reserve for own shares
    3 Reserves provided for by the articles of association
    4 Other reserves
  V Profit and loss account
  Minority interests

Balance sheet formats

Format 2

ASSETS

A Called up share capital not paid *(1)*

B Fixed assets
   I Intangible assets
      1 Development costs
      2 Concessions, patents, licences, trade marks and similar rights and assets *(2)*
      3 Goodwill *(3)*
      4 Payments on account
   II Tangible assets
      1 Land and buildings
      2 Plant and machinery
      3 Fixtures, fittings, tools and equipment
      4 Payments on account and assets in course of construction
   III Investments
      1 Shares in group undertakings
      2 Loans to group undertakings
      3 Interests in associated undertakings
         Other participating interests
      4 Loans to undertakings in which the company has a participating interest
      5 Other investments other than loans
      6 Other loans
      7 Own shares *(4)*

C Current assets
   I Stocks
      1 Raw materials and consumables
      2 Work-in-progress
      3 Finished goods and goods for resale
      4 Payments on account
   II Debtors *(5)*
      1 Trade debtors
      2 Amounts owed by group undertakings
      3 Amounts owed by undertakings in which the company has a participating interest
      4 Other debtors
      5 Called up share capital not paid *(1)*
      6 Prepayments and accrued income *(6)*

   III Investments
      1 Shares in group undertakings
      2 Own shares *(4)*
      3 Other investments
   IV Cash at bank and in hand

D Prepayments and accrued income *(6)*

LIABILITIES

A Capital and reserves
   I Called up share capital *(12)*
   II Share premium account
   III Revaluation reserve
   IV Other reserves
      1 Capital redemption reserve
      2 Reserve for own shares
      3 Reserves provided for by the articles of association
      4 Other reserves
   V Profit and loss account
   Minority interests

B Provisions for liabilities and charges
      1 Pensions and similar obligations
      2 Taxation including deferred taxation
      3 Other provisions

C Creditors *(13)*
      1 Debenture loans *(7)*
      2 Bank loans and overdrafts
      3 Payments received on account *(8)*
      4 Trade creditors
      5 Bills of exchange payable
      6 Amounts owed to group undertakings
      7 Amounts owed to undertakings in which the company has a participating interest
      8 Other creditors including taxation and social security *(9)*
      9 Accruals and deferred income *(10)*

D Accruals and deferred income *(10)*

Profit and loss account formats

Format 1

1 Turnover
2 Cost of sales *(14)*
3 Gross profit or loss
4 Distribution costs *(14)*
5 Administrative expenses *(14)*
6 Other operating income
7 Income from shares in group undertakings
   Income from interests in associated undertakings
8 Income from other participating interests
9 Income from other fixed asset investments *(15)*
10 Other interest receivable and similar income *(15)*
11 Amounts written off investments
12 Interest payable and similar charges *(16)*
13 Tax on profit or loss on ordinary activities
14 Profit or loss on ordinary activities after taxation
   Minority interests
15 Extraordinary income
16 Extraordinary charges
17 Extraordinary profit or loss
18 Tax on extraordinary profit or loss
   Minority interests
19 Other taxes not shown under the above items
20 Profit or loss for the financial year

Profit and loss account formats

Format 2

1 Turnover
2 Change in stocks of finished goods and in work-in-progress
3 Own work capitalized
4 Other operating income
5 (a) Raw materials and consumables
   (b) Other external charges
6 Staff costs: (a) wages and salaries
                (b) social security costs
                (c) other pension costs
7 (a) Depreciation etc. written off tangible and intangible fixed assets
   (b) Exceptional amounts written off current assets
8 Other operating charges
9 Income from shares in group undertakings
   Income from interests in associated undertakings
10 Income from other participating interests
11 Income from other fixed asset investments *(15)*
12 Other interest receivable and similar income *(15)*
13 Amounts written off investments
14 Interest payable and similar charges *(16)*
15 Tax on profit or loss on ordinary activities
16 Profit or loss on ordinary activities after taxation
   Minority interests
17 Extraordinary income
18 Extraordinary charges
19 Extraordinary profit or loss
20 Tax on extraordinary profit or loss
   Minority interests
21 Other taxes not shown under the above items
22 Profit or loss for the financial year

Notes on profit and loss account formats

14   Cost of sales, distribution costs, administrative expenses
State these items including any provisions for depreciation.

15   Income from other fixed asset investments, other interest receivable, etc.
Show separately income and interest derived from group undertakings.

16   Interest payable and similar charges
Show separately the amount payable to group undertakings.

17   Depreciation (Formats 1 and 3)
Disclose in a note any provision for depreciation of fixed assets (shown under Format 2, item 7(a) and Format 4, item A.4(a)).

Profit and loss account formats

Format 3

A   Charges
    1   Cost of sales *(14)*
    2   Distribution costs *(14)*
    3   Administrative expenses *(14)*
    4   Amounts written off investments
    5   Interest payable and similar charges *(16)*
    6   Tax on profit or loss on ordinary activities
    7   Profit or loss on ordinary activities after taxation
       Minority interests
    8   Extraordinary charges
    9   Tax on extraordinary profit or loss
       Minority interests
   10   Other taxes not shown under the above items
   11   Profit or loss for the financial year

B   Income
    1   Turnover
    2   Other operating income
    3   Income from shares in group undertakings
       Income from interests in associated undertakings
    4   Income from other participating interests
    5   Income from other fixed asset investments (15)
    6   Other interest receivable and similar income (15)
    7   Profit or loss on ordinary activities after taxation
       Minority interests
    8   Extraordinary income
       Minority interests
    9   Profit or loss for the financial year

Profit and loss account formats

Format 4

A   Charges
    1   Reduction in stocks of finished goods and in work-in-progress
    2   (a)   Raw materials and consumables
       (b)   Other external charges
    3   Staff costs: (a) wages and salaries
             (b) social security costs
             (c) other pension costs
    4   (a)   Depreciation etc. written off tangible and intangible fixed assets
       (b)   Exceptional amounts written off current assets
    5   Other operating charges
    6   Amounts written off investments
    7   Interest payable and similar charges *(16)*
    8   Tax on profit or loss on ordinary activities
    9   Profit or loss on ordinary activities after taxation
       Minority interests
   10   Extraordinary charges
   11   Tax on extraordinary profit or loss
       Minority interests
   12   Other taxes not shown under the above items
   13   Profit or loss for the financial year

B   Income
    1   Turnover
    2   Increase in stocks of finished goods and in work-in-progress
    3   Own work capitalized
    4   Other operating income
    5   Income from shares in group undertakings
       Income from interests in associated undertakings
    6   Income from other participating interests
    7   Income from other fixed asset investments *(15)*
    8   Other interest receivable and similar income (15)
    9   Profit or loss on ordinary activities after taxation
       Minority interests
   10   Extraordinary income
       Minority interests
   11   Profit or loss for the financial year

Appendix 6
Bibliography

The background and structure of company accounts
William H. Beaver (1998) *Financial Reporting: An Accounting Revolution*, 3rd edn, Prentice-Hall.

Andrew Higson (2003) *Corporate Financial Reporting: Theory and Practice*, SAGE Publications.

D. R. Myddelton (2004) *Unshackling Accountants*, Institute of Economic Affairs.

Analysing performance
George Foster (1986) *Financial Statement Analysis*, 2nd edn, Prentice-Hall.

C. A. Westwick (1987) *How to Use Management Ratios*, 2nd edn, Gower.

Measuring profit or loss
T. A. Lee (1986) *Income and Value Measurement*, 3rd edn, Nelson.

R. H. Parker, G. C. Harcourt and G. Whittington (eds) (1986) *Readings in the Concept and Measurement of Business Income*, 2nd edn, Philip Allan.

Capital structure
Richard Brealey and Stewart Myers (2004) *Principles of Corporate Finance*, 7th edn, McGraw-Hill.

D. R. Myddelton (2000) *Managing Business Finance*, Prentice-Hall.

Group accounts
Raymond Brockington (1996) *Accounting for Intangible Assets*, Addison-Wesley.

S. J. Gray and A. G. Coenenberg (eds) (1988) *International Group Accounting*, Croom Helm.

P. A. Taylor (1987) *Consolidated Financial Statements: Concepts, Issues, Techniques*, Harper and Row.

International accounting
Jon Flower with Gabi Ebbers (2002) *Global Financial Reporting*, Palgrave.

Christopher Nobes and Robert Parker (eds) (2004) *Comparative International Accounting*, 7th edn, Prentice-Hall.

Clare Roberts, Pauline Weetman and Paul Gordon (1998) *International Financial Accounting*, FT Pitman.

Inflation accounting
B. V. Carsberg and M. J. Page (eds) (1984) *Current Cost Accounting: The Benefits and the Costs*, ICAEW.

D. R. Myddelton (1984) *On A Cloth Untrue: Inflation Accounting, The Way Forward*, Woodhead-Faulkner.

David Tweedie and Geoffrey Whittington (1984) *The Debate on Inflation Accounting*, Cambridge University Press.

Interpreting company accounts
Ernst & Young (2004) *UK and International GAAP 2005*, 7th edn, LexisNexis.

Geoffrey Holmes and Alan Sugden (1997) *Interpreting Company Reports and Accounts*, 6th edn, Woodhead-Faulkner.

Terry Smith (1996) *Accounting for Growth*, 2nd edn, Century Business Books.

Appendix 7
Analysis forms

Blank forms for use in analysis are set out on the following pages. Please feel free to photocopy any or all of these forms for use as convenient.

COMPANY: YEAR:

SUMMARY OF KEY FIGURES AND RATIOS					
	20	20	20	20	20
Key figures £m (as in 5 year summary) Turnover Net assets Profit after tax Earnings per share					
Annual % change Turnover Net assets Profit after tax Earnings per share Retail Prices Index					
Profitability ratios (%) Return on equity Tax ratio Return on net operating assets Operating profit margin **Asset turnover ratios** Net operating asset turnover (times) Tangible fixed asset turnover (times) Stock (days) (COGS basis) Stock (days) (sales basis) Trade debtors (days)					

COMPANY: YEAR:

	20	20	20	20	20
SUMMARY OF KEY FIGURES AND RATIOS **(continued)**					
Financial status ratios Total debt/Capital employed % Total debt/Equity % Interest cover (times) Current ratio Acid test					
Stock market ratios Earnings per share Price/earnings ratio Dividend yield % Dividend cover (times)					
Stock market indicators Share price					
Annual % change Share price All share index Industry index					

PROFITABILITY   20   20

Return on equity %   _____ = _____ =   _____ = _____ =

Tax ratio %   _____ =   _____ =

Return on net operating assets %   (a) _____ = _____ =   _____ = _____ =

Operating profit margin %   (a) _____ =   _____ =

ASSET TURNOVER

Net operating asset turnover   (a) _____ =   _____ =

Tangible fixed asset turnover   _____ = _____ =   _____ = ____ =

Stock turnover (days)   _____ =   _____ =
   (COGS/stock)

Stock turnover (days)   _____ =   _____ =
   (sales/stock)

Trade debtor (days)   _____ =   _____ =
   (sales/trade debtors)

(a)   Exclude FA investments and related income if significant

FINANCIAL STATUS RATIOS   **20**   **20**

Solvency

Total debt/Capital employed %   (a)   _____ = _____ =   _____ = _____ =

Debt/Capital employed %   (b)   _____ = _____ =   _____ = _____ =

Total debt/Equity %   (a)   _____ = _____ =   _____ = _____ =

Debt/Equity %   (b)   _____ = _____ =   _____ = _____ =

Interest cover   _____ = _____ =   _____ = _____ =

Liquidity

Current ratio   _____ = _____ =   _____ = _____ =

Acid test   _____ = _____ =   _____ = _____ =

STOCK MARKET RATIOS

Earnings per share   _____   =   _____   =

Price/earnings ratio   _____   =   _____   =

Dividend yield %   _____ = _____ =   _____ = _____ =

Dividend cover (times)   _____   =   _____   =

Treating all interest-bearing short-term borrowings as (a) capital employed (b) current liabilities

PRODUCT ACTIVITY

Product group	Sales £m					Annual % sales growth					Net assets £m				
	20	20	20	20	20	20	20	20	20	20	20	20	20	20	20
Total															

Product group	Profit £m					Profit/Sales %					Profit/Net assets %				
	20	20	20	20	20	20	20	20	20	20	20	20	20	20	20
Total															

MARKET ACTIVITY

Geographical area	Sales £m					Annual % sales growth					Net assets £m				
	20	20	20	20	20	20	20	20	20	20	20	20	20	20	20
Total															

Geographical area	Profit £m					Profit/Sales %					Profit/Net assets %				
	20	20	20	20	20	20	20	20	20	20	20	20	20	20	20
Total															

RESTATED FUNDS/CASH FLOW STATEMENTS

		20	20	20	20	20
INTERNAL FUNDS/INVESTMENT						
Group operating profit						
Items not involving the flow of funds						
Depreciation						
Gross funds from operations						
Interest						
Tax						
Dividends						
Foreign exchange adjustments						
Net funds from operations						
Working capital (increase)/decrease						
Stocks (increase)/decrease						
Debtors (increase)/decrease						
Creditors increase/(decrease)						
FX on working capital						
Net cash available for fixed asset investment						
Sale of fixed assets						
Other fixed asset disposals						
Total cash available						
Fixed asset investment						
Fixed assets						
FA investments						
Acquisition of businesses						
Financing (requirement)/surplus	£m					
EXTERNAL FINANCING						
Ordinary share capital						
Minorities						
Loans						
Overdrafts						
Liquid resources						
Financing/(investment)	£m					

289

PUBLISHED FUNDS/CASH FLOW STATEMENTS

Insert descriptions from Annual Report

	20	20	20	20	20

ADJUSTMENTS TO PUBLISHED CASH FLOW STATEMENTS

Insert descriptions from Annual Report

	20	20	20	20	20

290

Solutions

1.5 The Acme Company Limited

THE ACME COMPANY LIMITED
Balance sheet at 30 June 2005

		£'000
Fixed assets		
Freehold shop		150
Fixtures and fittings		30
		180
Current assets		
Stock	60	
Debtors	40	
Cash	20	
	120	
Less: **Creditors due within one year**		
Trade creditors	30	
Taxation payable	20	
	50	
		70
Total assets less current liabilities		250
Capital and reserves		
Called up share capital		200
Profit and loss account		50
		250

Notes

1 Note the order of the items shown in current assets and in creditors due within one year.
2 Note the grouping of items and subtotals in each part of the balance sheet.

1.6 General Contractors Limited

GENERAL CONTRACTORS LIMITED
Profit and loss account
for the year ended 31 December 2004

	£'000
Turnover	1 250
Cost of sales	1 100
Trading profit	150
Interest payable	10
Profit before tax	140
Tax	40
Profit after tax	100

Notes

1 The heading for the profit and loss account

   (a) includes the name of the company
   (b) indicates that the account is 'for the year ended 31 December 2004'.

2 Turnover has to be disclosed; and deducting cost of sales determines the amount of trading profit.

3 Cost of sales is £1 050 000 plus depreciation £50 000.

4 Tax is not combined with interest payable; but separate subtotals are shown for

   (a) 'profit before tax'
   (b) 'profit after tax'.

1.7 The Marvel Trading Company Limited

THE MARVEL TRADING COMPANY LIMITED
Profit and loss account
for the year ended 30 June 2005

	£'000
Turnover	1 200
Cost of sales	1 100
Trading profit	100
Income from investments	12
	112
Interest payable	8
Profit before tax	104
Tax	26
Profit after tax	78

THE FINE FARE CATERING COMPANY LIMITED

Balance sheet at 31 March 2005

	£'000		£'000
Capital and reserves		**Fixed assets**	
Called up share capital	70	Leasehold restaurant	70
Profit and loss account	20	Fixtures and fittings	10
Shareholders' funds	90		80
Creditors due within one year		**Current assets**	
Trade creditors	10	Stock	20
Tax	10	Cash	10
			30
	20		
	110		110

**Profit and loss account
for the year ended 31 March 2005**

	£'000
Turnover	150
Cost of sales	120
Trading profit	30
Tax	10
Profit after tax	20

Note

We have chosen to present the balance sheet in the outdated 'horizontal account format'. You might care to re-present it in the more usual 'vertical format' which we have used up to now.

ANDREW HUNT LIMITED

Balance sheet at 30 September 2004

			£'000
Fixed assets			
Leasehold factory			600
Plant and machinery, net			450
			1 050
Current assets			
Stock	330		
Debtors	470		
Cash	200	1 000	
Less: **Creditors due within one year**			
Trade creditors	320		
Taxation	145	465	
			535
			1 585
Less: **Creditors due after one year**			
10% Debenture 2008			400
			1 185
Capital and reserves			
Called up share capital			750
Profit and loss account			435
			1 185

**Profit and loss account
for the nine months ended 30 September 2004**

	£'000
Turnover	3 400
Cost of sales	2 790
Trading profit	610
Interest paid	30
Profit before taxation	580
Taxation	145
Profit after tax	435

2.4 Worldchem plc (A): performance ratios

	2005	**2004**
Profitability		
(a) Return on equity	$\dfrac{91}{520}$ = 17.5%	$\dfrac{96}{490}$ = 19.6%
(b) Tax ratio	$\dfrac{46}{137}$ = 33.6%	$\dfrac{48}{144}$ = 33.3%
(c) Return on net assets	$\dfrac{137 + 15}{681 + 16}$ = 21.8%	$\dfrac{144 + 14}{638 + 26}$ = 23.8%
(d) Profit margin	$\dfrac{152}{1\,028}$ = 14.8%	$\dfrac{158}{923}$ = 17.1%
Asset turnover		
(e) Net asset turnover	$\dfrac{1\,028}{697}$ = 1.47 times	$\dfrac{923}{664}$ = 1.39 times
(f) Fixed asset turnover	$\dfrac{1\,028}{389}$ = 2.64 times	$\dfrac{923}{332}$ = 2.78 times
(g) Stock turnover	$\dfrac{1\,028}{205}$ = 5.01 times	$\dfrac{923}{178}$ = 5.19 times
(h) Days' sales in debtors	$\dfrac{211 \times 365}{1\,028}$ = 74.9 days	$\dfrac{182 \times 365}{923}$ = 72.0 days

Comments

1 Return on equity of Worldchem plc has declined due to a lower return on net assets (for which add 16 short-term borrowings to 681 net assets.)
2 Profit margins are much lower – down from 17.1% to 14.8%.
3 Net asset turnover is up due to lower liquid resources and an 11% increase in sales. Other asset turnover rates are all slightly down.
4 We use sales to calculate stock turnover, absent 'cost of sales'.
5 Similarly we use 'debtors and prepayments' for days' sales in debtors.

3.7 Worldchem plc (B): financial and stock market ratios

	2005	**2004**
Financial status ratios		
(a) Debt ratio	$\dfrac{161 + 16}{697}$ = 25.4%	$\dfrac{148 + 26}{664}$ = 26.2%
(b) Interest cover	$\dfrac{152}{15}$ = 10.1 times	$\dfrac{158}{14}$ = 11.3 times
(c) Current ratio	$\dfrac{531}{239}$ = 2.22 times	$\dfrac{536}{230}$ = 2.33 times
(d) Acid test	$\dfrac{326}{239}$ = 1.36 times	$\dfrac{358}{230}$ = 1.56 times
Stock market ratios		
(e) Earnings per share	$\dfrac{91}{(163 \times 4)}$ = 14.0p	$\dfrac{96}{(163 \times 4)}$ = 14.7p
(f) Price/earnings ratio	$\dfrac{136}{14.0}$ = 9.7	$\dfrac{142}{14.7}$ = 9.7
(g) Dividend yield (net)	$\dfrac{6.3}{136}$ = 4.6%	$\dfrac{5.1}{142}$ = 3.6%
(h) Dividend cover	$\dfrac{14.0}{6.3}$ = 2.22 times	$\dfrac{14.7}{5.1}$ = 2.88 times

Notes

(a) Short-term borrowings are shown as part of creditors due within one year in the balance sheet; but in practice they may often be regarded as part of the longer-term financing of the business. Hence we show 'debt' as 161 + 16 = 177, and 'debt + equity' (= 'net assets') as 681 + 16 = 697.
(c, d) Despite what is said above, we take a conservative approach, and include short-term borrowings as 'current' liabilities for the purpose of computing the liquidity ratios (as is almost always done).
(g, h) Dividend per share = £41m ÷ (163m x 4) = 6.3p (£33m ÷ 652 = 5.1p)

Comments

1 Gearing is slightly lower, but with lower profit the interest cover has declined.
2 The current and acid test ratios are both lower, reflecting the reduced liquid resources, but still look high for a chemical company
3 With profit after tax down and dividends up, the dividend cover has declined.

4.5 Chemical Products Company Limited (A)

CHEMICAL PRODUCTS COMPANY LIMITED
Balance sheet at 31 ~~July~~ 2004 *August*

				£'000
Fixed assets				
Plant at cost	a + 10		38	~~38~~ 28
Current assets				
Stock	d − 18		~~25~~	7
Debtors	b − 8	d + 15	~~15~~	22
Cash	a − 10	b + 8 c − 5	~~12~~	5
				~~52~~
			34	~~80~~
			72	

		£'000
Capital and reserves		
Called up share capital		50
Profit and loss account	d − 3	17 ~~20~~
		67 ~~70~~
Creditors due within one year		
Trade creditors	c − 5	5 ~~10~~
		72 ~~80~~

Note

Notice that there was a *loss* on the sale of goods. Sales proceeds were £15 000 while the goods had cost £18 000. The loss of £3 000 (being a negative profit) is *deducted* from the £20 000 balance on profit and loss account.

4.9 Whitewash Laundry Limited

WHITEWASH LAUNDRY LIMITED
Balance sheet at ~~1 January~~ 2005 *31 March*

			£'000
Fixed assets			
Laundry and equipment			50
Current assets			
Debtors	a + 60	c − 55	~~30~~ 35
Cash	c − 6 c + 55 d − 30 e − 15		~~10~~ 14
			49 ~~40~~
			99 ~~90~~
Capital and reserves			
Called up share capital			75
Profit and loss account	+ 9 (see above right)		24 ~~15~~
			99 ~~90~~

WHITEWASH LAUNDRY LIMITED
Profit and loss account
for the quarter ended 31 March 2005

		£'000
Turnover		60
Less: Supplies	6	
Operating expenses	30	
		36
Gross profit		24
Selling and administrative expenses		15
Trading profit		9

4.8 Abacus Book Shop Limited (C)

ABACUS BOOK SHOP LIMITED
Balance sheet at ~~31 January~~ 2005 *28 February*

			£'000
Fixed asset			
Leasehold shop	b + 6		6
Current assets			
Stock	c − 2 d − 1 e + 3 f + 2		~~6~~ 8
Debtors	d + 2		~~1~~ 3
Cash	a + 5 b − 6 c + 3 e − 3		~~2~~ 1
			12 ~~9~~
			18 ~~9~~
Capital and reserves			
Called up share capital			3
Profit and loss account	c + 1 d + 1		7 ~~5~~
			10 ~~8~~
Creditors due after one year			
10% Loan (secured)	a + 5		5
Creditors due within one year			
Trade creditors	f + 2		3 ~~1~~
			18 ~~9~~

Notes

1   Notice the two new balance sheet categories:
    Fixed asset: Leasehold shop
    Creditors due after one year: 10 per cent loan.
2   Did you remember to change the date of the balance sheet?

4.11 A Green Limited

Cash book

1 April	Balance	3 000	(d)	Operating expenses	2 000
(b)	Sales	15 000	(e)	Creditors (suppliers)	14 000
(f)	Debtors	3 000		Balance c/d	5 000
		£21 000			£21 000
	Balance b/d	5 000			

Ledger

Share capital

			1 April	Balance	3 000

Profit and loss account

			1 April	Balance	2 000

Trade creditors

(e)	Cash	14 000	1 April	Balance	3 000
	Balance c/d	5 000	(a)	Stock	16 000
		£19 000			£19 000
				Balance b/d	5 000

Van

1 April	Balance	4 000			

Stock

(a)	Creditors	16 000	(b)	Cost of sales	12 000
			(c)	Cost of sales	4 000
		£16 000			£16 000

Trial balance, 30 June 2005

	Total Dr	Total Cr	Profit and loss account Dr	Profit and loss account Cr	Balance sheet Dr	Balance sheet Cr
Share capital		3 000				3 000
Profit and loss account		2 000				2 000
Trade creditors		5 000				5 000
Van	4 000				4 000	
Stock						
Debtors	3 000				3 000	
Sales		20 000		20 000		
Cost of sales	16 000		16 000			
Operating expenses	2 000		2 000			
Cash	5 000				5 000	
Profit for quarter			2 000			2 000
	£30 000	£30 000	£20 000	£20 000	£12 000	£12 000

Debtors

1 April	Balance	1 000	(f)	Cash	3 000
(c)	Sales	5 000		Balance c/d	3 000
		6 000			6 000
	Balance b/d	3 000			

Sales

			(b)	Cash	15 000
			(c)	Debtors	5 000
					20 000

Cost of sales

(e)	Stock	12 000		
(c)	Stock	4 000		
		16 000		

Operating expenses

(d)	Cash	2 000		

A GREEN LIMITED

**Profit and loss account
for the three months ended 30 June 2005**

	£
Turnover	20 000
Cost of sales	16 000
Gross profit	4 000
Operating expenses	2 000
Trading profit	2 000

Balance sheet, 30 June 2005

		£
Fixed assets		
Van		4 000
Current assets		
Debtors	3 000	
Cash	5 000	
		8 000
		12 000
Capital and reserves		
Called up share capital		3 000
Profit and loss account		4 000
		7 000
Creditors due within one year		
Trade creditors		5 000
		12 000

Notes

1 Did you remember to include the £5 000 cash balance in the trial balance? The 'cash book' is a 'ledger account' too.

2 Notice how the £2 000 profit for the quarter is treated in the trial balance schedule:

  (a) It is shown as a (balancing) 'Dr' in the p + l account column and as a 'Cr' in the balance sheet.

  (b) It is then added to the £2 000 'balance brought forward' at 1 April to make a cumulative balance of £4 000 at 30 June.

4.12 Joseph Sillen Limited

Cash book £'000

1 July	Balance	40	(c)	Stock	250
(a)	Sales	350	(e)	Expenses	100
(g)	Debtors	130	(f)	Creditors	90
			Dec	Balance c/d	80
		520			520
1 Jan	Balance b/d	80			

Trial balance, 31 December 2004

£'000	Total Dr	Total Cr	Profit and loss account Dr	Profit and loss account Cr	Balance sheet Dr	Balance sheet Cr
Share capital		300				300
Profit and loss account		130				130
Trade creditors		90				90
Factory and machinery	250				250	
Stock	170				170	
Debtors	80				80	
Sales		900		900		
Cost of sales	660		660			
Expenses	170		170			
Tax expense	10		10			
Cash	80				80	
Profit for year			60			60
	1 420	1 420	900	900	580	580

Note

The balance shown on the profit and loss account in the ledger at 30 June, when the transactions for 2004 appear in separate ledger accounts, is the £130 balance as at 1 January 2004 not the £150 balance appearing in the balance sheet at 30 June. The difference is the £20 profit for the six months ended 30 June.

Ledger accounts

		£'000				£'000
			Share capital			
			||	1 July	Balance	300

Profit and loss account

			|| 1 Jan	Balance (150 – 20)	130

Trade creditors

(f)	Cash	90			1 July	Balance	100
	Balance c/d	90			(d)	Stock	80
		180					180
					1 Jan	Balance b/d	90

Factory and machinery

1 July	Balance	250	||

Stock

1 July	Balance	200			(a)	Cost of Sales	250
(c)	Cash	250			(b)	Cost of Sales	110
(d)	Creditors	80				Balance c/d	170
		530					530
1 Jan	Balance b/d	170					

Debtors

1 July	Balance	60			(g)	Cash	130
(b)	Sales	150				Balance c/d	80
		210					210
1 Jan	Balance b/d	80					

Sales

			|| 1 July	Balance	400
			|| (a)	Cash	350
			|| (b)	Debtors	150
							900

Cost of sales

1 July	Balance	300			
(a)	Stock	250			
(b)	Stock	110			
		660			

JOSEPH SILLEN LIMITED

Balance sheet, 31 December 2004

		£'000
Fixed assets		
Factory and machinery		250
Current assets		
Stock	170	
Debtors	80	
Cash	80	
		330
		580
Capital and reserves		
Called up share capital		300
Profit and loss account [= £130 + £60]		190
		490
Creditors due within one year		
Trade creditors		90
		580

Profit and loss account
Year ended 31 December 2004

	£'000
Turnover	900
Cost of sales	660
Gross profit	240
Expenses	170
Profit before tax	70
Tax	10
Profit after tax	60

Expenses

1 July	Balance	70			
(c)	Cash	100			
		170			

Tax expense

1 July	Balance	10	||

6.4 Anderson Tiles Limited

Closing stock valuation		£
3 000 cases at £5.00	=	15 000
2 000 cases at £4.75	=	9 500
1 000 cases at £4.25	=	4 250
		28 750

Cost of sales		
Opening stock 3 000 cases at £4.00		12 000
Purchases		41 500
		53 500
Less: Closing stock		28 750
		24 750

Cost of sales identified		
3 000 cases at £4.00 (opening stock)	=	12 000
3 000 cases at £4.25	=	12 750
		24 750

6.7 Kenton Limited

	Cut back production £m	Continue as normal £m
Cost of production in year:		
Direct materials	5m @ £8 = 40	6m @ £8 = 48
Direct labour	5m @ £4 = 20	6m @ £4 = 24
Production overheads	36	36
	96	108
Less: closing stock	1m/5m = (19.2)	2m/6m = (36)
Charged to P & L as cost of goods sold*	76.8	72

*In addition to cost of opening stock (assuming FIFO).

So gross profit before tax would be £4.8m higher if production continues at its normal level. This represents (1/3 − 1/5) x £36m, i.e. 2/15 x £36m, the extra fraction of fixed production overheads being carried forward in closing stock.

6.6 Berwick Paper Limited

BERWICK PAPER LIMITED

Date 2004	Stock	Tonnes	Average cost £	Amount £	Cost of Issues £
Jan	Opening	1 200	21.00	25 200	
March	Issues	900	21.00	18 900	...... 18 900
		300	21.00	6 300	
March	Purchases	1 800	18.00	32 400	
		2 100	18.4286	38 700	
June	Issues	1 700	18.43	31 329	...... 31 329
		400	18.43	7 371	
June	Purchases	2 400	15.00	36 000	
		2 800	15.4896	43 371	
Sept	Issues	1 400	15.49	21 686	...... 21 686
		1 400	15.49	21 685	
Sept	Purchases	1 200	25.00	30 000	
		2 600	19.8788	51 685	
Dec	Issues	1 900	19.88	37 770	...... 37 770
		700	19.88	13 915	
Dec	Purchases	1 800	20.00	36 000	
	Closing	2 500	19.9660	49 915	109 685

6.5 Newport Machines Limited

The overhead percentage is: $\dfrac{540\,000}{300\,000} = 180$ per cent on direct labour

The stock will therefore be valued as follows:

	£
Direct materials	30 000
Direct labour	20 000
Overheads (180% x 20 000)	36 000
	86 000

Note

The absorption cost method defers some *period* expenses by relating them to the *products* in stock. (Not all overheads, of course, need be period costs.)

7.10 Jonas Limited (C) (in £'000)

(a) The annual depreciation charge would be reduced from £14 (= £84/6) to £13 (= [£84 – £6] ÷ 6), that is by £1 (= £6/6). The net book value at the end of year 6 (the asset's expected life) would then be £6 (the asset's expected residual value) instead of zero.

(b) The cost of the improvement (£12) would have to be 'capitalized' and written off over the remaining three years of the asset's life, so the depreciation charge would be increased by £4 in each of years 4, 5, and 6. The net book value would therefore be increased by £8 at the end of year 4 (= £12 – £4) and by £4 at the end of year 5 (£12 – [2 x £4]).

7.13 Gilbert Limited and Sullivan Limited

		Gilbert £'000	Sullivan £'000
	Cost	72	72
Year 1	Depreciation	6	24
	Net book value	66	48
Year 2	Depreciation	6	16
	Net book value	60	32.0
Year 3	Depreciation	6	10.7
	Net book value	54	21.3
Year 4	Depreciation	6	7.1
	Net book value	48	14.2
	Sales proceeds	2	2.0
	Loss on disposal	46	12.2

7.15 Talmen Limited (A)

Net book value at 31 December 2002 = £228 000 (£300 000 – 3 x £24 000). The company needs to write off £228 000 – £20 000 (= £208 000) over the remaining four years of estimated life = £52 000 per year.

7.16 Talmen Limited (B)

Net book value at 31 December 2002 = £228 000 (as in case (A)). The company needs to write off £228 000 – £100 000 (= £128 000) over the remaining ten years of estimated life = £12 800 per year.

7.11 James Hillier Limited (A)

		(a) 50% £	33% £	(b) 40% £	36.5%* £
	Cost	8 000	8 000	8 000	8 000
Year 1	Depreciation	4 000	2 667	3 200	2 920
	Net book value	4 000	5 333	4 800	5 080
Year 2	Depreciation (x% of n.b.v.)	2 000	1 778	1 920	1 854
	Net book value	2 000	3 555	2 880	3 226
Year 3	Depreciation	1 000	1 185	1 152	1 178
	Net book value	1 000	2 370	1 728	2 048
Year 4	Depreciation	500	790	691	748
	Net book value	500	1 580	1 037	1 300
	Expected proceeds	750			
	Expected profit on sale	250			

Notes

1. It is not unusual to 'expect' some profit or loss on sale in advance. With declining balance depreciation it is not always easy to find a rate that will conveniently write the asset down to its precise expected residual value over its expected life.

2. The declining balance depreciation percentage uses the following formula:

$$r = \left[1 - (R/c)^{\frac{1}{n}} \right] \times 100$$

Where: r = rate of depreciation per period
c = original cost
R = Residual value
n = number of periods of useful life.

3. Any declining balance rate between 33 per cent and 40 per cent would seem appropriate to produce a net book value at the end of year 4 of around £1 300. Using the formula, a rate of 36.5 per cent can be calculated:

$$r = \left[1 - \sqrt[4]{\frac{1\ 300}{8\ 000}} \right] \times 100 = 36.5\%$$

7.12 James Hillier Limited (B)

(a) Depreciation schedule £

Year 4 Net book value 500

Year 5 Depreciation 250

Net book value 250

Year 6 Depreciation 125

Net book value 125

Sale proceeds 600

Profit on sale 475

(b) Journal entries in year 6

	Dr	Cr
(1) Depreciation expense	125	
Accumulated depreciation		125
Annual depreciation charge in year 6		
(2) Accumulated depreciation	7 875	
Disposal A/c	125	
Cost of fixed asset		8 000
Transfer net book value to disposal A/c		
(3) Cash	600	
Disposal A/c		600
Entering sales proceeds in disposal A/c		
(4) Disposal A/c	475	
Profit and loss account		475
Transfer profit on sale to P & L account		

(c) Ledger accounts for year 6

Cost of fixed asset

Balance b/f	8 000	Disposal a/c	8 000

Accumulated depreciation

Disposal a/c	7 875	Balance b/f	7 750
		Depreciation expense	125

Depreciation expense

Accumulated depreciation	125	Profit and loss account	125

Disposal account

Cost of fixed asset	8 000	Accumulated depreciation	7 875
P & L a/c: profit on sale	475	Cash	600
	8 475		8 475

7.14 Nick Saint plc

1 Total net book value of disposals in 2004 was £8 million:

Land and buildings	£3m – 0	= £3m
Plant and equipment	£32m – £27m	= £5m
		£8m

If proceeds from disposal were £9m, there would be a profit on sale of fixed assets of £1m. This would simply be deducted from depreciation expense. Being only a small amount it would not be disclosed separately.

2 Plant and equipment:

	Cost or valuation at 30.9.04	£866m
	Annual depreciation charge	£75m

Implied average useful life: 866/75 = 11.5 years.
Assumptions:
(a) A full year's depreciation has been charged on additions.
(b) No plant and equipment was fully written off before 30.9.04.
(c) There are no special adjustments in the £75m depreciation charge.

3

	Land and buildings £m	Plant and equipment £m
Cost or valuation		
At 1 October 2004	360	866
Additions	28	84
(Disposals)	–	(26)
At 30 September 2005	388	924
Depreciation		
At 1 October 2004	40	415
Provided in the year	8	77
(Disposals)	–	(21)
At 30 September 2005	48	471
Net book value: At 1 Oct 2004	320	451
At 30 Sept 2005	340	453

7.17 Annuity depreciation

The formula for annuity method depreciation is as follows:

$$\text{First year's depreciation} = C/S_{ni}$$

where:
- C = net cost of the fixed asset
- n = estimated asset life in years
- i = annual rate of interest
- S_{ni} = the sum to which an instalment of 1 per year will accumulate over n years at an interest rate of i per year.

Thereafter each year's depreciation increases by i per cent of the previous year's.

So if $n = 5$ and $i = 8\%$ a year, then $S_{ni} = 5.8666$; and $C/S_{ni} = 12\,000/5.8666 = 2\,045$.

So the depreciation schedule is as follows:

Year 1	2 045
Year 2	2 209
Year 3	2 386
Year 4	2 577
Year 5	2 783
Total	12 000

8.8 Kent Traders Limited

KENT TRADERS LIMITED
Balance sheet at 30 April 2005

		£'000
Fixed assets, net		750
Current assets		
Stock	260	
Debtors	190	
Cash	670	
	1 120	
Less: **Creditors due within one year**	240	
		880
		1 630
Less: **Creditors due after one year**		
Long-term loans		270
		1 360
Capital and reserves		
Called up share capital, 1.5 million ordinary 50p shares		750
Share premium account		450
Profit and loss account		160
= Shareholders' funds		1 360

Notes

1. A 1 for 4 rights issue involves issuing a quarter of the shares now in issue = 300 000. At 200p per share the proceeds will be £600 000, which must be added to the cash balance.
2. The £600 000 proceeds are split:

   (a) Nominal share capital: 300 000 at 50p = £150 000.
   (b) Share premium: 300 000 at 150p = £450 000.

3. Notice that, since a rights issue really increases the company's capital, in this case £600 000 is added both to shareholders' funds and to net assets.

ANTROBUS LATHES LIMITED

Balance sheet, end of 2004

Capital and reserves		Actual £'000	With loan converted £'000 End 2005
Called up ordinary £1 share capital		2 400	3 000
Reserves		1 100	2 000
Shareholders' funds		3 500	5 000
10% Convertible loan stock		1 500	–
8% Loan stock		1 000	1 000
Capital employed		6 000	6 000
Debt ratio		$\dfrac{2\,500}{6\,000} = 42\%$	$\dfrac{1\,000}{6\,000} = 17\%$

Profit and loss account 2004

	Actual	For 2005
PBIT	1 430	1 430
Loan interest payable	230	80
Profit before tax	1 200	1 350
Tax at 30%	360	405
Profit after tax	840	945
Earnings per share	$\dfrac{840}{2\,400} = 35.0\text{p}$	$\dfrac{945}{3\,000} = 31.5\text{p}$
Interest cover	$\dfrac{1\,430}{230} = 6.2$	$\dfrac{1\,430}{80} = 17.9$

Notes

1 The implied price of 250p per share gives a *premium* of 150p per share. Thus the share premium on conversion = 600 000 at 150p = £900 000.

2 Total capital employed has not changed.

3 Notice the significant reduction in the debt ratio and the increase in the interest cover. An analyst should be well aware of this *potential* change in the company's capital structure when analysing the 2004 accounts.

4 Finally, note that conversion reduces earnings per share by 10 per cent; even though profit after tax increases by 12½ per cent.

WESTERN ENTERPRISES LIMITED
Balance sheet, at 31 December 2004

	1 January 2004 £'000	Changes in year £'000			31 December 2004 £'000
Fixed assets					
Land and buildings, at valuation	700	b + 800			1 500
Plant, net	1 700				1 700
	2 400				3 200
Net assets	800	a + 150	d + 380	e – 270	1 060
	3 200				4 260
Less: **10% Loan stock**	1 200				1 200
	2 000				3 060
Capital and reserves					
Called up ordinary £1 shares	700	a + 50	c + 1 500	f + 150	2 400
Share premium	350	a + 100	c – 450		
Revaluation reserve		b + 800	c – 800		
Profit and loss account	950	d + 380	f – 150		660
		c – 250	e – 270		
	2 000				3 060

Notes

1 Did you remember to change the description of land and buildings from 'at cost' to 'at valuation'?

2 The bonus issue in (c) involves capitalizing reserves. Normal practice is to capitalize the most 'permanent' reserves first, that is, first share premium, then revaluation reserve, finally profit and loss.

3 The cash dividend of £270 000 in (e) is deducted from the £380 000 profit after tax, leaving retained profits for the year of £110 000.

4 The bonus issue in (f) would be excluded if it didn't actually happen until 2005.

8.11 Equivalent rights

n = number of existing shares in issue
p = current market price per share.

Basis for rights issue
s new shares for each existing share (meaning sn new shares) at a discount of d (which is $100d\%$) from p (i.e. at a price of p $(1 - d)$ per share).

Hence cash raised by rights issue = $sn.p$ $(1 - d)$.

Number of new shares to issue @ p to raise same cash as rights issue
= sn $(1 - d)$.

Bonus issue needs to issue $sn - sn$ $(1 - d)$ = $sn.d$ new shares.

So the terms of the bonus issue must be: $\dfrac{sn.d}{n + sn \ (1 - d)}$

8.12 Sadler Limited (A)

Profit and loss account extract
Year ended 31 December 2004

	£'000
Profit before interest payable and tax	48.0
10% Debenture interest	8.0
Profit before tax	40.0
Tax at 20%	8.0
Profit after tax	32.0
Dividends: 3.5% Preference Dividend	2.1
Profit available for ordinary shareholders	29.9

(a) Interest cover = $\dfrac{48.0}{8.0}$ = 6.0 times

(b) Ordinary dividend cover = $\dfrac{29.9}{16.0}$ = 1.87 times

(c) Earnings per share = $\dfrac{29.9}{200.0}$ = 14.95p.

8.13 Sadler Limited (B)

Balance sheet extract at 31 December 2004
Capital and reserves

	£'000
Called up ordinary £1 share capital	200
Reserves	60
Ordinary shareholders' funds	260
3½% Preference share capital	60
10% Debentures	80
Capital employed	400

(a) Debt ratio = 80/400 = 20 per cent.

(b) If net assets realize 125
    debentures amount to 80
    leaving for preference and ordinary shareholders ... 45
    but preference share capital is ... 60
    Therefore preference shareholders will get only 75 per cent of the nominal amount of their shares, that is, 75p per share. Ordinary shareholders will get *nothing*.

(c) If net assets realize 190
    debentures and preference capital amount to ... 140
    leaving for ordinary shareholders ... 50
    (= 25p per share)

Notes

1 In this case net assets realize enough to pay creditors (both short-term and long-term) in full. If there were not enough to do that, and assuming that all creditors were 'unsecured', every creditor would be paid *pro rata* (except for certain debts, such as amounts due for wages, and taxes, which have statutory priority). There is *no* priority for current as opposed to longer-term creditors.

2 As you know, balance sheets are prepared on a going concern basis, and do not purport to show the *realizable value* of *all* the company's assets. Balance sheets show the *unexpired costs* of those assets which have cost something. (Some valuable assets, for instance goodwill, may have cost nothing.)

3 Despite the above, some analysts refer to a calculation of 'book value per share' from time to time. This simply assumes that net assets could be realized for their book value: and divides the ordinary shareholders' funds by the number of ordinary shares in issue.
    For Sadler Limited, then, the 'book value per share' is 130p (260/200).

8.14 Bell Limited, Book Limited and Candle Limited

		Bell Limited £'000	Book Limited £'000	Candle Limited £'000
(a)	**2004**			
	PBIT	180	180	180
	Interest	60	20	–
	Profit before tax	120	160	180
	Tax at 20%	24	32	36
	Profit after tax	96	128	144
(i)	Return on net assets	18%	18%	18%
(ii)	Return on equity	24.0%	16.0%	14.4%
(iii)	Interest cover	3.0	9.0	–
(iv)	Earnings per share	64p	42.7p	36p
(b)	**2005**			
	PBIT	50	50	50
	Interest	60	20	–
	Profit (loss) before tax	(10)	30	50
	Tax at 20%	–*	6	10
	Profit (loss) after tax	(10)	24	40

*Tax refund of £2 might be available in respect of the loss.

(i)	Return on net assets	5%	5%	5%
(ii)	Return on equity	(2.5%)	3.0%	4.0%
(iii)	Interest cover	0.83	2.5	–
(iv)	Earnings per share	(6.7p)	8.0p	10.0p

9.6 Barber Limited and Jenkins Limited

Extracts from Jenkins Group 2005 accounts

	£'000		
Net assets	3 600	Profit after tax	600
Investment in subsidiary	500(a)	Dividend paid	300
	4 100	Retained profit for the year	300(a)

(a) Including Jenkins 100 per cent share of Barber's retained profits.

(b) If the subsidiary paid a dividend of £75 000 (all to the holding company), under the 'equity' method, Jenkins has already included all the subsidiary's 2005 profit of £100 000 whether or not any dividend is paid. Thus the only effect of Jenkins' subsidiary paying a £75 000 dividend would be on the balance sheet: to increase assets (cash) by £75 000, and to reduce the investment in the subsidiary by the same amount.

9.7 Woodley Limited and McNab Limited

WOODLEY LIMITED
Consolidated balance sheet at 1 April 2005

	Merger £m
Called up share capital (40 + 20)	60
Share premium account	–
Profit and loss account (20 + 15)	35
Shareholders' funds (= net assets)	95

9.8 Triple Enterprises Limited

TRIPLE ENTERPRISES LIMITED
Balance sheet at 1 April 2005

	Brighton Brands £'000	Corbett Chemicals £'000	Duckham Drugs £'000	=	Triple Enterprises £'000
Fixed assets, net	370	420	350	=	1 140
Net working capital	280	380*	110	=	770
Less: Long term debt	(150)	(200)	(60)	=	(410)
	500	600	400	=	1 500
Capital and reserves					
Called up share capital	120	200	80	=	400
Revaluation reserves	110	90	140	=	340
Profit and loss account	270	310*	180	=	760
Shareholders' funds	500	600	400	=	1 500

*After deducting £30 000 written off Corbett's stocks.

Notes
1　The revaluation makes merger accounting in this case very simple: just a question of adding the numbers together.
2　If the fixed assets were *not* revalued? Triple's balance sheet would simply show fixed assets, net at £800 000 (= 260 + 330 + 210); and would not include any revaluation reserves.

9.9 Philip Limited

No profit for sales between companies within a group should be included in consolidated accounts until the goods have been sold to a customer outside the group. Only then is profit 'realized' from the group's point of view.

Arising from sales to Philip in the year ended 31 March 2005, Sidney will have incorporated the following transactions in its accounts:

Sale	£80 000
Cost of sales	£50 000 = Profit £30 000

Thus Sidney has included in its accounts a profit of £30 000 in respect of intercompany sales, one quarter of which are still 'unrealized' by the group at 31 March 2005. Group profits should therefore be reduced by £7 500 (sales turnover down £20 000, cost of sales down £12 500); and stock should be reduced by £7 500. Any amount still owing by Philip to Sidney at 31 March 2001 will be cancelled out against the amount shown as debtors in Sidney's books.

11.5 Tesco plc

TESCO PLC: CASH FLOW STATEMENT
53 weeks ended 28 February 2004

	2004 £m	2003 £m
Net cash inflow from operating activities (FRS 1 format)	2 942	2 375
Interest received	41	37
Dividends from joint ventures and associates	60	11
(Interest paid)	(337)	(255)
(Taxation paid)	(326)	(366)
(Dividends paid)	(303)	(368)
Operating activities	**2 077**	**1 434**
(Purchase of tangible fixed assets)	(2 239)	(2 032)
Proceeds from disposals	62	32
(Purchase of subsidiaries)	(216)	(386)
(Purchase of interests in joint ventures and associates)	(56)	(50)
Investing activities	**(2 449)**	**(2 436)**
Net cash (outflow) before financing	**(372)**	**(1 002)**
Ordinary shares issued for cash	868	73
(Purchase of own shares)	(51)	(52)
Net (decrease)/increase in loans	(178)	950
(Increase)/decrease in cash less overdrafts	(267)	31
Financing activities	**372**	**1 002**

12.7 Parkside Limited (A): Closing rate method

(a) Blue Moon: Profit and loss account
Year ended 31 December 2005

	R$'000		£'000
Sales	7 000	@ 2.00	3 500
Depreciation	300	@ 2.00	150
Other expenses	6 560	@ 2.00	3 280
Profit	140	@ 2.00	70

Blue Moon: Balance sheet as at 31 December

	2005		2004	
	R$'000	£'000	R$'000	£'000
Fixed assets	1 200	600	1 500	500
Working capital	560	280	360	120
	1 760	880	1 860	620
(Long-term debt)	(720)	(360)	(960)	(320)
	1 040	520	900	300
Capital and reserves:				
Called up share capital	200	50	200	50
Retained profits	840	320	700	250
Exchange differences	–	150	–	n/a
	1 040	520	900	300

Exchange differences for year 2005

	£'000
Opening net assets (R$900) @ opening exchange rate (£1 = R$3.00)	=300
Opening net assets (R$900) @ closing exchange rate (£1 = R$2.00)	= 450
Exchange differences for year 2005	= 150

Retained profit at 31 December 2005

	£'000
Opening balance at 1 January 2005	250
Profit for the year	70
Closing balance at 31 December 2005	320

(b) Using the average rate, instead of the closing rate, to translate 2005 profits would produce a profit for 2005 of £56 (R$140 @ £1 = R$2.50) instead of £70. The difference of £14 would be an additional exchange difference in reserves.

12.8 Parkside Limited (B): Temporal method

Blue Moon: Profit and loss account
Year ended 31 December 2005

	R$'000		£'000
Sales	7 000	@ 2.50	2 800
Depreciation	300	@ 4.00	75
Other expenses	6 560	@ 2.50	2 624
Exchange losses	–		56
Profit for year	140		45

Blue Moon: Balance sheet as at 31 December

	2005		2004	
	R$'000	£'000	R$'000	£'000
Fixed assets	1 200	300	1 500	375
Working capital	560	280	360	120
	1 760	580	1 860	495
(Long-term debt)	(720)	(360)	(960)	(320)
	1 040	220	900	175
Capital and reserves:				
Called up share capital	200	50	200	50
Retained profits	840	170	700	125
	1 040	220	900	175

Exchange differences for year 2005

		£'000
Profit before depreciation R$440: @ average rate R$2.50	= 176	
@ closing rate R$2.00	= 220	
		+ 44
Opening net monetary liabilities R$600: at opening rate		
R$3.00	= 200	
at closing rate		
R$2.00	= 300	
		– 100
Exchange losses		– 56

306

Index